MANAGING TECHNOLOGY in the HOSPITALITY INDUSTRY

Educational Institute Books

UNIFORM SYSTEM OF ACCOUNTS FOR THE
LODGING INDUSTRY
Eleventh Revised Edition

PLANNING AND CONTROL FOR FOOD AND
BEVERAGE OPERATIONS
Ninth Edition
Jack D. Ninemeier

UNDERSTANDING HOSPITALITY LAW
Fifth Edition
Jack P. Jefferies/Banks Brown

SUPERVISION IN THE HOSPITALITY INDUSTRY
Fifth Edition
Jack D. Ninemeier/Raphael R. Kavanaugh

MANAGEMENT OF FOOD AND BEVERAGE
OPERATIONS
Sixth Edition
Jack D. Ninemeier

MANAGING FRONT OFFICE OPERATIONS
Tenth Edition
Michael L. Kasavana

MANAGING SERVICE IN FOOD AND BEVERAGE
OPERATIONS
Fifth Edition
Ronald F. Cichy/Philip J. Hickey, Jr.

THE LODGING AND FOOD SERVICE INDUSTRY
Eighth Edition
Gerald W. Lattin/Thomas W. Lattin/James E. Lattin

SECURITY AND LOSS PREVENTION MANAGEMENT
Third Edition
David M. Stipanuk/Raymond C. Ellis, Jr.

HOSPITALITY INDUSTRY MANAGERIAL
ACCOUNTING
Eighth Edition
Raymond S. Schmidgall

MANAGING TECHNOLOGY IN THE HOSPITALITY
INDUSTRY
Seventh Edition
Michael L. Kasavana

HOTEL AND RESTAURANT ACCOUNTING
Eighth Edition
Raymond Cote

ACCOUNTING FOR HOSPITALITY MANAGERS
Fifth Edition
Raymond Cote

CONVENTION MANAGEMENT AND SERVICE
Ninth Edition
James R. Abbey

HOSPITALITY SALES AND MARKETING
Sixth Edition
James R. Abbey

MANAGING HOUSEKEEPING OPERATIONS
Revised Third Edition
Aleta A. Nitschke/William D. Frye

HOSPITALITY TODAY: AN INTRODUCTION
Eighth Edition
Rocco M. Angelo

HOSPITALITY FACILITIES MANAGEMENT AND
DESIGN
Fourth Edition
David M. Stipanuk

MANAGING HOSPITALITY HUMAN RESOURCES
Fifth Edition
Robert H. Woods, Misty M. Johanson, and Michael P. Sciarini

RETAIL MANAGEMENT FOR SPAS

HOSPITALITY INDUSTRY FINANCIAL
ACCOUNTING
Fourth Edition
Raymond S. Schmidgall/James W. Damitio

HOTEL INVESTMENTS: ISSUES & PERSPECTIVES
Fifth Edition
Edited by Lori E. Raleigh and Rachel J. Roginsky

LEADERSHIP AND MANAGEMENT IN THE
HOSPITALITY INDUSTRY
Third Edition
Robert H. Woods/Judy Z. King

CONTEMPORARY CLUB MANAGEMENT
Third Edition
*Edited by Joe Perdue and Jason Koenigsfeld for the Club
Managers Association of America*

HOTEL ASSET MANAGEMENT: PRINCIPLES &
PRACTICES
Third Edition
Edited by Rich Musgrove, Lori E. Raleigh, and A. J. Singh

MANAGING BEVERAGE OPERATIONS
Second Edition
Ronald F. Cichy/Lendal H. Kotschevar

FOOD SAFETY: MANAGING WITH THE HACCP
SYSTEM
Second Edition
Ronald F. Cichy

SPA: A COMPREHENSIVE INTRODUCTION
Elizabeth M. Johnson/Bridgette M. Redman

REVENUE MANAGEMENT: MAXIMIZING REVENUE
IN HOSPITALITY OPERATIONS
Second Edition
Gabor Forgacs

FINANCIAL MANAGEMENT FOR SPAS
Raymond S. Schmidgall/John R. Korpi

MANAGING TECHNOLOGY in the HOSPITALITY INDUSTRY

Seventh Edition

Michael L. Kasavana, Ph.D., CHTP

AMERICAN HOTEL & LODGING
EDUCATIONAL INSTITUTE

Disclaimer

This publication is designed to provide accurate and authoritative information in regard to the subject matter covered. It is sold with the understanding that the publisher is not engaged in rendering legal, accounting, or other professional service. If legal advice or other expert assistance is required, the services of a competent professional person should be sought.

> — *From the Declaration of Principles jointly adopted by the American Bar Association and a Committee of Publishers and Associations*

The author is solely responsible for the contents of this publication. All views expressed herein are solely those of the author and do not necessarily reflect the views of the American Hotel & Lodging Educational Institute (AHLEI) or the American Hotel & Lodging Association (AHLA).

Nothing contained in this publication shall constitute a standard, an endorsement, or a recommendation of AHLEI or AHLA. AHLEI and AHLA disclaim any liability with respect to the use of any information, procedure, or product, or reliance thereon by any member of the hospitality industry.

©2016
By the AMERICAN HOTEL & LODGING
EDUCATIONAL INSTITUTE
2113 N. High Street
Lansing, Michigan 48906-4221

The American Hotel & Lodging
Educational Institute is a nonprofit
educational foundation.

Printed in the United States of America
   3 4 5 6 7 8 9 10 21 20 19 18

ISBN 978-0-86612-490-4

Editor: Peter Morris

Contents

About the Author

Michael L. Kasavana, Ph.D., CHTP, NCE5, is the NAMA-endowed Professor Emeritus in Hospitality Business in *The* School of Hospitality Business at Michigan State University, where he served as the School's resident technology expert for nearly four decades. Dr. Kasavana completed his undergraduate and graduate work at the University of Massachusetts—Amherst. He received a bachelor's degree in hotel, restaurant, and travel administration; a master of business administration in finance; and a doctorate in management information systems. He has written several books, instructional software packages, and a host of research journal and trade industry magazine articles.

Dr. Kasavana's teaching and research efforts have been sharply focused on automation applications for hotels, restaurants, clubs, casinos, and automated merchandising. He is an active consultant and a recipient of the MSU Distinguished Faculty Award, MSU Teacher–Scholar Award, and the Eli Broad College of Business Withrow Teacher/Scholar Award. He has presented numerous seminars on a variety of topics in the United States, Canada, Rome, Hong Kong, and other areas of the world. Dr. Kasavana is also a member of the International Technology Hall of Fame sponsored by Hospitality Financial and Technology Professionals and a recipient of the Distinguished Achievements Award from the Food Service Technology Consortium.

In addition to his past responsibilities in the MSU hospitality school, Dr. Kasavana served as the university's Faculty Athletic Representative to the NCAA, Big Ten, and CCHA athletic conferences, and chaired the MSU Athletic Council for twenty-six years.

Chapter 1 Outline

Evaluating Hospitality Technology
    Competitive Advantage
    Productivity Improvement
    Profitability Enhancement
Property Management Systems
    Reservations Module
    Rooms Management Module
    Guest Accounting Module
PMS Interfaces
Point-of-Sale Systems
Sales and Catering Systems
Hospitality Accounting Systems
E-Commerce
    Electronic Distribution
    Social Networking
    Internet Marketing
    Enterprise Systems
    Website Development

Competencies

1. Discuss the criteria used to evaluate hospitality technology. (pp. 4–6)

2. Describe the basic functions common to property management systems. (pp. 6–11)

3. Identify stand-alone technology systems that may interface with property management systems. (pp. 11–14)

4. Describe the basic functions of a point-of-sale system. (pp. 15–17)

5. Describe the basic functions of a sales and catering system. (pp. 17–19)

6. Identify hospitality accounting modules typically provided by back-office software packages. (pp. 19–21)

7. Explain the elements and impact of e-commerce on hospitality organizations. (pp. 21–30)

Hospitality Technology Systems

1

HOW MUCH DOES a manager need to know about technology to operate an automated system? About as much as a motorist needs to know about auto mechanics to drive a car. A motorist does not need to master the mechanical wonders of the internal combustion engine to drive a car. A driver simply needs to learn how to instruct the machine—how to turn the ignition key, push the gas pedal, apply the brake, and so on. Sparks jump, pistons pump, and gears turn, regardless of the driver's knowledge of mechanical engineering. However, if a motorist has some understanding of auto mechanics and basic auto maintenance skills, the car should perform even better and meet the driver's transportation needs for a longer period of time.

Similarly, in order to use technology, a manager does not need to learn the intricacies of electronic circuitry etched on silicon chips. The manager simply needs to learn the commands by which to instruct the system to carry out the desired functions. However, if a manager also has some basic knowledge about the essential operations of a system, he or she will be better equipped to use technology as an effective tool in managing information needs. A basic knowledge of the way systems operate enables managers to select technology applications that best meet the information needs related to operations, or to enhance and expand their present system functionality. Some knowledge of technology can be extremely helpful in identifying system capabilities.

Despite the increasing number of functions being built into sophisticated hospitality applications, no one system is likely to cover all areas a property may need to manage. At a minimum, a comprehensive property management system and select interfaced applications may be needed. If there is a bar or restaurant, a point-of-sale system will likely be needed. For operations with several function rooms and group meeting or banquet business, a sales and catering system would be an appropriate application. Properties with extensive food and beverage operations will also gain much from the cost controls provided by inventory control and purchase ordering applications.

Apart from these, there are a host of sub-systems that manage such functions as self check-in, call accounting, voice mail, electronic door locks, Internet and WiFi access, energy management, on-demand entertainment, mini-bars, bookings for spa/tennis/golf, and so on. Applications addressing these needs are produced primarily by specialists (not necessarily the main property management system vendor) and interact with the property management system through interfaces of varying degrees of complexity and capability. Getting the most efficient and effective outcomes from interconnected multiple systems at a single location depends, to a large degree, on the ease of data integration between component parts.

Evaluating Hospitality Technology

There have been many financial techniques, return on investment analyses, and other complicated schemes designed to evaluate application software both before and after purchase. Pre-implementation reviews, which can be somewhat complicated and time-consuming, often identify application needs, business parameters, functional metrics, system capabilities, and desired outcomes. In other words, pre-implementation reviews present a technology road map of what an application needs to accomplish (both directly and indirectly). Delineating objectives before implementing the application creates a benchmark that makes it possible to evaluate the application after implementation, which usually requires managers to conduct a system audit, develop a process review, or perform a workflow analysis. Suppose a hotel is evaluating whether to replace its front office system. A pre-implementation review of the current system may determine that this system is contributing to excessive wait times during registration because its rooms search function is too slow. The pre-implementation review has identified a need that any new system will be expected to address. Once the new front office application is installed, post-implementation review of the upgraded system's impact on average guest check-in time can be conducted. While a post-implementation review is usually easier than a pre-implementation review, a comparative analysis of the two provides a basis for establishing operational benchmarks as well as evaluating the application. Similarly, inventory management, point-of-sale data entry, departmental report generation, and additional system functions can be evaluated within pre- and post-implementation time frames. Industry practitioners considering adoption of such metrics usually are confused and dismayed by the breadth and depth required to perform a formal post-implementation review. Managers usually are challenged to conduct a system audit, develop a process review, or perform a workflow analysis.

Sometimes an application misses its intended target. Evaluating the application with a specific set of criteria both before and after implementation can help identify not only missed targets, but other application deficiencies as well. The criteria used should be measureable in order to better establish operations standards, and they should be simple so as to avoid the pitfalls that tend to accompany more complex analyses. Three highly useful criteria to use when evaluating an application are:

- Does it provide a competitive advantage?
- Does it improve productivity?
- Does it enhance profitability?

The following sections discuss each of the criteria in greater detail.

Competitive Advantage

Can technology produce a competitive advantage in the hospitality industry? The answer is a resounding yes! Consider a hotel company's website with self-reservation capability, a hotel lobby with a kiosk for self check-in, a restaurant point-of-sale system with frequent diner software, or an eatery with a table management system. Each application produces an outcome unparalleled by a nonautomated or semi-automated equivalent and, therefore, forms a basis for creating a **competitive advantage**.

Competitive advantage can be established in four ways. The first is via **product differentiation**—applying technology to produce a feature or product that is unique (e.g., a customized blog or photo-sharing site for frequent travelers). A product advantage arises when a feature or product has a distinctive characteristic that appeals to a market segment.

A second means for establishing competitive advantage is to use technology to improve customer service. This can be done through the use of customer relationship management (CRM) software, which is built on the proposition that knowledge of the customer is valuable to loyalty and revenue-generating programs. If customers appreciate the enhanced service that results, this can create a strong point of differentiation.

A third method to create competitive advantage is by producing a product at a lower cost. When technology is applied so that costs are reduced, margins are higher and/or selling prices are lower. Either way, competitive advantage can be gained.

A fourth approach is the use of market segmentation to create a competitive advantage. By using technology to target specific market segments, firms can expand market reach while exceeding customer expectations. Most hospitality firms have moved into the customer service phase of competitive advantage based on the realization that differentiation on price and quality alone tends to be insufficient.

Productivity Improvement

Select hospitality software applications may help to improve productivity. The usual measurable outputs for determining productivity are the number of transactions per hour, degree of process integration, efficient resource scheduling, and effective inventory control.

There are two aspects of productivity evaluation: workflow processing (which involves task sequencing, space management, and related physical elements) and data processing (which transforms input to output). From a data processing perspective, there are three categories of metrics. The first is minimizing the time it takes to transform data from input (raw facts) to output (information). When this time is minimized, the business is considered to be operating in an efficient manner. The second involves minimizing the number of times data must be handled. Each time a piece of data is processed, there is a chance of transposition or omission errors; an effective application will reduce data-handling procedures, thus minimizing chances for data entry error. For example, servers may take guests' orders using handheld devices that immediately send the orders to the point-of-sale system and any relevant kitchen or bar software, thus eliminating the need to reenter the same data again on those different systems. The third data processing metric is streamlining output. Modifying reports so that only the most relevant statistical and analytical information will be generated produces a more productive application. An example of streamlining is the dashboard and/or flash reporting available on many property management system applications. Additionally, system-generated reports need to be formatted efficiently to enable more effective managerial decision-making.

Profitability Enhancement

The use of proper technology will certainly enhance profitability, although this may be the most difficult criterion to measure accurately. Determining how an application directly and/or indirectly affects profitability can be complex. Stated simply, if the benefits of an application outweigh its costs, then the application has enhanced profit.

Property Management Systems

An automated lodging information system is commonly called a **property management system (PMS)**. Although the components of a PMS may vary, the term "PMS" is generally used to describe the set of application software that directly relate to hotel front office and back office activities.

A PMS does not actually manage a property in the commercial real estate sense; instead, it helps manage virtually every aspect of a guest's stay at a lodging property. Primary functions typically performed by a PMS include:

- Allowing for the management of a wide range of room rates, covering different room types, dates, and associated discounts (i.e., revenue management).

- Monitoring the availability status of all guestrooms and rates for at least the next twenty-four months (i.e., reservation horizon).

- Tracking the details of each guest's reservation, whether as an individual or as part of a group (i.e., reservation management).

- Identifying an appropriate room for the guest either on or before arrival (i.e., room and rate assignment).

- Monitoring the housekeeping status of all rooms in the property (i.e., room management).

- Facilitating the check-in process (i.e., registration management).

- Maintaining an accurate record of guest charges, either directly or through point-of-sale (POS) interfacing (i.e., guest accounting).

- Accepting full or partial payment for guest transactions (i.e., folio management).

- Reconciling accounts receivable from an approved account (i.e., account settlement).

Front office PMS applications consist of a series of programs (or modules) including reservations, rooms management, and guest accounting functions. A variety of stand-alone specialty applications may also be interfaced with an installed

PMS. Popular interfaces include point-of-sale systems, call accounting systems, electronic locking systems, energy management systems, handheld guest service devices, guest-operated devices, and others. Back office applications typically included in PMS packages contain modules covering general ledger accounting and internal control functions such as inventory, human resources, and purchasing. The following sections briefly describe some of the basic features of PMS front office applications, as outlined in Exhibit 1.

Reservations Module

A **reservations module** enables a hotel to rapidly process room requests and generate timely and accurate rooms, revenue, and forecasting reports. Exhibit 2 shows a sample PMS reservations screen. Reservations received at a central reservations office (CRO) or central reservation system website (CRS) can be processed, confirmed, and electronically communicated to the destination property. At the destination property, the PMS activates the reservation module to receive data directly from the reservation source, instantly updating in-house PMS reservation records, files, and revenue forecasts. In addition, the reservations data can be automatically reformatted into preregistration data and an updated expected-arrivals list can be generated. Functions performed by a PMS reservations module include:

- Establishing and displaying the availability of different room rates for different room types, dates, and guest types, including specific rates negotiated for individual groups and companies.

- Supporting preprogrammed length-of-stay restrictions, prepayments, or advance deposit policies as required by occupancy rules (demand).

- Monitoring bookings for individuals and groups, preferably checking guest history records automatically to determine guest history status.

Exhibit 1   PMS Front Office Applications

Reservations Module	Rooms Management Module
Availability/Forecasting Reservation Records Reservation Confirmations	Room Status Registration Room Assignments

Guest Accounting Module
Folio Management Credit Monitoring Transaction Tracking

Exhibit 2   Sample PMS Reservations Screen

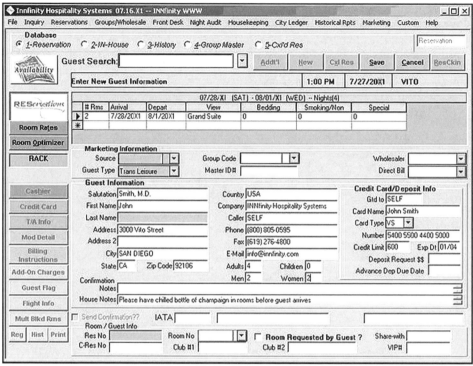

Courtesy of INNFINITY Software Systems, LLC. For more information, browse the company's website at www.innfinity.com.

- Blocking specific rooms for guests, when appropriate (VIP, handicapper, suites, etc.).

- Accommodating requests for shared rooms by guests from different market segments, different package plans, or different arrival and departure dates. The PMS typically will prompt rate adjustments among guests on overlapping days.

- Enabling rapid data entry for group bookings with differing numbers of room types blocked on varying nights.

- Generating and distributing confirmations as required, whether by e-mail, text messaging, fax, or regular mail.

- Setting up multiple folios as needed, with the ability to post charges automatically to the appropriate folio (for example, separating room and tax charges from all other charges for billing purposes).

- Creating specialty package plans consisting of various combinations of room rates, meal charges, and fees for other services (parking, spa, etc.) bundled into a single charge, but allocating the revenue appropriately to each department.

- Allowing for service charges and various federal, state, and city taxes to be applied automatically to appropriate guest and group folios.

- Allowing travel agent tracking by reservation, with financial reporting of commissions payable following check-out.

- Recording and applying prepayments and advance deposits to the correct guest account.

Rooms Management Module

A **rooms management module** maintains up-to-date information regarding the status of rooms, assists in room assignment during registration, and helps coordinate many guest services. Since this module replaces most traditional front office equipment, it often becomes a major determinant in the selection of one PMS over another. This module alerts front desk employees of each room's housekeeping status. A front desk employee can simply enter the room's number into the PMS and the current status of the room is displayed. Once a room becomes clean and ready for occupancy, the information is immediately communicated to the front desk staff through the PMS. Functions performed by a PMS rooms management module include:

Check-In

- Retrieving the guest's reservation, preferably by electronic capture of a debit or credit card, affinity card, or similar media.

- Displaying a list of available rooms that match the guest's requirements from which the front desk agent can select (or have the PMS automatically select) and check in the guest.

- Providing for a streamlined group check-in after guest names, room types, and room-sharing arrangements have been applied.

Housekeeping

- Automatically setting the status of all occupied rooms to "dirty" each night.

- Allowing the grouping of dirty rooms into housekeeping sections and automatically assigning sections to specific attendants and supervisors.

- Automatically updating each room's status (as cleaning and inspection routines progress) either through a housekeeping department workstation or through the attendants' use of a handheld terminal or cell phone.

- Identifying discrepancies between a room's occupancy status as recorded by the front office staff and as reported by the housekeeping department, to identify possible "skippers" (i.e., should be occupied, housekeeping reports it as vacant) or "sleepers" (i.e., should be vacant, reported as occupied).

- Changing a room's status to "out of order" to allow for correction of engineering or maintenance issues, preferably also linking to an engineering work order application.

Switchboard

- Providing instant access to the guest list for the current day, including guest arrivals and departures.

- Taking and posting messages for guests and ensuring delivery.

- Linking to a voice messaging application.

Guest Accounting Module

A **guest accounting module** increases the hotel's control over guest accounts and significantly modifies the traditional night audit routine. Guest accounts are maintained electronically, thereby eliminating the need for folio cards, trays, or posting machinery. The guest accounting module monitors predetermined guest credit limits and provides flexibility through multiple folio formats. When revenue centers are connected to the PMS, remote point-of-sale terminals communicate with the folio module to automatically post to the appropriate guest folio. At check-out, all outstanding account balances are transferred automatically to the city ledger (accounts receivable) for collection. Exhibit 3 shows a sample guest folio. Functions performed by a PMS guest accounting module include:

Exhibit 3   Sample PMS Guest Folio

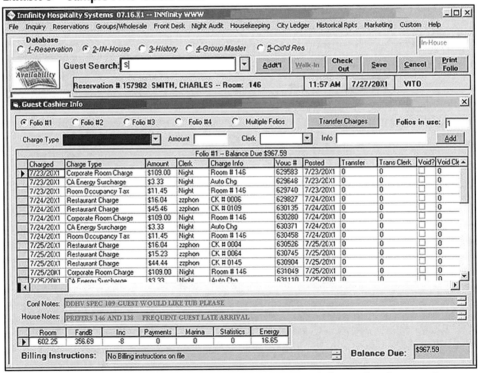

Courtesy of INNFINITY Software Systems, LLC. For more information, browse the company's website at www.innfinity.com.

Charge Posting

- Enabling cashiers at point-of-sale terminals to post charges for multiple departments directly to guest folios.

- Allowing for the automatic posting of charges to guest folios from interfaced applications such as point-of-sale systems, call accounting systems, in-room entertainment systems, and so on.

- Electronic transference of charge postings between one folio and another.

- Automated corrections to current day postings and adjustments to those from previous days. Corrections may be displayed for review, but generally are not printed on the final guest folio.

- Documenting a continuous audit of all postings and account adjustments.

- Tracking credit limits for each guest and reporting when a limit is exceeded. If a credit or debit card authorization interface is used, automatic authorization should be obtained.

Check-Out

- Posting payments and credits to guests' folios in the form of cash, checks, credit or debit card payments, or transfers to other folios for in-house guests and authorized direct-bill (third-party) accounts.

- Providing a streamlined check-out process for guests after appropriate reconciliation of outstanding guest folio balances.

End-of-Day

- Generating end-of-day reports to help the front office audit staff to close out the day's operations, including capturing cashiers' shift balances, resolving room rate discrepancies, and so on.

- Producing a detailed set of back-up records for the day's operations.

- Monitoring and updating accounting dates within the system.

- Automatically generating various sets of standard operating and financial reports for managerial access, review, and distribution.

PMS Interfaces

In order to enhance the effectiveness and efficiency of data processing, the property management system often includes several important interfaces. An **interface** involves connectivity and interactivity between two independent system components. The physical point of connectivity forms the hardware portion of the interface and may involve cabling or wireless applications. Once physical connectivity is achieved, software is needed to transport data and apply it appropriately. **PMS interfaces** involve data formats and application software that define data standards and capabilities. The following sections offer brief summaries of common PMS interfaces, some of which are included in Exhibit 4.

Exhibit 4   Common PMS Interfaces

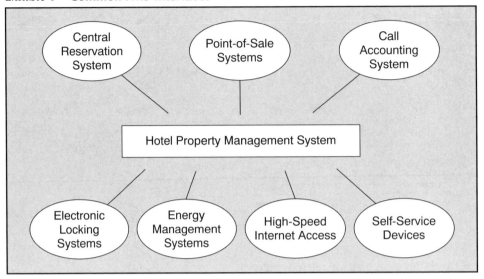

Central Reservations System (CRS). Reservation systems may involve simplex (one-way) or duplex (two-way) communications. A one-way interface receives guest bookings made through airlines/travel agencies, the hotel's website, third-party websites, property direct sales, or through the hotel chain's centralized booking facility. Bookings are merged automatically into the PMS reservations module, with certain exceptions (e.g., unusual requests or group bookings) that may require review and subsequent manual posting. Simplex systems are not very common or efficient. With a two-way interface, in addition to receiving bookings, the system automatically adjusts the room and rate inventory for the property and initiates a printed text message, or e-mail confirmation. For hotel companies that collect centralized guest history data from multiple properties, the interface may also transmit end-of-stay details following check-out.

Internet. This interface allows visitors to the property's own website to book reservations through an online process that automatically transports the data directly into the PMS reservation database. The PMS allows property management to restrict the room and rate types available. More sophisticated web booking engines allow group coordinators and event planners to access group bookings, create rooming lists, reserve meeting space, and so on, using a group or corporate code to book at negotiated rates. In addition, many properties offer wired or wireless **high-speed Internet access (HSIA)** in public spaces and directly in the guestroom. Sometimes this service is provided at no charge as an amenity; in other installations, an access fee may be applied. The choice is largely based on the property's guest mix and local demand for access. HSIA may require a dedicated server to issue temporary user names and passwords for access. Hotels offering HSIA service must be careful to maintain security and log-in procedures. When

HSIA access charges are applied, the fees should be programmed to automatically post to the guest's folio.

Sales and Catering. A sales and catering interface passes PMS guestroom availability to the sales and catering system to give sales managers an accurate profile of space availability, including function rooms and guestrooms. The interface also captures details of transactions dealing with nonroom sales (banquets, catering, meeting rooms, etc.) to establish a group master folio (and possibly other folios) in the PMS.

Point-of-Sale. A point-of-sale (POS) interface receives and responds to requests from a revenue center to verify and accept deferred payments as postings to a specific guest folio. The trend is to pass increasing levels of POS transactional detail to the PMS to reduce the number of disputed POS charges occurring at the front desk. PMS/POS interfaces have been developed that allow the PMS to:

- Retrieve details of a POS transaction from the guest's PMS folio using hyperlinked drill-down technology.

- Recognize when a POS transaction has been opened for a particular guest in a revenue center and set a corresponding location flag.

- Alert the POS cashier that the guest settling a transaction is actually registered to the room receiving the charge.

- Maintain an accurate folio balance from check-in to check-out, due to real-time account postings.

Electronic Payment Processing. At check-in, a credit or debit card reader automatically verifies the validity of the account and its ability to receive transaction activity. Subsequently, the interface should reserve a transaction amount based on the guest's declared length of stay plus an additional amount for estimated incidental expenditures. During the stay, if the guest's credit or debit limit is exceeded, the interface may automatically seek to increase the authorized amount. At check-out, the interface may manage settlement of credit or debit accounts and collect the funds due the property.

Revenue Management. A revenue or yield management interface relies on the frequent transference of levels of reservations booking activity in the PMS to the revenue management system. The system then analyzes availability and demand data against preset goals, rules, and historical trends and adjusts room rates for future dates and applies length-of-stay restrictions as appropriate.

Back Office Accounting. Since accounts receivable balances at check-out (e.g., credit and debit card transactions) become part of the PMS, the back office interface typically transfers electronic journal entries, reflecting end-of-day operational totals, to the general ledger.

Call Accounting. A **call accounting system (CAS)** enables a hotel to take control over local and long-distance telephone services and to apply a markup to switchboard operations. While call volumes have significantly declined as many guests prefer to use a personal mobile phone, call accounting continues to represent a revenue opportunity. A call accounting system automatically routes and prices outgoing calls placed over in-house phones installed on the property without operator intervention. The interface receives phone charges from completed phone calls and posts these charges to the guest's folio, with varying levels of detail.

Electronic Locking Systems. Electronic locking systems (ELS) dominate guestroom access control and are highly reliable. ELS/PMS interfacing enables lock codes to be changed on demand while providing unparalleled levels of security. For example, a front desk console can identify a series of access codes that permit guestroom entry and produce a magnetic stripe card (or alternate electronic medium) for the current guest to use. Once a code is entered and a card produced, all previous guest-issued codes for that lock are canceled so that guestroom access cards issued to previous guests are no longer valid.

Energy Management. An **energy management system (EMS)** interface receives a message from the PMS at check-in to change the guestroom thermostat to its predefined "occupied" setting and at check-out to set it back to the "vacant" setting. Interfacing energy management systems to a PMS links guestroom energy controls with room occupancy. An EMS is capable of monitoring guestroom and public area temperatures. EMS connectivity can often lead to significant reductions in energy consumption and thereby lower energy costs for the property. For example, in the cold winter months, an unoccupied room may be maintained at a temperature of 60°F (15.6°C). When a guest checks in and is assigned a specific guestroom, the EMS/PMS interface can adjust the room's temperature to a more comfortable 70°F (21.1°C). By the time the guest reaches the room, the temperature will be acceptable, and the hotel's energy costs will have been reduced accordingly.

Auxiliary Guest Service Devices. Automation has simplified many auxiliary guest services, such as the placement of wake-up calls, voice messaging, and e-mail services for guests. These functions are often performed by auxiliary guest service devices (such as electronic message-waiting systems and voice mail systems) that are often marketed as stand-alone systems that can be interfaced with a PMS. The interface sends signals to the PBX to turn on a light on the guestroom phone when a message is left for a guest and to turn it off again when the message has been delivered. Sometimes combined with the PBX interface, a voice mail system creates a new voice mailbox when a guest checks in and clears it at check-out. The interface receives a signal when a message is left in the voice mailbox to turn on the message-waiting flag in the PMS, and clears it when the guest retrieves the message. This interface may also alert the front desk cashier to the presence of any unretrieved messages still in the guest's mailbox at check-out.

Self-Service Devices. Guest-operated devices can be located in a public area of the hotel, in private guestrooms, or remotely via the Internet. A lobby self-check-in kiosk, for example, can be used to accelerate guest registration and can also function as a self-checkout device. In-room guest-operated devices (such as automated mini-bars, on-demand movies, and video games) are designed to be user-friendly systems. An assortment of devices can provide concierge-level service with minimal staff activity or involvement.

Point-of-Sale Systems

A **point-of-sale (POS) system** is a core technology for any revenue center at a lodging property. A POS system captures data at the time and place of a sales transaction. POS systems rely on devices that combine the functions of a cash register, an electronic media reader, and related payment mechanisms for instantly capturing transactional data. In restaurants, POS systems coordinate order entry, production, and service of menu items. As such, a POS device must be capable of handling different meal period menus (breakfast, lunch, and dinner) and different pricing at different times of the day. Exhibit 5 shows a sample POS touchscreen.

Orders can be entered on the system's workstations or handheld devices in the main dining area and are then automatically routed to remote display screens or printers in various production areas (e.g., hot or cold kitchen preparation areas or a service bar). POS systems allow all components of an order to be entered at once with the system grouping items into common production locations for preparation. Guest checks for settlement may be printed on demand.

Most POS systems can also be used as a time and attendance system by tracking employee clock-in/clock-out terminal entries; in addition, they may offer

Exhibit 5   POS Server Touchscreen

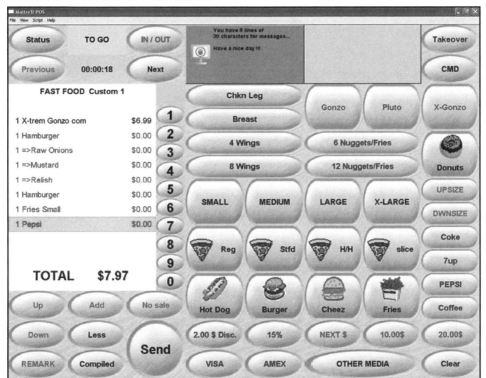

Courtesy of Maitre'D POS. For more information, browse the company's website at www.maitredpos.com.

inventory/purchasing capabilities, recipe details, and menu analysis. However, more specialized time and attendance and inventory/purchasing systems are commonly used to augment limited POS capabilities in these areas. The main functions performed by a POS system include:

Order Entry

- Allowing menu items to be sold at different prices at different meal periods in different outlets (restaurant, lounge, room service, catering, etc.).

- Creating both price and nonprice modifiers that can (or must) be applied to individual menu items, based on guest request.

- Allowing menu items to be grouped together into build-to-order combinations with a system-computed bundled price.

- Defining a default kitchen/bar printer or display screen where orders for each menu item will be routed, plus a secondary printer or display screen in case the first is unavailable or dysfunctional.

- Allowing some ordered items to be delayed for printing or display in the kitchen at a later time, either manually when the server judges that the timing for relaying the order is appropriate or automatically after a predetermined interval via **automatic coursing,** also known as auto-coursing. In automatic coursing, a POS system automatically sends orders to the kitchen based on production workload.

- Maintaining and updating servers with a current total of significant menu items in short supply, such as daily specials, based on a POS countdown feature that tracks the number of remaining portions of menu items.

- Providing for the rapid entry of quick-service items such as coffee, bar drinks, and desserts.

- Providing a simple way to re-order and account for menu items or a round of drinks on an open guest check.

- Allowing for the custom ordering of off-menu items, with special pricing.

Settlement

- Allowing for the straightforward splitting of charges on a check among the guests at a table, including dividing the cost of individual items or the entire check between two or more guests, in varying proportions (i.e., split checks).

- Allowing dining room guest checks to be transferred from one server to another.

- Combining dining room guest checks for multiple tables and/or servers.

- Automatically adding a preset gratuity percentage and/or service charge for parties exceeding a certain size or for special services such as room service.

- Managing distribution and reporting of wait staff tips.

- Recording the settlement of guest checks to cash, check, payment (credit or debit) card, guest folio, e-wallet, or gift card.

- Tracking guest checks for menu items that have been voided, corrected, or adjusted.

- Providing a set of operating reports, including cashier reconciliation, menu item popularity, server productivity, and so on.

In addition to a hotel PMS interface, POS systems may interface with a food and beverage inventory/purchasing system. This interface is capable of transmitting details of menu items sold to the inventory/purchasing system, which analyzes menu item sales by standard recipe ingredient quantities and projects remaining inventory on hand. A POS interface can also be configured to receive ingredient costs from a purchasing system to allow for effective menu item costing and pricing.

Sales and Catering Systems

To balance the number of rooms sold at discounted rates, some hotels allocate a block of guestrooms for group sales (usually defined as ten or more guestrooms). The sales and catering system is often used to manage the property's group sales efforts, as well as the scheduling of function rooms for meetings, banquets, weddings, conferences, and other events.

Sales and catering systems have traditionally been stand-alone applications that function independently from the PMS. The main functions performed by a sales and catering system include:

Group Sales

- Creating group master records, similar to individual guest profile records, that include links between corporate subsidiaries (across a parent company's multiple divisions).

- Facilitating contact management, including assignment of contacts to sales managers and tracking interactions with follow-up "tickler" reminders. Exhibit 6 shows a sample sales call information screen.

- Displaying availability of function rooms and guestrooms, showing for the latter both the number set aside for group business and the total available on specific dates.

- Creating and tracking group bookings at specified group rates for assigned function rooms and blocks of guestrooms.

- Allowing adjustment of the contracted number of rooms/guests to an expected level based on prior experience with the group/company (referred to as the "wash" percentage).

Function Rooms

- Creating function room records by square footage, capacity in various configurations (ballroom, conference, classroom theater, or other seating), and ability to be subdivided with movable walls (preferably incorporating photos—either still or panoramic—in typical room configurations).

Exhibit 6   Sample Sales Call Information Screen

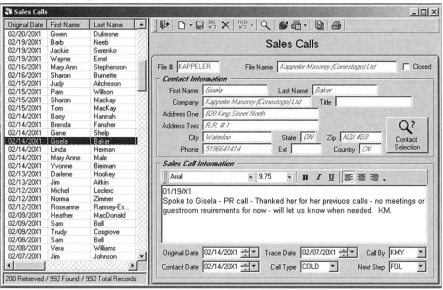

Courtesy of Agilysys, Inc.

- Displaying availability of function rooms graphically, showing the period each is booked by client.

- Creating and tracking room bookings, allowing for subdividable spaces and flags to indicate special considerations (priority ranking, sound level, arrival patterns, etc.).

- Facilitating the relocation of an event from one room to another.

- Creating pick-lists of standard-priced menu items that can be used for food and beverage ordering.

- Managing requests for audiovisual and other equipment and furniture (typically on a rental basis).

- Creating event contracts and banquet event orders (BEOs) for client signature. BEOs should specify room(s) booked by date and time, set-up configurations required, food and beverage services, audiovisual equipment, and other special items.

A sales and catering system may interface with a PMS, a room mapping system, and an event/meeting digital display system. The sales and catering system may exchange details of an event (number of guests, room configuration, furniture required, etc.) with an event management software package that generates a schematic of the room indicating all of the appropriate furnishings and equipment in position.

Catering-specific software monitors and controls the activities associated with each stage of catering service. In addition to containing data on all food and beverage products, catering files may also include data on such nonfood items as tables and chairs, serving utensils, production equipment, rental equipment, disposable items, and entertainment options. The more complete this information, the easier it becomes to assemble a catering service package and event contract.

Hospitality Accounting Systems

The number of accounting modules provided by a back office software package may vary widely. A back office system may contain application software designed to monitor and process accounts receivable and accounts payable transactions, payroll accounting, and financial reporting. Additional back office programs include inventory control and valuation, purchasing, budgeting, and fixed asset accounting. Exhibit 7 summarizes typical hospitality accounting applications. The primary functions performed by a PMS back office accounting system include:

- Creating a chart of accounts according to standard hospitality accounting practices and guidelines. (In the case of lodging properties, these are described in the *Uniform System of Accounts for the Lodging Industry,* currently the Eleventh Revised Edition.)

Exhibit 7   Hospitality Accounting Applications

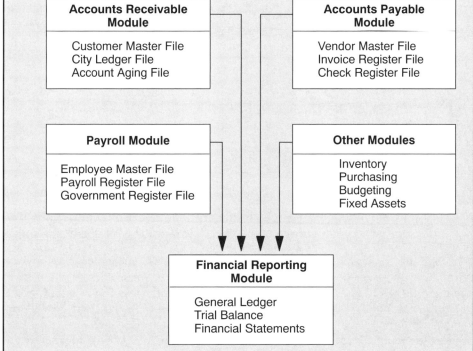

- Handling twelve or thirteen accounting periods per year, according to the property's preference.

- Permitting individual and batch postings of transactions and adjustments, with appropriate audit detail.

- Maintaining transaction details, including audit trails, for at least a complete fiscal year.

- Facilitating the creation and monitoring of operating and capital budgets with revenue and expense forecasts.

At the property level, a PMS back office accounting system may be responsible for comprehensive financial reporting. Payroll may be contracted to an outside agency or may be available through an in-house accounting module. Many properties use general accounting packages either at the property or, more commonly, in multi-property groups on a central server accessed remotely by users at individual properties.

The following sections present an overview of the applications that may be included in a PMS back office package.

Accounts Receivable. An **accounts receivable module** monitors outstanding balances of guest accounts. An account receivable is a dollar amount representing charged purchases made by a guest who has deferred payment for the products and services rendered by the hotel. Accounts receivable balances can be automatically transferred from front office to back office software. Once entered into the back office system, account collection begins. Account billings and the aging of accounts receivable will be monitored by back office software.

Accounts Payable. The **accounts payable module** normally tracks purchases, creditor positions, and the hotel's banking status. Accounts payable activities normally consist of posting purveyor invoices, determining amounts due, and printing checks for payment. Three major files maintained by an accounts payable program are the:

- Vendor master file
- Invoice register file
- Check register file

The vendor master file contains an index of vendor names, addresses, telephone numbers and vendor code numbers, standard discount terms (time and percentage), and space for additional information. An invoice register file is a complete list of outstanding invoices cataloged by vendor, invoice date, invoice number, or invoice due date. This file becomes especially important when management wishes to take advantage of vendor discount rates. The calculation and printing of bank checks or electronic transference of data for payment to vendors is monitored through a check register file or electronic funds transfer record. Payments are summarized into a payables report and reconciled with reconciliation statements.

Payroll Accounting. A **payroll accounting module** is a complex part of a back office package because of the variables involved in properly processing time and attendance records, unique employee benefits, pay rates, withholdings, deductions, and required payroll reports. The payroll accounting module must be capable of handling job codes, employee meals, uniform credits, tips, taxes, and other data that affect the net pay of employees. The unique nature of payroll data dictates that special care be taken to maintain an accurate payroll register, to closely control the issuing of payroll checks, and to protect the confidentiality and propriety of payroll data.

Inventory. A back office **inventory module** automates several internal control and accounting functions. Internal control is essential to efficient operations. By accessing inventory data maintained by an inventory master file, a back office inventory module is generally able to address three of the most common inventory concerns: inventory status, inventory variance, and inventory valuation. "Inventory status" refers to an account of how much of each item is in storage; "inventory variance" refers to differences between a physical count of an item and the balance maintained by the perpetual inventory system; and "inventory valuation" refers to the monetary or dollar value of items in inventory or the money necessary to replace the inventory.

Purchasing. A back office **purchasing module** maintains a purchase order file and a bid specification file. This module enhances management's control over purchasing, ordering, and receiving practices. Using minimum/maximum inventory-level data transferred from the inventory module, the purchasing module generates purchase orders based on an order point established through usage rate and lead-time factors. A purchasing module may also use a zero-based inventory system and generate purchase orders based on projected sales volume. Electronic purchasing (e-procurement) involves transmission of an electronic purchase order from the property to its supplier via the Internet.

Financial Reporting. The use of a **financial reporting module**, also considered part of the general management module, involves the specification of a chart of accounts (a list of financial statement accounts with account numbers) and a systematic approach to recording transactions. The design of this module is often crucial to an effective back office system. The financial reporting module is generally capable of tracking accounts receivable, accounts payable, cash, and adjusting entries. In addition, most financial reporting modules can access data from front office and back office modules to prepare comprehensive financial statements, which may include a balance sheet, an income statement (and supporting departmental schedules), and other reports for use by management.

E-Commerce

The **Internet** is a large and complex series of electronic networks designed to provide universal access to a wide range of information and communication services. It has created a communications and information explosion that routinely affects virtually every aspect of the hospitality industry. In an office environment, most networks connect individual access devices to a more powerful device called a **server**. The server controls the flow of information along the network. It can also be used to establish a gateway to other networks beyond the office environment. The Internet takes the concept of networks to its fullest application by seamlessly connecting large numbers of very complex networks. The Internet is an affiliation of several thousand private, commercial, educational, and government-supported networks around the world. When a user connects to the Internet, data and information can be shared with other users.

The **World Wide Web (www)**, also known simply as the web, is only one of the many different parts of the Internet. It is the best-known part because its user-friendly features have attracted users. The web offers an incredibly rich combination of text, images, sound, animation, and video. The graphic and video options of the web and the surging numbers of users have enticed businesses, organizations, educational institutions, government agencies, and individuals to create web pages and participate in the dissemination of information.

Much of the user-friendly nature of the web stems from the **HyperText Transfer Protocol (http)** that structures information on the web. This protocol is a set of file download commands embedded within the hypertext markup language (html) used to place text, graphics, video, and other information displays on the web. The "http" indicates that the web page can handle nonsequential links to other hypertext pages—a trait characteristic of nearly all web pages.

A **Uniform Resource Locator (URL)** designates the Internet address of a site, usually the site's homepage. A site's homepage is the first screen or web page presented when a destination site is located. URLs are usually built into the hypertext of a web document, enabling users to jump from site to site along the web. The URL for an organization, hotel, restaurant, club, or individual consists of a series of letters and punctuation marks. Each grouping of letters represents a section of the path that leads to a desired site. A hospitality company may secure multiple domain names for its website but have each address point to a singular main web page. These alternate addresses are referred to as **proxy URLs**.

The best way to find a website when its address is unknown to the user is to use a search engine. A **search engine** is a software program that reads indexed websites and creates lists and links to sites that match a user's inquiry. Most search engines provide tips on how to search efficiently for information. Generally, the more specific the query, the more relevant will be the list of sites the query generates. However, even if the resulting list is long, the user can usually scroll or page through the list and decide which sites are worth viewing. Then it's simply a matter of clicking on the link or URL to go directly to the web document.

E-commerce, like traditional commerce, involves the buying and selling of goods and services. In e-commerce, however, transactions are supported by the use of the Internet or another electronic medium. A hospitality company's e-commerce offering may be as simple as a set of web pages describing the company and its products and services or as sophisticated as an online scheduling and booking engine where reservations can be made for both guestrooms and function rooms. E-commerce offers instant access to information and, if warranted, the ability to quickly compare products, make choices, purchase items, and settle a transaction.

The Internet and e-commerce are having a dramatic effect on the supply chain in most industries, with the hospitality industry being a prominent participant.

The initial implementation of e-commerce in the hospitality industry dates back to when the first electronic hotel reservation was created by a travel agent and delivered to a hotel via telex or fax. Due to the vast amount of product and rate information that already exists in an electronic form, the implementation of e-commerce in the hospitality industry has been primarily focused on the front-end distribution of hotel rooms and restaurant food service.

Well beyond the sale of hotel rooms and food and beverage items, e-commerce has far-reaching implications for the hospitality industry. As industry consolidation continues, and operators and suppliers become more sophisticated in their business practices, an ever-increasing number of routine tasks and transactions are being conducted online. E-commerce does not end with the development of a stylish website or the ability to transact business. It has found its way into interactions with suppliers, accountants, payment services, government agencies, and even competitors. This online community changes the way business is conducted, from production to consumption, and affects companies that might otherwise not be considered part of an online economy.

What is driving the e-commerce revolution? Automation and networking options such as **electronic data interchange (EDI)** standards have existed for some time, but the Internet is the first ubiquitous two-way data communications platform that operates on a set of common standards. The wide availability and inexpensive nature of the medium have led to the development of business applications and supporting transaction standards that enable previously stand-alone systems to exchange data and communicate easily with one another. This reduces the cost of integrating systems, allowing free exchange of information while eliminating duplicate data entry and redundant manual processes.

Electronic Distribution

Historically, hotel management has relied on central reservations operations and direct property contact to control the pricing and distribution of overnight accommodations. As hotels continue to gain access to a broader set of reservation distribution channels, knowledge of online booking technologies becomes more important in practicing **electronic distribution**. Electronic distribution channels (EDC), which provide communication linkage between a hotel and its potential guests, can significantly expand marketing opportunities, promote specialty packages, encourage repeat visits, and provide a strategy for selling distressed inventory. The objective of channel distribution management is to optimize hotel room revenues through multiple exposure alternatives. Electronic distribution systems (EDS) can help streamline reservation management at the property level by providing direct linkage to the hotel's in-house PMS. This process typically entails the exchange of five informational items: room rates, rate rules, availability, amenities, and special services.

The Internet serves as the dominant electronic distribution channel. Determining how to identify essential touchpoints (potential guest contacts) becomes critical, since online channels can profoundly affect reservations management.

Relevant decisions about how hotel rooms are positioned, presented, priced, and procured through interactive websites take on new significance. When price is the dominant selection criterion, potential guests are treating hotel rooms similar to other commodities and thereby failing to differentiate properties by other characteristics. For example, when using an auction-bid format website to make a reservation, a potential guest is likely to select a destination hotel based on lowest price or relative ranking on an arbitrary rating scheme without regard to such factors as location, furnishings, services, amenities, or brand affiliation. The challenge for the hotelier is to develop an effective multiple-channel distribution strategy that differentiates lodging properties based on a multitude of factors and in a way that appeals to a broader spectrum of potential guests. In order to accomplish this goal, participation in multiple channels may be necessary.

Important to electronic distribution management is the need to effectively manage room rate integrity, reduce reservation transaction costs, and accurately monitor room availabilities. Reservation distribution channels have evolved into complex technological networks capable of providing a reliable base for operational efficiencies and profitability. The power of online services is sufficiently influential that for each reservation transaction completed online, it is assumed that there is a second reservation made through an off-line contact (e.g., travel agent, hotel call center, or property direct contact) as a result of online investigation. Industry practitioners estimate that a significant proportion of all hotel reservations emanate from online looking or booking.

When a hotel contracts a reservation network for distribution services, there is a risk that the hotel may only be able to set the price it earns for its inventory (net rate), while the reseller determines the eventual price set for the room (gross rate). When price is the main determinant in differentiating guestrooms, the services, amenities, and ambience of a property tend to be ignored. The availability of efficient search engines has made comparative room rate analysis simple and highly visible. Hotel operators do not generally want guests to make accommodation decisions based primarily on lowest room rate, as they need to avoid price dilution that results in devaluation of inventory and excessive discounting. In addition to concerns surrounding low pricing, how a hotel is portrayed on a website (text and graphics) will influence its sales performance. Hence, maintaining control over descriptive text and graphic components used in various distribution channels is of utmost importance. An individual hotel's competitiveness will be significantly diminished through poor web-based representation.

In order for online reservation systems to be effective, there must be accurate, timely, and identical room rate and availability data provided to all electronic distribution channels simultaneously. The best means to accomplish this is through single-image inventory technology. Simply stated, single-image inventory means giving all reservation distribution channels access to the same room availability, rates, rate rules, services, and amenities database. An effective **single image inventory** solution allows transmission of current pricing, policies, and availability data to all presentation outlets at the same time. Failure to have all distributors working from the same data source can be chaotic and lead to overselling or underselling, resulting in erratic levels of occupancy. A major advantage of single-image inventory technology is that all sellers engage in reservation transactions based upon identical information. Alternatively, not having the same information available at all representative outlets can lead to discrepancies over the rights to sell available rooms as well as the number of rooms that remain available.

The fastest growing hotel reservation booking source is the web. Many industry practitioners report that reservation traffic has rapidly moved from property-direct systems to web-based central reservation systems (CRS), **global distribution systems (GDS)**, and **Internet distribution systems (IDS)** applications. The issue for a hotel, regardless of size, no longer involves deciding whether to have a presence in cyberspace; now it is to determine the most effective reservation management scheme for maximum brand exposure and distribution efficiency. One of the main attractions of an online application is its ability to accept input from a dedicated reservation terminal, web page script, or from a web clipping on a mobile device.

In the past, hotel reservation systems were expensive, complex, and labor-intensive as access to the system required a dedicated workstation in the call center. Web-based reservation networks, on the other hand, operate in a much different manner. A basic online self-service application configuration includes a booking engine responsible for matching inquiry (data input) to availability (database content) to process the transaction. While there are many appealing features of a web-based reservation network, two in particular stand out. First, the process functions as a self-service application. The guest accesses the network and enters reservation inquiry data. Once the inquiry is matched with availability, a reservation record is created. This record can subsequently be transmitted to the hotel's in-house PMS reservations module. Second, an online application is available 24 hours a day, 7 days a week, 365 days a year, and requires no human intervention.

A web-based application can be an extension of the hotel's website, linked to a central reservations system website, or administered through a third party by an application service provider (ASP) or by a software as a service (SaaS) provider. When the reservation application is located at the hotel's website, there are minimal maintenance costs (keeping data current) with no variable transaction fees or commissions payable. An application at a central reservations site will likely incur a structured set of hosting and transaction fees, thereby presenting a higher cost per reservation than when handled at a property website. Typically, an ASP or SaaS provider develops and supports its own third-party website and charges a fee for lessening the burden on the hotel. Transaction fees may be a percentage of the booking revenue, a flat fee, or a combination of the two. Despite such fee scales, automated applications represent substantial savings over traditional reservation system processing that involved telephone operators and recordkeeping machinery.

Social Networking

Despite the fact that the concept of social networking has been available for quite some time, it is only since Internet usage has become so widespread that it has begun to be utilized to its full potential. Over the past several decades, the web has evolved from a one-way communication channel into a digital community that enables individuals to interact and engage with one another. From the time computers first became networked, regardless of whether the networks used were local area networks (LAN) or wide area (WAN) networks, the popularity of computer-mediated social activity began to increase.

An **online social network (OSN)** is a virtual community of people with similar interests. Individuals can join these communities by creating a personal profile, which allows them to establish a contact directory of "friends" who have also created profiles within the community. Other features that some OSN sites support include personal messaging, commenting, photo-sharing, video-sharing, and blogging. There are hundreds of online social networks worldwide, including such popular sites as Ning, Orkut, Twitter, Flickr, Facebook, Instagram, Tumblr, and LinkedIn, which, along with other networking sites, are being used daily by millions of people around the world. Many sites are used simply for meeting new people, establishing business contacts, or for communicating with others with similar beliefs or interests.

Social networking sites allow strangers to connect and exchange information, as well as create digital pipelines for interaction with industries, including the hospitality industry. Interconnectivity has changed the dynamics of business relationships between potential guests and experienced guests, employees, business associates, colleagues, and others. For example, guests have helped initiate a series of hotel and restaurant networks, which are often referred to as travel and entertainment networks. These types of social networks and others offer unparalleled marketing opportunities for the hospitality industry.

Internet Marketing

The trend toward global, daily use of and familiarity with social networking sites has huge implications for the hospitality industry. The industry is based on connecting with people and engaging guests, which makes OSNs a logical platform for industry application. Most industry observers recognize that the growth of Internet marketing in the industry has corresponded with the development of new innovative electronic media tools used to accelerate e-commerce, such as booking engines, sophisticated technology for greater business visibility, and interactive online sites that help to foster customer engagement. These tools allow e-marketers to build loyalty, boost competitive edge, and reinvent the guest experience by connecting with potential guests prior to, during, and after actual interaction with a hospitality property. Internet marketing involves contact with guests at every touch point in the purchase process.

Online social networking has significance for guests as well as management. The Internet allows users to critique businesses via third-party websites, which gives it the potential to have an impact on a company's reputation and image. Despite the lack of consistent evaluation criteria, users seem to find both anonymous and non-anonymous postings of ratings from consumer-generated content credible. This content includes blogs, forums, and communities, which many travelers and diners use to make purchase decisions. When a unique social network is created for a hospitality brand or property that enables consumers to create a profile and share stories, photos, and other memorabilia, it also creates a good opportunity to foster customer relations. Conversely, negative testimonials and statements shared on such networks can wreak havoc on operations regardless of whether they are deserved. If a consumer is loyal enough to provide content about a positive hospitality-related incident, however, most often the property will gain a competitive advantage, as potential guests can learn about previous guests' pleasant experiences. Many hospitality companies realize the potential impact of this aspect of social networking and thus often keep an eye on the social networks dedicated to their operations. By observing these networks, management can get a better idea of the company's public image and capitalize on it.

Immeasurable virtual conversations take place on a regular basis among interconnected consumers. Brand managers and e-marketers are wise to observe online exchanges, and can even participate in the conversation—without, of course, being invasive—which helps build customer engagement and brand equity. Engaging customers is important because those who are engaged tend to spend more money, come back more often, and pass information along to others. OSN statistics indicate that a majority of adult travelers watch posted video and audio clips, and many read blogs, share photos, and engage in virtual tours; however, fewer adult travelers actually post responses. The methods for determining the precise costs and benefits, both direct and indirect, of e-marketing remain unscientific, and no analysis has yet been made that captures the magnitude of OSN influence on the public.

Enterprise Systems

Property management systems, point-of-sale systems, and other technology systems discussed earlier in this chapter are, for the most part, property-based systems. An **enterprise system** addresses the technology needs of multi-property hospitality organizations, such as hotel and restaurant chains and management companies. An enterprise system often relies on web-based technology to eliminate the labor-intensive and duplicative efforts of central offices in updating corporate databases. An enterprise system accesses data in real time (or at predetermined intervals) directly from individual property systems. Property-level data is consolidated and analyzed, enabling the corporate office to compare operating results, generate aggregate reports, and provide timely feedback to properties.

For restaurant chains, enterprise systems enable individual units to focus on production and guest service, leaving the database administration tasks to the corporate office. Such systems offer the corporate office immediate access and a communication channel for implementing changes that affect such areas as:

- Menu offerings.
- Item promotions.
- Price changes.
- Recipe changes.
- Inventory changes.
- Tax table changes.
- Hours of operations changes.

For lodging companies, enterprise systems may include a central reservations application fully synchronizing room inventories and rate plans. This application may integrate with GDS and IDS providers. Enterprise systems for lodging companies may also provide detailed status reports based on real-time operational statistics. The reports can be consolidated by division, location, property type, or other categories designated by the lodging company. These systems also offer the central office the capability to adjust revenue management strategies based on key performance data such as:

- Average daily rate (ADR).
- Length of stay.
- Occupancy percentage.
- Revenue per available room (RevPAR).
- Rooms revenue.

Lodging companies can also monitor budget performance and provide feedback to properties that compares budgeted figures to actual results, with variances noted. Exhibit 8 shows a sample corporate consolidation report.

Enterprise systems go beyond simple database management and consolidation of financial information. Since the systems may directly access the technology systems at each property level, the central office can produce extensive individual guest histories (including current and past spending patterns) and group business reports (booking pace, spending pattern, billing information, etc.). The generation of guest histories and group reports are available for distribution to managers at properties company-wide.

Website Development

Hotel websites represent a cost-effective way to distribute hotel information, room rates, and room availability to potential guests. The challenge lies in creating and managing a site that can take advantage of sophisticated digital and social media capabilities while satisfying or exceeding users' expectations.

Compared with traditional advertising or printed collateral, websites are accessible 24/7/365, and content is relatively inexpensive to update. Since consumers demand current, correct information through cutting-edge technologies, sites require constant review, change, improvement, and creativity. The only interaction many guests have with a property before arrival is through its website. This virtual relationship should be nurtured just as carefully as if the guest were at the front desk interacting with staff. Therefore, management must use care in selecting a web developer.

A logical extension of a public website is an internal **intranet** designed to facilitate communication among staff. An intranet is a partitioned section of the public website that is password-protected to provide staff members with timely access to important work-related information.

In addition, some hospitality companies create a specialized partition of the website for corporate clients or suppliers. An **extranet** enables the hotel to transact business, share information with trading partners, and improve efficiency. While

Exhibit 8　Sample Corporate Consolidation Report

SAMPLE CORPORATE FLASH

Forecast: Jan 21

Current Day

Rooms	Rate	Revenue	RevPar	Occ %		Rooms	Rate	Revenue	RevPar	Occ %
158	$ 76.37	$ 12,065.95	$ 60.33	79%	Comfort Inn & Suites	2,970	$ 74.94	$ 222,584.25	$ 53.00	71%
71	$ 80.84	$ 5,739.76	$ 45.55	56%	Comfort Suites	1,581	$ 86.83	$ 137,279.75	$ 51.88	60%
184	$ 75.68	$ 13,925.98	$ 44.07	58%	Holiday Inn	3,387	$ 79.29	$ 268,566.69	$ 40.47	51%
154	$ 50.14	$ 7,721.23	$ 35.42	71%	Hotel Circle	3,618	$ 50.82	$ 183,859.14	$ 40.16	79%
147	$ 78.50	$ 11,539.55	$ 53.18	68%	Regency Plaza	2,544	$ 75.78	$ 192,790.09	$ 42.31	56%
714	$ 71.42	$ 50,992.47	$ 47.35	66%	West Coast	14,100	$ 71.28	$1,005,079.92	$ 44.44	62%
93	$ 65.67	$ 6,107.00	$ 48.47	74%	Barnabey's Resort	1,998	$ 76.40	$ 152,654.90	$ 57.69	76%
100	$ 74.05	$ 7,404.76	$ 41.60	56%	Holiday Inn	1,928	$ 72.29	$ 139,375.51	$ 37.29	52%
17	$ 58.31	$ 991.30	$ 17.09	29%	Jolly Roger	692	$ 75.18	$ 52,023.38	$ 42.71	57%
44	$ 82.29	$ 3,620.64	$ 19.06	23%	Seaside Inn	2,307	$111.21	$ 256,559.73	$ 64.30	58%
121	$141.13	$ 17,076.20	$ 90.83	64%	Watergate	3,246	$141.25	$ 458,503.20	$116.14	82%
417	$ 91.95	$ 38,343.00	$ 46.87	51%	East Coast	11,172	$103.20	$1,152,908.33	$ 67.12	65%
1,131	$ 78.99	$ 89,335.47	$ 37.68	48%	Total	29,326	$ 91.23	$2,675,402.39	$ 53.73	59%

Variance to Forecast

Rooms	Rate	Revenue	RevPar	Occ %		Rooms	Rate	Revenue	RevPar	Occ %
11	$(11.01)	$ (778.05)	$ (3.89)	6%	Comfort Inn & Suites	-27	$ (5.86)	$ (19,599.75)	$ (4.67)	-1%
-42	$ (7.31)	$ (4,221.24)	$(33.50)	-33%	Comfort Suites	-295	$ (4.00)	$ (33,115.25)	$(12.52)	-11%
-18	$ (3.54)	$ (2,078.02)	$ (6.58)	-6%	Holiday Inn	-522	$ (2.26)	$ (50,221.31)	$ (7.57)	-8%
31	$ (3.55)	$ 1,117.28	$ 5.13	14%	Hotel Circle	660	$ (4.20)	$ 21,111.54	$ 4.61	14%
-15	$(12.02)	$ (3,125.45)	$(14.40)	-7%	Regency Plaza	247	$ (5.89)	$ 5,180.09	$ 1.14	5%
-33	$ (9.01)	$ (9,085.48)	$ (8.44)	-3%	West Coast	63	$ (5.78)	$ (76,644.68)	$ (3.39)	0%
-8	$(15.37)	$ (2,078.00)	$(16.49)	-6%	Barnabey's Resort	125	$ (0.23)	$ 9,111.90	$ 3.44	5%
-24	$ 1.31	$ (1,614.24)	$ (9.07)	-13%	Holiday Inn	-382	$ (2.84)	$ (34,165.49)	$ (9.14)	-10%
-13	$(30.32)	$ (1,667.70)	$(28.75)	-22%	Jolly Roger	-140	$ 0.51	$ (10,101.62)	$ (8.29)	-11%
-36	$(10.48)	$ (3,800.94)	$(20.00)	-19%	Portofino Inn	-460	$ 5.06	$ (37,149.35)	$ (9.31)	-12%
1	$(18.65)	$ (2,096.80)	$(11.15)	1%	Watergate	209	$ 4.02	$ 41,744.20	$ 10.57	5%
-71	$ (9.19)	$ (11,011.58)	$(13.46)	-9%	East Coast	-617	$ 2.56	$ (33,484.75)	$ (1.95)	-4%
-387	$(22.95)	$ (65,413.06)	$(27.59)	-16%	Total	-795	$ (1.91)	$ (129,974.29)	$ (2.61)	-2%

Courtesy of Datavision Technologies. For more information, browse the company's website at www.datavisiontech.com.

intranet and extranet technology may be more complex and expensive than the cost of a basic website, the real value of web-based technology lies in its ability to improve and extend traditional business processes.

Website guidelines include:

- Feature interesting information about current hotel news and events.
- Include interesting graphics and photos of the property and specialized facilities.

- As new technologies become available and cost-effective, consider integrating them into the site.

- Position the site as a portal for guests to communicate, exchange information, relate experiences, and transact business.

- Consider implementing intranets and extranets as needs arise. Work schedules, employee newsletters, suggestions, evaluations, benefit administration, important developments, and web-based training programs can be included.

The amount of effort put into the development and ongoing maintenance of the hotel's website will have a direct impact on its success.

 **Key Terms**

Property Management Systems and Interfaces

accounts payable module—Tracks purchases, creditor positions, and the hotel's banking status.

accounts receivable module—Monitors outstanding balances of guest accounts.

automatic coursing or auto-coursing—A POS system function that automatically sends orders to the kitchen based on production workload.

call accounting system (CAS)—A property management system interface that enables a hotel to take control over local and long-distance telephone services and to apply a markup to switchboard operations.

competitive advantage—An advantage that can be established via product differentiation, use of technology, lower production costs, or use of market segmentation.

electronic locking system (ELS)—Interfaces with a property management system and allows the front desk to control the locking of rooms electronically.

energy management system (EMS)—Electronically monitors guestroom temperatures.

financial reporting module—Tracks accounts receivable, accounts payable, cash, and adjusting entries.

guest accounting module—Front office application software that maintains guest accounts electronically. The guest accounting module increases the hotel's control over guest accounts and significantly modifies the night audit routine.

interface—Connection and interaction between hardware, software, and the user.

inventory module—Automates several internal control and accounting functions.

payroll accounting module—Handles job codes, employee meals, uniform credits, tips, taxes, and other data that affect the net pay of employees.

point-of-sale (POS) system—Network of terminals that are combined with cash registers, bar code readers, optical scanners, and magnetic stripe readers for instantly capturing sales transactions. In restaurants, these systems manage the ordering and delivery of all menu items in one or more restaurants and/or bars.

product differentiation—The art of applying technology to produce a feature or product that is unique.

property management system (PMS)—Set of computer programs that directly relate to a hotel's front office and back office activities.

property management system (PMS) interfaces—Stand-alone technology systems that may be linked to a hotel's PMS; the formats and languages that define data that one system is capable of delivering to another.

purchasing module—Enhances management's control over purchasing, ordering, and receiving practices.

reservation module—Front office application software that enables a hotel to rapidly process room requests and generate timely and accurate rooms, revenue, and forecasting reports.

rooms management module—Front office application software that maintains up-to-date information regarding the status of rooms, assists in the assignment of rooms during registration, and helps coordinate many guest services.

single image inventory—A configuration in which all e-distribution channels operate from the same room availability database.

E-Commerce

e-commerce—All aspects of business and market processes enabled by the Internet and web-based technologies.

electronic data interchange (EDI)—Transfer of data between different companies using networks such as the Internet. As more and more companies are connected to the Internet, EDI is an increasingly important mechanism for companies to buy, sell, and trade information.

electronic distribution—Selling products or services over the Internet or some other electronic medium. Hospitality electronic distribution includes the GDS and Internet-based sales channels.

enterprise system—Addresses the technology needs of multi-property hospitality organizations, such as hotel and restaurant chains as well as management companies.

extranet—Portion of a public website that gives a company's corporate and business partners access to a password-protected portion of the site. A website administrator assigns access parameters for what documents, discussions, and areas can be viewed.

global distribution system (GDS)—Electronic networks used by travel agents and some Internet-based distribution channels to make airline, hotel, car rental, and cruise ship reservations.

high-speed Internet access (HSIA)—Any one of a variety of services that provide fast access to the Internet. The most common and cost-effective types of HSIA include DSL and cable modem services. Cable modem services are generally provided by a local cable TV provider and utilize cable facilities to provide fast

Internet access. Other forms of HSIA include satellite, private data line, and frame relay services.

HyperText Transfer Protocol (http)—Set of file download commands embedded within the hypertext markup language used to place text, graphics, video, and other information displays on the World Wide Web.

Internet—Interconnected system of networks that share standards and protocols connecting computers around the world.

Internet distribution system (IDS)—Internet-based services providing consumers with the ability to book airline, hotel, car rental, and cruise ship reservations.

intranet—Portion of a public website partitioned and password-protected for access by employees or special workgroups. This private, secure site is used to share documents, calendars, and event information. An intranet site is an ideal online communication tool for centralizing important company information, posting documents, creating schedules, and announcing events.

online social network (OSN)—A virtual community of people with similar interests.

proxy URLs—Alternative addresses for a company's website that all point to the same main web page.

search engine—Software that reads indexed websites and creates lists and links to sites that match a user's inquiry.

server—Controls the flow of information along a network and establishes a gateway to other computer networks.

Uniform Resource Locator (URL)—Designates the Internet address of a site, usually the site's homepage.

World Wide Web (www)—A user-friendly part of the Internet that offers an incredibly rich combination of text, images, sound, animation, and video.

Review Questions

1. Why is it important to delineate application objectives before implementation?
2. What is product differentiation?
3. What are the basic functions performed by a reservations module of a property management system?
4. What are the basic functions performed by a rooms management module of a property management system?
5. What are the basic functions performed by a guest accounting module of a property management system?
6. Why are property management system interfaces necessary?
7. What are the basic functions performed by a point-of-sale system?

8. What are the basic functions performed by a sales and catering system?

9. What are the basic functions performed by a hospitality accounting system?

10. How have hospitality businesses been affected by e-commerce?

11. How do enterprise systems interact with property management systems?

12. What advice concerning website development would you give to hospitality managers?

Internet Sites

For more information, visit the following Internet sites. Remember that Internet addresses can change without notice. If the site is no longer there, you can use a search engine to look for additional sites.

Hospitality Associations

American Hotel & Lodging Association
www.ahla.com

American Hotel & Lodging Educational Institute
www.ahlei.org

Club Managers Association of America
www.cmaa.org

Hospitality Finance and Technology Professionals (HFTP)
www.hftp.org

Hotel Electronic Distribution Network Association (HEDNA)
http://hedna.org

National Restaurant Association
www.restaurant.org

National Restaurant Association Educational Foundation
www.nraef.org

Hotels and Restaurants

Affinia Hotels
www.affinia.com

Best Western International, Inc.
www.bestwestern.com

Choice Hotels International, Inc.
www.choicehotels.com

Darden Concepts, Inc.
www.darden.com

Fairmont Hotels & Resorts
www.fairmont.com

Hard Rock Cafe International, Inc.
www.hardrock.com

Hilton Worldwide
www.hilton.com

Hyatt Hotels and Resorts
www.hyatt.com

InterContinental Hotels Group
www.ihgplc.com

Interstate Hotels & Resorts
www.interstatehotels.com

Marriott International, Inc.
www.marriott.com

McDonald's Corporation
www.mcdonalds.com

Radisson Hotels & Resorts
www.radisson.com

TGI Friday's Incorporated
www.tgifridays.com

The Spaghetti Warehouse
www.meatballs.com

Walt Disney World
http://disneyworld.disney.go.com

Starwood Hotels & Resorts
  Worldwide, Inc.
www.starwoodhotels.com

Wyndham Worldwide Corporation
www.wyndhamworldwide.com

Links to Hospitality Technology Companies

Ehotelier
www.ehotelier.com

Hospitality Upgrade
www.hospitalityupgrade.com

Chapter 2 Outline

Input/Output Components
    Keyboards
    Touchscreen Terminals
    Other Input Components
    Gesture Interfacing
    Monitors
    Printers
    Common Hospitality I/O Components
The Central Processing Unit
    Read-Only Memory (ROM)
    Random Access Memory (RAM)
External Storage Devices
    Magnetic Tapes
    Magnetic Disks
    Hard Disks
    USB Drives
    Optical Disks
Anatomy of a Computer
    Microprocessor Characteristics
    Bus System
    System Architecture
    Computer Add-Ons
    Hardware Configurations
    Interface Connections
Software
    The Operating System
Networks
    WiFi Networks
Internet Components

Competencies

1. Identify and describe system input components. (pp. 37–39)

2. Identify and describe system output components. (pp. 39–42)

3. Explain the function of a system's central processing unit and distinguish read-only memory from random access memory. (pp. 42–44)

4. Identify and describe common external storage devices. (pp. 44–46)

5. Explain how the processing capability and speed of a system are measured. (pp. 46–48)

6. Identify and describe components or devices commonly added on to a system. (pp. 48–49)

7. Explain computer hardware configurations and interface connections. (pp. 49–51)

8. Define the two broad categories of software and explain the function of an operating system. (pp. 52–53)

9. Discuss types of computer networks. (p. 53–54)

10. Identify and describe components fundamental to Internet operations. (p. 54–55)

2

Hospitality Technology Components

THE PHYSICAL EQUIPMENT of a computer system is called **hardware**. Computer hardware is visible, movable, and easy to identify. In order to have an automated system, three hardware components are required: an input/output (I/O) component, a central processing unit (CPU), and an external storage device.

Input/output components allow users to interact with the system. For example, users can input data through a keyboard and receive output on a monitor (also called a display screen) and/or on paper through a printer.

The central processing unit or CPU is the control center of the system. Inside are the circuits and mechanisms that process and store information and send instructions to the other components of the system. The system is said to *read* when it takes data in for processing, and to *write* when it sends processed data out as information. All input entering the system is processed by the CPU before it is sent to the internal memory or to an output device. Similarly, all output (sent to a monitor, printer, or other device) has first been processed by the CPU. Usually there is no direct link between input and output devices. Whenever information moves within an automated system, it passes through the CPU.

External storage devices retain data and/or programs that the CPU can access. Data and programs can be permanently stored on such external devices as magnetic tapes, magnetic disks, hard disks, USB drives, and optical disks.

This chapter examines these types of technology components, including processing systems, operating systems, networks, and Internet components.

Input/Output Components

Keyboards and touchscreen terminals are common input units. Display monitors and printers are common output units. For most data processing, the computer system needs a keyboard for input and a monitor for output. For a paper record of the processed data, a printer is also needed. Disk drives are also input/output devices; they are capable of sending stored data in either direction—for input to the central processing unit or for output to a monitor or printer.

Keyboards

A keyboard is the most common input device. While specialty keyboards can be uniquely configured, the number, positioning, and function of keys are relatively standard. Common groupings of keys are:

- Function keys
- Alphabet keys
- Cursor control keys
- Numeric keys

Function Keys. Function keys are usually spread across the top of a keyboard and are numbered F1 through F12. These keys perform different operations when used in conjunction with different software applications. That is, the operation performed by the F3 key in one software application may be entirely different from the operation the F3 key performs in another software application.

Alphabet Keys. These keys normally function like the keys on a typewriter. Since electronic word processing normally performs several functions automatically, the "enter" key is used to force a break in the automatic line return (such as at the end of paragraphs).

Cursor Control Keys. A keyboard's cursor control keys are used in conjunction with the display screen. The **cursor** is a marker on a display screen that indicates where the next character to be entered will appear. The cursor control keys are marked by arrows. When one of these keys is pressed, the cursor moves in the direction of the arrow indicated on the key. Cursor movement is often determined by the particular software application that is being run on the computer system. Individual software applications may have specifically defined instructions for the cursor control keys.

Numeric Keys. When the "Num Lock" key is on, the keys that make up the cursor control keypad are converted to a numeric keypad and perform much like the keys of an adding machine or calculator. Many keyboards also have alternate number keys that can function in combination with the shift key.

Touchscreen Terminals

Manufacturers have developed terminals that enable the user to enter data without having to type a command from a keyboard. One such device is the touchscreen terminal. A **touchscreen terminal** may employ a grid of tiny beams of light over a display screen. When the screen is touched in a sensitized area, the light beam is broken, causing a signal to be transmitted to the processor. A touchscreen terminal is especially appealing to those who cannot type well or those interested in streamlined input procedures. Since touch-sensitive screens can move large quantities of data quickly, they can be especially effective as order entry devices in food service, self-check-in kiosks, navigational screens, and in graphic business applications (such as charts, graphs, and so on).

Other Input Components

Other common input components include computer mice, scanners, voice recognition systems, and various types of handheld devices. A computer **mouse** is a small pointing device designed to fit comfortably under a user's hand. The mouse is connected to the processor by a serial cable or a wireless infrared sensor. A mouse is used in place of, or in combination with, a computer keyboard or touch-pad. With it, a user is capable of choosing commands, moving text and icons, and performing a number of other operations. Moving the mouse across a flat surface moves a pointer, which is equivalent to a traditional cursor. The pointer is a small graphic symbol that shows the user where the next entered character will appear.

A **scanner** is an input device capable of translating a page of text or graphic image into a machine-readable format. Scanners convert text and images into digitized information that can be input to and recognized by the computer.

Voice recognition input involves instructions spoken by human voice. Also referred to as automated speech recognition (ASR), this form of input converts spoken data directly into electronic form suitable for processing. Experimentation with voice recognition technology is of special interest to the hospitality industry. A hotel reservations program may generate a series of prompts or cues to which a potential guest responds by pushing designated buttons on a touch-tone telephone and/or by speaking into the mouthpiece of the headset. This automated application acknowledges the user's input and may subsequently generate an additional series of prompts. The potential impact of innovative voice recognition applications in the hospitality industry could prove significant.

Handheld devices, such as a mobile phone, palmtop PC, or personal digital assistant (PDA), can be used for a variety of data processing applications in addition to being organizers for personal information. Many handheld devices can serve such basic functions as a name and address database, Internet browser, and video device. Some devices are pen-based and use a stylus to tap selections on menus and to enter printed characters. The unit may also include a small on-screen keyboard. Data can be transferred and synchronized to a desktop system through a cable connection or wireless transmission to a docking station or other device.

Gesture Interfacing

Automated **gesture recognition applications** are based on hand motions (pointing/movements) or facial expressions (eye tracking/emotions) designed to replace physical interfaces such as keyboard, mouse, or touchscreen. Often referred to as human-machine interaction (HMI), recognition systems are capable of interpreting hand and face movements through complex mathematical algorithms built on vision-based techniques. Gesture recognition has evolved as an alternative to typed, touched, or spoken input. Reliance on a motion-sensing controller allows computing devices to efficiently detect and track user gestures for application in real-time computing.

Monitors

A **monitor** (also called a display unit or screen) is the most common output unit. The type of monitor selected often depends on the kind of system used and the needs of the user. In addition to traditional designs, flat-screen monitors and multi-screen applications are popular alternatives. Monitors typically are purchased as high-resolution units. High-resolution displays enable high-definition graphics with various foreground and background color combinations:

- CGA (color graphics adapter); low-end color screen also referred to as RGB (red, green, and blue).

- EGA (enhanced graphics adapter); a step up from CGA in screen resolution and clarity (uses digital signals).

- VGA (video graphics array); best for desktop publishing and computer-aided design software (uses analog signals).

- SVGA (super video graphics array); popular option among a variety of monitor units (uses digital and analog signals).

- LCD (liquid crystal display); blue or black letters on grayish white background (typically found on handheld units).

- GP (gas plasma); orange letters on a black screen (normally limited to handheld units).

Printers

Printers are considered output devices and part of the hardware of a system. They can be classified in relation to how they generate processed data. Printer speed may be measured in characters per second (cps), lines per minute (lpm), or pages per minute (ppm).

Although not very common in hospitality industry applications, an **impact printer** depends on the movement of a print head or paper-feeding mechanisms to place data on the page. The simplest printers, such as dot matrix printers, place characters in a row one after another, then return the carrier to the left margin as the paper is moved up to another line. A line-printing terminal (LPT) is an impact printer that prints one line of type at a time.

Dot matrix printers form characters by firing a vertical line of pins through an inked ribbon onto the paper. Each time a pin is fired, it strikes the inked ribbon and presses it against the paper to produce a dot. In the case of some dot matrix printers, the dot is about 1/72nd of an inch in diameter. The size varies slightly depending upon the age of the ribbon and the type of paper used. As the print head moves horizontally across the page, pins are fired in different patterns to produce letters, numbers, symbols, or graphics.

Some impact printers support high-speed bidirectional printing in which the print head goes from left to right only on every other line. On the alternating lines, it reverses itself and prints right to left, saving time. Otherwise the time the print head takes to go from the right margin back to the left would be wasted.

A **nonimpact printer** achieves accurate print positioning electronically and can use a greater range of type styles more quickly and efficiently than impact printers. Nonimpact printers are a part of many hospitality applications and include thermal, ink jet, and laser printers.

Thermal Printers. A thermal printer, also referred to as an electrothermal printer, works by burning a protective layer off specially treated paper to reveal ink.

Thermal (heat-sensitive) paper has a paper base covered with a layer of ink and a coating of aluminum. The printer forms characters by passing high voltage through printing wires for a fraction of a second. This high voltage burns away the aluminum coating to reveal the ink beneath. Thermal printers are quiet and reliable because they have few moving parts. However, because they require special heat-sensitive paper, their operating costs may be higher than those of other types of printers. Thermal printers are typically restricted to point-of-sale (POS) receipt printer applications.

Ink Jet Printers. An **ink jet printer** works by spraying a minute and finely controlled jet of ink onto paper. The printer establishes a high voltage between its paper roller and an ink rod. The ink rod is composed of carbon grains encased in a tube. A spark jumps between the paper roller and the ink rod carrying enough carbon from the nozzle to make a dot appear on the paper. The ink (carbon) is electrically charged as it is sprayed onto the paper. Once charged, the ink can be moved around by electric fields in much the same way an electron beam is used to produce a picture on a television set. Ink jet printers are extremely versatile because they can produce a wide range of characters and high-quality graphics in a broad spectrum of colors.

Laser Printers. A **laser printer** is relatively quiet, highly efficient, and somewhat more expensive than an ink jet printer. Many laser printers are similar in appearance to desktop photocopying machines and may be available as part of a multifunctional unit (a combined photocopier, fax, printer, and scanner). Laser technology enables printing to be measured on a page-per-minute basis. Given their speed of output, many laser printers are equipped with collating capabilities. In addition, optional font (print style) packages, advanced graphics, and high-quality color capabilities are available.

Common Hospitality I/O Components

Although the hospitality industry is quickly adopting touchscreen and handheld I/O units, the most common I/O unit used in the industry remains the CRT unit ("CRT" is an acronym for cathode-ray tube). The CRT unit is composed of a television-like video screen and a keyboard that is similar to a typewriter keyboard. Data entered through the keyboard can be displayed on the screen. The CRT operator can edit and verify the on-screen input before sending it for processing.

Other types of I/O equipment common in the hospitality industry include tablet PCs and keyboard-and-display units such as POS devices, kitchen monitors, and specialty handheld devices. POS devices are designed to record transactions and monitor account balances. With hotel property management systems, restaurant charges can be captured by a POS terminal in the restaurant and automatically transmitted to the property management system, where guest folios are updated with the charges.

One important difference among I/O units is the type of output they produce. A CRT unit displays output on a monitor for the user to examine; this type of output is referred to as **soft copy** because it cannot be handled by the user or taken from the system. Printers, however, generate a paper copy of the output called a **hard copy**. Most systems are designed so that they can produce both types of output. For example, a hotel's front desk might have a CRT unit that enables the front desk agent to view a soft copy of a guest's folio; at checkout, a hard copy of the folio will be generated and provided to the guest as a printed statement of account. Obviously, output displayed on a screen is much more temporary and its use more constricted than output printed on paper. Generally, hospitality managers will receive **dashboard and flash reports** (reports that are produced when predetermined parameters are attained and appear on a user's screen, but are not necessarily accompanied by hard copies) as well as essential documents in hard copy form, allowing storage outside the system and providing a base for information backup.

The Central Processing Unit

The **central processing unit** (CPU) is typically the most important hardware component found within an automated system. It is the "brain" of the system and is responsible for controlling most other system components. As shown in Exhibit 1, the CPU is composed of four subunits.

The first subunit is the arithmetic and logical unit (ALU), which performs all the mathematical, sorting, ranking, and processing functions.

The second subunit is the control unit, which is responsible for determining which peripheral devices in the system can be accessed by the CPU. If a unit is capable of interacting directly with the CPU, it is described as being "online"; "off-line" refers to the condition in which there is no direct connection between a peripheral device and the CPU. It is important to realize that an automated component may be switched on (powered up) but not online. For example, when a

Exhibit 1   System Hardware Components

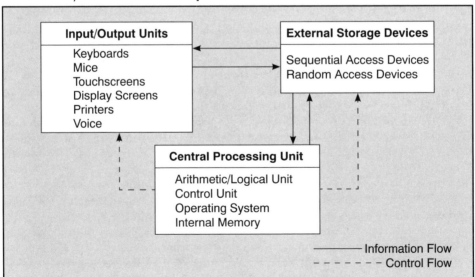

printer is connected to a CPU and its power switch is turned on, only the operating system or the application software can switch the printer to an online status. The printer can respond to commands from the CPU only when it is online.

The third subunit of the CPU houses a portion of the operating system. The **operating system** is responsible for orchestrating the hardware and the software within the system. It establishes the system's priorities and directs its resources to accomplish desired tasks. Operating systems are discussed in greater detail elsewhere in the chapter.

The final subunit of the CPU is the system's internal (or primary) memory, which is housed in a set of specialized circuits. One part of internal memory, called **read-only memory** (ROM), holds a permanent record of information that the system references each time it is started (booted). Another part of internal memory, called **random access memory** (RAM), holds a temporary version of the programs and/or data that the user is currently processing.

Read-Only Memory (ROM)

ROM (also known as PROM—permanent read-only memory) stores a permanent control program entered by the computer developer that may also house the operating system. The control program contains specific sets of commands and instructions that guide the most fundamental routines carried out by the system. For example, the control program contains instructions for the conversion of keyboard entries into binary codes for processing by the CPU.

Since ROM is composed of a limited syntax (vocabulary), a computer recognizes only its own preprogrammed commands. If a user tries to enter a different command, the computer will not recognize the input and may respond by reporting that a "syntax error" has occurred. For example, some application software will start when the user types "GO"; another may require the user to double-click an icon. Different ROM contents recognize different commands.

Storing the control program in ROM enables an automated system to "read" commands and instructions that program the fundamental operations of the system while preventing users from accidentally altering or erasing portions of the control program. Users cannot "write" or save information to the ROM area of the computer's internal memory. In fact, with many systems, users are prohibited from accessing, referencing, or reviewing any of the programs that are stored in ROM.

The ROM area of the internal memory does not require a constant power supply to retain the commands, instructions, or routines that the manufacturer includes as part of the control program. For this reason, ROM is described as **nonvolatile memory**. Programs stored in ROM are not lost when the system is turned off or otherwise loses electrical power.

Random Access Memory (RAM)

All data that are entered into the system are temporarily stored in the random access memory (RAM) area of the computer's internal memory. Since data stored in RAM can be accessed and/or altered by the user, RAM is often described as **read/write** memory: the user can both "read" from RAM (retrieve data), and "write" to RAM (store data).

Since all user operations are carried out in RAM, it is important that the amount of RAM supported by a particular system be sufficient to meet the user's needs. RAM size is typically designated in terms of the number of gigabytes that RAM is able to temporarily store. A 60 Gb machine has enough RAM capacity to temporarily store up to 60 gigabytes of data.

As a general rule, the larger the RAM, the more efficient the data processing. Since software application programs vary in the amount of RAM they require, RAM capacity is an important consideration in system configuration. There are two forms of RAM used in an automated system. The first is as described above; the second refers to storage media. RAM found in the CPU is referred to as **volatile memory**, since its contents are lost whenever power is lost or turned off. In order to save data held in RAM for future use, the user must save it on some type of external storage device in a nonvolatile-memory format.

External Storage Devices

An external storage device is the system component that retains data and/or programs that can be accessed by the CPU. Data and programs can be permanently saved on a variety of external storage devices.

An important factor in selecting the kind of external storage device for a particular system is the kind of access that users need to have to the stored data. User access to stored data will be addressed in the following sections, which discuss some of the more common external storage devices: magnetic tapes, magnetic disks, hard disks, USB drives, and optical discs.

Magnetic Tapes

A magnetic tape is an external storage medium that is made from a polyester base material coated with an oxide compound. It is this compound that gives the tape its durability and electromagnetic properties. Magnetic tape units are referred to as a **sequential access medium** because they store data in chronological sequence.

The way a user accesses data stored on magnetic tape is similar to the way in which anyone searches for a portion of a recording stored on a cassette tape recorder—the user must wind and rewind the tape until the desired portion of data is found. Since this can be a cumbersome process, magnetic tape is not a feasible storage device for many hospitality operations. However, using magnetic tapes to store back-up data may represent a significant cost advantage. Therefore, in some situations, magnetic tape may serve as a backup system on which to store data that are not required on a regular basis. However, if tapes are stored for very long periods of time, they must be periodically recopied or the tightly coiled magnetic surfaces may contaminate each other. Magnetic tape is classified as nonvolatile memory (memory that holds its content without electrical power).

Magnetic Disks

A **magnetic disk** (also called a "diskette") is an inexpensive external storage device used for transporting data and programs from one location to another. Magnetic disks are made of a hard plastic outer jacket and a thin, flexible-plastic inner disk.

The inner disk is coated with a magnetized oxide compound designed to hold electronic information. The size and density of the disk depend on the type of disk drive used.

The surface of a disk is divided into tracks, which are invisible concentric rings of magnetic zones. Each track contains a number of sectors. The tracks and sectors are numbered, enabling the computer to store information on the disk at specific locations (e.g., sector 7 of track 3, sector 4 of track 23, etc.). The number of tracks and sectors on a disk is largely determined by the computer operating system through a process known as formatting (also called initializing). **Formatting** creates the tracks and sectors on which the system is able to read and write information. Once formatted, magnetic disks are capable of storing large amounts of data.

Magnetic disks are a form of nonvolatile memory and are often referred to as a **random access medium**, because data can be stored in any available location on the disk. Since the tracks and sectors of the disk are numbered, the system records where data is stored and allows a user to access stored data quickly and easily. For example, when a flexible disk is inserted in the appropriate disk drive slot, the disk drive holds the jacket of the disk still and spins the inner disk, reading information from (or writing information to) the disk surface.

When a user instructs the computer to store information on a disk, the information is stored in an area of unused disk space. A user can also instruct the system to write over information that is already stored on the disk. This feature can be convenient for updating inventory records, personnel files, and so on. However, if information is written over old information, the old information will be erased and no longer accessible.

A high-capacity form of magnetic disk is the **zip disk**. This disk compresses data to conserve storage and requires a uniquely designed zip drive. Although no longer a preferred storage medium, zip disks are available in a variety of capacities.

Hard Disks

Hard disks (also called fixed or rigid disks) are external storage devices that tend to be much faster to use and store larger amounts of information than other forms of disks. Hard disks may be permanently online to the computer system or attached as a self-contained removable storage device.

Hard disk devices are manufactured in a dust-free environment and hermetically (heat) sealed to protect against foreign matter. The sealed hard disk device is mounted on a chassis that spins the disk at high speed. The hard disk drive has two recording heads, one below and one above the disk. Both recording heads are used to read and write to the disk's surfaces. The access time of a hard disk device depends on the mechanism used to move the recording heads across the disk.

Data stored on a hard disk are classified as nonvolatile. Users must take care to protect data stored on a hard disk.

USB Drives

Peripheral devices can be connected to a computer through a parallel port, serial port, or USB port. Parallel ports tend to transfer data much faster than serial ports, and USB ports are even faster. Traditional parallel and serial plugs are being replaced by a Universal Serial Bus (**USB**) connector that has evolved as a common fixture on desktop, laptop, and palmtop computers, monitors, servers, and other forms of hardware. A USB port enables a computer operating system to automatically detect and connect to a device (termed "plug-and-play installation"). More than one hundred devices can be simultaneously connected to a computer through a specialty device called a USB hub. A USB connector can be used to interface with a printer, mouse, keyboard, speakers, digital camera, scanner, mobile device, and external disk drive. A **USB drive**, also called a flash drive or thumb drive, is a form of external storage that can be connected to a USB port to provide high-speed, portable memory. A USB drive can be used in place of a low-capacity disk-based storage unit, such as a floppy disk or zip disk, and can be configured with extensive storage capacity. Additionally, a USB drive can be plugged into or unplugged from a port at any time without affecting other system activity (typically referred to as hot-swapping or hot-plugging).

Optical Disks

Common forms of optical storage media are compact disk (CD) and digital versatile disk (DVD). Two important characteristics of a CD are access speed and data transfer rate. The access speed is the elapsed time required to locate and retrieve stored data. The data transfer rate is the time it takes the system to display the retrieved data. The higher the drive speed, the faster the system can access data from the disk. While CD-R is read-only, CD-RW drives can both read and record (or write) information onto a compact disc and create separate files similar to those on a hard disk. A DVD is an optical storage device that operates similarly to a CD, except that its capacity can be significantly larger.

Anatomy of a Computer

The technical descriptions contained in this section closely parallel the operations and equivalent components often found in both small minicomputers and larger automated systems.

Microprocessor Characteristics

The microprocessor is the central processing unit of a computer. The number assigned to a microprocessor chip refers to the complexity of its CPU. The microprocessor is the chip that processes instructions and carries out system commands. Central processing units vary in the amount of information they can process. Older microprocessors process significantly fewer bytes of data than newer models. A byte of data is eight bits, or the amount of information contained in one character (a letter or numeral). The more information a computer can process at one time, the faster it operates.

In addition to the processing capability of a CPU, speed is an important factor. The speed of a CPU is termed its "clock rate" or "clock speed." Clock speed can be measured in **megahertz (MHz)**, **gigahertz (GHz)**, or higher speeds. One MHz is equivalent to one million cycles per second; a gigahertz is equivalent to one billion cycles per second. A 1 GHz computer, for example, will operate slower than a 3 GHz computer. Just as CPU processing ability can be compared to the lanes on a highway, the CPU clock speed can be related to the highway speed limit. The higher the clock speed, the faster the CPU can process data.

On the other hand, higher clock speeds also produce more heat, and over-heating can often be a significant barrier to clock speed increases. The critical component related to speed is termed an independent processing unit or core unit. The role of a core unit, or simply core, is to execute program commands (e.g., edit data, move data, save data, print data, etc.) efficiently. Computer processors initially had a single core component. As the problem of excess heat slowed the development of ever faster microprocessors, the search for greater speed turned to the use of more than one core processor, starting with the dual-core processor. As system capabilities continued to advance, multi-core processors (units with more than two independent cores) became readily available. As a result, multiple core units gained multitasking capabilities to run multiple instructions simultaneously, thereby increasing overall speed without corresponding heat gains. Improved performance, reduced power consumption, and completion of complex tasks are outcomes brought about by **core multi-processors (CMP)**. Nearly all hospitality technology solutions employ multiple core processors, including desktop, mobile and tablet computers, servers, and workstations.

Personal computers are most often identified by the model number or name of the microprocessor contained in the system unit.

Bus System

Inside a computer, there are channels through which signals travel. A **bus system** is defined as the electronic circuitry over which power, data, address, and other signals travel. Signals need to get from one location to another, and the system's bus architecture facilitates such movements.

There are three buses within a computer system; together they make up the BIOS (bus input/output system). One transports data (data bus), another directs operations (address bus), and another transmits instructions (control bus). A data bus is the electrical pathway over which data travels between the CPU, disk drives, and peripherals. The address bus is responsible for finding the specific address that contains the requested data, and the control bus transports instructions on what to do with addresses and data. Assume the CPU needs to send two instructions, such as "start reading data at address abc" and "stop reading data at address xyz." The messages "start reading data" and "stop reading data" will be carried on the control bus. The proper location of data elements would be accessed by the address bus. The requested data would be sent to the CPU through the data bus.

A computer's BIOS is important, since it transports signals among the different input and output devices and the computer's microprocessor. The BIOS is basically a platform into which peripheral devices (serial ports, parallel ports, network cards, etc.) are inserted. Add-ons to PCs are typically connected to the system's BIOS.

System Architecture

Advancements in input/output (I/O) architecture are changing the way in which computers process data. The capabilities of the I/O bus should match the number of bits a microprocessor can process at once. A BIOS clock speed is not the same as a CPU clock speed. Since bus speed is generally measured in nanoseconds (billionths of a second) and CPU speed is generally clocked in GHz (billions of cycles per second), I/O bus speed and CPU clock speed typically do not match exactly. Some variance in speeds is tolerable. Similar to differing speeds among motorists on merging highways, major imbalances between I/O bus and CPU speed may lead to traffic jams. Computer traffic jams are termed bottlenecks.

Historically, most computers were built using Industry Standard Architecture (ISA) in which I/O buses have fixed bit or byte widths (referred to as bandwidth). Given the increased capability of microprocessors, ISA is often too slow for CPUs with newer microprocessors that manage large amounts of data at a time. Extended Industry Standard Architecture (EISA) and Micro Channel Architecture (MCA) were developed in response to the need for a bus that is compatible with microprocessors that process larger quantities of data more quickly and efficiently. These systems are designed to more easily handle the workload created by faster, more powerful microprocessors.

Computer Add-Ons

Add-ons are components or devices that are added to a system to increase its storage capacity, modify its architecture, or upgrade its performance. An add-on may require the insertion of a special circuit board inside the computer unit or operate wirelessly through an external access point. Before expanding the capabilities of a system, the user must recognize the limitations placed on add-on components by the computer's power supply. The power supply provides electrical current to the computer. Power supply is expressed in watts. The higher the wattage, the more add-on components a computer will be able to support.

While there are many peripheral devices that may be connected to a computer system, the most popular add-on components are expanded memory, extended memory, modem devices, fax boards, interface boards, and network interface cards.

Expanded Memory. The additional memory that resides outside the computer's basic memory and that can be accessed in revolving blocks is referred to as **expanded memory**. Since expanded memory was developed in response to limited capabilities, it is usually available through add-on circuit boards. A circuit board is inserted into one of the computer's main board expansion slots. Expanded memory takes advantage of unused reserved memory that the computer believes is in use when, in reality, it is not. For example, the computer system may reserve several Mbs of space for the system monitor. Should the system monitor require only half of the reserved space, expanded memory can be used to take advantage of this opening. Expanded memory swaps blocks of memory located outside the computer for unused memory located within the computer. The borrowing of this available memory is commonly referred to as "bank switching." Some computer operating systems work better with expanded memory than others. Expanded memory is additional memory that enables large programs to use memory beyond conventional limitations. While expanded memory may be slower than extended memory, it is compatible with more software. Computers with extended memory can also take advantage of expanded memory, but the opposite is not true.

Extended Memory. The linear memory that reaches beyond a system's basic limits is referred to as **extended memory**. Extended memory often comes built into the system board of some microprocessing units or can be purchased as an add-on. Unlike expanded memory, which swaps unused computer memory within the system's limits, extended memory provides memory outside the system limits. Extended memory is usually required for advanced multitasking (running several applications simultaneously). Extended memory operates faster than expanded memory, but is compatible with fewer types of software.

Modem Devices. A modem is a telecommunications device that is used to transmit digital data over analog telephone lines (telephone modem) or via coaxial cable (cable modem). A modem board is installed on the computer's main board or externally cabled to an ethernet port. Once the modem detects an open channel, data file transfer can begin.

Fax Boards. "Fax" is an abbreviation of "facsimile." A fax board allows a computer user to send and/or receive images of documents. These documents can vary from text to pictures, diagrams, and maps. Fax boards prepare data files for transmission and then, using an internal modem, connect to a destination computer and transmit the document electronically.

Interface Boards. Peripheral devices often need more than a cable or wireless access point to communicate with a computer. An interface board (also referred to as an interface card) is composed of a series of microchips on a circuit board containing an I/O port. The interface board connects to the CPU and allows communications between the CPU and a remote device. It is the circuitry of the board that allows the peripheral to recognize information it receives from the computer. An interface board may be placed into an available expansion slot on the main board. The input/output port, or access point, of the interface board protrudes outside the computer for cable connections or for antenna attachment in the case of wireless transmission.

Network Interface Cards. A network interface card (NIC), also referred to as a "network adapter card," enables a computer to communicate on a network. The NIC basically performs bi-directional functions: it sends and receives data. Some NICs contain a memory chip and are capable of storing incoming and outgoing data. NICs must be compatible with the network cabling or wireless protocol used to establish connectivity within the network.

Hardware Configurations

The most common hardware configuration for property-based systems is the client-server model. This model uses a powerful file server PC to hold the software application and all relevant data, and communicates with the individual PC workstations over a local area network (LAN). Sometimes systems vendors require separate servers for their products.

There is much justification for using multiple servers, in that keeping the software applications separate does reduce the chance of one application interfering with another and makes troubleshooting easier. However, sometimes the vendors err on the side of caution, requiring a hotel or restaurant to spend more money on hardware than may be necessary. Going too far in the other direction and putting as many applications as possible on a single server may save hardware costs, but it increases the property's vulnerability to server failure, as multiple systems could be lost at once.

This is less of a problem than it used to be, given increasingly failure-resistant servers that often feature redundant disk drives and power supplies, but unless fully redundant servers are installed, failure will always remain a possibility. It is always worth analyzing a property's actual combination of systems before ordering specific hardware. Typically, at least two servers are required: one for hotel-specific applications and one for general-purpose software (such as Microsoft Office, anti-virus programs, etc.) and network management.

The other systems configuration that is seeing growing interest is the web-hosted or cloud computing model, more properly called a remote-server model. In this scenario, the application software is physically located somewhere other than at the property, such as at the vendor's or hotel chain's headquarters or even at a third party's satellite location. The users' workstations at the property are connected to the server over a wide area network (WAN), and the applications are paid for on a monthly rental or a per-transaction fee basis.

Much of the publicity cloud computing has received comes from the emergence of the Internet (the "cloud") as an inexpensive way to implement a distant configuration, but a remote application can also be used (and with greater guarantees of security and performance) over virtual private networks (VPN). Several mission-critical hotel and restaurant applications are available in a cloud computing version, and use the Internet or a VPN for data security.

The benefit to the property is the removal of worries about server reliability, data backups, and software upgrades, since the cloud application vendor takes care of them. The trade-offs are the long-range cost of using the system (transaction-based costs work out about the same as lease payments, but are continuous), and the vulnerability of the operation to the loss of the network connection. However, networks have proven themselves to be extremely reliable, especially if configured with backup links with automatic connection in case of primary failure, and practical experience has removed many fears on this score. The ongoing cost of accessing software on this monthly service basis is still a factor, but once a traditional system has been paid for, there are still operational costs arising from disruptions if it is not kept up to date (with the vendor's application enhancements and with anti-virus and anti-spam software upgrades), and if it's not backed up or supported properly from a hardware viewpoint. It's an analysis all potential users have to work out for themselves, but there's a great deal of merit in paying a steady fee to have access to a professionally maintained, always-current cloud computing system.

Cloud Computing

Cloud computing, also known as virtual computing, is the term used to describe off-premises, as opposed to on-site, automation. The "cloud" represents the Internet, with application software located at various websites. Cloud computing allows users to access programs and data from anywhere there is an Internet connection. While not all functions lend themselves to cloud application, there are some hospitality areas that may be well-suited to an off-premises model. Historically, there have been many designs promoted as remote hospitality computing applications. Such terms as outsourced, web-hosted, application service provider (ASP), and software as a service (SaaS) have been used to describe designs for cloud computing systems, in which data is transported from the host property to an application provider's website for processing and storage.

Property management computing has generally been applied to individual workstations under the cloud, with the system's in-house memory components storing operational and transactional data. Some hospitality companies do, however, recognize the potential benefits of centralized management and control of data, and have moved to an automation model where data is stored on, and many applications are performed from, an in-house server. The possibility for moving applications and data storage farther away from the hotel or restaurant, into the cloud, is also an option. Several cloud platforms are available from various industry technology suppliers; security concerns, however, are an important challenge with cloud-based applications, since systems can be accessed by unauthorized parties more easily than with applications that are based in-house. Precautions users can take include installing firewall and other types of protection software.

Interface Connections

One other systems hardware issue worth mentioning is the equipment used to implement the interfaces that link the sub-systems with the PMS and with each other. The basic need is to establish communication between the file server and its interface partner.

Sometimes, in the simplest configuration, the servers are fitted with communications boards that enable the interface connections directly. More commonly, a separate device sits between the two servers to handle the interface traffic. To some extent, this configuration off-loads communications traffic from the application servers, thereby boosting performance, but it will create a need for more space, given the extra hardware.

Some vendors use standard PCs as interface servers, with various restrictions as to the number of sub-system interfaces (usually from two to ten) that each can control to preserve satisfactory performance. A widely used alternative is Comtrol's Lodging Link, a specialized interface communications unit that handles up to eight interfaces. While having the advantages of small physical size and quick implementation, the Comtrol unit provides interfaces among the most widely used system components.

Software

The hardware of a computer system does nothing by itself. In order for hardware components to operate, there must be a set of instructions to follow. Instructions that command an automated system to perform useful tasks are called **software**. Software programs direct data processing procedures through hardware operations.

There are two broad categories of software: system software and application software. System software, which is managed by the system supplier, is responsible for diagnostics and maintenance of hardware components. Application software is under the user's control and may be generic or industry-specific. Examples of generic software include word processing, electronic spreadsheet, database management, and communication programs. Examples of industry-specific software are property management systems, restaurant management systems, catering systems, and club management systems.

Experienced system users are familiar with system software, which must be present for application software to establish a connection with system hardware components. The discussion of system software in this chapter focuses primarily on operating systems.

The Operating System

A significant portion of system software is the operating system. Like other types of system software, the operating system controls interactions between hardware components of an automated system and application software programs. An operating system is necessary for a system to be able to carry out instructions generated by application software programs. The operating system manages routine computer functions while maintaining system priorities. The operating system controls how the system receives, transfers, and outputs information at the most fundamental levels. The computer cannot function without an operating system.

A computer system must have a control mechanism if it is to run application software programs without constant intervention from the user. When a user directs the system to save a program or data to an external storage device, something must happen within the system so that the entered command successfully initiates the proper sequence of operations for storing the program or data. The management of such routine functions is handled by the operating system.

In simplest terms, the operating system is the program that controls the execution of other programs. Think of the operating system as the traffic controller of a busy metropolis, directing the flow of traffic by controlling the signals at every intersection. Like the traffic controller, the operating system is at the center of system activity, directing the flow of data and instructions from application software to the various hardware components of the system.

Common operating systems include Windows (Windows 7, Windows 8, etc.), Mac OS, Linux, and others. The various Windows systems account for the majority of operating systems employed in the hospitality industry.

Operating systems rely on a graphical user interface (GUI) that contains several user-friendly files. A GUI allows a mouse (or other pointer or touch-sensitive device) to interact with display screens containing icons (small pictorial representations) and drop-down and pull-down menus. To select a program, the user merely moves the cursor to the appropriate icon or menu item and clicks the mouse. Unlike a character user interface (CUI), which requires the user to enter text commands, a graphical user interface relies upon cursor control and icon selection. GUI was one of the original aspects of Windows that helped distinguish it from other operating systems.

An important characteristic of a multi-tasking operating system is that multiple programs and files can be open and used simultaneously. In addition, the operating system should incorporate a standardization of design among compatible programs. By learning the basics of one GUI-based application, the user becomes familiar with other GUI applications.

Newer versions of operating systems support several user interfaces, including the traditional GUI interface, the multi-media user interface (MUI), and network-enabled (and Internet-enabled) interfaces. A network-enabled interface combines the functionality of the operating system with an Internet browser-like screen in which icons function like hyperlinks on the web. These versions feature advancements in user interfacing, work productivity design, enhanced system security, improved digital entertainment, and ease of mobile device connectivity. From a networking perspective, the operating system supports a variety of connectivity options as well as several forms of data encryption and automated backup techniques. Operating systems are designed to provide effective data processing, sharing, storage, and security, and are considered appropriate for complex business applications that seamlessly connect a variety of users to networked applications needed for collaborative work. In addition, an efficient operating system will have built-in defenses against spyware and malware, as well as outstanding firewall security.

Networks

A **network** is a configuration of workstations that enables users to share data, programs, and peripheral devices. Data-sharing allows systemwide communications, and program-sharing enables users to access infrequently used programs without the loss of speed or memory capacity that would normally result if those programs were installed at each workstation. From an economic perspective, device-sharing is an important benefit derived from networking. Expensive peripheral devices, such as high-capacity storage devices and high-definition color laser printers, can be made available to all clients connected to a network server.

A network environment can be configured as client-server (c/s) or peer-to-peer (p/p). A client-server environment links a powerful computer (file server) to several (a handful, dozens, or even hundreds) of other, less powerful computers (clients). Clients may access a variety of programs stored on the server and draw upon the server's processing power to perform tasks more quickly and more efficiently than if they operated in a stand-alone mode.

An advantage of the client-server environment is that the server can handle multiple client requests simultaneously. Client-server networks also improve system performance by managing communications (e-mail) and providing network administration (monitoring and security).

Unlike the client-server network, in a peer-to-peer network, each workstation functions as both a client and a server. Since any client can be a server and any server can be a client, the devices are considered to have equal, or peer, status. Peer-to-peer networks, like client-server networks, support communications, database management, and file sharing. Unlike client-server networks, peer-to-peer networks tend to achieve lower levels of performance and be more prone to security and access control problems.

WiFi Networks

High-frequency radio-wave technology can be used to support a wireless network, also referred to as a **WiFi (wireless fidelity) network**. WiFi networks are based on a universally adopted standard known as 802.11. In a WiFi network, the originating system component converts data into a radio signal and transmits it using an antenna device. The signal is then picked up, decoded, and forwarded by a device called a **router**. In turn, the data is broadcast to the network. This process also works in reverse, enabling a network computer to communicate data through an access point that converts the data to radio signals and sends it to the originating system component. The ease of installation, basically involving a network router and wireless access point, presents minimum hurdles to creating a WiFi network (also called a hot spot). The creation of hot spot areas within hospitality properties (hotels, restaurants, clubs, and casinos) serves as a WiFi platform for the business to apply internal wireless applications, while providing guests a workspace for public Internet access and other forms of remote computing. Given there is no need for wires or cables, WiFi networks are more flexible, yet remain capable of operating at levels of reliability and speed comparable to or greater than hard-wired networks.

Internet Components

The Internet is a collection of diverse networks. Data transmitted on the Internet will likely travel between several types of networks, computers, and communication lines before reaching a final destination. Special hardware components of the Internet are designed to move data from network to network in a seamless operation. Such devices as bridges, gateways, and routers are essential to effective Internet operations.

A **bridge** connects two or more networks that use the same data transfer protocol (the same address format). A bridge enables attached networks to operate as a single network. The purposes of a bridge are to extend network capabilities and to isolate network traffic.

A **gateway** provides a means for two incompatible networks to communicate. A gateway simply converts the sending computer's request into a format that the receiving computer can understand. A dial-up phone or cable modem are examples of gateway devices.

Internet host computers are connected to routers that direct messages between different areas of the Internet. A router interprets the protocol used in a data packet (a group of data being sent over the Internet) and translates between sending and receiving protocols. Routers are used to connect networks that incorporate different protocols.

 **Key Terms** ───────────────────────────────

Input/Output

cursor—A flashing marker on a display screen that indicates where the next character to be entered will appear.

dashboard and flash reports—Reports that are produced when predetermined parameters are attained and appear on a user's screen, but are not necessarily accompanied by hard copies.

gesture recognition applications—Applications designed to respond to hand motions or facial expressions rather than physical interfaces such as keyboard, mouse, or touchscreen.

hard copy—A printed paper copy of system-processed information.

impact printer—An electronic printer, such as a dot matrix printer, that prints character by character and line by line.

ink jet printer—An electronic nonimpact printer that works by spraying a minute and finely controlled jet of ink onto paper. The ink (carbon) is electrically charged as it is sprayed onto the paper. Once charged, the jet of ink can be moved around by electric fields in much the same way that an electron beam is used to produce a picture on a television set.

laser printer—A high-speed electronic nonimpact printer similar in appearance to desktop photocopying machines. While other printers print one character at a time, laser technology enables these devices to print an entire page all at once.

monitor—A system output device that is usually capable of displaying both text and graphics (e.g., graphs, pie charts, etc.) in soft copy. Also, these output units may be programmed to various foreground and background color combinations while operating many software applications.

mouse—A small manual input unit used in place of, or with, a keyboard or touchscreen. Designed to fit comfortably under a user's hand, it controls the cursor or pointer on the display screen. It can also be used to choose commands, move text and icons, and perform a number of other operations.

nonimpact printer—A category of electronic printers that includes thermal, ink jet, and laser printers.

scanner—A system input device capable of translating a page of text into a machine-readable format by converting the images on a page into digitized information that the system can recognize.

soft copy—Output on a monitor that cannot be handled by the operator or be removed from the system.

touchscreen terminal—A terminal that contains a unique adaptation of a screen and a special microprocessor to control it. The self-contained microprocessor displays data on areas of the screen that are sensitive to touch. Touching one of the sensitized areas produces an electronic charge that is translated into digital signals telling what area was touched for transmission to the microprocessor. This signal also instructs the microprocessor to display the next screen.

voice recognition—A form of input that converts spoken data directly into electronic form suitable for processing.

System Components

bus system—The electronic circuitry over which power, data, address, and other signals travel.

central processing unit (CPU)—The control center of a system. Inside are the circuits and mechanisms that process and store information and send instructions to the other system components.

core multi-processor (CMP)—A CPU containing two or more microprocessors that permit more effective multitasking of separate applications running simultaneously or of a single application written to take advantage of multi-threading.

expanded memory—The additional memory capacity that resides outside the system's basic memory. It can be accessed in revolving blocks, and is available as add-on boards that are inserted into one of the system's expansion slots.

extended memory—Memory that reaches beyond a system's basic limits; usually required for advanced multitasking (running several applications simultaneously).

gigahertz (GHz)—A unit of electrical frequency equal to one billion cycles per second; used to measure the speed of a system's central processing unit.

hardware—A systems term referring to the physical equipment of a system. Hardware is visible, movable, and easy to identify. In order to have a system, three hardware components are required: an input/output (I/O) component, a central processing unit (CPU), and an external storage device.

megahertz (MHz)—A unit of electrical frequency equal to one million cycles per second; used to measure the speed of a system's central processing unit.

nonvolatile memory—Memory that holds its content without power. A term describing ROM (Read Only Memory); programs stored in ROM are not lost when the system is turned off or otherwise loses electrical power.

operating system—Responsible for orchestrating the hardware and the software within the system. It establishes the system's priorities and directs its resources to accomplish desired tasks.

random access memory (RAM)—Often abbreviated as RAM, a portion of a system's internal memory that holds a temporary version of the programs or data that users are processing.

read-only memory (ROM)—Often abbreviated as ROM, a portion of the internal memory of a system that holds a permanent record of information that the system needs to use each time it is turned on.

read/write—A system is said to "read" when it takes data in for processing, and "write" when it sends processed data out as information. RAM is often described as read/write memory; the user can both read from RAM (retrieve data) and write to RAM (store data).

software—A systems term referring to a set of programs that instructs or controls the operation of the system's hardware components. Software programs tell the system what to do, how to do it, and when to do it.

USB—Universal Serial Bus; a peripheral device connector that is much faster than parallel or serial ports.

volatile memory—A systems term used to describe random access memory (RAM). When the memory device loses electrical power, or is deliberately turned off, all user data stored in RAM is lost. In order to save data stored in RAM for future use, the user must instruct the system to save it on a nonvolatile storage device.

External Storage

formatting—A process that creates the tracks and sectors of a disk on which the system is able to read and write information.

hard disks—External storage devices that are much faster to use and store far greater amounts of information than magnetic disks. Hard disks are permanently online to the system.

magnetic disks—External storage media, also called diskettes or floppies, frequently used for shipping data and programs from one location to another. They are made of thin, flexible plastic that is protected by a jacket. The plastic is coated with a magnetized oxide compound designed to hold electronic information. The size of the disk (eight-inch, five-and-one-quarter inch, or three-and-one-half inch) depends on the type of system used.

random access medium—A characteristic of an external storage medium (such as magnetic disks) permitting data to be stored in any available location on the disk. Since the tracks and sectors of the disk are numbered, the system allows a user to access stored data quickly and easily.

sequential access medium—A systems term referring to an external storage medium, such as a magnetic tape, which stores data in chronological sequence.

USB Drive—A data storage device that connects to a USB port.

zip disk—Compresses data to conserve storage space and requires a unique zip drive to operate.

Internet Hardware

bridge—A hardware component of the Internet that connects two or more networks that use the same data transfer protocol. A bridge makes attached networks appear to operate as a single network. The purposes of a bridge are to extend network capabilities and to isolate network traffic.

cloud computing—Term used to describe off-premises, as opposed to on-site, automation.

gateway—A hardware component of the Internet that provides a means for two incompatible networks to communicate. A gateway simply converts the sending system's request into a format that the receiving system can understand.

network—A configuration of workstations that enables users to share data, programs, and component devices (such as monitors and printers).

router—A hardware component of the Internet that directs messages between different areas of the Internet.

WiFi network—A local area network that uses a wireless transmission protocol.

 Review Questions

1. What does the term "hardware" mean? Identify the three hardware components necessary for a computer system, and describe their functions.

2. What are the various types of keys typically found on a computer's keyboard?

3. What is the difference between an impact printer and a nonimpact printer? Give examples of each type of printer.

4. What is the difference between RAM and ROM?

5. What are examples of external storage devices?

6. What is the difference between a sequential access medium and a random access medium?

7. What terms do the following abbreviations represent: I/O, CPU, CRT, CD-R, CD-RW, DVD?

8. What is meant by the term "software"?

9. What are the various functions performed by most operating systems?

10. What comprises a network? What are the two ways networks can be configured?

11. What are three hardware components essential to effective Internet operations? What are their functions?

 Internet Sites

For more information, visit the following Internet sites. Remember that Internet addresses can change without notice. If the site is no longer there, you can use a search engine to look for additional sites.

Apple, Incorporated
www.apple.com

Compaq
www.compaq.com

Dell
www.dell.com

Gateway
www.gateway.com

Hewlett-Packard Development
  Company, L.P.
www.hp.com

IBM Corp.
www.ibm.com

Intel Corporation
www.intel.com

Maitre'D POS
www.maitredpos.com

MICROS Systems, Inc.
www.micros.com

NEC Corporation
www.nec.com

Radiant Systems, Inc.
www.radiantsystems.com

Sony Corporation of America
www.sony.com

Tyco Electronics
www.elotouch.com

Chapter 3 Outline

Electronic Distribution Channels
    Global Distribution Systems
    Internet Distribution Systems
    DSP Connectivity
    Extranet Connectivity
Intersell Agencies
Central Reservation Systems
    Affiliate and Nonaffiliate Systems
    CRS Functions
Property-Level Reservation Systems
    Reservation System Elements and
        Procedures
Distribution of Revenues
    Merchant Model
    Wholesaler Model

Competencies

1. Describe the role played by e-distribution systems and distinguish global distribution systems from Internet distribution systems. (pp. 62–65)

2. Explain the use of distribution service providers and extranets in meeting the needs of hotels and the e-distribution channels they use. (p. 65)

3. Summarize the services provided by intersell agencies. (p. 66)

4. Distinguish affiliate from nonaffiliate central reservation systems. (pp. 66–68)

5. Identify the basic functions and services performed by a central reservation system. (pp. 68–71)

6. Explain the elements and procedures of a property-level reservation system. (pp. 71–76)

7. Describe the revenue effects of using various distribution channels and explain the difference between the merchant model and the wholesaler model. (pp. 76–78)

3

Reservation Systems

WHILE MANY INDUSTRIES automated several decades earlier, the hospitality industry did not actively pursue automation until the 1970s. This comparatively late start enabled the hospitality industry to benefit from advances in technology. While other industries were struggling to upgrade their existing systems, hoteliers and restaurateurs received greater value for dollars spent on newer hardware components and easier-to-operate software modules. This is especially true in regard to the first generation of hotel reservation systems. However, lodging reservation systems became less efficient as technological advances linked reservations directly to comprehensive property management systems (PMSs), central reservation systems (CRSs), and electronic distribution systems (EDSs). Soon, second-generation systems matured and expanded their processing capabilities. The implementation of next-generation reservation systems included Internet distribution systems and myriad intermediary and referral networks. These worldwide reservation systems more effectively linked hotel reservations to systems developed for airlines, car rental agencies, travel agencies, cruise lines, and other travel-related businesses. The popularity of online self-reservations and third-party rooms promotions has further changed the reservations landscape; for example, the burden of making room sales has been shifted from hotel staff to online content and website applications, and it has become more difficult for revenue management to identify upcoming high or low demand periods, which influence rate setting.

The proper handling of reservation information is critical to the success of hotel companies and individual properties. Reservations can be made for individuals, groups, tours, or conventions. Each request for accommodations creates a need for an accurate response in relation to the availability of room types and rates at a given point in time, making it critical that all distribution channels have access to current availability information.

The online sale of overnight rooms has exploded into multiple distribution channels, with hotels encouraged to participate in all available channels. In addition to property-direct reservations that are entered locally into the hotel PMS, there are property online reservations, central reservation systems, global distribution systems, Internet distribution systems, and intersell arrangements. To ensure transaction integrity, online applications may employ enhanced encryption security techniques and promotional materials such as photographs, virtual tours, and multimedia presentations of candidate hotel properties. In order to maintain current room and rate inventory information, online distribution systems may rely on a distribution service provider (DSP) and/or a hotel extranet application. Exhibit 1 lists the various types of reservation channels and sample providers.

Exhibit 1 Reservation Channel Examples

Global Distribution Systems
    Sabre
    Galileo
    Amadeus
    WorldSpan

Internet Distribution Systems
    Hotwire
    Priceline.com
    Orbitz
    Hotels.com
    Expedia
    Travelocity

Central Reservation System
    Affiliate Reservation Network (Hotel Chains)
    Nonaffiliate Reservation Networks
        Leading Hotels of the World
        Preferred Hotels
        Distinguished Hotels

Intersell Agencies
    Airline and Other Travel and Club Affiliates

Property Direct
    PMS Reservations Module

This chapter examines reservations management systems, including electronic distribution systems, global distribution systems, Internet distribution systems, DSP connectivity, extranet connectivity, central reservation systems, intersell arrangements, and property-direct reservation systems.

Electronic Distribution Channels

Electronic distribution, or **e-distribution**, is the means by which hotels make products and services available via electronic channels, including travel agents, wholesalers, consolidators, and consumers. Such channels are widely viewed as more convenient for those constituents that have online access and are often a less expensive source of bookings than traditional channels. Electronic distribution includes the following two major categories: global distribution systems (GDS) and Internet distribution systems (IDS).

Competing hotel companies may participate in the same global or Internet distribution systems. Therefore, e-distribution channels must provide a security system that protects the proprietary nature of room and rate availability data. Security is usually maintained through passwords, data encryption, firewalls, and other security methods. Users of a system may be issued passwords that restrict access to proprietary data. Although passwords may need to be changed frequently, they can offer effective measures of security.

Global Distribution Systems

Global distribution systems (GDSs) are often formed as joint ventures linking a number of diverse businesses. By directly linking the reservation systems of hotel, airline, car rental, and travel agency companies on a worldwide basis, global distribution systems provide access to travel and tourism inventories around the world. A global distribution system can represent a significant portion of reservations business for many airport, convention center, and resort properties.

Most central reservation systems connect with one or more of the global distribution systems. The largest and best known GDSs are Sabre (www.sabre.com), Amadeus (www.amadeus.com), and Galileo and WorldSpan (which can both be found at www.travelport.com). Historically, each GDS was owned by an airline company or consortium of airline companies. Over the years, GDS companies have evolved into electronic marketing agencies with a propensity to promote hotel bookings over airline traffic. The Hotel Electronic Distribution Network Association (HEDNA) tracks GDS industry statistics and researches channel traffic patterns.

GDSs provide worldwide distribution of hotel reservation information and allow selling of hotel reservations around the world. GDSs also provide distribution of airline tickets, automobile rentals, and other services that may be required by travelers. Through mergers and acquisitions, several GDS companies also control Internet travel sites.

Selling hotel rooms is usually accomplished by connecting the hotel company reservation system with the GDSs. Most online travel agents (OTAs) around the world have terminals connected to one or more of the many airline reservation systems to book airline travel. By having hotel accommodations and automobile rentals available in the reservation system at the same time, most GDSs provide single-source access to most of the travel agent's selling requirements. In one transaction, an OTA is able to sell an airline ticket, hotel room, and automobile rental.

Although many global distribution systems perform similar functions, each maintains unique internal system formats in relation to room rate, room type, and availability, confirmation, and settlement information. A key to the success of distribution systems is the **smart switch**. This switch translates reservations transactions into as many unique formats as required by diverse network interconnections, thereby allowing participating firms to share data from diverse reservation systems without having to deal with complex formats, files, and operating systems. The smart switch can access reservation system files and convert the data into an easy-to-use format.

Travel agents were once reluctant to book hotel rooms through GDSs because room availability and rates were not always accurate and the hotel confirmation process was not always foolproof. Hotel companies now, however, have their central reservation systems linked to GDSs, which allows travel agents to book reservations directly into hotel systems and verify room availability and rates in real time. This process is called **seamless integration**. Confirmations come from the hotel companies' systems, eliminating the concern about the inaccuracy of data or the unreliability of the confirmation process. In a seamless configuration, all distribution channels operate from the same database, a concept termed single image inventory.

Since most airlines have leisure travel departments, airline reservations agents often also sell hotel rooms. With several hundred thousand terminals around the world, GDSs represent a powerful force in hotel reservations.

Internet Distribution Systems

Internet distribution systems (IDSs) are consumer-oriented reservation systems that function as self-service e-distribution channels. In contrast to GDSs, consumers themselves typically use these systems to book airline, hotel, restaurant, car, and cruise ship reservations. The wealth of information available to consumers has never been greater, and consumers are willing to do the research necessary to find satisfactory accommodations online. As a consequence, the online environment has become highly competitive. Discount sites and last-minute travel bargain notifications have provided an outlet for the hospitality industry to dispose of distressed or otherwise under-utilized inventory.

Typically, IDSs are operated by independent website sponsors that implement an online reservation booking engine. IDS sites can connect to a property in at least three ways:

1. Connection to the company's central reservation system

2. Connection to a switching company that connects to a central reservation system

3. Connection to a GDS that connects to a central reservation system

The web supports two IDS processing models: transparent sites and opaque sites. While both models tend to feature a proprietary property rating or private star ranking system, there is at least one major difference between the two. In a transparent application, the names and locations of candidate hotels appearing in the qualifying range of the prospect's search criteria are identified; this is not true for an opaque site. Expedia (www.expedia.com), Hotels.com, Lastminute.com, and Travelocity (www.travelocity.com) are examples of transparent IDS sites.

At an opaque site, a hotel room tends to be marketed by price and/or star stratification without revealing a brand affiliation or any other property specifics. The services, amenities, and ambiance of individual properties are not considered. The hotel brand, location, and features are hidden from the buyer until the transaction is complete. Since the hotel's identity is not disclosed until after the sale is completed, branding or defining whether the guest is a customer of the e-commerce site or the hotel can be challenging and confusing. Since both hotel and travel sites tend to offer loyalty club points or frequent shopper rewards, this can be an important concern for hotel management.

Opaque sites sometimes work on an auction basis. Potential guests may specify a rate they are willing to pay and the site then determines available inventory in that price range. If it has no inventory to sell in the price range specified, it may contact alternative participating hotels to see if they will accept the bid price. Since these rates may be significantly below the published or even usual discounted rates of the hotel, profit margins are reduced. For this reason, many hotel companies do not offer loyalty club points or upgrades for reservations made through opaque sites. Examples of opaque sites include Priceline.com and Hotwire (www. hotwire.com).

IDS reservations can incur hosting and transmission fees, processing costs, sales commissions, and other expenses and tend to have the highest transaction cost of online options. The final cost of the reservation transaction is directly attributable to the electronic distribution interchange (movement of data) of the booking from the IDS to the hotel PMS.

DSP Connectivity

A **distribution service provider (DSP)**, also called a switching company, provides a link between a room and rate data source and an electronic distribution channel provider. The role of the DSP in the reservations network is to communicate room and rate availability data from a CRS to participating online GDS and IDS entities, and, in turn, transport completed reservation records to the CRS. DSPs are especially important to hotels that participate in multiple distribution channels, as the DSP will ensure that identical and timely rate and inventory information goes to all sites simultaneously. Simply stated, DSPs form linkages so that hotels do not have to individually communicate room and rate information to each member of a CRS, GDS, or IDS network directly. Instead, the DSP receives updated reservation data and forwards it to affiliated distribution channel members using push technology. In addition to populating availability databases, a DSP can also provide competitive benchmarking of booking performance metrics unavailable through alternate sources. Examples of DSP companies include Pegasus (www.pegs.com) and TravelCLICK (www.travelclick.net).

Extranet Connectivity

Instead of relying on a DSP, a hotel can employ a secure external website for linkage to e-distribution channel participants. An extranet is a website, or a partitioned and password-protected portion of a website, that is available to a restricted number of authorized users. While extranets are not as popular as DSPs for transmitting proprietary room and rate data, an extranet can simplify data transmission and acquisition needs. With an extranet, the hotel places current data onto the extranet site and allows participant companies access to the data using pull technology. Once captured, the current data is uploaded and replaces legacy data at the distributor's site.

Hotels may also create extranets to serve high-volume customers. For example, a major hotel brand may create an extranet for its largest corporate customers to use. When corporate clients access the extranet, they are provided specially negotiated room rates for room types addressed in the corporate contract. Examples of hotel distribution channels that rely on extranet site updating include Hotels.com and PlacesToStay.com.

Intersell Agencies

Domestic competition for hotel reservation commissions is intense since other segments of the travel industry (consolidators, wholesalers, booking agencies, etc.) may also operate reservation systems. Airline carriers, travel agencies, car rental companies, and chain hotels offer stiff competition to independent central reservation systems entering the reservations marketplace.

The term **intersell agency** refers to a reservation network that handles more than one product line. Intersell agencies typically handle reservations for airline flights, car rentals, and hotel rooms. The spirit of an intersell promotion is captured by the expression "one call does it all." Although intersell agencies may channel reservation requests directly to individual hotels, some elect to communicate with central reservation systems or electronic distribution channels.

It is important to note that a local, regional, or national intersell arrangement does not preclude a hotel property from participating in a GDS or IDS or from processing reservations directly from its own website or via contact with the hotel's reservation department.

Although there are a variety of options for interconnecting various intersell agencies with individual properties, the goal of integrating operations is to minimize suspense time. Suspense time refers to the elapsed time from reservation request to response. Minimal suspense time results when, instead of communicating with participating individual properties, intersell agencies are able to automatically access reservation system information (rate and room availability). Information-sharing provides intersell reservation agents with a simplified method for booking a guest's complete travel requirements, and also provides participating hotels with a way to simultaneously update the central reservation system. Intersell systems enhance product distribution while providing a basis for cost-effective CRS operations. The CRS simply increases its exposure while reducing its operating expenses.

Central Reservation Systems

Vacation travelers, business travelers, corporate travel offices, and international visitors are all able to use the web to arrange for their own travel and accommodation needs. The variety of potential guests accessing Internet sites to place reservations has prompted travel and hospitality companies to develop simple, user-friendly reservation procedures. Large and small hotels alike have a presence on the Internet. One of their most important tools is the central reservation system.

Since the early 1970s, the hospitality industry has seen many independent central reservation systems enter and leave the marketplace. Demand for their services was not the problem. Rather, it was difficult to service the demand at an acceptable profit. Expensive equipment (hardware components and communication devices), high overhead, and extensive operating costs have made it difficult for independent central reservation systems to succeed. The staff required to process individual reservation requests and to maintain diverse reservation records for a multitude of hotel properties can lead to dwindling revenues and soaring operating costs.

Increased online interaction between hotel property management systems, central reservation systems, and electronic distribution channels decentralizes the reservation function but centralizes marketing and sales efforts in relation to the reservations process. This results in greater control of reservations handling at the property level and increased sales efforts across various distribution channels on behalf of the participating properties.

Affiliate and Nonaffiliate Systems

There are two types of **central reservation systems**: affiliate (chain-operated) and nonaffiliate (independent) systems. An **affiliate reservation system** is a hotel chain's central reservation system in which all participating properties are contractually related. Each property is represented in the system database and is required to provide room availability and inventory data to the central reservation system on a timely basis. Chain hotels link their operations in order to streamline reservations processing and reduce total system costs. Typically, a central reservation system of an affiliate system performs the following functions:

- Deals directly with public access

- Advertises a website address or contact information

- Provides participating properties with network technology

- Communicates individual property room rate and availability data to e-distribution channels and nonaffiliate reservation systems based on information supplied by individual properties

- Performs data entry services for remotely located or nonautomated properties

- Transmits reservations and related information to individual properties quickly and cost-effectively

- Maintains statistical information on the volume of contacts, conversion rates, denial rates, and other statistics (conversion rate is the ratio of booked business to total number of inquiries; denial rate refers to reservation requests that were turned away)

- Performs customer relations management functions for guest recognition and loyalty programs

- Maintains a property profile of statistical information about online viewers

- Manages a commission or payment exchange for reservation transaction

Some affiliate systems enter into agreements with non-chain properties, allowing them to join the system as overrun facilities. An **overrun facility** is a property selected to receive reservation requests after chain properties have exhausted room availabilities in a geographic region.

A **nonaffiliate reservation system** is a subscription system linking independent properties. A hotel subscribes to the system's services and takes responsibility for updating the system with accurate room rate and availability data. Examples of nonaffiliate reservation systems are The Leading Hotels of the World, Preferred Hotels & Resorts, and Distinguished International Hotels, Residences and Resorts.

Nonaffiliate systems generally provide the same services as affiliate systems, thus enabling independent hotel operators to gain benefits otherwise available only to chain operators. However, many nonaffiliate systems process reservations solely on the basis of the availability of room types. With this method, room types are classified as either "open" or "closed." Most affiliate systems process reservations on the basis of a declining inventory of both room types and room rates. This method helps participating properties to maximize revenue potential and occupancy.

Affiliate and nonaffiliate central reservation systems often provide a variety of services in addition to managing reservations processing and communications. A CRS may also serve as an inter-property communications network, an accounting transfer system, or a destination information center. For instance, a CRS is used as an accounting transfer system when a chain hotel communicates operating data to company headquarters for processing. When a CRS communicates reports on local weather, special events, and seasonal room rates, it serves as a destination information center.

CRS Functions

Central reservation services are provided by the **central reservation office (CRO)**. The CRO manages room rate and availability information from participating properties. Information from connected properties is typically sent over communication lines and enters the database directly. In a CRS network configuration, the responsibility and control of room and rate information lies at the property level. The key to successful central reservation management is that the individual properties and the central system have access to the same room and rate availability information in real time. When this is the case, the system is able to confirm room rates and availability at the time of reservation.

The timely transfer of reservation confirmations from a CRS to individual properties is vital. Many chain systems provide multiple delivery alternatives to ensure that properties receive all new reservations, modifications, or cancellations. For example, most central reservation systems relay processed transactions to member properties through online interfaces. Although online interfacing between central reservation offices and property-level systems is fast and effective, some networks may also e-mail or fax the information to properties to ensure successful completion of the reservation process.

The goals of a CRS are to improve guest service while enhancing profitability and operating efficiency. A CRS accomplishes these goals by:

- Providing access to special room rates and promotional packages.

- Instantly confirming reservations.

- Communicating with major airline, travel, and car rental agencies.

- Creating comprehensive reservation records.

Basic services provided by most central reservation systems include automatic room availability updating and corporate-wide marketing.

Automatic Room Availability Updating. As a room is sold, whether through an e-distribution channel, a CRS, an individual property, or a remote intersell agency, the inventory of rooms available for sale is simultaneously updated for all reservation tracking systems. Having current, synchronized room availability information for each participating distribution channel provides the ability to automatically close out room types without obtaining direct property approval. Under a single image inventory system, reservationists (at any distribution channel) can directly confirm room rates and availability at the time reservations are made.

In the past, a CRS primarily was provided intermittent room availability data from participating properties at regularly scheduled intervals. This meant that when a property booked its own reservations, there would be no immediate notice of status change sent to the CRS; updating waited until the next scheduled reporting period. As the CRS booked reservations for a property, messages were sent to the property, printed, and stored. The property was often required to manually enter the printed transactions into its in-house reservation system so that accurate room availability data could be recalculated. In turn, this recalculated data was sent back to the CRS as an update on room availability. Advances in technology now allow for single image inventory that enables all distribution sources to work from the same data.

Corporate-Wide Marketing. A CRS can function as a powerful marketing resource. The CRS normally contains important marketing data on individual guests and may provide participating properties with profiles of groups holding reservations. CRS technology allows hotels to vary room rates for each room type on a daily basis. Varying conditions of supply and demand may cause the room rates to slide within the ranges prescribed by each individual property.

Guest history data can be extremely helpful in processing reservations for returning guests. These data also serve as the basis for determining demographic and geographic patterns of guests staying at participating hotel properties. Repeat guests may qualify for special frequent traveler or other loyalty program rewards offered by a hotel chain or individual property. By accessing guest history data, central reservation systems are usually able to direct and support a variety of marketing-oriented programs. Guest profile data may include:

- Guest identification number.
- Full name and preferred salutation.
- Membership status in the program.
- Home and business addresses and telephone numbers.
- Type of guestroom preferred.
- Amenities, such as king-sized bed, non-smoking room, or pillow preference.
- Preferred form of account settlement.

For each guest's stay, the system may track the guest's arrival and departure dates, number of room nights by room type, and a revenue breakdown by room, food and beverage, and other categories. In addition, special promotions, packages, and/or recreational activities may be noted.

Additional Services. In addition to maintaining up-to-date information about room availability and rates, a comprehensive CRS may maintain such data as:

- Room types
- Room rates
- Room décor
- Room location
- Promotional packages
- Travel agent discounts
- Alternative booking locations
- Guest recognition programs
- Special amenities
- Weather conditions and news reports
- Currency exchange rates
- Connectivity to affiliate websites
- Connectivity to the company's loyalty program
- Connectivity to local area attractions and events

In addition to processing reservations, a CRS may perform a variety of other services. A reservation system may serve as an administrative network for inter-property communications. The reservation system may also be used as the preferred platform to transfer accounting data from individual properties for processing at company headquarters. In addition, the system may operate as a destination information center by serving as a communications channel (portal site) for local weather, news, and reports on special hotel features. Central reservation systems can report:

- Travel or airline agent performance statistics
- Effectiveness of promotional packages
- Sales forecasting information

Many systems enable participating hotels to build in specific rules and procedures for each of the hotel's promotional packages or products. Some central reservation systems expand basic services to include such functions as:

- Revenue or yield management
- Centralized commission reporting
- Links to intersell agencies
- Deposit/refund accounting
- Links to electronic-distribution channels

Revenue management, also called yield management, is a set of demand forecasting techniques used to develop pricing strategies that maximize rooms revenue for a lodging property. Centralized commission reporting details the amounts payable to travel agencies (and others) booking commissionable business with a hotel through the hotel's CRS. Hotel companies that require advance deposits to ensure reservations may find the CRS helpful in maintaining pre-arrival accounting records. Records can be kept of deposits made with reservation requests and of amounts refunded to individuals or groups who cancel reservations within the allotted time and procedures specified by management.

Property-Level Reservation Systems

Prospective guests will sometimes contact a property directly to make reservations. This contact may involve the property's own website (property online reservations) or it may involve a phone call or other direct communication with a person in the reservations department (property direct reservations).

Online reservations booked at an individual hotel's website rely on a simple interchange operation. Interactive script at the website is used to capture reservation and guest information used in creation of a reservation record. Once the record exists, the system takes responsibility for placing the record in the reservations database. With the lowest associated cost per online transaction, direct reservations are the least expensive of all reservation options. Unlike other online formats, property online reservations incur expenses associated only with maintaining current room rate and inventory updating at the site. There are no transactional fees or commissions paid for bookings at a property online application.

Property direct reservations involve a guest contacting the hotel's reservation department to ascertain room rate and availability information. An on-site staff member processes the reservation inquiry through the hotel's property management system (PMS) and completes the transaction locally.

Reservation System Elements and Procedures

Property-level reservation systems are designed to meet a property's particular needs. A PMS typically supports a reservation module designed to streamline reservations handling and distribution channel management. The specific needs and requirements of individual properties determine whether stand-alone reservation management software is operated separately or as a part of an overall reservation system network.

A PMS carries out a number of front- and back-office functions, including property-direct reservations processing. Once the data is captured, a property-level application can streamline operations by enabling the reservations module to rapidly process room requests and generate timely and accurate rooms, revenue, and forecasting reports. Electronic reservation files can be reformatted into pre-registration and registration records capable of monitoring guest cycle transactions. Interfacing an external reservation network to an in-house application provides an enhanced data-handling procedure.

A PMS reservation module may also enable a staff reservationist to respond quickly and accurately to requests for future accommodations. This module can also connect to the CRS for seamless reservation processing. The module significantly reduces paperwork, physical filing, and other clerical procedures, providing the reservationist with more time for personal attention to callers and marketing various services the hotel offers. Stored information can be accessed quickly, and many of the procedures for processing requests, updating information, and generating confirmations are simplified.

A guest can contact a hotel reservation network or property directly and work with a reservationist who can create a **reservation record**. Alternatively, the guest can access a hotel reservation network or property website and create their own reservation record through completion of an electronic form. Reservation records identify guests' special requests prior to their arrival at the property and enable the hotel to personalize guest service and appropriately schedule needed staff and resources. In addition, reservation modules can generate a number of important reports for management's use. The following sections describe typical activities associated with the use of a PMS reservation module. These activities also apply to a majority of the booking engines used in e-distribution channels. These activities include:

- Reservation inquiry

- Determination of availability

- Creation of the reservation record

- Confirmation of the reservation

- Maintenance of the reservation record

- Generation of reports

Reservation Inquiry. A reservation request can be received in person; over the telephone; via postal delivery, facsimile, or e-mail; or through an online interface with an external reservation distribution channel. Regardless of its origin, the reservation request is formulated into a **reservation inquiry** by the reservationist or automatically by the software application. This inquiry typically contains the following data:

- Date of arrival

- Type and number of rooms requested

- Number of room nights

- Room rate code (standard, special, package, etc.)

- Number of persons in party

The online guest or reservationist enters the preliminary data through a software template according to rigidly defined inquiry procedures. Simultaneous processing occurs in real time, meaning that the reservationist receives the necessary feedback from the system in order to respond immediately to the inquiry. The **real time capability** of many reservation modules is designed to provide instant responses (less than three seconds) and, therefore, enables the reservationist to edit, alter, or amend the inquiry. Once the inquiry is matched with rooms availability data, the PMS can be programmed to automatically block a room, thus removing that room from the availability database.

Determination of Availability. Once entered, the reservation inquiry is compared to rooms availability data according to a predetermined inventory algorithm. The algorithm may be an automated formula designed to sell rooms in a specified pattern (by zone, floor, block, etc.). Processing a reservation request may result in one of several system-generated responses, including:

- Acceptance or rejection of the reservation request.

- Suggestions of alternative room types or rates.

- Suggestions of alternative dates.

- Suggestions of alternative hotel properties.

Exhibit 2 presents a sample room availability search screen.

Creation of the Reservation Record. Once the reservation request has been processed and the room blocked, the system requires completion of the reservation record by filling in necessary fields, such as:

- Guest's contact data (name, address, e-mail address, and telephone number)

- Time of arrival

Exhibit 2   Sample Room Availability Search Screen

Booking Name	MGR	Tot Rms	Avg Rate	Total Revenue	Fri 03/16	Sat 03/17	Sun 03/18	Mon 03/19	Tue 03/20	Wed 03/21	Thu 03/22	Fri 03/23	Sat 03/24	Sun 03/25	Mon 03/26	Tue 03/27
Definite Totals		1605	94	150,217	80	99	80	0	1	1	1	80	80	1	1	85
Tentative Totals		312	95	29,718	41	0	0	0	3	8	14	35	35	0	1	0
Other Totals		32	99	3,168	0	0	0	0	0	0	0	0	0	0	16	16
Ceiling					140	140	105	105	105	105	105	140	140	105	105	105
Professional Engineers of I	EMJ	11	105	1,150	11											
20XX IASM Annual Conve	JDF	30	0	0	10	10	10									
20XX Annual Meeting	JDF	165	139	22,980	55	55	55									
Manulife Bank	CLB	30	100	3,000	30											
20XX IASM Annual Conve	MMM	30	0	0	10	10	10									
SMITH WEDDING	JDF	10	150	1,500	5	5										
20XX Annual IASM Conve	JDF	0	0	0	0	0	0									
Witzel Party	CLB	19	99	1,881		19										
National Ballet School	DAB	5	99	495			5									
IAPA	MAT	3	90	270					3							
Mark Markusoff Inc.	CLB	6	120	720					1	1	1	0	0	1	1	1
Wescast Industries	MAT	8	99	792						8						
Center for Behavioral Res	WED	42	88	3,696								14	14	14		
Waterloo M.B. Church	SAB	20	99	1,980									10	10		
Chatham Maroon Oldtimer	DAB	20	99	1,980									10	10		
Pentecostal Assembly	EMJ	120	97	11,640									60	60		

Courtesy of INNFINITY Software Systems, LLC.

- Reservation classification (advance, confirmed, guaranteed)

- Confirmation number

- Caller data (agency or secretary)

- Special requirements (handicapper, crib, no smoking, etc.)

Exhibit 3 presents a sample reservation record screen.

A major benefit of automated processing is the streamlining of the initial inquiry and the collection of secondary reservation record data. This prevents the waste of time that occurs when the data is collected at the outset and the system then denies the reservation request.

Confirmation of the Reservation. Property management systems can automatically generate reservation confirmation notification following reservation processing. Information can be retrieved from the reservation record and placed in a template designed for mailing, emailing, texting, or faxing. While there are many formats and styles of confirmation letters, acknowledgments within confirmation letters generally include:

- Guest's name and address

- Date and time of arrival

- Type, number, and rates of rooms

- Number of nights

- Number of persons in party

Exhibit 3   Sample Reservation Record Screen

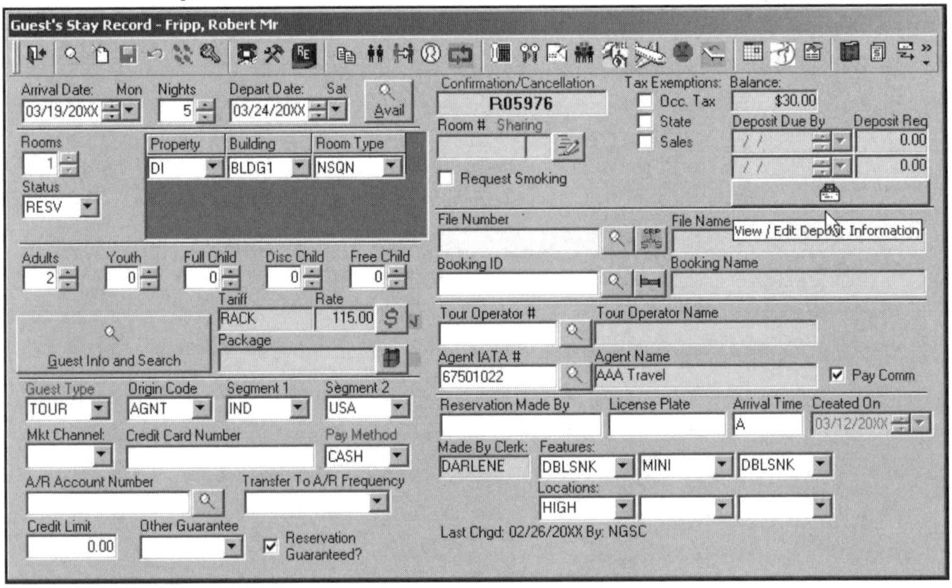

Courtesy of INNFINITY Software Systems, LLC.

- Reservation classification (advance, confirmed, guaranteed)
- Special services requested by the guest
- Confirmation number
- Request for deposit or prepayment
- Update of original reservation (reconfirmation, modification, or cancellation)
- Cancellation policy
- Transportation directions or options

Reservation confirmations may be distributed immediately as part of placement of the reservation into the database. This process is often part of the system update. A **system update** performs many of the same functions as those routinely performed by a night audit in nonautomated properties. System updates are run daily to allow for report production, system file reorganization, system maintenance, and to provide an end-of-day time frame.

Room Reservation Record Maintenance. Reservation records are stored in a database and commonly segmented by date of arrival (year, month, day), group name, and guest name. File organization and the method of file retrieval are critical to an effective reservation module because guests frequently update, alter, cancel, or reconfirm reservations. For example, should a guest request a cancellation, the online application or staff reservationist must be able to quickly access the correct reservation record, verify its contents, and process the cancellation. In turn, the reservation module typically provides a system-generated cancellation code number.

Data from reservation records is also used to generate preregistration reports. Reservation records can also serve as preregistration folios for presale guest cycle transactions. Prepayments, advance deposits, and cash payouts are examples of transactions that can be posted to the reservation record and later transferred to the guest's in-house folio.

In addition, the reservation module has the ability to interface with other front office functions. Reservation record data can be:

- Used to generate preregistration reports that help accelerate the check-in process.
- Used to create electronic guest folios and information lists (alphabetical listings or sequential room number listings).
- Transferred to commission agent files for later processing.
- Formatted for eventual inclusion in a guest history file.

Generation of Reports. Similar to many PMS applications, the number and type of reports available through a reservation module are functions of the user's needs, software capability, and database contents. A PMS reservation module is designed to maximize room sales by accurately monitoring room availabilities and providing a detailed forecast of rooms revenue. A **rooms availability report** lists, by room type, the number of rooms available each day (net remaining rooms in each category). A **revenue forecast report** projects future revenue by multiplying predicted occupancies by assigned room rates. A PMS reservation module can also compile and generate:

- Reservation transaction records
- Expected arrival and departure lists
- Commission agent reports
- Turnaway statistics

A **reservation transaction record** provides a daily summary of reservation records that were created, modified, or canceled. Reservation modules may also generate supplemental summaries of specialized activities, such as cancellation reports, blocked room reports, and no-show reports. **Expected arrivals lists** and **expected departures lists** are daily reports showing the number of guests expected to arrive and depart, the number of stayovers (the difference between arrivals and departures), and the names of guests associated with each transaction. **Commission agent reports** delineate reservation transactions and commissions payable, by agent. Agents having contractual agreements with a hotel may earn commissions for the business they book at the property. A **turnaway report**, also called a refusal report, tracks the number of room nights refused because rooms were not available for sale for specified date(s). This report can be especially helpful to hotels that experience peak demand periods.

Advancements. Since reservations management was the first functional area of hotels to be automated, it has received a great deal of vendor research and development. Additionally, the airline industry has spent millions of dollars developing its own reservation techniques, many of which have been adapted to the needs of hotels. One of the more interesting developments in reservations technology is experimentation with automated speech recognition (ASR).

Interactive multi-media and virtual reality presentations for independent travelers, meeting planners, and travel agents remain under development. The addition of voice input/output seems the next step as lodging companies continue to develop panoramic photography and full-motion property tours through property websites. Experimentation with verbal recognition/synthesis technology (spoken commands) is promising and may significantly affect hotel reservation modules in the future.

Distribution of Revenues

Revenues derived by hotels (suppliers) and agents (sellers) engaged in online distribution channels vary widely across channels. While there are no agent transaction fees for property-direct reservations, central reservation systems typically charge affiliate properties either a fixed rate per night per room regardless of reservation activity or a transaction fee based on bookings, or both. The amount of revenues earned by the CRS depends on the financial negotiations contracted between the chain and its member properties. GDS companies derive residual revenues by levying transaction fees, transmission fees, and/or operating on a merchant or wholesaler model. For example, a hotel selling a room for $100, nets $100; but when a GDS agent sells the room for $100 the hotel receives less money. Why? There are multiple fees that reduce the net revenue for the hotel. For example, the seller—assume an online travel agency—earns a 10 percent commission ($10 in this case) and the GDS may be paid a $3 transaction fee. In addition, the reservation transaction may be processed through the chain's CRS, reducing the net revenue by an additional amount—perhaps $5. In this example, the hotel nets $82 for the sale of a $100 room rate, while $18 is paid for commissions and fees associated with the reservation transaction. Similarly, Internet distribution system websites produce revenues based on a merchant model or wholesaler model (discussed below).

When hotel room rates are discounted, the property's occupancy is likely to increase as its revenues per room decrease, thereby creating a conflicting set of conditions. The tactic is used in hopes that the decrease in rate will be more than offset by the increase in occupancy. An additional concern for hotel management is arbitrage. **Arbitrage** is defined as the simultaneous purchase and sale of an asset in order to profit from a price difference. For example, when an IDS company purchases a hotel room at a discounted price, applies a price multiplier, and resells the room for a higher price, arbitrage is created. The price difference, sufficient to offset commissions, may raise questions about the fairness of the transaction from the hotel's perspective, as the same room type may be available in multiple channels at different rates. The IDS company likely would argue that without the IDS exposure, the room probably would have remained unsold.

Merchant Model

The **merchant model**, also called the markup model, is an e-commerce strategy that involves the negotiation of reduced room prices with a supplier hotel. The participating hotel provides rooms at a discounted rate that may be 20 to 35 percent below the lowest published rate for the room type. This discounted rate is called the net rate. In turn, the merchant (i.e., seller) takes on the responsibility for marketing the rooms that are allocated to it by the hotel at the discounted net rate. The merchant then multiplies the net rate by a factor to achieve the gross rate. For example, assume a standard room has a lowest published rate of $100. The net rate to the merchant is found by applying the agreed-upon discount rate, which in this example is 25 percent. The hotel's net rate is therefore $75. The merchant then determines the new selling price (gross rate) for the room by multiplying the net rate by a percentage markup (assume a 25 percent markup factor). This generates a gross rate of $93.75.

In this example the merchant earns a gross margin (gross rate minus net rate) of $18.75 and the guest pays $6.25 less than the normal $100 rack rate. In essence, the purchaser experiences a discount of 6.25 percent. This formulation supports the strongest argument of an online merchant, which is that the gross rate allows the hotel to remain price-competitive (the offered rate remains close to the $100 published rate). In addition, merchant sites tend to rank the presentation of a hotel higher with more features in its display list based on the lowest net rate offered to the merchant. For example, two competing hotels both have published rates of

$100 that also appear on their own websites. Hotel A offers a net rate to a merchant model website of $75, or a 25 percent discount. Hotel B offers a net rate to the same merchant model website of $70, or a 30 percent discount. If the website chooses to mark up the rates from Hotel B by 35 percent, it will earn more than if it marks up the rate by 25 percent for Hotel A. As a result, the website may market or promote Hotel B more strongly than Hotel A. In doing so, the merchant tends to be more successful in its negotiations of net rate through content and ranking incentives provided by the hotel. In other terms, the hotel bargains for more preferential positioning and treatment on the merchant's website by offering a lower net rate. However, many hotel managers feel pressured to provide significant discounts to merchant model websites out of fear that their hotel will not be promoted as well as their competition. Examples of merchant model sites include Hotels.com, Lowestfare.com, Orbitz (www.orbitz.com), Lodging.com, and Travelocity.

Wholesaler Model

The **wholesaler model**, also called the commission model or agent model, is an alternate e-commerce strategy for determining room rates for inventory from a supplier hotel. In a wholesale transaction, the hotel pays a commission to the wholesaler based on a percentage of the hotel's net rate. In this model, the hotel maintains greater control over the end price paid by the guest. Simply stated, the hotel sets the selling price and the wholesaler receives an agreed-upon sales commission. For example, consider a hotel company that offers a room with a rate of $100 to a wholesaler at a net rate of $80. If the hotel agrees to pay the seller a 10 percent commission, the room will have a gross rate of $88. The difference between the gross rate and net rate is the seller's gross margin, in this case, $8. Although the guest pays $12 less than the published rate, the seller tends to earn less in the wholesaler model than the merchant model. It is for this reason that sellers tend to favor the merchant model, while hotels tend to favor the wholesaler model. Wholesalers will tend to give preference to those rooms that provide the greatest margin for the seller. When negotiated commission rates are similar, then the hotels offering the lowest net rates will be the most preferred by the wholesaler. Some wholesalers, like Priceline and Hotwire, may negotiate a minimum margin to be added to the net rate rather than work on percent commission. Examples of wholesaler model sites include Expedia, Trip.com, Hotwire, and Priceline. Orbitz, like several other travel sites, offers both a merchant model and a wholesaler model platform.

🔑 Key Terms

affiliate reservation system—A hotel chain's reservation system in which all participating properties are contractually related. Each property is represented in the computer system database and is required to provide room availability data to the reservations center on a timely basis.

arbitrage—The simultaneous purchase and sale of an asset in order to profit from a price difference.

central reservation office—Typically deals directly with the public, advertises a central telephone number, provides participating properties with necessary communications equipment, and bills properties for handling reservations.

central reservation system—An external reservation network. *See also* affiliate reservation system *and* nonaffiliate reservation system.

commission agent report—Delineates reservation transactions and commissions payable, by agent.

distribution service provider (DSP)—An intermediary between a CRS and e-distribution channels that provides single image inventory information to participating online GDS and IDS entities and communicates reservation information back to the CRS. Also called a switching company.

e-distribution—The selling of products or services over the Internet or some other electronic medium. Hospitality e-distribution includes the GDS and Internet-based sales channels.

expected arrivals list—A daily report showing the number of guests and the names of guests expected to arrive with reservations.

expected departures list—A daily report showing the number of guests expected to depart, the number of stayovers (the difference between arrivals and departures), and the names of guests associated with each transaction.

global distribution system (GDS)—Electronic networks used by travel agents and some Internet-based distribution channels to make airline, hotel, car rental, and cruise ship reservations.

Internet distribution system (IDS)—Internet-based services providing consumers the ability to book airline, hotel, car rental, and cruise ship reservations.

intersell agency—A reservation network that handles more than one product line. Intersell agencies typically handle reservations for airline flights, car rentals, and hotel rooms.

merchant model—An e-commerce strategy in which a seller negotiates a discounted rate with a supplier hotel and then adds its own markup factor and sells the rooms to consumers. Also called the markup model.

nonaffiliate reservation system—A subscription system linking independent properties. A hotel subscribes to the system's services and takes responsibility for updating the system with accurate room availability data.

overrun facility—A hotel property selected to receive reservation requests after chain properties have exhausted room availabilities in a geographic region.

real time capability—Refers to simultaneous processing. For example, real time capability enables a reservationist to receive necessary feedback from the system immediately in order to respond to a caller's requests during a telephone call.

reservation inquiry—A reservation request is formulated into a reservation inquiry by the reservationist. This inquiry typically collects the following data:

date of arrival, type and number of rooms requested, number of room nights, room rate code (standard, special, package, etc.), and number of persons in party.

reservation record—A record created before guests arrive at the property to identify the guests and their needs. Such records enable the hotel to personalize guest service and appropriately schedule needed personnel.

reservation transaction record—Provides a daily summary of reservation records that were created, modified, or canceled.

revenue forecast report—Projects future revenue by multiplying predicted occupancies by current house rates.

revenue management—A set of demand forecasting techniques used to develop pricing strategies that maximize rooms revenue for a lodging property.

rooms availability report—Lists, by room type, the number of rooms that are available each day (net remaining rooms in each category).

seamless integration—The ability of travel agencies to book reservations directly into hotel reservation systems, as well as verify room availability and rates.

smart switch—Translates reservations transactions into as many unique formats as required by diverse network interconnections, thereby allowing users to share data from different reservation systems without having to deal with complex formats, files, and operating systems. The smart switch can access reservation system files and convert the data into easy-to-use formats and files.

system update—Performs many of the same functions performed by a traditional night audit routine in nonautomated properties. System updates are run daily to allow for report production, system file reorganization, and system maintenance, and to provide an end-of-day time frame.

turnaway report—Also called a refusal report, tracks the number of room nights refused because rooms were not available for sale. This report is especially helpful to hotels with expansion plans.

wholesaler model—An e-commerce strategy in which a seller negotiates a discounted rate with a supplier hotel and then adds a standard markup factor and sells the rooms to consumers. Also called the commission model.

 Review Questions ————————————————————————————

1. Why is data security a concern of electronic distribution systems?

2. What role might the Internet play in a global distribution system?

3. How do affiliate reservation systems differ from nonaffiliate reservation systems?

4. What does the term "intersell agency" mean?

5. What services are provided by a central reservation system?

6. What are the typical activities associated with the use of a PMS reservation module?

7. What data is collected through reservation inquiry procedures?

8. What data is generally included in confirmation letters produced by property-level reservation systems?

9. How can a property use data maintained by reservation records?

10. What kinds of reports can be produced by PMS reservation modules?

11. What are the merchant model and the wholesaler model? How are they different?

Internet Sites

For more information, visit the following Internet sites. Remember that Internet addresses can change without notice. If the site is no longer there, you can use a search engine to look for additional sites.

Internet Reservation Sites

Expedia
www.expedia.com

Priceline.com
www.priceline.com

Hotel Online
www.hotel-online.com

Resorts Online
www.resortsonline.com

HotelTravel.com
www.hoteltravel.com

Travelocity
www.travelocity.com

Orbitz
www.orbitz.com

Technology Sites

CSS Hotel Systems
www.csshotelsystems.com

INNFINITY Software Systems, LLC
www.innfinity.com

Execu/Tech Systems, Inc.
www.execu-tech.com

iTesso
www.myhotelsoftware.com

Hospitality Financial and
  Technology Professionals
www.hftp.org

MICROS Systems, Inc.
www.micros.com

Hotellinx Systems Ltd.
www.hotellinx.com

Newmarket International
www.newmarketinc.com

Chapter 4 Outline

Rooms Management Module
    Room Status
    Room and Rate Assignment
    Guest Data
    Housekeeping Functions
    Generation of Reports
Guest Accounting Module
    Types of Accounts
    Posting to Accounts
    Front Office Audit
    Account Settlement
    System Update

Competencies

1. Identify features and functions of the rooms management module of a hotel property management system. (pp. 83–89)

2. Define room status terms and explain the importance of eliminating room status discrepancies in hotel operations. (pp. 84–87)

3. Explain how managers can use various reports commonly generated by the rooms management module of a hotel property management system. (pp. 89–90)

4. Identify features and functions of the guest accounting module of a hotel property management system. (pp. 90–97)

5. Describe the different types of folios that a guest accounting module may use to monitor transactions. (pp. 91–94)

6. Explain how managers can use various reports commonly generated by the guest accounting module of a hotel property management system. (p. 97)

4

Rooms Management and Guest Accounting Applications

An automated property management system (PMS) monitors and controls a number of front office and back office functions. A rooms management module is always an essential component of front office software. A rooms management module maintains current information on the status of rooms, assists in the assignment of rooms during registration, and helps coordinate many guest services. Similarly, a guest accounting module processes and monitors financial transactions that occur between guests and the hotel. When remote point-of-sale devices, situated at various revenue centers throughout the hotel, are interfaced with a guest accounting module, guest charges are communicated to the front desk and automatically posted to the appropriate PMS-based guest folios.

Rooms Management Module

The rooms management module is an important information and communications branch within a PMS. It is primarily designed to strengthen the communication links between the front office and the housekeeping department. Most rooms management modules perform the following functions:

- Identify current room status.
- Assist in assigning rooms to guests at check-in.
- Provide in-house guest information.
- Organize housekeeping activities.
- Provide auxiliary services.
- Generate timely reports for management.

A rooms management module alerts front desk employees of the status of each room, just as room racks used to do in nonautomated operations. A front desk employee simply enters the room's number into the PMS to retrieve and display the current status of the room. Once a room becomes clean and ready for occupancy, housekeeping staff may change the room's status through a workstation terminal in the housekeeping department, a guestroom phone, or a wireless handheld device. The updated room status information is in turn communicated to the rooms management module. Rooms status reports may be generated at any time for use by management. Exhibit 1 illustrates one type of **rooms status report**.

Rooms management modules may also automatically assign room and rate at check-in. In addition, their ability to display guest data on screens at the front desk, switchboard, concierge station, self-check-in kiosks, and other guest service locations eliminates the need for traditional front office equipment such as room racks and information racks. A rooms management module also enables management to efficiently schedule housekeeping staff and to review detailed housekeeping productivity reports. In addition, automated wake-up systems and message-waiting systems can be interfaced with the rooms management module to provide greater control over these auxiliary guest services. Exhibit 2 summarizes primary functions performed by a rooms management module.

Room Status

Before assigning rooms to guests, front desk employees must have access to current, accurate information on the sales status of guestrooms in the property. The current status of a room can be affected by information about future availability (determined through reservations data) and information about current availability (determined through housekeeping data).

Exhibit 1 Sample Rooms Status Report

```
ROOM STATUS REPORT — KELLOGG CENTER
05/19      18:56
RU–PAGE 1                                     FLOOR(S) 2, 3, 4, 5, 6, 7

      201  OOO    202  O/D    203  CO     204  V/C    205  V/C    206  O/C
      207  V/C    208  V/C    209  V/C    215  O/C    216  V/C    217  V/C
      219  OOO    220  V/C    222  O/D    223  OOO    224  OOO    225  OOO
      227  V/C    230  OOO    231  V/C    232  V/C    233  O/C    301  V/C
      302  O/D    303  O/D    304  O/D    305  O/D    306  O/D    307  O/C
      308  O/C    309  O/D    311  O/C    312  O/D    313  O/C    314  V/C
      316  V/D    317  O/D    319  OOO    320  V/C    322  V/C    323  V/C
      325  OOO    327  V/C    328  V/C    329  O/D    330  O/D    331  O/D
      332  O/D    333  O/D    401  V/C    402  V/C    403  V/C    404  V/C

      715  V/C    716  V/C    717  V/C    719  V/C    720  V/C    722  V/C

      77  V/C    2  V/D    18  OOO    54  OCC    5  CO
```

Courtesy of Kellogg Center, Michigan State University, East Lansing, Michigan.

Exhibit 2 Functions of a Rooms Management Module

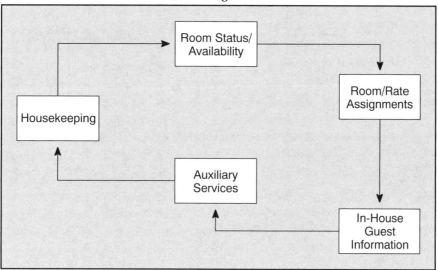

Information about future availability is important because it may affect the length of stay of in-house guests. Access to rooms availability data that extend several days into the future gives front desk employees reliable **room status** information and enhances their ability to satisfy the needs of guests while maximizing occupancy. Consider the following example.

Mr. Gregory checks in on Thursday for a one-night stay. However, during the course of his work on Friday, he finds it necessary to stay over through the weekend. The front desk employee may be inclined to approve this extension based on the fact that Friday night's business is light. Later, upon checking reservations data, the employee learns that although the hotel has a low occupancy forecasted for Friday evening, all rooms are reserved on Saturday night. This obviously poses a problem that needs to be resolved according to hotel policy, but it is better for the problem to surface Friday than on Saturday night when all guestrooms are expected to be occupied.

The housekeeping description of the current status of a room is crucial to the immediate, short-run selling position of that room. Common room status definitions are presented in Exhibit 3.

Information about current availability is absolutely essential in order for front desk employees to properly assign rooms to guests at the time of check-in. In the past, nonautomated front office systems often experienced problems because of a breakdown in communication between housekeeping staff and front desk employees. Automated front office applications, on the other hand, ensure timely communications by converting data input by front desk employees, housekeepers, or guest services personnel into messages that are available at several locations throughout the lodging operation.

Exhibit 3   Room Status Definitions

Occupied: A guest is currently registered to the room.

Complimentary: The room is occupied, but the guest is assessed no charge for its use.

Stayover: The guest is not checking out today and will remain at least one more night.

On-change: The guest has departed, but the room has not yet been cleaned and released for resale.

Do not disturb: The guest has requested not to be disturbed.

Sleep-out: A guest is registered to the room, but the bed has not been used.

Skipper: The guest has left the hotel without making arrangements to settle his or her account.

Sleeper: The guest has settled his or her account and left the hotel, but the front office staff has failed to properly update the room's status.

Vacant and ready: The room has been cleaned and inspected and is ready for an arriving guest.

Out-of-order: The room cannot be assigned to a guest. A room may be out-of-order for a variety of reasons, including the need for maintenance, refurbishing, and extensive cleaning.

Lock-out: The room has been locked so that the guest cannot re-enter until he or she is cleared by a hotel official.

DNCO (did not check out): The guest made arrangements to settle his or her account (and thus is not a skipper) but has left without informing the front office.

Due out: The room is expected to become vacant after the following day's check-out time.

Check-out: The guest has settled his or her account, returned the room keys, and left the hotel.

Late check-out: The guest has requested and is being allowed to check out later than the hotel's standard check-out time.

In addition to traditional front desk check-in procedures, some hotels are placing kiosks in the lobby area enabling self check-in. When kiosks are used, they rely on the same information that the front desk employee would use. Self check-in depends on efficient room status reporting.

The hotel PMS routes data through the rooms management module and thereby helps coordinate the sale of rooms. Hotel technology is capable of instantly updating the housekeeping status of rooms, which enables front desk employees to make quick and accurate room assignments to guests at the time of check-in. For example, when a housekeeping attendant informs the PMS that a room's status has been changed from on-change to vacant and ready, notification is automatically relayed within the rooms management module.

Room status discrepancy is a term that refers to situations in which the housekeeping department's description of a room's status differs from the room status information that guides front desk employees in assigning rooms to guests. Room status discrepancies can seriously affect a property's ability to satisfy guests and maximize rooms revenue. Nonautomated properties experience room status discrepancies not only because of time delays in communicating room status information from the housekeeping department to the front desk, but also because of the cumbersome nature of comparing housekeeping and front desk room status information. Consider the following scenario.

Mr. Gregory checks out of a nonautomated hotel and the desk clerk forgets to change his room's status in the room rack—giving the impression that Mr. Gregory remains an in-house guest. When housekeeping attendants clean the room, they may notice that Mr. Gregory's luggage and belongings have been removed (since the room has been vacated). However, if the housekeeping report does not indicate that Mr. Gregory is a check-out and not a stayover, the actual status of the room may go undetected. As long as this room status discrepancy exists, the hotel will not sell Mr. Gregory's vacated room because the room rack at the front desk will erroneously continue to indicate that the room is occupied. Unfortunately, this situation, termed a **sleeper**, arises all too often in nonautomated hotels. Why is it called a sleeper? Since the guest's registration card remains undisturbed in the room rack, it is described as being asleep.

An automated PMS operates without a room rack. Instead, the rooms management module generates a **rooms discrepancy report** that signals to management the specific rooms whose status must be investigated to resolve discrepancies. The report notes any variances between front desk and housekeeping room status updates. This is an important dimension of the rooms management module and provides an aspect of control that may otherwise be difficult to achieve.

Room and Rate Assignment

Rooms management modules may be programmed to assist front desk employees in assigning rooms and rates to guests at the time of check-in. Modules may make automatic assignments or require front desk personnel to input data to initiate room assignments.

Automatic room and rate assignments are made according to parameters specified by hotel management. Rooms may be selected according to predetermined floor zones (similar to the way in which guests are seated in a dining room) or according to an index of room usage and depreciation schedules. The system may track room histories (frequency of use) and rank rooms according to usage data. The system may then use this information to assign rooms on a basis that evenly distributes occupancy loads across the full inventory of rooms.

Interactive room and rate assignments are popular automated applications in the lodging industry. Such applications provide front desk personnel direction in decision-making situations while increasing control over actual room assignments. For example, in a property with 800 rooms, a front desk employee can narrow the search routine by clarifying the guest's needs through a series of room and rate category queries. In addition, the front desk employee may use the rooms management module to display an abbreviated list of available rooms selected by type and rate. This abbreviated list enables the front desk employee to quickly select or suggest a room to a guest at check-in. This ensures a more efficient and quicker check-in process than would a less-directed search through an extensive rooms availability listing.

To accommodate guest preferences and to ensure smooth check-in procedures, rooms management modules typically feature an override function that front desk employees can use to bypass the room or rate assignments automatically generated by the system. An override function is often a useful feature, since guest preferences may be difficult to anticipate. For example, most automatic room-and-rate-assignment programs will assign guests only to rooms whose status is "clean and available for occupancy." However, many times it may be necessary to assign a particular guest to a room whose status is on-change. For example, a guest may arrive in advance of the hotel's check-in time and have to leave immediately to attend a lunch meeting. An override function permits the front desk employee to complete the necessary check-in procedures while informing the guest that the room won't be available for occupancy until later in the day.

Guest Data

The rooms management module is also designed to provide a limited review of guest data. Guest data can be displayed on workstation screens, handheld devices, or other media, enabling a guest services coordinator, front desk employee, or concierge to quickly identify the name and room number of a particular guest. This function of the rooms management module also contributes to the elimination of such traditional information sources as information racks, room racks, and telephone lists. Workstation terminals on handheld devices may also be located at room service order stations, concierge stations, parking garage outlets, and other high-guest-contact areas to enhance employees' recognition of guests, thereby creating opportunities to personalize services.

Guest data may also be transferred from a rooms management module to a point-of-sale (POS) area to expedite the verification and authorization of guest charge purchases. When a POS terminal is interfaced with the hotel's PMS, guest data can be reviewed before charges are accepted. This capability allows cashiers to verify that a particular room is occupied and that the correct guest name is on the room folio. Access to this data minimizes the likelihood of charges being accepted and/or posted to the wrong guest folios, including the folios of guests who have already checked out or have been denied charge privileges.

Housekeeping Functions

Important housekeeping functions performed by the rooms management module include:

- Forecasting the number of rooms requiring service.
- Identifying rooms to be cleaned.
- Scheduling room attendants.
- Assigning housekeeping workloads.
- Measuring housekeeping productivity.

A rooms management module forecasts the number of rooms that will require cleaning by processing current house counts and the expected number of arrivals. After identifying rooms that will require cleaning, the rooms management module may generate schedules for individual room attendants and assign a specific number of rooms to each attendant on the basis of property-defined standards.

Upon first entering a room to clean it, a room attendant may use a handheld device or room telephone interface to the PMS to enter an employee identification code, room number (not always necessary), and a housekeeping status code number to communicate the room's current status. The system may automatically log the time of the call. When the room is clean and ready for inspection, the room attendant may again use a handheld device or room telephone interface to notify the PMS that the room is now ready for inspection. The system may once again record the time of the call. The cycle completes when an inspector confirms the room's readiness for sale.

The log of room attendants' times in and out enables the rooms management module to determine productivity rates. Productivity rates are determined by calculating the average length of time an attendant spends in a room and the number of rooms attended during a work shift. Productivity reports keep management apprised of potential inefficiencies while also tracking the whereabouts of housekeeping personnel throughout a work shift.

Generation of Reports

The number and types of reports that can be generated by a rooms management module are functions of the property's needs, software capacity, and the contents of the rooms management database. A wide variety of reports are possible because the rooms management module overlaps several key areas, such as the rooms department, the housekeeping department, and auxiliary services. Most rooms management modules are designed to generate reports that focus primarily on near-term room availability, room status, and room availability forecasting. These reports are designed to assist management in scheduling staff and distributing workloads.

A **rooms allotment report** summarizes rooms committed (booked or blocked) by future date. One type of **expected arrival/departure report** is shown in Exhibit 4. A **registration progress report** provides the rooms department with a summary of current house information. The report may list present check-ins, the number of occupied rooms, names of guests with reservations who have not yet registered, and the number of rooms available for sale. A registration progress report may also profile room status, rooms revenue, and average room rate. A **rooms activity forecast** provides information on anticipated arrivals, departures, stayovers, and vacancies. This report assists managers in staffing front desk and housekeeping areas. An **actual departures report** lists the names of guests who have checked out and their room numbers, billing addresses, and folio numbers.

A **housekeeper assignment report** is used to assign floor and room numbers to room attendants and to list room status. This report may also provide space for special messages from the housekeeping department. System-generated **housekeeper productivity reports** provide productivity information for each house-

Exhibit 4   Sample Expected Arrival/Departure Report

ARRIVALS, STAYOVERS, DEPARTURES FOR KELLOGG CENTER
DA-PAGE 001
05/13   8:40

DATE	ARRIVE	STAYON	DEPART	GUESTS	SOLD	UNSOLD	REVENUE
05/13	27	112	23	143	139	7	6,435.00
05/14	27	117	22	151	144	2	6,593.00
05/15	20	126	18	162	146	0	6,806.00
05/16	72	21	125	143	93	53	4,907.00
05/17	35	16	77	62	51	95	2,460.00
05/18	43	41	10	100	84	62	3,995.00
05/19	27	33	51	72	60	86	2,837.00
05/20	53	21	39	86	74	72	3,874.34
05/21	14	26	48	49	40	106	2,002.00

Courtesy of Kellogg Center, Michigan State University, East Lansing, Michigan.

keeper by listing the number of rooms cleaned and the amount of time taken to clean each room.

At the end of each month, quarter, and year, rooms management modules are capable of generating **rooms productivity reports** that rank room types by percentage of occupancy and/or by percentage of total rooms revenue. Rooms management modules may also produce a **rooms history report** depicting the revenue history and use of each room by room type. This report is especially useful to those properties using an automatic room-assignment function based on a rotational usage of rooms.

Guest Accounting Module

The most critical component of a hotel front office system is the guest accounting module. The creation of electronic folios enables remote POS terminals to post charges directly to guest and non-guest accounts. The guest accounting module gives management considerable control over financial aspects of the hotel guest cycle. This front office module is primarily responsible for automatic charge postings, file updating (auditing), maintenance, and folio display/printing upon demand. In addition, guest accounting modules may provide electronic controls over such areas as folio handling, account balances, cashier reconciliation, outlet guest-check control, account auditing, and accounts receivable. Exhibit 5 diagrams the sequence of activities involved in the process of guest accounting. The following sections discuss guest accounting modules in relation to:

• Types of accounts (also referred to as folios).

• Account postings.

• Account auditing.

Exhibit 5   Guest Accounting Activities

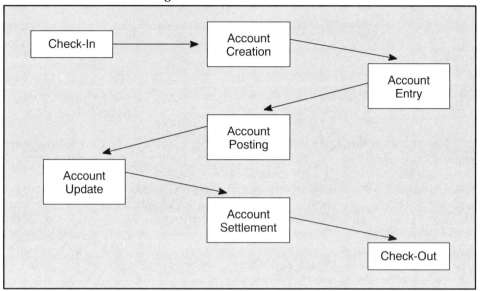

- Account settlement.
- System update and reports.

Types of Accounts

A PMS ensures that preregistration folios are prepared for guests arriving with reservations. Preregistration folios are typically produced by the PMS reservations module when a reservation record is created. When guests arrive without reservations, front desk employees capture and enter the necessary data into the PMS at check-in. The PMS uses select registration data to create an individual or group folio. Data elements needed to create a folio are referred to as header information. Common header elements include:

- Guest name.
- Street address.
- E-mail address.
- Room number.
- Folio number.

If self-check-in kiosks or handheld devices are available at the property, guests may enter the necessary data themselves by responding to system-generated queries. Information collected by kiosks will be transmitted to the PMS and used in folio creation.

While not all hotel guest accounting modules offer the same folio formats, common types of electronic folios include:

- Individual folios.

- Master folios.

- Non-guest folios (city accounts).

- Employee folios.

- Control folios.

- Semi-permanent folios.

- Permanent folios.

Individual folios (also referred to as "room folios" or "guest folios") are assigned to in-house guests for the purpose of charting their financial transactions with the hotel. Exhibit 6 presents a sample guest folio. **Master folios** (also referred to as "group folios") generally apply to more than one guest or room and contain a record of transactions that are not posted to individual folios of group members. Master folios are commonly created to provide the kind of billing service required by most groups and conventions. For example, consider the needs of the International Gymnastics Conference. While attendees at this conference are responsible for their own food and beverage expenses, the sponsoring organization has agreed to pay room and room tax charges. As participants dine at various food and beverage outlets in the hotel, their deferred payments are posted to their individual folios. Each night's room and room tax charges,

Exhibit 6   Sample Guest Folio

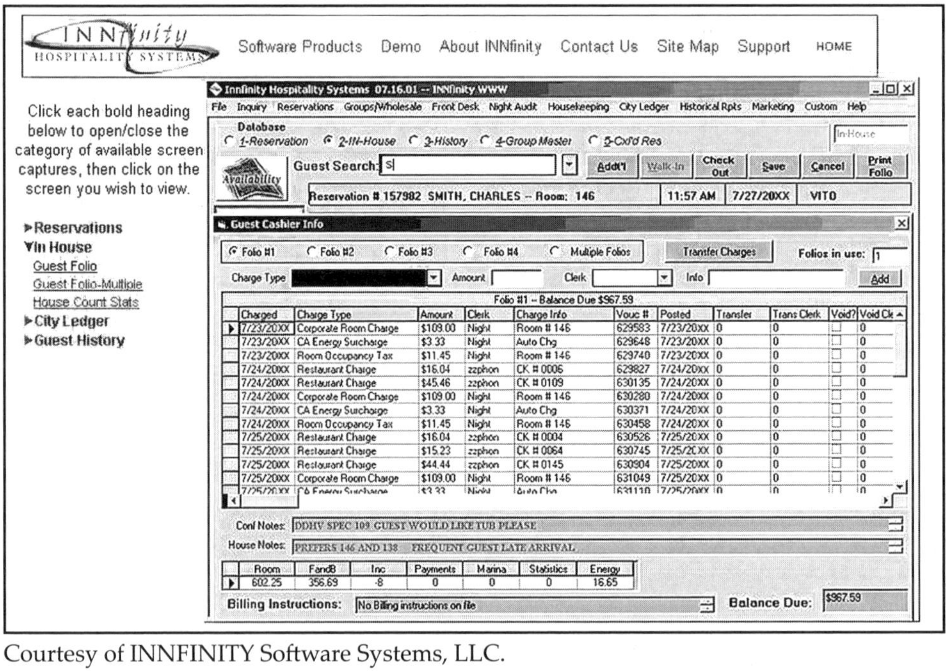

Courtesy of INNFINITY Software Systems, LLC.

however, are posted to the group's master folio. At check-out, each guest receives a folio documenting only the charges for which he or she is responsible. The conference administrator is responsible for settling the master folio containing the room and room tax charges.

Non-guest folios are created for individuals who have in-house charge privileges but are not registered guests in the hotel. These individuals may include health club members, corporate clients, recreation club members, political leaders, or local celebrities. Non-guest account numbers are assigned at the time that the accounts are created and may be printed (or imprinted) on specially prepared paper or plastic account cards. When purchases are charged to non-guest accounts, cashiers may request to see the account card as a verification that a valid posting status exists.

Procedures for posting transactions to non-guest folios are similar to those required for automatic posting of transactions to individual folios. Instead of inputting a room number, the cashier, front desk employee, concierge, or auditor inputs the non-guest's assigned account number. The use of a unique billing number alerts the guest accounting module to the type of account being processed. For example, a six-digit account number may signal a non-guest account, while a four-digit number may signal an in-house guest account. A major difference between accounting for non-guest and in-house guest transactions lies in the area of account settlement. Individual folios are settled at check-out; terms for settlement of non-guest accounts are usually defined at the time of account creation. The term "settlement" refers to bringing an active outstanding folio to a zero balance either by posting cash received or by transferring the outstanding folio balance to the city ledger or credit/debit card processor for eventual settlement.

When properties offer charge privileges to employees, transactions may be processed in a manner similar to non-guest accounts. **Employee folios** can be used to record employee purchases, compute discounts, register expense account activity, and separate authorized business charges from personal expenditures.

The efficiency of a guest accounting module in carrying out continuous posting and auditing procedures often depends on the existence of control folios. **Control folios** may be constructed for each revenue center and used to track all transactions posted to other folios (individual, master, non-guest, or employee). Control folios provide a basis for double-entry accounting and for cross-checking the balances of all electronic folios. For example, as an in-house guest charges a purchase in the hotel's restaurant, the amount is posted (debited) to the appropriate individual folio, and the same amount is simultaneously posted (credited) as a deferred payment to the control folio of the restaurant. Control folios serve as powerful internal control documents and represent ongoing auditing functions.

A **semi-permanent folio** is used to track "bill to" accounts receivable. A guest who establishes credit privileges before check-in may be allowed to settle his or her folio balance by billing a sponsoring organization or individual. The front desk agent will reconcile the account by transferring the guest's folio balance to a semi-permanent folio, thereby enabling the back office to track the billing and subsequent collection of payment from the approved third party (bill-to agency). Once the outstanding balance is paid, the semi-permanent folio is closed. It is for this reason it is referred to as semi-permanent.

A **permanent folio** can be used to track guest folio balances that are settled to credit card and debit card accounts. A permanent folio is established for each external entity with which the hotel has a contractual payment program. For example, a hotel could establish a permanent folio for American Express, Discover, Visa, and MasterCard. When the guest charges a folio balance to an acceptable form of deferred payment, the guest accounting module transfers the balance to the appropriate permanent folio for monitoring. A permanent folio enables the tracking of receivables beyond the guest's stay. Permanent folios exist as long as the hotel continues to maintain a business relationship with the outside entity.

Posting to Accounts

Account entries can be made from workstation terminals at the front desk or from remote POS terminals that interface with the PMS guest accounting module. Account entries can also be made internally—that is, from within the guest accounting module itself. For example, during the system update routine, room rates and room taxes may automatically be posted to all in-house guest folios. Although guest accounting modules vary in operation, most modules rely on specific data entry requirements to ensure that amounts are properly posted to appropriate folios. Data entry requirements may consist of the following sequence:

- Room number (or account number for non-guest transactions)
- Identification code
- Reference code
- Charge total

After a room number (or account number) is entered in a posting routine, the guest accounting module may require that an identification code also be entered. This is generally done by inputting the first few letters of the guest's last name. An **identification code** enables the guest accounting module to post a charge to the correct folio when multiple accounts exist under the same room number. In these situations, simply inputting a room number does not guarantee that the correct folio is accessed for transactional posting. To help ensure proper posting, an identification code may be part of the required data entry sequence.

Before a charge can be posted to a folio, the guest accounting module may also require that a **reference code** be entered. This is typically done by inputting the serial number of a departmental source document or a unique departmental identifier. Departmental **source documents** may be serially numbered for internal control purposes. This numbering system helps the guest accounting module maintain precise records should it become necessary to conduct investigative searches or analyze account entries made through remote POS terminals.

The final data entry requirement in an account posting procedure is to input the amount of the charge. However, before accepting a charge and posting it to a folio, the guest accounting module may initiate a **credit monitoring routine**. This routine compares the current folio balance with a predetermined credit limit (also called a **house limit**) that is determined by hotel management. Although most guest accounting modules allow managers to specify a single house limit, some provide for further options based on guest history information, such as whether the guest is a repeat customer or a known business associate. Other options may include setting a house limit on the basis of the type of reservation or the credit authorization limits established by individual credit card and debit card companies.

Regardless of how a guest's credit limit is established, an attempt to post a charge to an account initiates a credit monitoring routine, thus ensuring that the outstanding balances during a guest's stay do not exceed the account's credit limit. When hotel policy dictates that a line of credit is not to be extended to a guest, a folio can be set at a no-post status. The guest accounting module will not permit charges to be posted to a folio with a no-post status.

When in-house guests make charge purchases during a hotel stay, they are typically asked to present a room keycard as verification that a valid posting status exists. Some PMS procedures allow for keycard swiping to authorize the posting of charges to the guest's folio from POS terminals. If a guest presents a keycard for an unoccupied room (an account with a no-post status) or a guest account that already has been closed (settled), the system will not permit the cashier to post the charge. Entering the guest's identification code (the first few letters of the purchaser's last name) may provide further evidence that the person making the charge may not be authorized to do so.

Front Office Audit

Front office modules of a PMS enable several audit functions to be performed continuously throughout the guest cycle. Automated systems enable the front office auditor to spend more time auditing transactions and related activities and less time performing postings and bookkeeping entries, as with prior nonautomated systems. Monitoring account balances and verifying account postings require a standardized procedure that compares guest ledger and non-guest ledger audit data with the front office daily report for balancing. When these documents are out of balance, there is usually an internal computational problem or an unusual data processing error. For example, the interface between the POS system may have been inoperative for a short time during the day. The POS system may show the total number and amount of the day's transfers to the front desk system, but the front desk system may have different totals due to the system problem. The front office auditor must reconcile the differences and post the adjusting entries to the guest ledger to bring the two systems in balance.

An automated guest accounting application retains previous balance information for guest and non-guest accounts, along with appropriate transactional details, in a comprehensive database. Automated guest accounting applications calculate current balances very quickly and make balances readily available to guests (through TV review) and front desk staff (through access procedures) and contain programs for account corrections.

The guest accounting application performs numerous mathematical verifications to ensure postings are correct. For example, a range check will recognize postings of unusual size, such as a $15 charge being posted as $1,500. Since most guest accounting applications are capable of tracking each posting by time, shift, employee, folio number, and revenue center, a detailed audit trail of transactional activity is created.

Guest accounting applications also offer rapid access to information, thereby enabling front office management to more knowledgeably manage operations. Reports detailing revenue data, occupancy statistics, advance deposits, arrivals, no-shows, room status, and other operational information can be generated on request, or as part of the regular system update routine.

Account Settlement

The ability to prepare clear itemized guest statements (with reference code detail) may significantly reduce guest disputes relative to folio postings. For example, assume that at check-out time Ms. Nessy has found what she believes to be a discrepancy in a long-distance telephone charge appearing on her folio. The front office cashier uses the reference code number on the folio to locate the proper telephone call record. The cashier then verifies the source (room number) from which the call was placed and the telephone number that was called. This drill-down procedure enables the cashier to quickly, objectively, and efficiently resolve the dispute.

PMS update routines may be programmed to generate a printed set of folios (usually by 7:00 A.M.) for guests expected to check out that day. Preprinting folios significantly speeds up the check-out process and minimizes guest discrepancies. When additional charges are posted to folios that have already been preprinted, the preprinted folios are simply discarded and updated folios, with the corrected account balance, are printed at check-out.

Automatic, instantaneous posting of all charges helps avoid or manage late charges or charges made under false pretenses. **Late charges** are charged purchases that are posted to folios after account settlement. For example, assume Mr. Bradley checks out of the hotel, then enters the hotel's restaurant. At the conclusion of his meal, he charges it to his folio. The restaurant cashier will have trouble posting the transaction, since the folio has been closed. Mr. Bradley will then have to present an alternate form of payment. To state it simply, electronic folios should be closed at the time of settlement. Accounts that are accidentally closed can be reopened. Check-out, however, typically triggers a communication to housekeeping relative to a change in room status and internally sets the account to a no-post status. Since the guest accounting module is interconnected with other front office modules, enhanced communications among staff members and more comprehensive reports are achieved.

System Update

A system update is intended to accomplish many of the functions of the traditional account audit routine it replaces. System updates are performed automatically, according to a predetermined schedule, to enable report production and system file consolidation, reorganization, and maintenance, as well as to establish an end-of-day closure.

Since guest accounting modules continuously audit transactional postings as they occur, there may be little need for the auditor to perform additional account postings. Instead, the auditor should routinely review interface procedures to ensure the proper handling of automatically posted transactions from the hotel's revenue centers. In the case of guaranteed reservation no-shows, for example, postings may be programmed to flow automatically to a billing file. If a transaction needs to be manually posted, the guest's electronic folio can be accessed for posting. Once complete, the updated folio is returned to electronic storage.

The balancing of front office and department accounts is continuously monitored through a double entry transactional accounting system. As a charge purchase is entered at a remote POS terminal, for example, the charge may be simultaneously posted to an electronic guest folio and revenue center control folio. The control folio serves as an internal accounting file that supports account postings originating from an operating department. To balance departments, the system tests all non-control folio entries against total control folio transactions. An imbalance is just as likely to identify a problem in automatic posting techniques as a shortcoming in front office accounting procedures. Detailed departmental reports can be generated and checked against account postings to prove account entries at any time.

Guest accounting modules are capable of producing a myriad of formatted statements and reports summarizing financial transactions that occur between guests and the hotel, activities within revenue centers, and audit findings. The analytical capacity of this module has simplified traditional hotel auditing procedures while providing increased control over guest accounting procedures. The ability to generate accurate guest and non-guest folios at any time during the guest cycle provides management with important accounting information on a timely basis. Room statistics and revenue reports detailing occupancy loads, room and non-room revenues, and projected departmental activity provide essential information on occupancy percentages, average rate (per-room and per-guest), and departmental revenue summaries.

Ledger summary reports present guest, non-guest, and credit/debit card activity by beginning balance, cumulative charges, and credits and debits. **Revenue center reports** show cash, charge, and paid-out totals by department and serve as a macro-analysis of departmental transactions. **Guest check control reports** compare guest checks used in revenue outlets, such as in food and beverage outlets, with source documents to identify discrepancies. Transfers to non-guest (city) ledgers from guest accounts are automatically logged onto a **transfer report**, along with the creation of an initial dunning letter. A dunning letter is a request for payment of an outstanding balance (account receivable) owed by a guest or non-guest to the hotel.

🔑 Key Terms

Rooms Management Module

actual departures report—Lists the names of guests who have checked out and their room numbers, billing addresses, and folio numbers.

expected arrival/departure report—A daily report showing the number and names of guests expected to arrive with reservations, as well as the number and names of guests expected to depart.

housekeeper assignment report—Used to assign floor and room numbers to room attendants and to list room status. This report may also provide space for special messages from the housekeeping department.

housekeeper productivity report—Provides a relative-productivity index for each housekeeper by listing the number of rooms cleaned and the amount of time taken to clean each room.

registration progress report—Provides the rooms department with a summary of current house information; may list present check-ins, number of occupied rooms, names of guests who have reservations but are not yet registered, and the number of rooms available for sale; may also profile room status, rooms revenue, and average room rate.

room status—The state of a hotel room in terms of its availability and cleanliness. Information about current room availability is essential in order for front desk employees to properly assign rooms to guests at check-in. The current status of a room is crucial to the immediate, short-run selling position of that room.

room status discrepancy—A situation in which the housekeeping department's description of a room's status differs from the room status information that guides front desk employees in assigning rooms to guests.

rooms activity forecast—Provides information on anticipated arrivals, departures, stayovers, and vacancies. This report assists managers in staffing front desk and housekeeping areas.

rooms allotment report—Summarizes rooms committed (booked or blocked) by future date.

rooms discrepancy report—Signals to management the specific rooms whose status must be investigated to avoid sleepers. The report notes any variances between front desk and housekeeping room status updates.

rooms history report—Depicts the revenue history and use of each room by room type. This report is especially useful to those properties employing an automatic room assignment function.

rooms productivity report—Ranks room types by percentage of occupancy and/or by percentage of total rooms revenue.

rooms status report—Indicates the current status of rooms according to housekeeping designations, such as on-change, out-of-order, and clean and ready for inspection.

sleeper—A vacant room that is believed to be occupied because the room rack slip or registration card was not removed from the rack when the guest departed (in nonautomated hotels) or because of room status report discrepancies or errors (in automated hotels).

Guest Accounting Module

control folio—Constructed for each revenue center and used to track all transactions posted to other folios (individual, master, non-guest, or employee). Control folios provide a basis for double entry accounting and for cross-checking the balances of all electronic folios.

credit monitoring routine—Compares a guest's current folio balance with a credit limit (also called a house limit) that is predetermined by management.

employee folio—Used to track employee purchases, compute discounts, monitor expense account activity, and separate authorized business charges from personal expenditures.

guest check control report—Compares guest checks used in revenue outlets, such as in food and beverage outlets, with source documents to identify discrepancies.

house limit—A credit limit predetermined by management.

identification code—Generally, the first few letters of a guest's last name. An identification code enables the guest accounting module to process a charge to the correct folio when two separate accounts exist under the same room number.

individual folio—Assigned to an in-house guest for the purpose of charting the guest's financial transactions with the hotel.

late charges—Charged purchases made by guests that are posted to folios after guests have settled their accounts.

ledger summary report—Presents guest, non-guest, and credit card activity by beginning balance, cumulative charges, and credits.

master folio—Generally applies to more than one guest or room and contains a record of transactions that are not posted to individual folios. Master folios are commonly created to provide the kind of billing service required by most groups and conventions.

non-guest folio—Created for an individual who has in-house charge privileges but is not registered as a guest in the hotel. Individuals with non-guest folios may include health club members, corporate clients, special club members, political leaders, or local celebrities.

permanent folio—Used to track guest folio balances that are settled to a credit card company.

reference code—Generally, the serial number of a departmental source document.

revenue center report—Shows cash, charge, and paid-out totals by department and serves as a macro-analysis of departmental transactions.

semi-permanent folio—Used to track "bill to" accounts receivable.

source document—A printed voucher, usually serially numbered for internal-control purposes, from a revenue-producing department showing an amount that is charged to a folio.

transfer report—Shows transfers to non-guest (city) ledgers from guest accounts.

Review Questions

1. What primary functions does a rooms management module perform?

2. How does a rooms management module help reduce room status discrepancies?

3. How does a rooms management module automatically perform room and rate assignments? Explain how an override option may be useful to management.

4. How can a rooms management module be used to schedule housekeeping staff and measure the productivity of room attendants?

5. What are some of the reports that a rooms management module can generate?

6. What are the primary functions a guest accounting module performs?

7. What types of folios might a guest accounting module use? Give brief descriptions of each.

8. Why are identification codes and reference codes important to online posting procedures?

9. What are some of the advantages of the system update routine performed by a guest accounting module?

10. How are account settlement procedures influenced by a guest accounting application?

Internet Sites

For more information, visit the following Internet sites. Remember that Internet addresses can change without notice. If the site is no longer there, you can use a search engine to look for additional sites.

Hotel Property Management Systems

CMS Hospitality
www.cmshospitality.com

Hotel Information Systems
www.hotel-online.com/Trends/
HotelInformationSystems/

INNFINITY Software Systems, LLC
www.innfinity.com

MICROS Systems, Inc.
www.micros.com

PAR Technology Corp.
www.partech.com

Chapter 5 Outline

System Interface Issues
Central Reservation Systems
Point-of-Sale Systems
Call Accounting Systems
    Features of Call Accounting Systems
    CAS/PMS Interfacing
Electronic Locking Systems
    Hard-Wired Locks
    Micro-Fitted Locks
    ELS Features
    ELS Reports
Energy Management Systems
Auxiliary Guest Services
Guest-Operated Devices
    Self-Check-In/Self-Check-Out Systems
    In-Room Entertainment Systems
    In-Room Vending Systems
    Guest Information Services

Competencies

1. Identify ways in which managers can minimize the risks associated with interfacing various stand-alone systems with a hotel property management system. (pp. 103–105)

2. Explain how a central reservation system interfaces with a hotel property management system. (pp. 105–106)

3. Explain how a point-of-sale system interfaces with a hotel property management system. (pp. 106–108)

4. Describe the features and functions of a telephone call accounting system and discuss the advantages of interfacing call accounting systems with hotel property management systems. (pp. 108–114)

5. Distinguish between hard-wired and micro-fitted electronic locking systems and identify electronic locking system features and reports. (pp. 114–116)

6. Identify the features and functions of an energy management system. (pp. 116–118)

7. Identify and discuss examples of auxiliary guest services that can interface with a hotel property management system. (pp. 118–119)

8. Describe guest-operated devices that may interface with a hotel property management system. (pp. 119–126)

5

Property Management System Interfaces

A FULLY INTEGRATED property management system (PMS) provides management with an effective means with which to monitor and control many front office and back office activities. Other areas of a lodging operation may also benefit from automation. Rather than function as part of a PMS, some automated systems may perform more effectively as independent, stand-alone devices that can be interfaced with the PMS. Interfacing permits the PMS to access data and information processed by stand-alone systems, without affecting the primary structure of the PMS. This approach is often referred to as "best in breed" since each application area employs the most appropriate solution while maintaining connectivity with the overall PMS.

This chapter presents a detailed discussion of PMS interfaces. Important interfaces for hotel operations include:

- Central reservation systems (CRS).
- Point-of-sale systems (POS).
- Call accounting systems (CAS).
- Electronic locking systems (ELS).
- Energy management systems (EMS).
- Auxiliary guest services.
- Guest-operated devices.

Some hotels have gone beyond installing basic property management systems by offering a variety of automated guest-operated devices. These devices are described in the final sections of this chapter. As the traveling public becomes more familiar with and skilled in using technology, there will be additional growth in many lodging service applications.

System Interface Issues

While it may seem logical to interconnect all hospitality technology applications at a property, a number of questions arise:

- Which applications should be interfaced?
- How will the lodging operation benefit from the interface?

- Which of the application vendors should perform the interface?

- How can management be sure that the interface is working properly?

- Will the interface maintain the integrity of the data?

- Will vendor support be compromised by the interface?

Connecting separate applications to a PMS is not without risk. If unsuccessful, data may be lost, application capabilities may be compromised, functionality may be slowed or lost, and overall confidence in the system may be shaken. Connecting two hardware components is not as troubling as software and networking issues. Running a serial cable or establishing a wireless connection is relatively easy; getting the devices to share information is more complex. The five C's of interfacing may help managers minimize risks associated with interfacing hospitality technologies:

- Confidence—test each system separately. Be sure each is functioning properly.

- Contracts—analyze existing provisions and look for any prohibitions.

- Communications—determine the "what, when, and how" of information exchange.

- Comparisons—contact users who succeeded with the same interface. What did they do?

- Contingencies—develop procedures for downtime in case the interface stops working.

Confidence. Before interconnecting two stand-alone applications (for example, a POS system and a PMS), be sure to test each system separately. There should be a high level of confidence in each system's operational capabilities before attempting to link them together. If there should subsequently be an interface problem and the components were not tested before being connected, troubleshooting the problem will be more difficult.

Contracts. Before attempting to connect separate systems, management should commission a legal review of all involved product vendor contracts. There may be contractual interface restrictions requiring direct involvement of the original product vendor when attempting an interface. By analyzing existing contract provisions, management may avoid actions that will violate existing contracts and possibly void warranties or cause other significant problems.

Communications. When contemplating an interface, determine the content, frequency, and format of the information to be exchanged. In addition, determine whether a copy of transmitted data should remain at the original source system or whether it should be permanently moved to the receiving system. Knowing what, when, and how interfaced data streaming is to occur is important to effective interface design. For example, in the case of POS interfacing, how much order entry detail should be transmitted to the PMS? The details of order entry are important to the food and beverage department, but not the accounts receivable module of a guest accounting system. Hence, perhaps only total revenue amounts from the food and beverage outlet should be exchanged. When should the POS data be sent to the PMS? Since the revenue center is going to bill its guests following service, there is probably no need to transmit POS data as it occurs (real time). Instead, it makes more sense to wait until a guest check is closed, or, if feasible, consider batching the POS data until the end of a meal period or some later time. What about data format? A workable data transmission format will be dictated by the requirements of the receiving system in the interface.

Comparisons. One of the biggest mistakes hospitality managers can make is not contacting current users to determine the best means by which to accomplish an interface. Product vendors normally have a detailed list of installed users and are usually aware of successful (and failed) interfaces to and from their product line. By contacting properties of a similar size and scope, managers can gain invaluable insight into interface solutions. For example, when considering interfacing a POS system with a PMS, the most efficient approach would be to ask the PMS vendor which of its installed users currently have successful POS interfaces.

Contingencies. Managers must be sure that staff members are trained to operate the lodging operation efficiently should the interface fail. In addition, it is wise to stock spare parts for components most likely to wear out or be troublesome. For example, when interfacing a POS system to a PMS, there needs to be a set of provisions governing backup procedures so that proper processing can be accomplished even if the interface is not operational.

The decision to interface stand-alone hospitality system applications requires planning. While the technical aspects of the interface warrant careful management review and active participation, there are additional considerations. Remember the three "nevers" of interfacing:

1. Never be the first user of an interface.

2. Never be the largest user of an interface.

3. Never be the last user of an interface.

Central Reservation Systems

A central reservation system (CRS) can be interfaced to a PMS as a one-way (simplex) or two-way (duplex) communication network. In a simplex interface, information flows in one direction only and, therefore, guest reservations made through an electronic distribution system (GDS or IDS) or a central reservation office (CRO) will be received by the PMS. The PMS is unable to communicate confirmation or other data as the reservation communication flow is inward only. Once received, reservation records are merged automatically into the PMS reservations module, assuming availability, with the exception of those reservations requesting special accommodation or additional consideration.

In a duplex CRS interface, the PMS, in addition to receiving reservations made through external sources, can automatically adjust room and rate inventory data held in the CRS to reflect changes in the PMS, such as guests who unexpectedly extend (stayover) or shorten their stay (understay). For hotels belonging to an affinity or rewards program, the collection of relevant data following a guest's stay can be transmitted to the central guest history system upon check-out.

Additionally, the CRS can be programmed to automatically transfer levels of reservation activity in the PMS to a stand-alone revenue management application. The revenue management system can then analyze business flows against a predetermined set of rules, goals, and trends designed to control the opening and closing of room rate categories as well as length of stay restrictions, if any.

Point-of-Sale Systems

A point-of-sale system is made up of a network of POS terminals that typically interface with a remote central processing unit. A **point-of-sale terminal** is normally configured as an independent, stand-alone unit. This device contains all the necessary components of an automated system: an input/output component, a central processing unit, and storage (memory) capacity. Some POS terminals may not have their own CPU and, therefore, may have to be connected to a remote CPU. In these cases, in order for POS transactions to be processed, the terminals must be connected to a remote CPU. In some cases, data transfer via the Internet may be the mode of relay.

POS system designs often link terminals within a local area network. Each terminal is networked to form an integrated POS system that functions without a separate, remote CPU. This system architecture is referred to as a **PC-based register configuration**.

When the main processor of a POS system interfaces with a property management system, data can be directly transferred from the POS system to various front office and back office PMS modules for further processing. This interface accomplishes the basic objectives of electronic data processing. The amount of time required to post transactions to guest folios is significantly reduced, and the number of times various pieces of data must be handled is minimized. Relaying data collected by POS terminals to the PMS also significantly reduces the number of posting errors while minimizing the possibility of late charges.

The number and location of POS terminals throughout a lodging property is a function of such factors as:

- Size and type of operation.
- Physical design dimensions.
- Communication requirements.
- Security considerations.

For example, a large hotel may place one or more terminals at every revenue center, including:

- Restaurants.
- Bar and lounge areas.
- Room service stations.
- Concession stands.

- Gift shops.

- Pool and spa areas.

- Pro shops.

Although a POS/PMS interface offers lodging properties significant advantages, there are also important concerns to address. Interface problems that may arise include these:

- Data transferred from the POS system may not meet the specific needs or data format of the PMS.

- POS system data may be lost, or misapplied, during the PMS's system update routine.

- General limitations and downtime situations of interface technology may interfere with effective system operations.

- The interface may not comply with payment card industry data security standards (PCI DSS).

The amount and type of data communicated from a POS system to a PMS vary in relation to the particular type of POS system and PMS design. Problems may arise when the type of data needed by front office or back office PMS modules cannot be easily collected, extracted, or transferred from the POS system. For example, a POS system may not be able to:

- Divide revenues from the total amount of a guest check into separate food and beverage amounts, or into smaller groups within each category.

- Transfer data relating to special hotel meal plans and promotions.

- Track taxes and tips.

Management officials may also have to address questions such as:

- Will individual transactions or consolidated transactions be transmitted?

- Will data be transmitted as it is collected or batched and sent at a later time?

- How much data will be stored in PMS files and how much will be retained by the POS system?

- How and when will settlement affect stored transaction data?

- What audit procedures will be followed to ensure proper posting and monitoring of transactions?

- Will data be carried forward indefinitely?

- What contingency plans will be executed should an interface failure occur?

A hotel's PMS undergoes a system update routine on a daily or more frequent basis. The update generally occurs sometime during the slower evening hours. While the system is being updated, the POS interface may be inoperable. Careful planning can help ensure that the interruption of data flow along the interface channel does not result in lost transactions or bottlenecks at either the POS or PMS end. For this reason, many properties schedule the system update when food and beverage outlets and other revenue centers are closed or during slack business hours. In the case of a system or interface failure, nonautomated procedures may have to be implemented at revenue outlets for the duration of the failure.

Before interfacing a POS system to a PMS, management may have to resolve problems related to interface technology. For example, a POS system may be dependent upon a unique set of application software unrelated to the needs of the PMS. Should this be the case, the primary application software of the POS system may need to be enhanced before the system is connected and synchronized with the PMS.

Interfacing a POS system to the PMS enables electronic posting from the revenue center to a guest's electronic folio. Initially, the PMS receives and responds to requests from the POS system related to a guest charging a purchase to his or her room account. The POS, in turn, displays the name(s) of the registered guest(s) assigned to the guestroom. The cashier then applies the POS charge against the selected guest's folio balance by identifying and selecting the correct guest. The breakdown of information communicated in a POS-to-PMS interface usually involves the separation of food detail, beverage detail, tax detail, and tip detail data. Advanced POS/PMS interfaces are capable of retrieving complete transaction detail via a drill-down technique related to the guest's folio. In addition, the POS device is capable of alerting the cashier to notify the guest of a message waiting in the PMS or enabling a guest to check out of the hotel via the POS terminal rather than at the front desk.

Some POS interfaces are set up to transfer revenue subtotals for all POS settlement types (not just room charges) to the PMS at the end of the day, thereby enabling the PMS to generate a summary report of daily revenue center transactions (often referred to as a flash report).

Protecting the payment card data of guests is a longstanding concern in the hospitality industry. That concern has been magnified by the growing number of points-of-sale and related touch points that allow access to cardholder data. Fortunately, the payment card industry has established data security standards (PCI DSS) that provide a framework for preventing fraudulent access, theft, and other security breaches. While the PCI DSS initially focused on compliance with a checklist of specific security requirements, it has evolved into a more proactive approach to addressing physical and virtual security concerns. This enables management to increase staff awareness of data security and to routinely test that the systems and processes are performing as expected. There is a specialized set of requirements for the software applications used to process payments called PA-DSS (Payment Application Data Security Standards), which includes instructional documentation and training programs.

Call Accounting Systems

Since 1981, it has been legal for lodging properties to resell telephone service to guests. This resale capability has enabled the hotel's telephone department, traditionally a loss leader, to potentially earn a profit. In recent years, however, guest use of property telephones has significantly declined as more and more guests now carry cellular phones or personal digital assistants (PDAs).

Despite the overall decline in guest use, guests still expect lodging properties to provide telephone services, making it important to find ways to continue to offer those services while controlling the associated expenses. A call accounting system (CAS) enhances management's control of expenses relating to local and long-distance telephone services. While a CAS may operate as a stand-alone system, it is typically interfaced with a hotel's PMS. Generally, a CAS is able to handle direct-distance dialing, distribute calls through a least-cost routing network, and price outgoing calls. When a CAS is interfaced to the PMS, the PMS receives telephone call charges emanating from the CAS and posts the charges to the proper guest folio. Posting detail typically includes the phone number called, the duration of the call, and the charge for the call. Since there is no way for the PMS to know which guest registered in a room made the call, the CAS charge is normally posted to the folio of the guest who checked in first. This is referred to as *prime folio posting*.

Call accounting systems conserve valuable space and often reduce maintenance and labor costs associated with traditional telephone systems. CAS hardware takes up less space and requires less maintenance than the bulky switchboard equipment it replaces. Labor costs decrease since a telephone operator is not involved in CAS call placement and distribution functions. Similarly, the automatic pricing of calls eliminates the need for manually calculating and posting telephone charges.

Exhibit 1 diagrams a CAS designed to monitor administrative (non-guest) and guest telephone traffic. The hotel's PBX (private branch exchange) system serves as a primary control device for the entire call accounting system. The PBX usually contains a station message detail record (SMDR) that takes responsibility for charting and monitoring telephone traffic.

Features of Call Accounting Systems

Exhibit 2 presents a simplified flowchart of the operation of a call accounting system. CAS functions may include:

- Call placement or automatic identification of outward dialing (AIOD).
- Call distribution or automatic route selection (ARS).
- Least-cost routing (LCR).
- Call rating program (CRP).
- Call record.

Call accounting systems have significantly simplified the sequence involved in call placement. Guests can direct-distance dial, eliminating operator intervention. The **automatic identification of outward dialing** (AIOD) feature of a CAS immediately identifies the extension from which a call is placed.

As an outgoing call is placed, the CAS's call distribution equipment is engaged. How and where a specific call is routed are essential in determining its cost. With a **passive call accounting system**, there are no options available to

Exhibit 1   Overview of a Call Accounting System

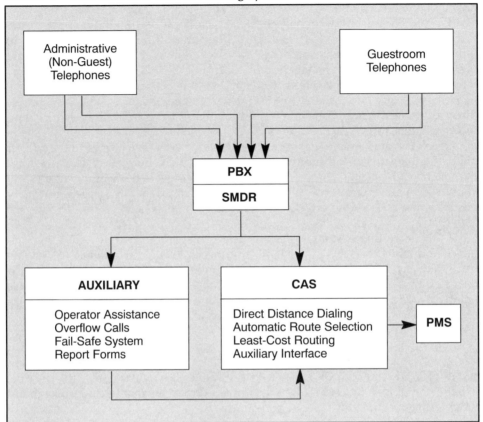

the call distribution network. Selection of a route is based on convenience rather than on minimizing expense. An **active call accounting system**, on the other hand, employs an automatic route selection switch with a least-cost routing device. The **automatic route selection** (ARS) feature has become an essential CAS component and is usually capable of connecting with a variety of common carriers. A **common carrier** is any recognized entity that transmits messages or other communication for general use at accepted rates. The **least-cost routing** (LCR) capability directs calls over the least-cost available line, regardless of carrier. When the least-cost line is busy, the LCR automatically prompts the CAS to seek the next least expensive line. This search procedure is performed at high speed and with remarkable precision.

The manner by which a call is priced or rated will vary in relation to vendors, equipment packages, and electronic switches. A **station message detail record** (SMDR) is used to chart and monitor telephone traffic. The data collected by the SMDR is used to rate calls. Some systems base calls on a ringback mechanism; others incorporate a timeout feature. With a **ringback mechanism** or auto-answer detection software, the guest is charged only for calls that are answered. With a

Exhibit 2   Simplified Flowchart of a CAS Operation

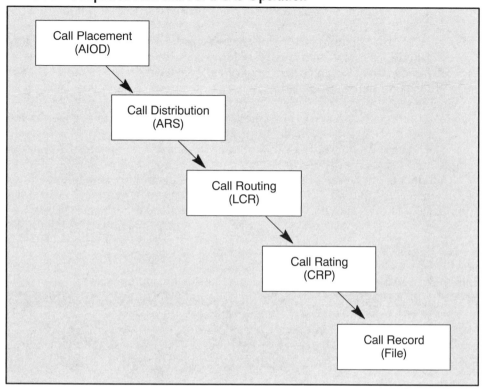

timeout feature, callers begin paying for calls after a predetermined amount of placement time. After a call is rated, it is entered into a call record file.

A call record is used to monitor details regarding calls processed by the CAS. This file may include:

- Date.
- Guestroom extension number.
- Telephone number dialed.
- Time call was placed.
- Duration of call.
- Cost of call (per carrier charges).
- Tax and markup charges.
- Amounts posted to guest folio.

Most call rating systems calculate the price and tax of a call and automatically post the necessary data to appropriate call records. A **call record** is electronic or hard-copy documentation containing essential transactional support data for individually placed and rated telephone calls. Call records are referenced on a guest folio and provide a means for resolving guest discrepancies relating to telephone charges.

Call records are automatically logged in a traffic transaction file. The **traffic transaction file** maintains data necessary for generating reports for management. Typically, records are organized by time of call placement (chronological file) or room extension number (sorted file). The extent of report detail is a function of management needs.

Telephone activity reports can be generated by date and/or time covering the entire company, a specific division, an individual property, a particular revenue center, or even individual extensions or specific call destinations. Exhibit 3 is a sample report showing details for the most recently processed calls.

Call details can be seen in order of extension, date and/or time, phone number called, etc. Exhibit 4 shows some of the detail that can be accessed regarding a specific call placed through a CAS. In addition, statistical reports and "real time" alerts (by pager or e-mail) can inform managers of potential abuses of the phone

Exhibit 3   Sample Telephone Activity Report Listing Recent Calls

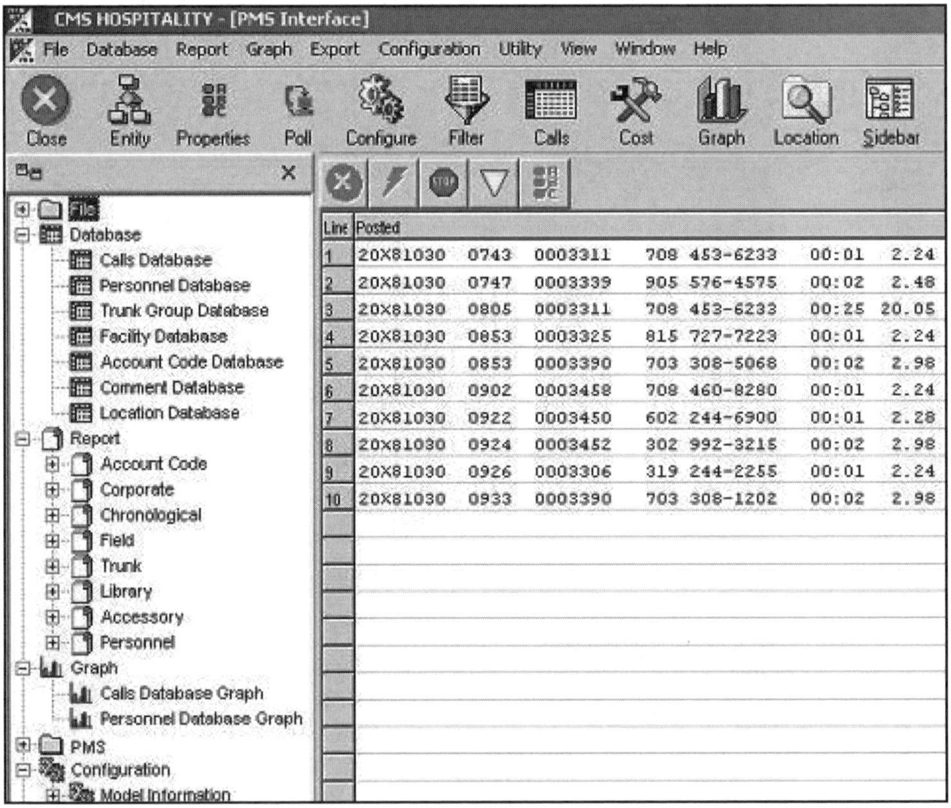

Courtesy of Resource Software International (RSI).

Exhibit 4 Sample Call Detail

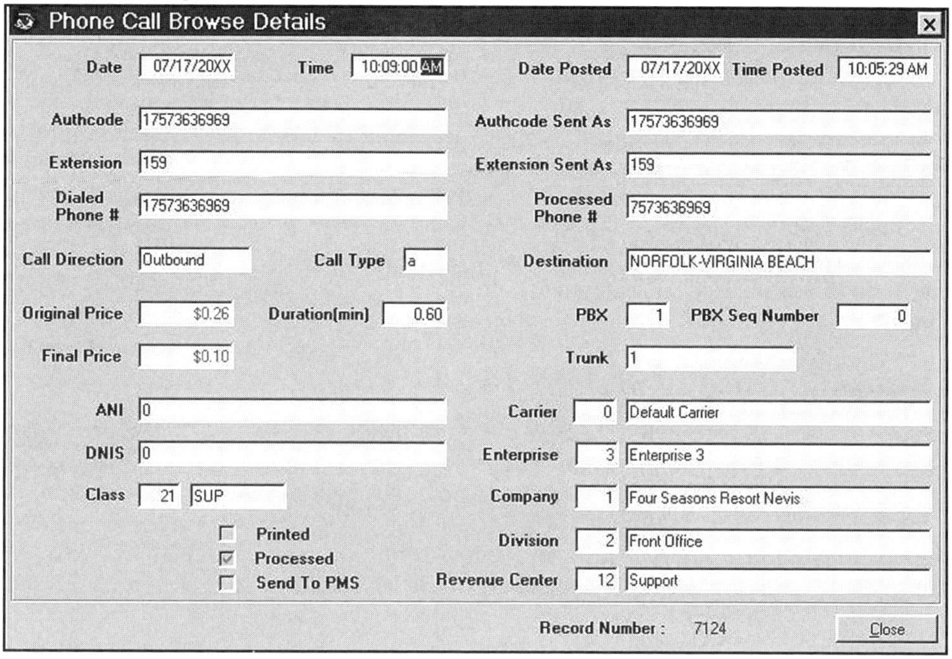

Source: RBS Computer Corporation.

system by indicating most expensive calls, longest calls, most frequently called numbers, etc.

CAS/PMS Interfacing

A CAS/PMS interface offers lodging properties a number of significant advantages, such as:

- Enhanced guest services and guest satisfaction.
- Improved communications networking.
- Improved call pricing methods.
- Minimized telephone traffic expenses.
- Automatic charge posting to guest folios.
- Automatic call detail records.
- Detailed daily reports of telephone transactions.

Since the CAS reduces operator intervention, the hotel telephone department can become more efficient with less labor. Eliminating telephone meter readings and reducing guest telephone charge discrepancies can also contribute to faster checkout times and more effective front desk operations.

Contingency backup procedures are a major concern when a CAS is interfaced with a PMS. Energy backup concerns for the CAS usually mandate access to an uninterruptible power supply.

Another important CAS concern is the storage and distribution capacity of the system. Before purchasing and installing a CAS, management must be sure that telephone traffic throughout the hotel has been properly evaluated so that the proposed CAS will have adequate storage and distribution capacity for processing and storing telephone traffic data. Management may also wish to ensure that the proposed system is able to distinguish administrative (non-guest) calls from guest calls. Other important concerns focus on system maintenance, service, and vendor support. In many cases, management officials may need to initiate new telephone maintenance programs.

Electronic Locking Systems

An electronic locking system (ELS) replaces traditional brass keys and mechanical locks with sophisticated guestroom access devices. Installing electronic locks on existing guestroom doors may involve a major reconstruction effort. Some systems require only the drilling of a small hole for wires to pass from the outside to the inside portion of the lock. In some cases, existing deadbolt and latch hardware are retained as part of the new lock. Other systems require new hardware, or even new doors.

In an ELS/PMS interface, the check-in procedure requires the PMS to transmit the room number and number of keys requested, as well as the dates and times for which the keycards will be valid, to a keycard encoder. The encoder, in turn, will record data onto the magnetic stripe (or other storage medium) contained on the keycard. There are a variety of electronic locking systems available to lodging properties. These systems are either hard-wired or micro-fitted locking systems, depending on the property's age and/or management preference.

Hard-Wired Locks

Hard-wired locks operate through a centralized master code console interfaced to every controlled guestroom door. The console may be a slotted switching device centrally located at the front desk. With this type of **hard-wired electronic locking system**, a front desk employee follows a prescribed check-in procedure and creates a new keycard. The console immediately transmits the keycard's code to the remote guestroom door lock. By the time the guest leaves the front desk, the issued keycard is the only workable guestroom access key. Keycards issued to previous guests who occupied the same room become invalid.

Since, with a hard-wired configuration, every controlled door must be cabled to the master console, hard-wired systems present both a challenge (expensive design) and an opportunity (improved security). Before such a system is installed, management should identify emergency procedures and energy backup sources. Hard-wired locking systems use AC (house current) as their primary energy source, with DC (battery pack) serving as emergency backup. Management must also determine when keycards are to be created (initially encoded) and how they are to be created, re-issued, recycled, and maintained.

Micro-Fitted Locks

Micro-fitted locks operate as individually configured stand-alone units, thus avoiding the complex dedicated circuitry required by hard-wired locking systems. Each door has its own microprocessor that contains a unique, predetermined sequence of codes. A terminal at the front desk contains a database of code sequences for each door and is connected to a key encoding device. With a **micro-fitted electronic locking system**, the front desk employee completes guest check-in by encoding a keycard with the next code in the predetermined sequence of codes for an assigned room.

With hard-wired systems, codes are directly communicated from the master code console to the controlled doors. Micro-fitted systems do not possess this kind of communications capability. The front desk terminal and the microprocessors of controlled doors are separate units. What connects them is the predetermined sequence of codes. This means not only that the front desk terminal must be programmed with the same predetermined sequence of codes that is contained within each door's microprocessor, but also that the terminal and each microprocessor must agree on which code in the sequence is currently valid. If the units are out of synchronization, the locking mechanism will need to be reset.

For example, assume that at check-in a family requests two rooms with an inside connecting door. The parents plan to stay in one of the rooms while their children stay in the other. Upon reaching the rooms, the family enters the first room and finds the connecting door to the other room already open. The next morning, the family checks out of both rooms, having never used the second room's keycard. The locking mechanism in the second room's door will not advance to the next code in the predetermined sequence because the keycard was never used. The terminal at the front desk, however, will automatically advance to the next code in the sequence when another guest checks into that room because it assumes that the last issued keycard was used. Should this happen, the new guest (receiving the next keycard) will find that the issued keycard fails to activate the lock. A hotel employee must then use a specially designed keycard to reprogram the room door's microprocessor so that the current code synchronizes with the front desk control console.

An important energy feature of micro-fitted electronic locking systems is that the microchips in each door are powered by battery packs and therefore do not require wiring to an external energy source. Some systems employ penlight size batteries, some D-size cells, while others use special battery units.

ELS Features

Electronic locking systems may produce various levels of master keys. Most systems provide several distinct levels of security. One level may be established for housekeeping personnel, another for hotel security officers, and yet another for property management.

Some ELS designs provide a "do not disturb" option for guests. This option typically employs an indicator that displays a notice when the guest wants privacy. The notice is often given by a flashing red light located within the locking mechanism. This indicator may be triggered when a room attendant inserts a keycard into the locking mechanism. No longer must the housekeeping staff knock on the door or test the door's chain to realize that the guest is still in the room.

A safety feature built into some electronic locking systems prevents the door from opening while the keycard remains in the lock. This prevents a guest from entering a guestroom while forgetting to take the keycard from the lock. One system permits entry without keycard removal; however, it tracks the length of time the keycard is in the door. If the keycard remains in the locking mechanism beyond a predetermined time interval, the system destroys the keycard by scrambling its code. The reason for scrambling a keycard's code relates to guestroom security. A keycard that remains in a lock may be taken by someone other than the room's occupant. To avoid problems, hotel staff must inform guests that failure to promptly remove the keycard will cause it to become invalid.

Other types of electronic locks do not require guests to possess keys or keycards at all. With an alternative system, guests may set the locking mechanism by programming a personal code number, recording biometric data (fingerprint, palm-print, or face geometry), or using a mobile device with the room access code or quick-response (QR) code. These systems are likely to become more widely adopted as guest acceptance, an overwhelming factor in determining the success of such systems, continues to increase. In the past, some electronic locking system vendors provided additional technology that enabled guests to use a credit card for room entry. At the time of check-in, the guest's credit card would be swiped through a magnetic strip reader. The reader would then encode guestroom access information on the card's magnetic stripe. When the guest arrived at the assigned room, the credit card would then operate as the room key. This idea has not received much support.

ELS Reports

One of the most significant advantages of an electronic locking system is that management can find out which keycards opened which doors, by date and time. This method of lock integration has helped reduce the number of unauthorized guestroom access incidents.

An ELS typically maintains an audit trail of all activities involving the use of system-issued access codes. Some systems generate reports detailing activities in chronological sequence. A system that records events as they occur generally may do so to optimize limited memory. Other systems record and store activity data that can be formatted to provide reports on demand. The creation of reports, as well as other system functions, should be controlled by operator identification and password security codes.

Energy Management Systems

Heating, lighting, ventilating, and air-conditioning equipment are essential to a hotel's existence. Efficient equipment better serves the needs of the hotel and its guests. Energy management systems may conserve energy, contain energy costs, and tighten operational controls over guestroom and public space environments. An important feature of these systems is their ability to minimize the building's energy needs while not significantly affecting the hotel's comfort conditions.

An energy management system may be a central feature of the rooms management module or operate as a stand-alone application. Historically, these systems were marketed as stand-alone systems and connectivity to the rooms management module was not very common.

An energy management system (EMS) is an automated system designed to manage the operation of mechanical equipment in a lodging property. The programming of this system enables management to determine when equipment is to be turned on or off or otherwise regulated. For example, if the meeting rooms of a property will be used from 10 A.M. to 2 P.M., the system controller can be programmed to automatically conserve energy during the hours the rooms will not be in use, while ensuring that by 10 A.M. the rooms reach a satisfactory comfort level for guests. This programming technique can usually be applied to equipment affecting various public spaces throughout the property. Similarly, when the EMS is interfaced to the PMS, the PMS can send an electronic message to the EMS at time of check-in to change the guestroom thermostat to a predefined setting for occupancy. At check-out, a similar message can be set to direct the EMS to return the thermostat to the unoccupied guestroom setting.

Although actual operating features of energy management systems vary, common energy control designs include:

- Demand control.
- Duty cycling.
- Room occupancy sensors.

Demand control maintains usage levels below a given limit by shedding energy loads in an orderly fashion. Equipment units assigned to demand control programs are those that can be turned off for varying periods without adversely affecting environmental comfort conditions. Unfortunately, hotels and motels do not have very many equipment units that can be shed without adversely affecting the overall operation of the property and the comfort of its guests.

Duty cycling turns off equipment sequentially for a predetermined period of time each work cycle. Heating, ventilating, and air-conditioning systems may be duty-cycled to reduce energy consumption while maintaining space comfort conditions. Duty cycling is not normally applied to large horsepower motors that cannot be stopped and started on a frequent basis without overheating.

Room occupancy sensors use either infrared light or ultrasonic waves to register the physical occupancy of a room or zone. Whenever a guest enters a monitored space, sensors turn on whatever devices are under their control, such as lights, air-conditioning equipment, heating equipment, and so on. When a guest leaves a monitored room, sensors react and, after a short delay, turn off or dim the lights and/or automatically reset the temperature.

An EMS/PMS interface offers a number of opportunities for energy control. For example, assume that, on a particular night, a 50 percent occupancy is forecasted for a 300-room property. Minimizing the hotel's energy consumption on this night becomes a factor in determining which rooms to sell. One approach would be to assign guests only to the lower floors of the property and significantly reduce the energy demands of rooms on the upper floors. By interfacing an energy management system to a front office rooms management module, it is possible to automatically control room assignments and achieve desired energy cost savings. In many cases, energy cost savings are tracked through specially created databases or electronic spreadsheets.

Comfort conditions in guestrooms, meeting and function rooms, public spaces, administrative offices, and other EMS-monitored areas can be controlled through a centralized system console. Energy management systems typically provide rapid access to heat, ventilating, and air conditioning levels at remote locations and display these readings on the console screen.

No matter how sophisticated an energy management system may be, energy controls are virtually worthless if they are operating an energy system that is poorly designed or inadequately maintained.

Auxiliary Guest Services

Automation has simplified many auxiliary guest services, such as the placement of wake-up calls, voice messaging, and Voice over Internet Protocol (VoIP). These functions are often performed by devices marketed as stand-alone systems that can be interfaced to the rooms management module of a PMS.

Perhaps the main reason for interfacing auxiliary guest services to a PMS lies in the comprehensive coordination and tracking of guest-related functions. While automated wake-up call devices are often best operated as stand-alone units, it may be beneficial to interface a guest-messaging system to the PMS. The ability to notify guests about messages waiting for them depends on access to the PMS mechanism that links with guestroom telephones and televisions.

An automated wake-up system permits front desk employees to input a guest's room number and requested wake-up time. At the specified time, the system automatically rings the room and calls back at predetermined intervals until the guest answers the phone. If there is no response on the third or fourth try, the system stops calling and makes note of the guest's failure to answer. If the guest answers the call, the system completes a prerecorded morning greeting and then disconnects. Some sophisticated wake-up devices require that the guest actually speak into the phone to confirm that he or she is awake. A notation of the answered call is often stored for the day within the system.

Electronic message-waiting systems and voice messaging systems are designed to let a guest know that a message is waiting and can be retrieved through the phone, television set, or other in-room device. Traditional message-waiting devices are capable of flashing a light on a telephone or television in the guest's room. Some systems can display messages on the television screen in the guest's room. Other systems employ an automatic telephone calling pattern similar to that used in automated wake-up systems. The system's ability to keep calling until the guest answers is more economical and efficient than employing the time, patience, and persistence of a switchboard operator. Hotels also use voice mailboxes, which are devices that record telephone messages for guests. A caller who wishes to leave a message for a guest simply does so over the phone, and the message is recorded for the guest to access later. To retrieve a message, the guest typically dials a special telephone number, connects with the voice mailbox, and listens to the message delivered in the caller's own voice. By interfacing the voice mailbox service with the PMS, the recording of the message trips the message-waiting mechanism in the guestroom, leaving the switchboard staff free to perform other productive tasks. Some hotels offer e-mail messaging as an alternative to voice mail.

Voice over Internet Protocol involves converting speech into digital signals for transmission over the Internet. Hotels that invest in guestroom high-speed Internet access may consider using the Internet as an in-room replacement for a traditional switchboard-based telephone system. While a VoIP connection requires specialty hardware, it produces the same result as a phone connection for both local and long-distance dialing. Once the guest enters the phone number to be contacted, the VoIP connection is made and the caller's speech is digitized and sent to the destination receiver. If the receiver is not also using a VoIP device, the caller's digitized speech is converted to a regular telephone signal before it reaches the destination. VoIP allows telephone traffic to originate directly from a computer, a VoIP phone, or a traditional phone connected to a VoIP adapter. In addition, on-premises wireless access locations outside the guestroom may also enable guests to connect to the Internet for VoIP service. VoIP service may provide the hotel with significant cost savings, since the hotel avoids paying for Internet connectivity and telephone carrier access (trunk) lines. In addition, a VoIP system may offer basic features that typically are available on an extra-fee basis on a traditional commercial phone plan.

Guest-Operated Devices

The adoption of self-service technologies is changing the high-touch tradition of the lodging industry. Guest-operated devices can be located in a public area of the hotel or in private guestrooms. In-room guest-operated devices are designed to be user-friendly. An assortment of devices provides concierge-level service with in-room convenience. Guest-operated devices discussed in the following sections include:

- Self-check-in/self-check-out systems.
- In-room entertainment systems.
- In-room vending systems.
- Guest information services.

Self-Check-In/Self-Check-Out Systems

Self-check-in/self-check-out functionality exists in various formats. Some hotels use self-service kiosks placed in hotel lobby areas. Some allow guests to access their accounts through guestroom televisions or telephones. Some even allow for online check-in before arrival. Regardless of which kind of guest-operated device is used, self-check-in/self-check-out terminals and in-room interfaces can significantly reduce the time it takes to process guest registrations, check-ins, and checkouts. In addition, some automated terminals have enhanced video capability that enables the property to introduce guests to the facilities and amenities available.

Automated check-in and check-out devices can free front office employees to spend more time with those guests who require personal attention.

Kiosks. Many hotel companies use self-service kiosks. Some kiosks resemble automatic bank teller machines, while others are unique in design. All possess audiovisual capability. Some are part of a wireless network that allows the hotel to move them easily as needed.

One type of system has a secured face plate that mounts on an interior or exterior wall. For the convenience of guests, step-by-step instructions are printed on the face plate. The only way to access the machine's contents is from the rear of the machine, which generally opens into the manager's office or another secure area. As a security precaution, the system does not disburse cash. If a late-arriving guest uses the system and a credit is due from a cash overpayment, the guest is instructed to receive the change at the front desk in the morning. When a guest pays by credit or debit card, authorization is secured by telecommunications capability. If the guest's use of a credit or debit card is declined, special instructions can be displayed asking the guest to use another card or to pay by cash.

A fully functional kiosk can handle guest identification, room and rate assignment, keycard dispensing, and account reconciliation. Two additional kiosk-based applications include providing departing guests access to a preferred airline website to print a boarding pass and providing them access to the guest's frequent-guest account for profile update and account review functions.

Kiosk-based applications are designed to be intuitive and user-friendly. In order to use self-check-in, a guest typically must arrive at the hotel with an advance reservation and possess a valid credit (or debit) card. The guest initiates the self-registration process by inserting the credit card into the terminal. The terminal then prompts the guest to use a keypad or touchscreen display to enter necessary information. After collecting registration data, the kiosk may display room types and rates. Since most kiosks are interfaced to a PMS rooms management module, automatic room and rate assignment is possible. Once a room and rate have been assigned, the kiosk may automatically dispense an electronic keycard (or tell the guest how to obtain a room key) along with a welcome letter and a map to the assigned room.

Lobby kiosks may also handle self-check-out procedures. Typically, the guest uses the credit or debit card used at check-in to access the appropriate folio and review its contents. After the guest completes the designated check-out procedures, the PMS interface will automatically close the guest folio and post the account balance to the credit or debit card for billing. The kiosk can then dispense an itemized statement for the guest or request an e-mail address for distribution.

The two most frequently cited reasons for using kiosks are reduced check-in and check-out time for guests and lower cost per transaction for hotels. Since a high percentage of frequent travelers have been using self-service technology, such as bank ATMs, for several years, the products tend to be well accepted as an effective alternative to traditional hotel registration. In addition to providing check-in and check-out services, some self-service kiosks are able to print guest messages (communications), upgrade an assigned guestroom (upselling), or print in-house promotional coupons (marketing).

Self-Service Technologies

Guests have grown tired of encountering long waiting lines and closed doors when they try to do business on the road or after typical business hours. To overcome such frustrations, an increasing number of hospitality firms are choosing to provide self-service technology options for guests. The successful implementation of applications such as self-check-out lanes at retail stores, pay-at-the-pump gas stations, self-check-in kiosks at airports, online banking and stock trading, and a variety of others has led to the development of hotel and restaurant self-service applications. The hospitality industry has embraced the transition from customer service to self-service in many ways. For example, user-friendly touchscreen terminals are capable of handling somewhat complicated tasks, while lodging providers and food service operators have confidence in face-to-monitor activity at a variety of unattended points of sale.

Self-service as a model and a market trend has gained momentum as consumers increasingly accept and often prefer self-service to assisted service. Most businesses report that self-service applications lead to a reduction in operating expenses while markedly improving customer satisfaction. For example, in banking the phrase "full service" was formerly used to refer to a bank teller's handling of transactions with checking accounts, saving accounts, and safe-deposit boxes, as well as processing of mortgage and loan account payments. Over time, "full-service" banking has evolved to comprise a wide range of self-service technological alternatives provided by the bank, such as Internet banking, automated teller machines, and interactive voice response (IVR) systems, which are designed to discourage customers from engaging in teller-based transactions. This allows the bank to hire fewer employees, which reduces labor costs, and allows employees to spend more time focusing on the customer and his or her needs. Additional customer satisfaction comes from the customer's ability to control his or her transactions at the pace and time of day he or she prefers, rather than having to rely on the bank, which might not satisfactorily cater to the customer's needs or circumstances or be available at the time of day the customer needs service.

Service Platforms

The three most popular self-service technology platforms are vending, kiosk, and web applications. While vending focuses on product presentation and delivery, kiosks are typically limited to dispensing information and deferred services, while the web provides unparalleled search and e-procurement capabilities. Today more kiosk applications are being built with product distribution in mind and web connectivity overlaps every aspect of transaction, which means management will likely transfigure vending into a more expansive and comprehensive unattended point-of-sale application. A list of self-service characteristics includes:

- *User interface*. In product selection, vending machines incorporate push-buttons, kiosks utilize touchscreen monitors, and the web relies on clicks and hypertext linkages.

- *Information*. Vending machine information is limited to product pricing; kiosks and web applications are best known for their information search and retrieval techniques, which can provide detailed data about a multitude of factors.

(continued)

(continued)

- *Product display*. Vending machines traditionally place products behind a glass front; unless a kiosk supports a product delivery mechanism, there is no product delivery, only information referencing; websites feature a variety of products, presented in digital format, with delayed shipping requirements.

- *Architecture*. Vending machines are governed by a vending machine controller (VMC) that monitors inputs, processes, and outputs; kiosks are PC-based devices that normally run a Windows or Linux operating system; the web consists of networks that are amenable to a variety of computing platforms.

- *Payment processing*. Vending machines are equipped to primarily handle coins and currency payments, and occasionally open (credit and debit card) or closed (paykey, RFID, payroll-direct) payments; kiosks are built with a high expectation of electronic payment transactions, but may be equipped to handle cash payments; the web is strictly a non-cash payment business.

- *Marketing*. Vending machines feature product packaging displayed behind a clear panel that conforms to mechanical (spiral and coil) restrictions; kiosks and web marketing usually incorporate dynamic digital displays with multiple product views as well as extensive product information. Many applications also provide a mechanism for package customization or personalized purchasing.

- *Products*. Vending machines are limited in product offerings based on the number of columns or selection options on a machine; kiosk screens can feature a large number of products and product sizes and, unless connected to a delivery mechanism, are flexible in product mix; websites can feature an almost infinite array of products through hyperlinks and search engine capabilities.

- *Services*. Vending machines are incapable of offering concierge services and are limited to the product inventory of the machine; kiosks and websites can link to the power of the Internet and numerous remote sites for access to a wide variety of concierge services.

Self-service also tends to involve such hidden features as:

- *Upselling*. The ability to suggestively "upsell" at the time of purchase by offering add-ons, modifiers, and/or bundling options; for example, in addition to flight registration, airlines are also using the web and self-check-in kiosks to upsell preferred bedding or seating based on fees or reward points, as well as to promote special amenities (e.g., single-day spa membership or theatre package). Both the web and the kiosk are more effective at upselling than a live agent.

- *History*. The application's ability to track, store, and recall prior purchases by customer account. For example, recalling a customer's last purchase can help accelerate order entry and/or settlement, as retrieved data remains accurate. This feature strengthens CRM and customer loyalty.

- *Affinity*. The account creation and administration of loyalty reward programs to track purchases for points, rewards, discounts, or special promotions to be applied at website and kiosk locations.

- *Savings.* The development of intuitive programming that enables processes to be completed without human intervention. It is estimated that customer check-in with an airline agent costs about $3 per transaction versus about $0.14 at a kiosk and less at a website.

As experts proclaim, self-service technology must make a process faster, cheaper, or better for customers, or it is not worth the effort. Given the capabilities of self-service platforms, it appears that a convergence of technologies may be on the horizon. The trend for vending machines is to market an array of non-traditional and higher-value items (e.g., electronic gadgetry, clothing, and restaurant-quality meals). For kiosks, designs are reengineered to facilitate more product distribution, while online connectivity overlaps every aspect of transaction management. A convergence of these formats creates a more expansive and comprehensive set of unattended point-of-sale applications. By combining the best technical aspects of these applications, the hospitality industry may well be capable of implementing more self-service applications at a lower operating cost, thereby becoming more profitable.

Despite the use of lead-through technology, hotel kiosks may present usability problems to guests that are technologically challenged or disabled. For this reason, some hotel companies are placing a kiosk service agent (KSA), or kiosk concierge, nearby to ensure smooth and accurate transactions. This is similar to a supermarket assigning an experienced cashier to oversee customer-operated self-check-out scanners. The emphasis is on maintaining functionality and operational efficiency.

In-Room Check-Out. At many properties, guests have the opportunity for both in-room folio review and **in-room check-out**. These systems may use in-room terminals, the property's television cable station, or guestroom telephones to access and display guest folio data on the guestroom television screen. When in-room terminals are interfaced with a PMS guest accounting module, they are able to access folio data and provide guests with a means to approve and settle their accounts. Some in-room folio review technology uses a guestroom telephone interfaced with the PMS to provide computer-synthesized voice responses. This system provides guests with folio totals (or details) and directs a self-check-out procedure. Folio copies are typically available for guests to pick up at the front desk or can be faxed or e-mailed to the departing guest.

Web-Based Check-In. Although wireless lobby kiosks have proven successful in handling a significant percentage of check-in volume, the high cost of development and installation are often major concerns. Web-hosted check-in, on the other hand, is a self-service application that is a comparatively low-cost alternative to kiosks. Hotel companies offering website check-in configure the application to allow online, remote check-in from several hours to several days before the destination property's check-in time on the day of arrival. Hotels have found that this application helps to reduce the number of no-shows (as commitment is firm before arrival) and accelerate the on-premises arrival and room allocation process at the front desk (the guest exchanges web-generated paperwork for a room keycard and hotel information packet). Web-based hotel check-in, described as "online, not *in* line," should become more commonplace within the next several years.

In-Room Entertainment Systems

In-room entertainment systems can be interfaced with a hotel's PMS or can function as independent systems. When interfaced with the PMS, in-room movie systems provide guestroom entertainment either through synchronous programming (with specific start and end times) or asynchronous programming (on demand). The interface includes a timing device. After a special programming channel has been tuned in for a predetermined amount of time (usually several minutes), the device triggers an automatic charge posting to the appropriate guest folio.

Guest-disputed charges have plagued in-room entertainment systems since their inception. A guest may inadvertently turn on a special programming channel for background entertainment, only to discover at check-out that the set was tuned to a pay channel. Incorporating a free preview channel introducing the special programming offered can significantly reduce the number of disputed charges resulting from guests unknowingly selecting a pay-to-view channel. The preview channel permits a guest to view a small segment of each special program. In order to view an actual program, the guest must then physically switch the television from normal viewing to a pay-to-view mode.

In addition to movies, in-room entertainment systems may include:

- On-screen controls (offering DVD/CD functionality).
- Video library access.
- Digital music channels.
- Online digital media access.
- Video and casino games.

In-Room Vending Systems

In-room vending systems are able to monitor sales transactions and determine inventory replenishment quantities. A popular in-room vending system is an in-room beverage system. There are two types of in-room beverage service systems: nonautomated honor bars and microprocessor-based beverage devices.

Nonautomated honor bars typically involve stocks of items that are held in both dry and cold storage areas within a guestroom. Changes in the bar's beginning inventory level are noted either by housekeeping room attendants during their normal rounds or by designated room service employees. In either case, the employee typically uses a hand-held portable computer terminal or the touchtone telephone in the guestroom to connect with the remote dedicated bar computer. Once connection has been made, the employee enters the product code numbers of items that have been consumed. The bar system's CPU relays guestroom information and charges for consumed items to the PMS for proper folio posting and issues a stock replacement report.

Although nonautomated honor bar systems are extremely convenient for guests, they may pose several problems for the hotel. For example, since the bar is always open, consumption is almost impossible to regulate. This service problem could result in underage access to alcohol or frequent late charges. Another potential problem is the high labor costs associated with taking the necessary physical inventory of each in-room bar.

Microprocessor-based beverage devices contain beverage items in see-through closed compartments. The compartment doors may be equipped with fiber optic sensors that record the removal of stored products. Once triggered, the sensors relay the transaction to a built-in microprocessor for recording. Individual room microprocessors are typically cabled to a remote CPU, which stores recorded transactions. This CPU converts transactions into accounting entries, and relays them to the property management system guest accounting module for folio posting. The bar system's CPU also maintains perpetual inventory replenishment data, which directs the restocking of vending units.

Microprocessor-based systems avoid some of the problems associated with honor bars. For example, hotel managers may use a remote central console to lock in-room vending units. Some systems enable guests to lock their in-room bar units with their guestroom keys. In addition, PMS interfacing minimizes late charges. Also, since microprocessor-based devices maintain a perpetual inventory record, labor costs associated with manual inventory tracking are reduced.

Guest Information Services

Just as shopping malls have installed information terminals, so too have many hotels. Automated **guest information services** include kiosks in public hotel areas and on in-room televisions and PCs that allow guests to inquire about in-house events and local activities. Transient guests, conference attendees, and casual observers alike can access information about the hotel, its outlets, and surrounding attractions.

Guest information systems, also called in-room electronic services, have evolved into an important guest amenity. These systems may connect to cable broadcast systems, wire news services, transportation schedules, flash graphic files, and restaurant and room service menus, as well as provide Internet access. Through access devices, guests are able to connect to the following:

- Airline schedules

- Local restaurant guides

- Entertainment guides and ticketing

- Stock market reports

- News and sports updates

- Shopping catalogs and transactions

- Video games and casino games

- Weather reports

Such connectivity enables the property to keep in-house guests and convention attendees informed about events and functions, provide tourists with information about local attractions, and inform business travelers about support services provided by the property.

Key Terms

Point-of-Sale Systems

PC-based register configuration (PCR)—A POS system design that networks terminals to form an integrated system that functions without a large, remote CPU.

point-of-sale terminal—Contains its own input/output component and may even possess a small storage (memory) capacity, but usually does not contain its own central processing unit.

Call Accounting Systems

active call accounting system—Enables a hotel to take control over local and long-distance services and apply a markup to switchboard operations. Call accounting systems are capable of placing and pricing local and long-distance calls.

automatic identification of outward dialing—A feature of a call accounting system that immediately identifies the extension from which an outgoing call is placed.

automatic route selection—A feature of a call accounting system that provides the capability of connecting with a variety of common carriers.

call record—Electronic or hard copy documentation containing essential transactional support data for individually placed and rated telephone calls.

common carrier—Any recognized entity that transmits messages or other communication for general use at accepted rates.

least-cost routing—A feature of an active call accounting system that directs calls over the least-cost available line, regardless of carrier.

passive call accounting system—Under this system, no options are available to the call distribution network. Selection of a route is based on convenience rather than on minimizing expense.

ringback mechanism—A feature of a call accounting system that ensures that a guest is charged only for calls that are answered.

station message detail record—A feature of a call accounting system that charts and monitors telephone traffic.

timeout feature—A feature of a call accounting system that ensures that callers begin paying for calls only after a predetermined amount of time, thus allowing for wrong numbers.

traffic transaction file—Part of a call accounting system that maintains data necessary for generating reports for management.

Voice over Internet Protocol (VoIP)—Communication network requiring specialty hardware and Internet access that enables worldwide connectivity.

Electronic Locking Systems

hard-wired electronic locking system—An electronic locking system that operates through a centralized master code console that is interfaced to every controlled guestroom door.

micro-fitted electronic locking system—An electronic locking system that operates as a stand-alone unit. Each door has its own microprocessor that contains a unique, predetermined sequence of codes. A master console at the front desk contains a record of all code sequences for each door.

Energy Management Systems

demand control—A feature of an energy management system that maintains usage levels below a given limit by shedding energy loads in an orderly fashion.

duty cycling—A feature of an energy management system that turns off equipment on a sequential basis for a given period of time each hour.

room occupancy sensors—Sensors that use either infrared light or ultrasonic waves to register the physical occupancy of a room.

Guest-Operated Devices

guest information services—Automated information devices in public hotel areas that allow guests to inquire about in-house events and local activities.

in-room check-out—When in-room computers are interfaced with a computer-based property management system's guest accounting module, they are able to access folio data and provide guests with a way to approve and settle their accounts.

in-room entertainment system—When interfaced with a hotel property management system, an in-room movie system provides guestroom entertainment through a dedicated television pay channel.

in-room vending system—A system capable of monitoring sales transactions and determining inventory replenishment quantities for in-room vending sales. Two popular in-room beverage service systems are nonautomated honor bars and microprocessor-based vending machines.

microprocessor-based beverage device—A guestroom vending machine that contains beverage items in see-through closed compartments. The compartment doors may be equipped with fiber optic sensors that record the removal of stored products. Once triggered, the sensors relay the transaction to a built-in microprocessor for recording. Individual guestroom microprocessors are typically cabled to a large CPU, which stores recorded transactions.

nonautomated honor bar—Typically involves stocks of items that are held in dry and cold storage areas within a guestroom. Changes in the bar's beginning inventory level are noted either by housekeeping room attendants during their normal rounds or by designated room service employees.

self-check-in/self-check-out terminals—Typically located in the lobbies of fully automated hotels, some resemble automatic bank teller machines, while others are unique in design and may possess both video and audio capability.

 # Review Questions

1. What issues should hospitality managers consider before interfacing separate applications with a property management system?

2. How does the choice between simplex and duplex communication affect an interface between a central reservation system and a property management system?

3. What are typical POS data entry requirements for posting charges to appropriate guest folios?

4. What are some concerns that management should address in relation to interfacing a POS system to a PMS system?

5. What data are maintained by a CAS call record file, and how may these data be useful to management?

6. What are the major differences between hard-wired and micro-fitted electronic locking systems, and what are the advantages and disadvantages of each system?

7. What are three energy control strategies that may be used by an energy management system?

8. What are some examples of auxiliary guest services that have been simplified by automation?

9. How can lodging properties benefit from automated self-check-in/self-check-out systems?

10. What are two in-room vending systems? Explain the advantages and disadvantages of each.

11. What external information services may guests be able to access from in-room computer terminals?

 # Internet Sites

For more information, visit the following Internet sites. Remember that Internet addresses can change without notice. If the site is no longer there, you can use a search engine to look for additional sites.

Agilysys
www.agilysys.com

Hitachi Communication Technologies
America, Inc.
www.hitachi-cta.com

INNCOM International Inc.
www.inncom.com

Inn Room Video
www.innroomvideo.com

Metropolis Technologies, Inc.
www.metropolis.com

NCR Corporation
www.ncr.com

Shift4 Corporation
www.shift4.com

SONIFI Solutions
www.sonifi.com

Squirrel Systems
www.squirrelsystems.com

System Concepts, Inc.
www.foodtrak.com

VingCard Elsafe
www.vingcardelsafe.com

Chapter 6 Outline

POS Order Entry Units
    Keyboards and Monitors
    Touchscreen Terminals
    Handheld Terminals
    Tablet POS Systems
POS Printers
    Guest Check Printers
    Receipt Printers
    Workstation Units
    Journal Printers
Account Settlement
    Power Platforms
    Smart Cards
    Debit Cards
    Cashless Payments
    Contactless Payments
PCI Compliance
    Cardholder Data and POS System
        Compliance
    PCI Requirements
Managing Guest Accounts
POS Software
    Menu Item File
    Labor Master File
    Inventory File
    Consolidated Reports
    Frequent Diner Applications
    Gift Cards
Automated Beverage Control Systems
    Order Entry Devices
    Delivery Networks
    Dispensing Units

Competencies

1. Describe the features and functions of keyboards and monitors typically used by point-of-sale systems. (pp. 131–137)

2. Distinguish touchscreen point-of-sale terminals from wireless terminals. (pp. 137–140)

3. Describe the features and functions of various types of point-of-sale printers. (pp. 140–144)

4. Describe the features and functions of point-of-sale account settlement devices such as magnetic strip and RFID readers, power platforms, smart cards, debit cards, cashless payment, and contactless payment. (pp. 144–149)

5. Discuss data typically found on payment cards and within POS systems, and identify PCI DSS objectives and requirements. (pp. 149–151)

6. Identify the major files typically maintained by point-of-sale software, describe how managers can use the various reports commonly generated by point-of-sale software, and discuss frequent diner applications and gift cards. (pp. 151–160)

7. Describe the features and functions of an automated beverage control system. (pp. 160–163)

6

Point-of-Sale Technology

WHILE AUTOMATED HOTEL PROPERTY MANAGEMENT SYSTEMS tend to consist of modules, restaurant management systems often involve specialty hardware and a wide variety of application software. This chapter focuses on applications that rely upon point-of-sale (POS) technology to monitor service area transactions through remote workstation printers, displays, and network controllers.

This chapter begins by identifying the necessary order entry units of a restaurant-wide POS system. Input/output devices such as keyboards, monitors, touchscreen terminals, OCR terminals, and wireless terminals are discussed in detail. POS printers—guest check printers, receipt printers, workstation printers, and journal printers—and POS account settlement devices—electronic payment systems—are also discussed. In addition, guest checks are examined in relation to enhancing management's control of operations. The chapter then goes on to outline the PCI standards required for hospitality properties that accept payment cards in account settlement.

Like other hardware components, POS terminals require software programs to instruct what to do, how to do it, and when to do it. POS software not only directs internal system operations, it also maintains files and produces reports for management's use. The chapter examines the types of data stored in most POS files and the kind of information used to produce aggregated reports.

The chapter closes with a section on automated beverage control systems. The discussion focuses on order entry devices, delivery networks, and dispensing units.

POS Order Entry Units

In this chapter, the term **cashier terminal** refers to a POS device that is connected to a cash drawer. A terminal without a cash drawer is commonly called a **precheck terminal**. Precheck terminals are used primarily to enter orders, not to settle accounts. For example, a server can use a precheck terminal located in a dining room service station to relay orders to the appropriate kitchen and/or bar production areas, but can only use the terminal to settle electronic payments. Only cashier terminals are used for cash settlement.

Since POS devices are generally sold as modular units, everything but the basic terminal is considered optional equipment. The cash drawer is no exception. Management may connect several cash drawers to a single cashier terminal. Multiple cash drawers may enhance management's cash control system when several cashiers work at the same cashier terminal during the same shift. Each cashier can be assigned a separate cash drawer so that, at the end of the shift, cash drawer receipts are individually reconciled.

A POS device with a cash drawer normally supports both prechecking and cashiering functions. For example, an employee at a cashier stand in a hotel restaurant may serve as the cashier for the food service outlet and as an order entry person for room service. When answering room service calls, the employee uses the cashier terminal as a precheck terminal. The terminal relays the room service orders to the appropriate kitchen and/or bar production areas. Before delivering the room service order, a room service employee may need to stop at the cashier station and pick up the printed guest check from the cashier. After delivering the order, the room service employee presents the settled or signed guest check to the cashier, who then uses the cashier terminal to close the guest check or transfer the folio charge within the system.

POS order entry units may be touchscreen or composed of keyboards and monitors. The following sections discuss these components. Keyboards are examined in relation to keyboard design, types of keys, and keyboard overlays. Touchscreen terminals are examined from an efficiency perspective. The section on monitors addresses important concerns, such as the size and function of operator displays and handheld devices. Touchscreen POS devices, multimedia readers, and handheld devices are traditional order entry devices. These devices are described in detail later in the chapter.

Keyboards and Monitors

The two primary types of keyboard surfaces are micro-motion and reed style. The micro-motion keyboard design has a flat, wet-proof surface. The reed keyboard design contains wet-proof keys raised above the surface of the keyboard. More important than the physical design of the device's surface is the number of hard and soft keys the keyboard or screen provides. **Hard keys** are dedicated to specific functions assigned by the manufacturer. **Soft keys** can be programmed by users to meet specific needs.

Keyboard designs can usually support interchangeable menu boards. A **menu board** overlays the keyboard surface and identifies the function performed by each key during a specific meal period. Menu boards can be developed to meet the specific needs of individual properties. Exhibit 1 shows a sample menu board for a dinner period. Menu boards for both micro-motion and reed style keyboard designs can identify a number of different types of key functions. Key types may include:

- Preset keys (or screen icons).
- Price look-up keys (or screen icons).
- Function keys.
- Settlement keys.
- Modifier keys.
- Numeric keys.

Exhibit 1　Sample Menu Board

CARAFE WHITE WINE	CARAFE RED WINE	BOURBON	VODKA	DECAF COFFEE	COFFEE	SALAD	BAKED POTATO	HASH BROWNS	FRENCH FRIES	SOUR CREAM	TIME IN
CARAFE ROSE WINE	SCOTCH	SODA	WATER	BLOODY MARY	TEA	WITH	WITH-OUT	BREAD	STEWED TOMATO	VEGETAB	TIME OUT
RARE	GIN	TONIC	COLA	SCREW-DRIVER	MILK	HOUSE DRESS	FRENCH DRESS	VINEGAR & OIL	EXTRA BUTTER	MUSHRM SAUCE	ACCOUNT #
MEDIUM	WELL	SAUTEED MUSHRMS	SHRIMP COCKTAIL	FRENCH ONION SOUP	CRAB MEAT COCKTAIL	OYSTERS ON 1/2 SHELL	ITALIAN DRESS	BLEU CHEESE DRESS	COUPON 1	COUPON 2	COUPON 3
PRIME RIB	T-BONE	SHRIMP	LOBSTER	CIGARS	CASH BAR	CLEAR	ERROR CORRECT	CANCEL TRANS	CHECK TRANSFER	PAID OUT	TIPS PAID OUT
CHATEAU-BRIAND	FILET	CLAMS	TROUT	CANDY	SERVER #	TRAN CODE	SCREEN	NO SALE	CASHIER #	EMPL DISC	MGR DISC
TOP SIRLOIN 16 OZ	TOP SIRLOIN 12 OZ	SEA BASS	SCALLOPS	SNACKS	VOID ITEM	7	8	9	QUANTITY	ADD CHECK	CREDIT CARD 2
PORTER-HOUSE	CHOPPED SIRLOIN	OYSTERS	ALASKAN KING CRAB	# PERSONS ADD ON	REVERSE RECEIPT	4	5	6	VOID TRANS	CHARGE TIPS	CREDIT CARD 1
STEAK & CHICKEN	SURF & TURF	RED SNAPPER	SEA FOOD PLATTER	DINING ROOM SERVICE	PRICE LOOK UP	1	2	3	NEW CHECK	CASH BAR TOTAL	CHARGE
LEG OF LAMB	ROAST DUCK	PORK CHOPS	CHICKEN LIVERS	LOUNGE SERVICE	MODE SWITCH	0		MENU 1	PREVIOUS BALANCE	CHECK TOTAL	CASH TEND

Servers enter orders by using preset keys and price look-up (PLU) keys. Modifier keys may be used in combination with preset and PLU keys to detail preparation instructions (such as rare, medium, well-done) for food production areas. Modifier keys may also be used to alter prices according to portion sizes (such as small, medium, and large). A numeric keypad facilitates various data-entry operations and enables cashiers to enter items by price when prices for items are not identified by preset keys or PLU numbers. Function keys and settlement keys are used to correct and complete transactions.

Generally, restaurant managers determine the positioning of most keys on a keyboard overlay. By positioning keys for similar items and functions together and arranging groups logically, managers can improve system performance and enhance operational controls. The following sections briefly discuss the types of keys commonly found on POS system keyboards.

Preset Keys. These keys are programmed to maintain the price, descriptor, department, tax, and inventory status for a select group of menu items. Automatic menu pricing speeds guest service, eliminates pricing errors, and permits greater menu flexibility. An item descriptor refers to the abbreviated description of a menu item, such as "SHRMPCKT" for shrimp cocktail or "PRIME" for prime rib. Although

Menu board overlay. (Courtesy of NCR.)

systems vary in the number of descriptor characters they can accommodate, most support descriptors of at least eight to ten characters long.

Each **preset key** (or screen icon) is normally associated with a department code and a printer routing code. A department code is used to describe the menu category to which the preset item belongs—appetizer, entrée, dessert, and so on. A printer routing code, also used in conjunction with a remote monitor or kitchen display unit (KDU), is used to direct preparation instructions to the proper production area. For example, the porterhouse steak on the keyboard in Exhibit 1 would have a department code associated with entrée items and a printer routing code designating it as an item prepared at the hot food production area of the kitchen. Other items on the same keyboard (salad, wine, etc.) can be assigned different department and printer routing codes.

Once a preset key is selected, a description of the item and its price are retrieved from memory and may be displayed on a monitor. This data may also be relayed (along with preparation instructions) to the appropriate production station and may be printed (or retained for later printing) on a guest check. In addition, the dollars represented by this transaction are retained for revenue reporting. Sales data for individual items are important for guest check totaling and management reports.

Price Look-Up Keys. Since terminals have a limited number of preset keys, **price look-up keys** (or screen icons) are used to supplement transaction entries. PLU keys operate like preset keys, except that they require the user to identify a menu item by a unique reference code number (up to five digits) rather than by its name or descriptor. A server entering an order for prime rib on a preset keyboard would merely press the item's preset key or use the designated PLU keys. In the absence of a prime rib preset key, the server would enter the item's code number (e.g., 7807) and then press the PLU key. PLU keys perform the same functions as preset keys but require more keystrokes. Preset keys and PLU keys enable the system to main-

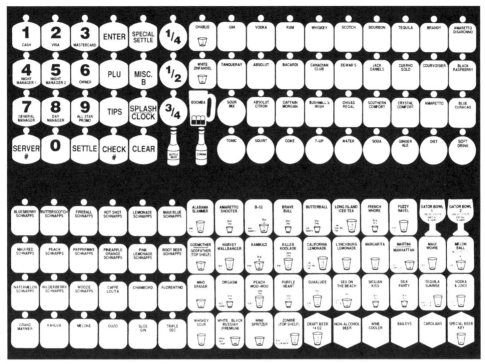

Keyboard for an automatic dispensing system.

tain a large inventory of menu items in terms of price, descriptor, tax, department, and inventory status.

Function Keys. While preset and PLU keys are used for order entry purposes, **function keys** assist the user in processing transactions. Sample function keys include: clear, discount, void, and no-sale. Function keys are important for error correction (clear and void), legitimate price alteration (discount), and proper transaction pricing and handling (no-sale). For example, a restaurant may attempt to increase weekly lunch sales by issuing coupons to nearby local businesses. When a coupon is used at the time of settlement, the cashier typically enters the value of the coupon and then presses the "discount" key. The value of the coupon is credited to the guest check and the remainder of the bill is settled through standard settlement procedures. The success of the promotion can be tracked if the POS system is capable of retaining itemized discounts and daily discount totals.

Settlement Keys. These keys are used to record the methods with which accounts are settled: by cash, credit card, house account, charge transfer, debit card, paykey, gift card, smart card, or other payment method. **Settlement keys** enhance revenue accounting controls because they classify transactions at the time of settlement. Although restaurants may use a number of revenue accounting methods, most operations use cashier banking or server banking. Server banking places the responsibility for guest check settlement on the server. Cashier banking involves a non-server handling account settlement. In either case, tracking the identification of the banker and the transaction settlement method facilitates a fast and accurate sales reconciliation.

Modifier Keys. Modifier keys allow servers to relay preparation instructions (such as rare, medium, or well-done) to remote workstation printers or monitors located in food and beverage production departments. Typically, a server enters the item ordered and then presses the appropriate preparation modifier. Modifier keys may also be used to legitimately alter menu item prices. For example, modifier keys may be useful to a restaurant that sells house wine by the carafe and half-carafe. Instead of tying up two preset keys (one for carafe, the other for half-carafe), a single preset key can be designated for house wine by the carafe and a modifier key can be programmed as a half-portion modifier. When a half-carafe is sold, the server simply presses both the carafe preset key and half-portion modifier key to register a half-carafe sale. The system will post wine revenue by adding the dollar amount for the half-carafe sale only. In addition, a countdown feature can be used to enable the POS system to accurately track inventory. A forced modifier may be built into the system. A forced modifier requires the server to respond to a specific cue before processing the order further. By requiring the server to respond, the system is intended to provide enhanced guest service.

Numeric Keypad. Numeric keys can be used to ring up menu items by price, access PLU data by menu item code number, access open guest check accounts by serial or transaction reference number, record the number of items sold, and perform other data entry operations. For example, if the cashier terminal is used to record and store payroll data, employee identification numbers can be entered as employees begin and end their workshifts. In addition, menu item code numbers may be entered through the numeric keypad to access various files in order to make adjustments approved by management. The numeric keypad may also be used to enter report codes that initiate the production of management reports.

Monitors. A micro-motion or reed style POS terminal typically contains an **operator monitor** and may also support a customer display unit. An operator monitor is generally a standard system component that enables the operator to view and edit transaction entries. The unit allows a server to monitor transactions in progress and also may serve as a prompt for various system procedures. The length and number of lines displayed are often an important consideration when selecting POS devices. Historically, line lengths have ranged from seven to eighty characters, and the number of lines available has varied from one to twenty-four or more. Graphic icons and color-coded tones are popular menu item format options. An operator monitor is typically encased in the primary housing of the POS device. This is not always the case for customer display units.

The designs of **customer display units** include those that rest atop, inside, or alongside the POS device. Although customer display units are more restricted in size and scope than operator monitors, they permit a guest to observe the operator's entries. In many table service restaurants, settlement activities often take place outside the view of guests; therefore, a customer display unit may not be warranted. In restaurants where guests can view settlement transactions, the use of a customer display monitor is often recommended.

Customer display units also permit management to spot-check cashier activities. For example, an employee operating a cashier terminal without a customer display unit might ring up a $5 transaction as $0.50. Later, to balance the cashier terminal's cash, the employee might take the $4.50 difference for personal use. This kind of theft is riskier when the terminal contains a customer display unit because a manager or the customer might observe the bogus $0.50 entry and take appropriate corrective action or request an explanation. Customer monitors are often more important for internal control purposes than for the assurance they offer guests.

The importance of practical, easy-to-use, fast, and reliable input devices has prompted the development of touchscreen terminals and handheld wireless server terminals. The following sections discuss each of these devices.

Touchscreen Terminals

There is perhaps no area of POS hardware that has received more attention than touchscreen technology. Color touchscreen terminals dominate the marketplace across all types of food service operations, including those that allow customers to use self-service order entry kiosks.

A **touchscreen terminal** contains a unique adaptation of a screen and a special microprocessor to control it. The self-contained microprocessor displays data on areas of the screen that are sensitive to touch. Touching one of the sensitized areas produces an electronic charge that is translated into digital signals for transmission to the microprocessor. This signal also instructs the microprocessor to display the next screen.

Although terminal design varies by vendor, a touchscreen terminal requires significantly less counter space than the traditional POS terminals it replaces. Many touchscreen devices measure only a few inches thick and can be mounted from walls, ceilings, counters, or shelving units. Flat screens offer restaurants additional flexibility in determining where to locate the terminals.

Touchscreens simplify data entry and are often selected over traditional screens and POS keyboards. A touchscreen provides prompts to guide servers through order entry or settlement procedures. For example, after a server enters an order for a menu item that needs preparation instructions (such as a New York strip steak), the screen shifts to display the appropriate modifiers (rare, medium rare, medium, medium well done, well done) or forced modifiers. Forced modifiers will not allow the user to proceed with order entry until a response is indicated. This reduces the possibility of servers sending incomplete orders to production areas. The interactive nature of a POS system also decreases the time it takes to train new employees.

Self-Service Order Entry. Some restaurant operations have installed countertop-recessed or lobby stand-up touchscreen terminals that enable customers to place their orders without interacting with staff members. This self-service option is intended to reduce labor costs and provide more efficient customer service. Some systems have highly attractive graphic components that help simplify order entry.

For example, icons (graphic images) or photographs can be used along with logos representing specific beverage choices. Condiments can also be creatively displayed—with a lasso indicating ranch salad dressing, the Eiffel Tower indicating French salad dressing, and so on.

A quick-service system may allow the customer to activate the touchscreen terminal by pressing a start feature on the screen. The screen then shifts to a display asking the customer to indicate whether the order will be taken out or eaten on-premises. Next, the screen shifts to display menu options. To order, the customer simply touches the desired item on the screen. As items are touched, a "video receipt" appears on the right side of the screen that maintains a running total during the ordering process. When the order is complete, the customer touches a "finished" box on the screen. At this point, a suggestive selling display may appear, asking the customer if he or she would like additional items or desserts (if not ordered). The final screen displays the total amount due and settlement options and instructions.

Handheld Terminals

Wireless order entry terminals offer unique POS opportunities. Since these units are palm-sized, they are labeled **handheld terminals** (HHTs). Through skillful programming, an HHT is able to perform most of the functions of a precheck POS terminal. Wireless technology can be a major advantage for establishments with drive-through facilities, long distances between service stations, outdoor dining areas, or in athletic stadiums or anywhere a precheck terminal would be impractical. Service may be greatly enhanced, since servers do not have to wait to use a precheck terminal during busy times and orders can be entered tableside.

HHT order entry operations rely on either sequential screen progression or written character recognition. HHTs with two-way communications not only allow a server to include special instructions, such as "no salt" or "medium rare" as part of an order, but also enable production staff or management to immediately alert a server if an item is out of stock or ready for pick-up. Typically, when an order is ready for pick-up, the server receives a page and/or displayed message.

Since all menu items must be entered through a server's handheld unit, the frequent problem of beverages or desserts inadvertently left off guest checks may be eliminated. Some wireless configurations enable managers to monitor all parts of service through a more powerful handheld device. See Exhibit 2 for examples of different order entry modes.

Exhibit 3 diagrams one type of hardware configuration for handheld server terminals. The handheld units have low-frequency FM radio transmitters and receivers. As orders are entered, signals are sent to **antenna units** (**access points**) located within the service area. These antenna units relay transmitted signals to a **radio base station** where the information is digitized and sent to remote workstation printers or monitors. A charged battery pack powers each handheld terminal. Fully charged, these battery packs may last for hours. It is recommended that two fully charged battery packs be available for each handheld unit to maintain service continuity.

Exhibit 2 Order Entry Methods

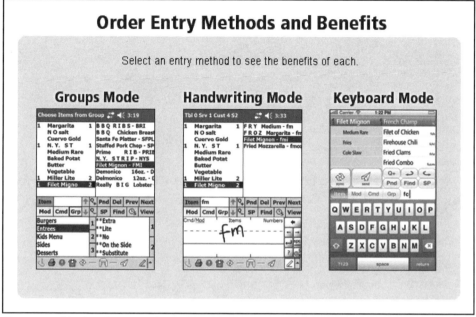

Courtesy of Action Systems, Inc., at www.rmpos.com.

Several antenna units may be connected to a radio base station. Before installation, a site survey should be conducted to determine the optimum locations for each access point. The location of interference structures within the restaurant is an important installation concern.

Tablet POS Systems

A typical hospitality industry stationary point-of-sale (POS) system requires both a significant upfront investment ($3,000 to $6,000 per terminal) and an annual software licensing and maintenance/support agreement fee (usually 10 to 15 percent of the system cost). By contrast, a switch from a tethered, hard-wired POS terminal to a comparable cloud-based POS system utilizing a handheld tablet PC or portable mobile device can be accomplished without a significant investment of time or money and can yield significant financial savings.

Those savings begin with reduced hardware costs, which typically represent only a fraction of the expenses associated with a stationary system. Use of a tablet is also accompanied by lower fees for software upgrades, system support, and auxiliary functionality (e.g., integrated sales and inventory analysis, reservations and table management monitoring, digital loyalty programs, and additional stand-alone applications). In many cases, these functions are not readily available in stationary POS systems.

Another benefit of a cloud-based platform is that its use enables the POS software to be updated remotely without operational downtime. In addition, unlike

Exhibit 3   Sample Hardware Configuration for Wireless Handheld Server Terminals

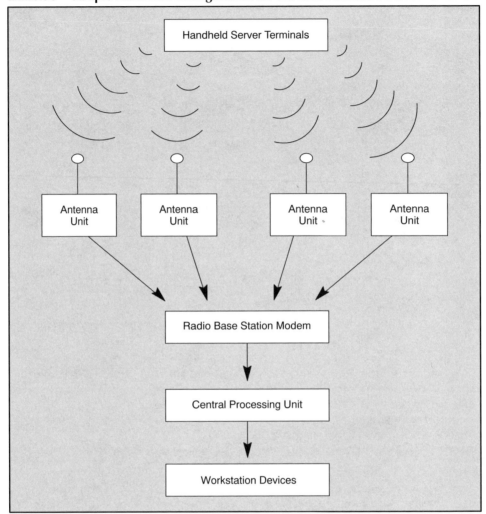

traditional POS devices that often require installation of an external payment card reader, a tablet PC is likely to be equipped with a payment processing reader. Given the streamlining associated with tablet POS technology, many operators are able to reduce technology support staff as well as parts inventory by replacing a traditional POS terminal system with a tablet POS system.

POS Printers

Cashier terminal printers are sometimes described as either on-board or remote printing devices. On-board printing devices are normally located within six feet of the terminal they serve. These devices include guest check printers and receipt printers. Remote printing devices include workstation printers and journal printers located more than six feet from the terminal they support. Each remote printing device will likely require separate cabling or wireless connectivity.

One of the most important peripheral devices in a POS system with remote workstation devices is the **network controller**, also called a printer controller. A network controller coordinates communications between cashier or precheck terminals and workstation printers or remote monitors, while ensuring that servers need only enter orders once. Exhibit 4 diagrams the function of a network controller.

When several precheck terminals send data to the same workstation printer or display monitor simultaneously, the network controller processes data from one of the terminals immediately and temporarily stores (buffers) other communications until the remote device becomes available. As the remote printer or monitor outputs data sent from one terminal, the network controller sends the next set of data, and so on, until all orders are printed or displayed. Since remote workstation units tend to move quickly, the time delay between order entry and printout or display is minimal—even for those orders temporarily buffered by the network controller.

Without a network controller, a remote workstation unit would be able to receive and print only one set of data at a time. When the remote unit is receiving data from one POS terminal, servers entering orders at other precheck terminals might encounter a "bottleneck" situation, much like a telephone busy signal. Without an effective network controller, orders likely would have to be re-input, since the original orders would not have been stored anywhere in the POS system—it is for this reason that a network controller is considered a buffer memory device.

Exhibit 4   The Function of a Network Controller

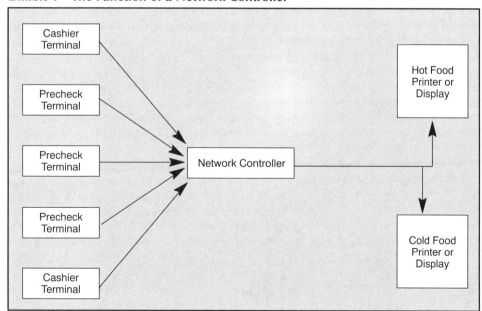

Guest Check Printers

Sometimes called slip printers, **guest check printers** of most POS systems can operate in the following modes:

- Immediate check printing

- Delayed check printing

- Retained check printing

Immediate check printing mode refers to the ability of the system to print items as they are entered at a POS terminal; delayed check printing mode means items will be printed at the end of a complete order entry; and retained check printing mode enables the guest check to be printed at any time following order entry. There are two types of guest checks: hard checks and soft checks. A **hard check** is a stiff-paper card that is stored outside the cashier terminal system. A **soft check** is made of lightweight receipt paper and is by far the preferred receipt format. Hard checks are rarely used since soft check printers have replaced hard check printers in a majority of food service operations. Hard check printers may be equipped with automatic form number reader (AFNR) and automatic slip feed (ASF) capabilities. Since hard checks tend to be serially numbered and printed sequentially as orders are entered, these features are quite important. Soft check printers are much easier to use and do not require serial numbering, since the complete guest check is available on demand. Soft check devices are popular because credit or debit card settlement can be recorded directly on the guest check as well as promotional messages and artwork.

In a hard check system, an **automatic form number reader** facilitates order entry procedures. Instead of a server manually inputting a guest check's serial number to access the account, a bar code imprinted on the guest check provides the check's serial number in a machine-readable format. The server simply slides the guest check into the terminal's AFNR unit, and the AFNR provides rapid access to the stored guest check account.

An **automatic slip feed** capability prevents overprinting items and amounts on hard checks. POS systems without ASF capability require that a server insert a guest check into the printer's slot and manually align the printer's ribbon with the next blank printing line on the guest check. This can be an awkward procedure for servers to follow during busy meal periods. If the alignment is not correct, the guest check appears disorganized and messy, with items and amounts printed over one another or with large gaps between lines. A system with ASF capability retains a record of the line number of the last line printed for each open guest check. The server simply aligns the top edge of the guest check with the top edge of the printer's slot, and the terminal automatically moves the check to the next available printing line and prints the order entry data.

Exhibit 5 presents an itemized hard check produced by a guest check printer with an automatic form number reader and automatic slip feed capability. The machine-readable bar code is printed in the upper right-hand corner of the guest check. The printed order follows food service coursing and not the sequence in which the server actually entered the order at a precheck terminal.

Exhibit 5 Sample Hard Guest Check

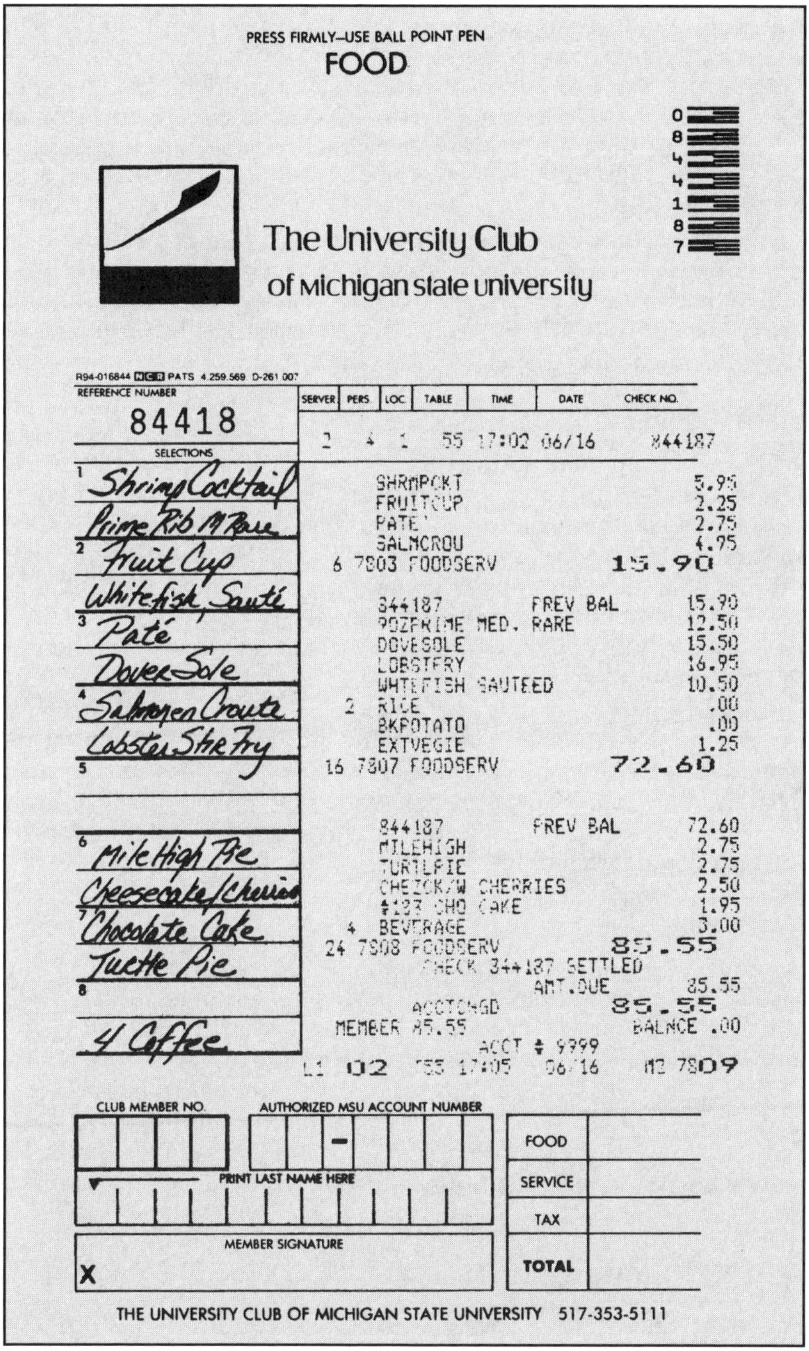
PRESS FIRMLY—USE BALL POINT PEN

FOOD

0844187

The University Club
of Michigan state university

R94-016844 NCR PATS 4 259 569 D-261 007

REFERENCE NUMBER

84418

SERVER	PERS.	LOC.	TABLE	TIME	DATE	CHECK NO.
2	4	1	55	17:02	06/16	844187

SELECTIONS

1 Shrimp Cocktail
Prime Rib M Rare
2 Fruit Cup
Whitefish, Sauté
3 Paté
Dover Sole
4 Salmon en Croute
Lobster Stir Fry
5
6 Mile High Pie
Cheesecake/Cherries
7 Chocolate Cake
Turtle Pie
8
4 Coffee

SHRMPCKT 5.95
FRUITCUP 2.25
PATE' 2.75
SALMCROU 4.95
6 7803 FOODSERV 15.90

844187 PREV BAL 15.90
PRIME MED. RARE 12.50
DOVESOLE 15.50
LOBSTFRY 16.95
WHTEFISH SAUTEED 10.50
2 RICE .00
BKPOTATO .00
EXTVEGIE 1.25
16 7807 FOODSERV 72.60

844187 PREV BAL 72.60
MILEHIGH 2.75
TURTLPIE 2.75
CHECK/W CHERRIES 2.50
#133 CHO CAKE 1.95
4 BEVERAGE 3.00
24 7808 FOODSERV 85.55
CHECK 844187 SETTLED
AMT.DUE 85.55
ACCTCHGD 85.55
MEMBER 85.55 BALNCE .00
ACCT # 9999
L1 02 55 17:05 06/16 M3 7809

CLUB MEMBER NO.

AUTHORIZED MSU ACCOUNT NUMBER

PRINT LAST NAME HERE

MEMBER SIGNATURE

X

FOOD

SERVICE

TAX

TOTAL

THE UNIVERSITY CLUB OF MICHIGAN STATE UNIVERSITY 517-353-5111

Courtesy of The University Club, Michigan State University, East Lansing, Michigan.

Receipt Printers

A **receipt printer** produces copy on narrow, flimsy paper tape. In addition to printing soft checks, a receipt printer may help control the production and accounting of menu items not prepared at departments receiving orders through remote display or printing devices. For example, when servers prepare their customers' desserts and the pantry area is not equipped with a remote communication device, desserts could be served without being entered into the POS system. When this happens, it is also possible that desserts will be served without ever being billed or paid for. This situation can be avoided by placing a receipt printer in the pantry area. Servers preparing desserts may be required to retrieve a receipt in the pantry area as proof that the items are properly posted to guest checks for eventual settlement. This procedure ensures that every menu item served is tracked somewhere in the POS system, thereby enhancing internal control.

Workstation Units

Remote printers or monitors are usually placed at kitchen preparation areas and service bars. As orders are entered at precheck terminals, they are sent to a designated remote **workstation printer** or **kitchen display unit (KDU)** to initiate production. Exhibit 6 shows printouts produced by remote workstation printers. The printouts correspond to items appearing on the sample guest check illustrated in Exhibit 5. This communication system enables servers to spend more time meeting guests' needs while significantly reducing traffic between the dining room and both the kitchen and the service bar.

If the need for hard copy output in production areas is not critical to an operation's internal control system, a remote KDU may be a viable alternative. Since these units display several orders on a single screen, kitchen employees do not have to handle numerous pieces of paper. An accompanying cursor control device enables kitchen employees to easily review previously submitted orders simultaneously by scrolling partial or full screens.

Journal Printers

A remote **journal printer** produces a continuous detailed record of all transactions entered anywhere in the POS system. Journal printers are usually located in secure areas (often in the manager's office or a security area) away from service and production areas. Hard copy may be produced on narrow register tape (usually twenty columns wide) or printed on letter-size paper and provides management with a thorough system audit. In addition to providing an audit trail, journal printers may also be used to print a variety of operational reports. Management routinely reviews journal printouts to verify that the system is functioning properly.

Account Settlement

Magnetic strip readers and **radio frequency identification (RFID) readers** are optional data capture devices that connect to a cashier terminal to facilitate electronic forms of settlement. Magnetic strip readers do not replace keyboards,

Exhibit 6   Sample Workstation Printouts

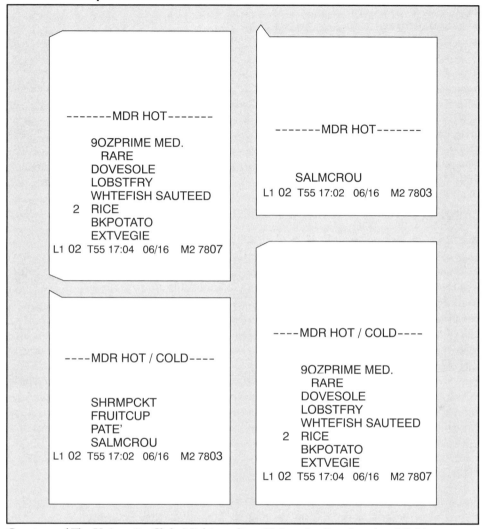

Courtesy of The University Club, Michigan State University, East Lansing, Michigan.

touchscreen devices, or optical character recognition terminals. Instead, they extend system capabilities. Magnetic strip readers are capable of collecting data stored on a magnetized film strip typically located on the back of a credit card, debit card, gift card, smart card, or loyalty or proprietary card. Terminals equipped with magnetic strip readers can also be used by employees with compatible identification cards to sign into the system. With magnetic strip readers, credit card, debit card, and related account transactions can be handled directly within a POS system. The connection of a magnetic strip reader to a cashier terminal allows rapid data entry and efficient settlement processing. It is also possible to add an

RFID reader to a POS terminal. The RFID reader can be used to process contactless transactions. RFID is discussed further later.

Power Platforms

Processing credit, debit, and gift card transactions can be greatly simplified when a **power platform** is used to consolidate electronic communications between a hospitality establishment and a remote authorization application. A POS power platform can connect all POS terminals at a location to a single processor for transaction reconciliation. This eliminates the need for redundant or individual POS terminal connectivity. Power platforms can capture transaction authorizations in seconds, and this swift data retrieval helps reduce the time, cost, and risk associated with deferred settlement.

Smart Cards

Smart cards are made of plastic and usually are the same shape and size as a credit card. Microchips embedded in smart cards store information that can be accessed by a specially designed reader. Smart cards can store information in several storage locations on the chip that can be accessed for different functions. For example, a smart card could store a person's vital health statistics, dietary restrictions, credit card number, frequent diner number, and bank account information. The security of information stored in smart cards is usually controlled through a personal identification number (PIN) or a biometric characteristic that must be used to access files.

Since smart cards contain the necessary information for completing electronic purchases, a specially designed reader may process a transaction and reduce the cash value stored on the chip by a corresponding amount. With a proprietary smart card, a closed system is used, which means no bank or credit card company authorizations are required.

Debit Cards

Debit cards differ from credit cards in that the cardholder must have money deposited into a linked bank account in order to establish settlement value. The cardholder deposits money in advance of purchases through a debit card center, bank, online financial outlet, or ATM. As purchases are made, the balance in the debit account is reduced accordingly. For example, a cardholder who has deposited $300 to a debit card account has $300 available for transaction settlement. As the cardholder makes purchases, the value of the debit account decreases to reflect the use of funds. To settle a transaction, the money is electronically transferred from the customer's account to the business account. There are two types of debit card transactions: online and offline. In an online debit transaction, the cardholder uses a PIN to authorize the transaction. In an offline debit transaction, the cardholder provides a signature to complete the transaction. An offline transaction is processed in a time frame and manner similar to a credit card transaction.

Cashless Payments

There are two distinct cashless payment systems: open systems and closed systems. An open system, also called an open loop system, involves acceptance of bank-sponsored credit card and debit card transactions (e.g., Visa, MasterCard, American Express, and Discover). Open system payment processing requires external authorization, processing, and settlement through an automated clearinghouse (ACH). When a guest completes a transaction with a credit or debit card, the transaction must be approved by the bank.

A closed system, also referred to as a closed loop system, relies on pre-payment, direct payment, or stored value payment at select point-of-sale locations supported by the issuer. Contrary to open systems, in a closed system there is no need for external verification or authorization, as the entire transaction is handled by the host location. A hospitality business that issues guests a paykey or branded pre-payment card, for example, is considered a closed system because the entire transaction is handled internally. The renewal or recharging of closed system media (e.g., a paykey or prepaid card) typically involves both open and closed system transactions, as a credit card is typically used to renew the value of the payment medium, which the guest can then use to make purchases.

Contactless Payments

Contactless payments, also referred to as proximity payment technology, involve settlement of a cashless transaction initiated and completed without physical contact between the payment media and payment reader. Purchase transactions are conducted with a wave or tap of an RFID chip embedded in a plastic card, tag, mini-card, or keychain fob, not with the swipe of a magnetic stripe. Settlement data is exchanged through contactless linkage using a passive RFID reader. It is the transmission and receipt of radio signals between a POS-based reader and the RFID payment medium that automatically initiates and completes the transaction. Near field communication (NFC) technology is also an effective contactless payment processing approach.

RFID Technology. Much contactless payment technology relies on RFID signal connectivity to operate. An RFID system consists of three components: a transponder (tag), an integrated RF circuit and antenna, and a transceiver (reader). Basically, a transceiver transmits radio frequencies to, and receives them from, a transponder via antenna relay. The transceiver subsequently transfers data to a processing device for reconciliation.

There are two types of RFID configurations: passive and active. Contactless payment systems are passive in nature. In a passive system, the reader broadcasts an RF signal that creates a magnetic field. The tag is empowered by this magnetic field and returns a signal to the reader to acknowledge its presence. In a passive system, the transponder need not have its own power source; instead, the reader serves as its energy source. This external power supply allows a passive RFID tag to be small and lightweight. By contrast, in an active system, both the transponder and transceiver send and receive signals and each has its own power source. An active configuration, therefore, is able to establish an extensive and broader range of detection and readability.

Once a passive RFID tag enters the electromagnetic detection area, it is activated and empowered to encode and exchange signals through its embedded antenna. The signal used to activate the tag's transmitter establishes authorization between the transponder and transceiver. The reader subsequently moves the transactional data to a POS or external data-processing system for settlement. Such terms as "tap 'n' go," "touch 'n' go," and "blink" are popular contactless technology terms meant to emphasize the non-contact nature of the transaction. It is important to note that most contactless media continue to feature a magnetic stripe and display of account information, thereby permitting transaction processing at locations where contactless technology is not available.

RFID has many advantages over competing contactless, cashless technologies such as bar coding and infrared. The primary advantage is that RFID is a non-line-of-sight technique. RFID tags can be read with great speed without attention to positioning, orientation, or clear sight line. A tag can be read at high speed with a high level of accuracy. The infrastructure necessary to conduct contactless settlement, as compared to cashless settlement, is minimal since, once the RF data is captured, settlement processing parallels contact media reconciliation. It is for this reason that an RFID application is considered the front-end of electronic data capture with subsequent settlement procedures identical to other forms of cashless settlement.

NFC Technology. For mobile devices, such as cell phones and personal digital assistants (PDAs), near field communications are used in place of RFID because NFC possesses superior interconnectivity capabilities and supports a wider range of interface standards. NFC-enabled cell phones and PDAs replace RFID contactless credit and debit media. Unlike plastic cards, keychain fobs, or tags, cell phones and PDAs offer the user an interface that provides rapid transaction settlement with an option to require entry of a secure PIN to authorize transactions. In addition, NFC technology can also provide a basis for audio and video downloading.

NFC-equipped cell phones, for example, enable users to pay for food and beverage service by waving an NFC-enabled phone near a contactless POS reader. The phone's NFC chip is used to establish a radio link that allows for transmission of the consumer's payment data without the need for a card swipe. Technically, NFC-enabled phones permit wireless provisioning based on service discovery. Wireless provisioning is defined as the automatic transmission of content via near-field connectivity (basically a push technology application). This feature may be most compelling in changing consumer buying habits from cash to cashless to contactless. For example, wireless provisioning can enable the automatic downloading of electronic coupons (to an NFC cell phone) just by passing nearby an NFC-enabled banner, sign, or device. Rather than broadcasting paper coupons through the mail or after settlement, an NFC-transmitted coupon can be applied immediately, thereby allowing the operator to influence consumer behavior before purchase.

Through an innovative process known as service discovery, NFC enables the transmission of optional content downloads from a smart display (a pull technology application). When an NFC-enabled chip is placed near a smart poster or sign, content downloads—including entertainment, animations, games, and nutritional data—can be selected. The smart display contains an NFC chip able to detect other NFC chips. Once it detects another chip, the display starts the download process and sends download instructions to the phone's browser. The user then chooses which, if any, downloads to execute.

PCI Compliance

A hospitality property accepting payment card settlement (credit cards and debit cards) must be in compliance with Payment Card Institute Data Security Standards (PCI DSS). PCI DSS contain a set of comprehensive requirements for payment account data security on a global basis; in other words, the PCI guidelines have an impact on businesses worldwide. Noncompliance can lead to excessive financial and operational penalties as well as expose guests to insurmountable monetary difficulties associated with identity theft. The most frequently cited PCI DSS requirement of which hospitality operators need to be mindful involves tracking and monitoring access to proprietary personal settlement resources. Hospitality management, in addition to standard property management system and point-of-sale practices, must be aware of the special vulnerability associated with wireless transaction processing and the need to safeguard payment data through complex encryption techniques.

There are at least two stages of transaction settlement in which data is especially prone to tampering, the first being data-at-rest (when data is being stored on the premises) and the second being data-in-transit (when data is being transferred). Surprisingly, the majority of unauthorized data acquisitions occur as the data is being transacted, either through the eavesdropping (i.e., unauthorized monitoring or tracking) of a payment device or theft of proprietary transaction data as it passes to or through a payment network.

Cardholder Data and POS System Compliance

Cardholder data refers to any information that can be found on a guest's payment card or other medium (e.g., keychain fob, tag, paykey, e-wallet, etc.). The cardholder data may be printed on the card's surface, stored on the card's magnetic stripe, or embedded via a contactless chip. Data typically includes cardholder name, account number, and account expiration date. There may also be additional sensitive data for personal authentication and/or transaction authorization. In general, no payment card data should ever be stored at the property. Management must use technical precautions to train staff and safeguard data during processing, settlement, and reconciliation procedures.

Since a hospitality property relies on its POS system for processing, storing, and transmitting settlement information to an external source (i.e., automated clearinghouse), the POS system must be certified as PCI-compliant. Under PCI specifications, credit and debit card data, account information, and transaction detail must be kept confidential and secure. This is especially important since accessible payment card information, in combination with other accountholder information, can lead to identity theft.

PCI Requirements

The objectives of PCI DSS are to a) build and maintain a secure network, b) protect cardholder data, c) maintain a vulnerability management program, d) implement strong access control measures, e) regularly monitor and test networks, and f) maintain an information security policy. Exhibit 7 provides a list of the twelve requirements that accompany the PCI DSS objectives.

Exhibit 7   PCI DSS Objective Requirements

The core of the PCI DSS is a group of principles and accompanying requirements, around which the specific elements of the DSS are organized:

Build and Maintain a Secure Network

Requirement 1: Install and maintain a firewall configuration to protect cardholder data.

Requirement 2: Do not use vendor-supplied defaults for system passwords and other security parameters.

Protect Cardholder Data

Requirement 3: Protect stored cardholder data.

Requirement 4: Encrypt transmission of cardholder data across open, public networks.

Maintain a Vulnerability Management Program

Requirement 5: Use and regularly update anti-virus software.

Requirement 6: Develop and maintain secure systems and applications.

Implement Strong Access Control Measures

Requirement 7: Restrict access to cardholder data by business need-to-know.

Requirement 8: Assign a unique ID to each person with computer access.

Requirement 9: Restrict physical access to cardholder data.

Regularly Monitor and Test Networks

Requirement 10: Track and monitor all access to network resources and cardholder data.

Requirement 11: Regularly test security systems and processes.

Maintain an Information Security Policy

Requirement 12: Maintain a policy that addresses information security.

Courtesy of the PCI Security Standards Council (www.pcisecuritystandards.org).

Data security standards are applied to secure the cardholder data that is stored, processed, or transmitted by hospitality properties and payment processors. PCI requirements have been developed based on security technologies and best business practices related to securing sensitive information. These PCI standards govern all hospitality businesses, retailers, and organizations that store, process, or transmit card settlement data. Compliance is mandatory and enforced by the major card brands (Visa, American Express, Discover, JCB International, and MasterCard Worldwide). As a result, hospitality management is strongly encouraged to ensure that all cardholder payment devices are PCI-compliant. Keep current with PCI standards and supporting documentation at www.pcisecuritystandards.org.

Managing Guest Accounts

Managing guest accounts is important regardless of whether a precheck or cashier terminal or a hard check or soft check receipt system is used. Before entering an order, the server may "open" a guest check within the system by inputting an employee identification number, biometric, or other type of authorization. Once the system has recognized the server and a new guest check has been opened, menu items can be entered and relayed to remote devices in production areas. The same items (along with selling prices) are posted to the guest check.

Once a guest check has been opened, it becomes part of the system's **open check file**. For each opened guest check, this file may contain the following data:

- Terminal number where guest check was initialized
- Guest check serial number (if appropriate)
- Server identification
- Time guest check was created
- Menu items ordered
- Selling prices of items ordered
- Applicable tax
- Gratuity (if appropriate)
- Total amount due

A server adds subsequent menu item requests to the guest check by accessing the open check via inputting a serial number (or other identifier) which matches that of the guest check at a POS terminal, and then entering the additional items.

There are many variations of this automated sequencing. As described earlier in this chapter, while most systems use soft checks, some use hard checks (guest checks with bar codes) with pre-printed serial numbers. Bar coding on a guest check eliminates the need for servers to manually input the guest check's serial number when opening a hard check or when adding items to guest checks already in use. When the guest check is placed in the guest check printer, the system reads the bar code and immediately accesses the appropriate file and line number.

Soft check systems eliminate the traditional externally stored guest check altogether. Soft check systems maintain only an electronic file for each open guest check. A receipt-like guest check can be printed at any time during service, but is usually not printed until after the meal when the server presents a final version of the check to the guest for settlement. Since no paper forms are used during service, the table number often is the tracking identifier for the order. With some systems, seat numbers can also be used for tracking multiple checks per table. When presenting soft checks to guests for settlement, the receipt-like guest checks can be inserted in high-quality cardboard, vinyl, or leather presentation jackets.

Most POS systems feature a soft guest check that can also be formatted to include a section for printing a credit card, debit card, smart card, or gift card receipt. This often reduces the time it takes servers to settle guest checks and assures customers of actual charges. Instead of presenting the guest check, collecting the guest's cashless payment media, printing an invoice, transferring information from the guest check to the invoice, and then presenting the invoice to the guest to sign, servers are able to present the guest check and a receipt simultaneously.

POS technology simplifies guest check control functions and eliminates the need for time-consuming manual audit procedures. Automated prechecking functions eliminate mistakes servers make in pricing items or calculating guest check totals. When items must be voided, an authorized supervisor can access the guest check and delete the items. Generally, automated systems can produce a report that lists all guest checks with voided or discounted items. It is important for automated systems to distinguish voided from discounted items because discounted items will appear in inventory usage reports, while voided items may not. If an item is voided after it has been prepared, the item typically is classified as "returned."

The status of a guest check changes from open to closed when payment is received from the guest and is recorded in the POS system. Most automated systems produce an **outstanding checks report** that lists all guest checks (by server) that have been opened but not settled. The report may list guest check number, server identification number, time guest check was opened, number of guests, table number, and revenue check total. This feature can help management determine responsibility for unsettled guest checks.

At any point, managers and supervisors can access the POS system and monitor the status of an open or closed guest check. This check-tracking capability can help identify potential walkouts, reduce server fraud, and tighten guest check and sales income control.

POS Software

As stated previously, the hardware of any system does nothing by itself. There must be a set of software programs directing the hardware in what to do, how to do it, and when to do it. POS application software not only directs internal system operations, but also maintains files and produces reports for management. Files that may be stored and maintained by a POS system include:

- Menu item file.

- Labor master file.

- Inventory file.

Data maintained by these files (and others) can be accessed by a POS terminal or connected PC, thereby enabling flexibility in report generation. The following sections briefly examine POS files and the types of data that may be stored in each.

Menu Item File

A **menu item file** contains data related to each menu item tracked by the POS system. Records contained within this file may contain the following menu item data:

- Identification number

- Descriptor

- Selling price

- Taxable item identifier

- Applicable modifier keys

- Ingredient quantities for inventory tracking

- Remote device routing code

This file is generally linked to a POS touchscreen map, menu keyboard, or selection panel. Management can control information stored for each current menu item for various meal periods. Operational reports can be produced by meal period identifying menu item descriptor, price, and applicable tax. When menu items, prices, or taxes need to be changed, the menu item file is accessed and changes are entered according to procedures indicated in the user's manual or on-screen instruction.

Labor Master File

Some food service operators employ a POS system as a labor tracking front-end device to a labor management application. Given that the POS system has a built-in time clock, its touchscreen or keyboard provides an input component for employees to sign in and sign out. The software can then compute gross time worked and associated labor cost based on the application of data maintained in the labor master file. The **labor master file** of a POS system contains one record for each employee and typically maintains the following human resources data:

- Employee name

- Employee number

- Social Security number

- Authorized job codes

- Hourly wage rates

This file may also contain data required to produce labor management reports. Each record in the labor master file may accumulate:

- Hours worked.

- Gross hourly wage(s).

- Declared wages.

- Tips (or tip credits).

- Credits for employee meals.

- Number of guests served (if appropriate).

- Gross sales generated.

Many POS systems are unable to compute net pay figures because of restricted processing ability and limited memory capacity. Data accumulated by the labor master file can be used to produce a number of reports, such as a labor master report and daily, weekly, and period labor reports. The labor master file can also be exported to a back office payroll accounting software package to generate a comprehensive set of labor reports and produce payroll checks.

A POS-based **labor master report** contains general data maintained by the labor master file. This report is commonly used to verify an employee's hourly rate(s), job code(s), or Social Security number.

A POS-based **daily labor report** typically lists the names, employee numbers, hours worked, wages earned, and wages declared for each employee. A **weekly labor report**, which contains similar information, may be used to identify the names of employees whose work schedule indicates they are approaching overtime pay rates. A **period labor report** generally lists hour and wage information for each employee who worked during the period.

Data stored in the POS labor master file may also be used to produce daily, weekly, and period employee meal reports that show amounts for meals provided to employees. Also, a weekly and period employee tips report may be generated to illustrate the appropriate total tips expected to be reported by each employee.

Inventory File

The **inventory file** maintained by a POS system may not meet the inventory control needs of all properties. Most POS systems are incapable of tracking the same item as it passes through the control points of receiving, storing, issuing, and production. Inventory data must be specific to each of these control points because purchase units (case, drum, etc.) commonly differ from storeroom inventory units (#10 can, gallon, etc.), which, in turn, differ from standard recipe units (ounce, cup, etc.). Many systems are not able to support the number of conversion tables necessary to track menu items through ingredient purchase, storage, and use.

Since most operators do not purchase menu item ingredients on a pre-portioned basis, there often are significant problems when trying to implement a POS-based inventory control system. In addition, the initial creation of an ingredient file and the subsequent file updates (daily, weekly, monthly, etc.) can be an overwhelming task for some operations. For example, a restaurant company typically carries an average of 450 menu items and an average inventory of 1,500 ingredients and monitors at least twelve to eighteen high-cost inventory items on a perpetual basis. POS systems may not be able to support the files necessary for effective inventory control on such a large scale.

Consolidated Reports

POS systems may access data contained in several files to produce consolidated reports for management use. Such reports typically include daily revenue reports, sales analysis reports, summary **activity reports**, and productivity reports. Data captured by a POS system can be exported to a back office software package for more extensive report generation.

A POS **sales and payment summary report** provides managers with a complete statement of daily or monthly sales (by shift and/or by food and beverage category). The report may also summarize settlement methods. Exhibit 8 illustrates a sample sales and payment summary report.

A POS **sales by time of day report** enables management to measure the sales performance of individual menu items by department or product category within certain time intervals (often called "day parts"). Time intervals may vary in relation to the type of food service operation. Quick-service restaurants may desire **sales analysis reports** segmented by fifteen-minute intervals, table-service restaurants in hourly sections, and institutional food service operators by meal period. A sales analysis report allows management to track individual item sales, analyze product sales movement, and monitor advertising and sales promotional efforts. A sample sales by time of day report is shown in Exhibit 9.

Exhibit 8   Sample Sales and Payment Summary Report

SALES		LUNCH	DINNER	BRUNCH	TOTAL
1 NUMBER OF CUSTOMERS		110	89	.	199
2 TAXABLE FOOD TOTAL		2455.50	2093.00	.	4558.50
3 TAXABLE BEVERAGES TOTAL		1371.00	1382.75	.	2753.75
TOTAL FOOD & BEVERAGE (before tax)		3826.50	3475.75	.	7302.25
SALES TAX		315.69	286.75	.	602.44
4 NONTAXABLE FOOD TOTAL		.	.	.	.
5 NONTAXABLE BEVERAGE TOTAL		.	.	.	.
TOTAL		4142.19	3762.50	.	7904.69
% OF SALES		52.40	47.60	.	

PAYMENTS	#CKS	TAXABLE	NONTAX.	TAX	TIPS	GROSS	CARD FEE	NET
6 CASH	3	482.50	.	39.81	.	522.31	.	482.50
7 CHECK	3	318.25	.	26.26	.	344.51	.	318.25
8 HOUSE CH.	3	1017.00	.	83.90	57.00	1157.90	.	1017.00
9 AMEX	40	5484.50	.	452.47	298.50	6235.47	222.64	5261.86
10 DC	0	.	.	.	.	.	.	.
11 VISA/MC	0	.	.	.	.	.	.	.
CARD SUBTOT	40	5484.50	.	452.47	298.50	6235.47	222.64	5261.86
TOTAL	49	7302.25		602.44	355.50	8260.49	222.64	7079.61

Exhibit 9   Sample Sales by Time of Day Report

	Stn	Date 8–30 Time 5:31 A.M. SALES BY TIME OF DAY									
		--------- CURRENT ---------					--------- TO DATE ---------				
	Stn	Sales	Trans	Cvrs	Avg $/Trns	Avg $/Cvr	Sales	Trans	Cvrs	Avg $/Trns	Avg $/Cvr
08:01– 09:00	01–	141.85	9	25	15.76	5.67	141.85	9	25	15.76	5.67
	02–	372.75	13	43	28.67	8.67	372.75	13	43	28.67	8.67
	–	514.60	22	68	23.39	7.57	514.60	22	68	23.39	7.57
09:01 – 10:00	01–	12.30	2	5	6.15	2.46	12.30	2	5	6.15	2.46
	–	12.30	2	5	6.15	2.46	242.40	18	36	13.47	6.73
10:01 – 11:00	01–	183.85	10	34	18.39	5.41	183.85	10	34	18.39	5.41
	02–	464.90	13	74	35.76	6.28	1,173.80	50	196	23.48	5.99
	–	648.75	23	108	28.21	6.01	1,357.65	60	230	22.63	5.90
11:01 – 12:00	01–	22.75	1	2	22.75	11.38	22.75	1	2	22.75	11.38
	02–	24.55	2	4	12.28	6.14	178.40	12	35	14.87	5.10
	–	47.30	3	6	15.77	7.88	201.15	13	37	15.47	5.44
12:01 – 13:00	01–	54.20	3	6	18.07	9.03	54.20	3	6	18.07	9.03
	02–	45.20	4	8	11.30	5.65	45.20	4	8	11.30	5.65
	–	99.40	7	14	14.20	7.10	99.40	7	14	14.20	7.10
13:01 – 14:00	01–	31.15	2	8	15.58	3.89	31.15	2	8	15.58	3.89
	02–	38.90	2	4	19.45	9.73	38.90	2	4	19.45	9.73
	–	70.05	4	12	17.51	5.84	70.05	4	12	17.51	5.84
Total	–	1,392.40	61	213	22.83	6.54	2,485.25	124	397	20.04	6.26

Exhibit 10 presents a sample POS **daily transactions report** that provides an in-depth analysis of sales transactions by individual server. POS **productivity reports** typically detail sales activity for all active food service servers. Daily productivity reports may be generated for each server on a guest count, total revenue, and average revenue per guest basis.

Frequent Diner Applications

A direct descendant of the airline industry's frequent flyer clubs, frequent diner applications enable a restaurant to gain valuable marketing information while rewarding brand loyalty and building future sales. The benefits are balanced: while the restaurant builds a guest history database, the guest reaps the rewards offered through the frequent diner program.

Customers are generally able to enroll in a frequent diner program in a number of different ways: in person, over the telephone, by fax, via e-mail, or online. During the enrollment process, restaurants obtain data such as customer name,

Exhibit 10   Sample Daily Transactions Report

```
              Date   8-30
              Time   5:31 A.M.          DAILY TRANSACTIONS
```

Guest Check	Tabl/ Covrs	Employee	ID	Time In	Time Out	Elapsed Time	Food	Bar	Wine	Guest Total	Tax	Tip	Settlement Method	Settlement Amount
11378	2–2	Jones	4	8:23	9:00	0:37	13.75	0.00	3.50	17.25	0.87	2.00	CASH	20.12
11379	2–1	Jones	4	8:25	9:00	0:35	2.35	0.00	0.00	2.35	0.12	0.00	COMP 1 0004	2.47
11380	3–3	Jones	4	8:32	9:01	0:29	13.15	0.00	5.50	18.65	0.93	0.00	CASH COMP 2 0033	9.58 10.00
11381	4–4	Jones	4	8:34	9:16	0:42	9.05	0.00	0.00	9.05	0.47	0.00	MC	9.52
11382	3–2	Jones	4	8:40	9:18	0:38	6.20	0.00	5.50	11.70	0.60	0.00	Cancelled	
11383	3–2	Jones	4	8:41	9:19	0:38	4.35	0.00	0.00	4.35	0.22	0.00	COMP 1 0004	4.57
11384	4–4	Jones	4	8:43	10:16	1:33	33.80	11.00	0.00	44.80	2.25	0.00	AMEXPRESS	47.05
11385	4–2	Jones	4	8:46	10:17	1:31	0.00	9.75	0.00	9.75	0.49	0.00	VISA	10.24
11386	4–5	Jones	4	8:51	10:17	1:26	0.00	18.50	0.00	18.50	0.91	0.00	MC	19.41
11387	8–2	Jones	4	8:54	10:18	1:24	14.65	2.50	0.00	17.15	0.85	0.00	COMP 1 0004	18.00
11388	4–3	Jones	4	9:23	10:17	0:54	4.70	3.00	0.00	7.70	0.39	1.00	CASH	9.09
11389	2–2	Jones	4	9:34	10:16	0:42	4.60	0.00	0.00	4.60	0.24	0.00	CASH	4.84
11398	3–2	Jones	4	12:09	12:10	0:01	11.35	0.00	0.00	11.35	0.57	0.00	CASH	11.92
11399	3–2	Jones	4	12:20	12:21	0:01	10.25	2.00	0.00	12.25	0.61	0.00	CASH	12.86
21615	3–2	Jones	4	11:39	11:41	0:02	13.15	0.00	0.00	13.15	0.65	0.00	CASH	13.80
21616	1–2	Jones	4	11:40	11:41	0:01	7.90	0.00	3.50	11.40	0.58	0.00	CASH	11.98
Total cancelled			11.70											
**** Totals							143.05	46.75	12.50	202.30	10.15	3.00		215.45

street and e-mail addresses (home and work), demographics (such as family status and birthday dates), special interests, and preferred frequent dining plan (if options exist). An enrollment fee is usually credited back to the member's account or is offset by discount incentives or redeemable points.

Upon completion of enrollment, an electronic file is created and the member may be issued a frequent diner card—a plastic card with a magnetic stripe or a smart card with an embedded microchip. Automated frequent diner programs post transactions at the point of sale. The member presents a card at the point of purchase and the transaction is posted to the database. As part of the transaction, the member accrues awards (points, discounts, merchandise, etc.) based on the number of visits and the value of the transaction.

Member account balances can be maintained in a database (locally, regionally, or nationally) or they can be stored on a member's smart card. A current account balance is the accumulation of points attained less the points used to redeem appropriate rewards. An important consideration in account tracking is that the member should be able to view the account balance, either at each point of sale or through online access.

Depending on the format of the databases, restaurants may be able to pose complex queries and search multiple databases containing transactional data, accrued points, issued vouchers, and redemption activity. Most frequent diner applications can identify and generate information in categories such as:

- Best customers (revenue generated)

- Customer frequency (number of visits)
- Popularity of menu items (indexing)
- Purchase patterns (menu mix)
- Bundled purchases (upscaling)
- Redemption points (reward programming)
- Marketing/advertising campaign success
- Special promotion effectiveness

Frequent diner applications vary in terms of the method used to capture transactions. Some POS systems have built-in frequent diner applications. These applications poll detailed customer transaction information captured at the time of sale and automatically post amounts to member accounts. Electronic data capture (EDC) is another method. An EDC-based application relies on the data-processing features of an external credit, debit, or smart card banking service to recognize, sort, and apply qualified transactional data to member accounts. The external company (or its intermediary) uses software capable of separating transactions by enrolled member and award criteria. A third option exists with stand-alone frequent diner applications that operate similarly to POS-based applications.

Gift Cards

Gift cards can be branded, personalized, and customized and offer the benefits of comprehensive usage tracking and a variety of redemption options. Gift cards can be used to recruit, recognize, motivate, and provide incentives for consumers. Sales of gift cards can have a significant impact on revenues for a hospitality business. An effective gift card program often involves the distribution of a branded prepaid card through multiple channels (POS, kiosk, retail display, or online), in any denomination, and is instantly redeemable. Gift cards are known as stored value media since purchasing power is posted and carried on an embedded chip or magnetic stripe on the card. The term *breakage* is used to describe the amount of stored value that will never be redeemed. Industry estimates reveal a breakage level of 10 to 12 percent. *Upspending* describes the situation in which the consumer purchases goods and services at a higher dollar value than carried on the gift card. In order to complete the transaction, the consumer must apply additional funds. It is estimated that the average gift card upspending is 1.4 times the value of the card.

Gift cards can be processed using existing electronic payment readers (credit/debit card readers) and therefore eliminate the need for separate gift card processing hardware or communication software at the point of sale. POS equipment can be used to activate new cards, increase the value of existing cards (recharging), perform balance inquiries, and redeem the card for purchases.

Several hospitality industry gift card programs are operated as stand-alone, third-party contracted applications. The third-party firm is a gift card specialty processor not directly affiliated with the hotel or restaurant operator. The processor manages account data, transaction posting, account reconciliation, and system reporting. In order to work efficiently, the processor needs to seamlessly interface with the in-house POS system. The POS system is used to create, activate, post, and process gift card transactions. The processor must program the system to conform to the expiration date, administrative fee structure, and other requirements for the location of the transaction. With most processor-based gift card solutions, the gift card management company holds the money. When the card is used, the processor credits the property's account for the amount of the transaction. The gift card processor, in addition to tracking account balances, can also provide web services to gift cardholders through a special website. Part of the role of the card processor is to handle card security, production, packaging, transaction processing, database management, reporting, and help desk support. Web-based reporting of real time account activity for hotel and restaurant clients is an important aspect of gift card accounting and financial tracking.

Gift cards fall into two general categories: cards issued by banks (open loop network) and cards sold by retail establishments (closed loop network). Open loop cards (with brands like Visa, MasterCard, and American Express) have a wide degree of negotiability and are akin to a debit card. As the name implies, open loop cards can be used at any hospitality establishment that accepts a debit card or ATM transaction. This is not true for a closed loop card that can be redeemed only at participating outlets. Closed loop gift cards are limited in scope and negotiability and rely on a proprietary network provided by a processor or fulfillment agency. From a hospitality industry perspective, a closed loop card provides a means to build customer loyalty and gain new customers, as the card must be used at participating locations. Closed loop cards are governed by state laws, which vary widely. Some states, for example, do not allow gift cards to expire, while others place limits on non-use and administrative fees imposed if the card is not used in a specified period of time.

Gift Card Accounting. The issuance of a gift card is a currency exchange, not a sale. The sale is deferred until the guest redeems the card as a form of payment. From an accounting perspective, the sale of a gift card represents a current liability, as payment is collected for a promise of future benefit. Under standard accounting practices, the amount later received in payment for goods or services should not be recognized as revenue. As gift cards are used, revenue represented by the rendered goods and services is recognized through gift card bank withdrawal and the liability reduced accordingly. In order to account for monies derived from gift card sales, a separate entry and fund deposit is normally created to chart redemption activity and to hold the funds securely for some period of time—maybe up to five years—per state-governed liability limitations. If a credit or debit card is used to purchase a gift card, some gift card management companies create a separate bank and deposit cash in the amount of the transaction to the bank. As a result, monies collected for gift cards in one accounting period often will not appear as revenue until a future period. Despite the fact that a gift card is sold for cash, the retailer or designated agent is obligated to hold the money from the sale until the consumer uses its stored value. It is important to note that in the United States, several states have adopted legislation to restrict the use of gift card expiration dates, dormancy fees, or both. Lost or unused gift cards are often referred to as "drift cards."

Automated Beverage Control Systems

Automated beverage control systems reduce many of the time-consuming management tasks associated with controlling beverage operations. While automated beverage systems vary, most systems can dispense drinks according to the operation's standard drink recipes, monitor the number of drinks poured, and report the associated revenues.

Automated beverage systems can be programmed to dispense both alcoholic and nonalcoholic products with varying portion sizes. An automated beverage control system can also generate projected sales information based on different pricing period forecasts. With many systems, the station at which drinks are prepared is connected to a guest check printer that records transaction data as drink orders are dispensed. As a control technique, systems may require that a hard guest check be inserted into the printer before a drink can be dispensed. With a soft guest check system, there must be a roll of paper in the printing unit. The goal is to automatically track all sales generated through automated beverage dispensing equipment.

With one type of automated beverage system, liquor is stored at the bar. Price-coded pourers (special nozzles) are inserted into each bottle. These pourers cannot dispense liquor without a special activator ring. The bartender slips the ring over the neck of a liquor bottle (with the price-coded pourer already inserted) and prepares the drink with a conventional hand-pouring motion. A cord connects the activator ring to a master control panel that measures the liquid flow and converts and records the number of drinks poured at each price level. The master control panel is typically connected to a POS terminal for transaction control. Reports indicate the number of drinks poured at different price levels and the total expected revenue from each dispensing station.

With another type of automated beverage system, liquor is stored in racks in a locked storage room located away from the bar area. The bartender prepares a drink by pushing the appropriate key on a dispensing device. The liquor and associated mixes required by the drink recipe travel to a dispensing location at the bar through separate, high-quality plastic tubing. The system pours the drink when the bartender holds a glass under the dispensing device. The drink may then be manually garnished and served to the guest.

Automated beverage control systems may employ several types of sensing devices to increase operational controls while maintaining data integrity within the system. Three common sensing devices are glass sensors, guest check sensors, and empty bottle sensors. A **glass sensor** is an electronic mechanism located in a bar dispensing unit that will not permit liquid to flow from the dispensing unit unless there is a glass in place to catch the liquid below the dispensing head. **Guest check sensors** prevent the system from fulfilling beverage orders unless first recorded on an open guest check. When a server places a beverage order whose ingredients are close to becoming out-of-stock, an **empty bottle sensor** relays a signal to the order entry device that product inventory needs replenishment.

Automated beverage control systems can enhance production and service capabilities while improving accounting and operational controls. Systems can record data input through order entry devices, transport beverage ingredients through a controlled delivery network, dispense ingredients for ordered items, and track important service and sales data. The following sections examine the basic components of an automated beverage control system: order entry devices, delivery networks, and dispensing units.

Order Entry Devices

In an automated beverage control system, the primary function of an order entry device is to initiate activities involved with recording, producing, and pricing beverage items requested by guests. There are two basic order entry devices: preset keys on a dispensing unit and keyboard units that function as precheck POS terminals.

A group of preset buttons on a dispensing unit is a popular order entry device format. Preset key devices may operate at a lower overall level of cost, since the dispensing unit serves as both an order entry device and a delivery unit. However, since dispensing units may support a limited number of preset buttons, the number of beverage items under control of the system is severely limited.

Keyboard units, which can also be touchscreen, function like precheck terminals; beverage dispensing is performed by a separate piece of hardware. Since keyboards support a full range of keys (including preset keys, price look-up keys, and modifier keys), these units place a large number of beverage items under the control of the automated system. Keyboard units may be equipped with a guest check or receipt printer and may feature a colorful array of keys or icons in graphical form.

Delivery Networks

An automated beverage control system relies on a **delivery network** to transport beverage ingredients from remote storage areas to dispensing units. The delivery network must be a closed system capable of regulating temperature and pressure conditions at various locations and stages of delivery. To maintain proper temperature conditions, the delivery network typically employs a cooling sub-system that controls such mechanisms as cold plating, cold boxes, and cold storage rooms.

Most systems are able to deliver beverage ingredients by controlling pressure sources such as gravity, compressed air, carbon dioxide, and nitrous oxide. Gravity and compressed air are normally used for delivering liquor, nitrogen or nitrous oxide for wine, compressed air for beer and perishable items (mixes, garnishes, etc.), and a carbon dioxide regulator for beverage post-mix products. The post-mix dispenser places syrup and carbonated water together at a soft drink dispenser instead of storing, transporting, and distributing the drink as a finished product.

The particular pressure source selected to transport a specific ingredient is a function of its effect on the taste and wholesomeness of the beverage item. For example, if carbon dioxide were attached to a wine dispenser, the wine would become carbonated and spoiled. Similarly, if compressed air were connected to a post-mix soft drink dispenser, the dispensed beverage would not have any carbonation. Pressure sources not only affect the quality of finished beverage items, but may also affect the timing, flow of mixture, portion size, and desired foaming.

Almost any brand of liquor and accompanying liquid ingredient can be stored, transported, and dispensed by an automated beverage control system. Portion sizes can be specified with remarkable accuracy. Typically, systems can be calibrated to maintain portion sizes ranging from one-half ounce to three and one-half ounces.

Dispensing Units

Once beverage item ingredients are removed from storage and transported by the delivery network to a service area, they are ready to be dispensed. Automated beverage control systems may be configured with a variety of dispensing units. Common dispensing units include:

- Touch-bar faucet.
- Hose and gun.
- Console faucet.
- Mini-tower pedestal.
- Bundled tower.

A touch-bar faucet can be located under the bar, behind the bar, on top of an ice machine, or on a pedestal stand. Touch-bar faucet devices do not have the versatility, flexibility, or expandability of other dispensing units. Typically, these units are dedicated to a single beverage type and are preset to one portion size output per push on the bar lever. A double shot of bourbon, for example, will require the bartender to push twice on the bar lever.

A hose and gun device features control buttons on the handle of a gun-like device that can be connected to liquors, carbonated beverages, water, and wine tanks. A hose and gun dispenser can be installed anywhere along the counter of a bar and is considered standard equipment on portable bars and service bars. Pressing a control button produces a pre-measured flow of a desired beverage. The number of beverage items under the control of a hose and gun dispensing unit is limited to the number of control buttons the device supports.

Console faucet dispensing units are similar to touch-bar faucet devices in that they can be located in almost any part of the bar area. In addition, these units may be located up to 300 feet from beverage storage areas. Unlike touch-bar faucet devices, console faucet units can dispense various beverages in a number of portion sizes. Using buttons located above the faucet unit, a bartender can trigger up to four different portion sizes of the same product from the same faucet head. An optional feature of a console faucet device is a double hose faucet unit that provides the capability to transport larger quantities of liquids in shorter amounts of time.

The mini-tower pedestal dispensing unit combines the button selection of a hose and gun device with the portion size capabilities of a console faucet unit. In addition, the mini-tower concept offers increased operational controls of bar procedures. In order for a beverage to be dispensed, the mini-tower unit requires that a preset key be pressed and a glass placed directly under the dispensing head. This automated dispensing unit is designed for dispensing beverage items that need no additional ingredients (items like wine, beer, and call brand liquors). A mini-tower unit can also be located on a wall, ice machine, or pedestal base in the bar area.

The most sophisticated and flexible dispensing unit is the bundled tower unit, also referred to as a tube tower unit. The bundled tower unit is designed to dispense a variety of beverage items. Beverage orders must be entered on an interfaced POS device, not on the tower unit. Bundled tower units may support in excess of 110 beverage products and contain a glass-sensing element. Each liquor has its own transportation line to the tower unit, and a variety of pressurized systems can be used to enhance delivery from distant storage areas. While other units sequentially dispense beverage item ingredients, the bundled tower unit simultaneously dispenses all ingredients required for a specific drink recipe. The bartenders merely garnish the finished product. Like the console faucet unit, this dispensing unit can be located up to 300 feet from beverage storage areas.

 ## Key Terms

POS System Hardware

automatic form number reader (AFNR)—A feature of a guest check printer that facilitates order entry; instead of a server manually inputting a guest check's serial number to access the account, a bar code imprinted on the guest check presents the check's serial number in a machine-readable format.

automatic slip feed (ASF)—A feature of a guest check printer that prevents overprinting of items and amounts on guest checks.

cashier terminal—A POS device that is connected to a cash drawer.

customer display unit—A display screen that may rest atop, inside, or alongside the POS device for the customers' viewing.

function keys—When part of a POS system terminal, function keys help the user process transactions; they are important for error correction (clear and void), legitimate price alteration (discount), and proper cash handling (no-sale).

guest check printer—A POS on-board printing device that is sometimes called a slip printer. A sophisticated guest check printer may be equipped with an automatic form number reader and may possess automatic slip feed capabilities.

hard checks—Guest checks that are made of stiff-paper cards. Hard checks are stored outside the cashier terminal system.

hard keys—Keys on a POS system terminal dedicated to specific functions programmed by the manufacturer.

journal printer—A remote printing device of a POS system that produces a continuous detailed record of all transactions entered anywhere in the system. Hard copy is produced on narrow register tape (usually twenty columns wide) and provides management with a thorough system audit.

kitchen display unit (KDU)—A video display unit capable of displaying several orders on a single screen.

menu board—A keyboard overlay for a POS system terminal that identifies the function performed by each key during a specific meal period.

modifier keys—Parts of a POS system keyboard used in combination with preset and price look-up keys to detail preparation instructions (such as rare, medium, and well-done) for food production areas; also used to alter prices according to designated portion sizes (such as small, medium, and large).

network controller—Part of a POS system that coordinates communications between cashier or precheck terminals and workstation printers or kitchen monitors, while ensuring that servers need enter orders only once. Also called a printer controller.

operator monitor—Part of a POS system terminal enabling the operator to review and edit transaction entries.

precheck terminal—A POS system terminal without a cash drawer; usually used to enter orders, although it is sometimes used to settle non-cash payments.

preset key—Part of a POS system keyboard programmed to maintain the price, descriptor, department, tax, and inventory status of a menu item.

price look-up (PLU) key—Part of a POS system keyboard that operates like a preset key, except that it requires the user to identify a menu item by its reference code number (up to five digits) rather than by its name or descriptor.

receipt printer—On-board printing devices that produce hard copy on narrow register tape.

settlement keys—Part of a POS system keyboard used to record the methods with which accounts are settled: by cash, credit card, house account, charge transfer, or other payment.

soft checks—Guest checks made of flimsy receipt paper.

soft keys—Parts of a POS system keyboard that can be programmed by users to meet the specific needs of their restaurant operations.

workstation printer—Remote printing devices usually placed at kitchen preparation areas and service bars.

POS System Software

activity report—A report generated by automated systems providing an in-depth analysis of sales transactions and actual labor hours during selected time periods.

daily labor report—A report generated by automated systems listing the names, employee numbers, hours worked, wages earned, and wages declared for each employee on a given workday.

daily transactions report—A report generated by automated food and beverage systems providing an in-depth analysis of sales transactions by individual server.

inventory file—A computer-based record of items in storage.

labor master file—A file maintained by sophisticated POS systems containing one record for each employee; it typically maintains the following data: employee name, employee number, Social Security number, authorized job codes, and corresponding hourly wage rates. This file may also contain data required to produce labor reports for management.

labor master report—A file maintained by sophisticated POS systems containing general data maintained by the labor master file; it is commonly used to verify an employee's hourly rate(s), job code(s), or Social Security number.

menu item file—A file maintained by sophisticated POS systems containing data for all meal periods and menu items sold. Important data maintained by this file may include: identification number, descriptor, recipe code number, selling price, ingredient quantities for inventory reporting, and sales totals.

open check file—A file maintained by sophisticated POS systems that maintains current data for all open guest checks; it is accessed to monitor items on a guest check, add items to a guest check after initial order entry, and close a guest check at the time of settlement.

outstanding checks report—A report produced by automated point-of-sale equipment that lists all guest checks (by server) that have not been settled; information may include the guest check number, server identification number, time at which the guest check was opened, number of guests, table number, and guest check total.

period labor report—A report generated by automated systems listing hour and wage information for each employee who worked during a period specified by management.

productivity reports—In relation to automated food and beverage systems, reports that detail sales activity for all assigned server sales records; may be generated for each server and cashier in terms of guest count, total sales, and average sales.

sales analysis report—A report generated by automated food and beverage systems that enables management to measure the sales performance of individual menu items by department or product category over various time intervals.

sales and payment summary report—A report generated by automated food and beverage systems providing managers with a complete statement of daily or monthly sales (by shift or broken down by food and beverage categories) and a listing of settlement methods.

sales by time of day report—A report generated by automated food and beverage systems enabling managers to measure the sales performance of individual menu items by department or product category within certain time intervals.

weekly labor report—A report generated by automated food and beverage systems listing the names, employee numbers, hours worked, wages earned, and wages declared for each employee on a given workday; may be useful for determining which employees are approaching overtime pay rates.

Other Peripherals

access point—Device in a wireless network capable of receiving and transmitting signals.

antenna units—Part of a system that supports the use of wireless, handheld server terminals. Antenna units relay signals from handheld terminals to a radio base station.

debit card—Debit cards differ from credit cards in that the cardholder must deposit money in order to give the card value. The cardholder deposits money in advance of purchases through a debit card center or an electronic debit posting machine; as purchases are made, the balance on the debit card falls.

gift card—A stored value media device containing prepaid deposits for future transactions.

handheld terminal—Wireless server terminal that performs most of the functions of a precheck terminal and enables servers to enter orders at tableside.

magnetic strip reader—Optional input device that connects to a POS system register or terminal capable of collecting data stored on a magnetized film strip typically located on the back of a credit card or house account card.

power platform—Consolidates electronic communications between a hospitality establishment and a credit card authorization center. Power platforms can capture credit card authorizations in three seconds or less. A POS power platform connects all POS terminals to a single processor for transaction settlement.

radio base station—Part of a wireless system supporting the use of handheld server terminals that relays signals received from antenna units to a digital computer's processing unit.

radio frequency identification (RFID) readers—Radio frequency identification units capable of emitting a broadcast signal used to locate passive RFID tags; useful for contactless payment transactions.

smart card—Smart cards are made of plastic and are about the same size as credit cards. Microchips embedded in them store information that can be accessed by a specially designed card reader. Smart cards can store information in several files that are accessed for different functions, such as a person's vital health statistics, dietary restrictions, credit card number, and bank balance. Information stored in smart cards is secured by a personal identification number (PIN) that must be used to access files.

touchscreen terminal—A terminal that contains a unique adaptation of a CRT or LCD screen and a special microprocessor to control it. The self-contained microprocessor displays data on areas of the screen that are sensitive to touch.

Automated Beverage Control Systems

delivery network—Part of an automated beverage control unit that transports beverage item ingredients from storage areas to dispensing units.

empty bottle sensor—Can be part of an automated beverage control unit; relays a signal to the order entry device.

glass sensor—Part of an automated beverage control unit; an electronic mechanism located in a bar dispensing unit that will not permit liquid to flow from the dispensing unit unless there is a glass positioned to catch the liquid below the dispensing head.

guest check sensor—Part of an automated beverage control unit preventing the system from fulfilling beverage orders unless they are first recorded to an open guest check.

Review Questions

1. What are the necessary hardware components of a POS system? What are the varieties of each component?

2. How do preset keys differ from PLU keys?

3. What functions do modifier and numeric keys perform?

4. How can a customer display unit on a POS terminal enhance management's internal control system?

5. What are two important features available for traditional guest check printers?

6. What information might be found on a guest's payment card?

7. How are guest checks opened and closed within a POS system?

8. What types of data are kept by the major files maintained by POS systems?

9. Why would managers prefer touchscreen, handheld, or wireless terminals to conventional keyboard order entry devices?

10. What kinds of sensor devices do some types of automated beverage systems have?

11. What are the basic components of an automated beverage control system?

Internet Sites

For more information, visit the following Internet sites. Remember that Internet addresses can change without notice. If the site is no longer there, you can use a search engine to look for additional sites.

Agilysys, Inc.
www.agilysys.com

Ameranth, Inc.
http://www.ameranth.com/
products_21stcenturyrestaurant.html

Comtrex Systems Corporation
www.comtrex.com

Elo TouchSystems
www.elotouch.com

MICROS Systems, Inc.
www.micros.com

NCR Corporation
www.ncr.com

POSitouch
www.positouch.com

Squirrel Systems
www.squirrelsystems.com

System Concepts, Inc.
www.foodtrak.com

Chapter 7 Outline

Recipe Management
    Ingredient File
    Recipe File
    Menu Item File
Sales Analysis
Menu Management
    Menu Item Analysis
    Menu Mix Analysis
    Menu Engineering Summary
    Four-Box Analysis
    Menu Engineering Graph
    Engineering the Menu
Menu Item Pricing
    Cost-Plus Pricing
    Cost-Multiplier Pricing
    ACM Pricing
Integrated Food Service Software
    Generic Software
    Precosting/Postcosting Applications
Automated Beverage System Reports

Competencies

1. Identify the files typically maintained by recipe management software applications for food and beverage operations. (p. 169)

2. Describe how information from recipe management software applications helps managers control food and beverage operations. (pp. 169–174)

3. Explain how food and beverage managers use various reports generated by sales analysis software applications. (pp. 174–176)

4. Explain the features and functions of menu engineering software. (pp. 176–183)

5. Discuss the different menu item pricing strategies used by food and beverage operations. (pp. 183–184)

6. Describe the advantages of integrated food and beverage software in relation to precosting and postcosting functions. (pp. 184–187)

7. Explain how managers use reports generated by automated beverage control systems. (pp. 187–190)

7

Food and Beverage Management Applications

RESTAURANT MANAGERS are constantly challenged to find new ways to increase revenues while controlling and reducing costs. A major stumbling block for many managers is the lack of detailed, current information about restaurant operations. Managers need timely feedback to measure effectiveness and plan business strategies. The cost of collecting information manually is often prohibitive. In contrast, an automated food service management system can quickly provide reports that help improve productivity and enhance managerial control.

Food and beverage management applications process data related to back-of-the-house food service activities. This chapter examines popular food service management applications such as:

- Recipe management
- Sales analysis
- Menu management

This chapter also discusses the importance of integrated food service software for precosting and postcosting applications, as well as reports generated by sophisticated automated beverage control systems.

Recipe Management

A recipe management software application maintains three of the most important files of an automated restaurant management system:

- Ingredient file
- Recipe file
- Menu item file

Most other food service applications access data contained within these basic files in order to effectively complete processing functions.

Ingredient File

An **ingredient file** contains important purchase, storage, and usage data on each purchased ingredient. The ingredient file is often referred to as the food item data file (FIDF). Important data maintained by this file may include:

- Ingredient code number.

- Ingredient description.

- Purchase unit (how a product arrives at the property).

- Purchase unit cost.

- Issue unit (how a product is tracked in the storeroom).

- Issue unit cost.

- Recipe unit (how a product is used in recipes).

- Recipe unit cost.

Some ingredient files may specify more than one recipe unit. For example, the recipe unit for bread used for french toast may be a slice; however, the recipe unit for bread used for stuffing may be an ounce. In addition, most restaurant operations enter non-food items into an ingredient file to ensure that the ingredient file contains a complete list of all purchased products. This list becomes especially important when purchase orders are generated to replenish depleted inventory or used for online purchasing or e-procurement.

Additional data contained in the ingredient file may provide the basis for effective inventory control. **Conversion tables** can be maintained to track ingredients (by unit cost) moving through purchasing/receiving, storing/issuing, and production/service control points. In order to efficiently maintain a perpetual inventory record, a food service system must be able to automatically convert purchase units into issue units and recipe units (also called usable units).

Assume that an ingredient is purchased, issued, and used in different units of measurement. When a shipment of the ingredient arrives, it should be easy to update the inventory record by simply entering the number of purchase units received. The system should then automatically convert this entry into issue units. Without this conversion capability, it would be necessary to manually calculate the number of units that will be stored and adjust the inventory record accordingly. Similarly, at the end of a meal period, the system should update the inventory record by entering the number of recipe units used to prepare menu items. If the food and beverage system cannot convert issue units into recipe units, these calculations must be performed manually and the corresponding inventory counts decreased accordingly.

The system should also track the costs associated with these various ingredient units. Assume that bottled ketchup is purchased by the case (twenty-four 12-ounce bottles), issued from the storeroom to the kitchen by the bottle, and used in recipes by the ounce. Given information regarding the purchase unit's net weight and cost, the system should extend costs for issue and recipe unit(s). If the purchase unit's net weight is eighteen pounds and its purchase price is $20.40, the system computes issue unit cost at $0.85 and recipe unit cost at slightly more than $0.07. To arrive at these costs through manual calculations, an employee would first compute the price per ounce of the purchase unit. This is done by first converting eighteen pounds to 288 ounces and then dividing $20.40 by 288 ounces to arrive at the recipe unit cost of $0.07 per ounce. Multiplying $0.07 by twelve ounces (the ounces contained in each bottle) yields the issue unit cost of $0.85. Performing manual calculations for every ingredient purchased would be a tedious and error-prone process. An ingredient file application package can perform these calculations in fractions of a second. Care must be taken to ensure that the ingredient file contains the necessary data, conversion definitions, and relational formulas.

Recipe File

A recipe file contains standardized recipes for all menu items. The recipe file is often referred to as the recipe item data file (RIDF). Important data maintained by the file may include:

- Recipe code number.
- Recipe name.
- Number of portions (batch size).
- Portion size.
- Recipe unit (ingredient metric).
- Recipe unit cost.
- Menu selling price.
- Food cost percentage.
- Contribution margin.

Exhibit 1 presents a sample screen shot from a typical recipe file. A limited number of ingredients can be listed for each standard recipe. A popular feature of a recipe record is the "high warning flag," which signals when the current food cost exceeds a predetermined level of concern as set by management. Recipe records are integral to purchase order systems, because stored recipes can indicate needed quantities for projected production and provide an index of perpetual inventory replenishment following production.

Some data in the standard recipe file may overlap data within the ingredient file. This simplifies the creation and maintenance of recipe records, because data will not have to be manually re-entered. Recipe management applications can access specific elements of data contained in ingredient and recipe files and generate a host of management reports.

Recipe management applications also provide space for preparation instructions (also called assembly instructions) that are typically found on standard recipe cards. Although this information is not accessed by other food service management applications, it allows management to print recipes for production personnel. This can be a useful feature when batch sizes (number of portions yielded by a particular standard recipe) need to be expanded or contracted to accommodate forecasted demand. For example, if a standard recipe is designed to yield 100 portions (batch size), but 530 portions are needed, the recipe application can be programmed to proportionately adjust the corresponding ingredient quantities. When a set of quantities is multiplied to reflect larger yields, there is an assumption of linearity among ingredients—this may not always be the case. When batch size can be

Exhibit 1   Sample Recipe File Screen

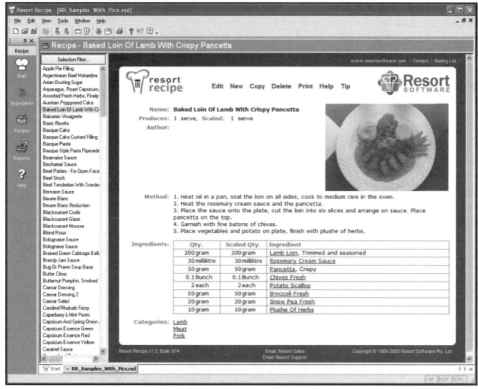

Courtesy of Resort Software Pty. Ltd. (www.resortsoftware.com).

modified, unique recipes can be printed that include preparation information and provide a complete plan for recipe production.

Few restaurants purchase all menu item ingredients in ready-to-use or pre-portioned form. Some ingredients are made on the premises. This means that the ingredients within a standard recipe record may be either inventory items or references to other recipe files. Recipes included as ingredients within a standard recipe record are called **sub-recipes**. Including sub-recipes as ingredients for a particular standard recipe is called **recipe chaining**. Chaining recipes enables the system to maintain an efficient record for a particular menu item that requires an unusually large number of ingredients. When ingredient costs change, automated recipe management applications must be capable of updating the costs of standard recipes, as well as the cost of sub-recipes that use the ingredient. If not, updated cost data would have to be entered into each sub-recipe record. Exhibit 2 illustrates the recipe-building feature of a recipe management program. The program also automatically reprices recipes as needed and can convert recipes to desired yields. Once a menu item's recipe cost is known, the difference between its selling price and the cost defines the item's contribution margin. Exhibit 3 presents a sample recipe printout with customized preparation instructions.

Exhibit 2   Sample Recipe Management Screen

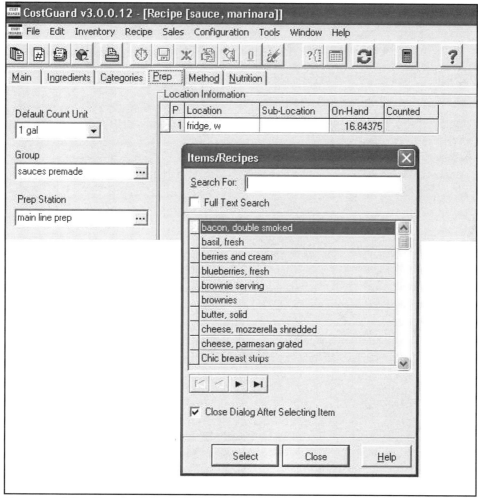

Courtesy of CostGuard (www.costguard.com).

Menu Item File

A **menu item file** contains data for all meal period offerings and menu items sold. The menu file is often referred to as the menu item data file (MIDF). Important data maintained by this file may include:

- Identification number (meal period index).
- Descriptor (meal period).
- Recipe code number.
- Selling price.

Exhibit 3   Sample Recipe Printout

```
Date: 8/19/20XX
Time: 1:31 PM
```

BBQ Pork Sandwich w/ Fries

Description:
    Yield: SERVING   Cost: $1.99   Type: Serving
    Portion: SERVING   Cost: $1.99   Portions In Yield: 1

	Cost	Sells For	FC %	Margin $
Current:	$1.99	$5.95	33.44%	$3.96
Target:		$6.22	32.00%	$4.23

L	Quantity and Unit	Ingredient or Recipe	Net	Purchase	T	Prep Notes
	1 Piece	Bread-Burger Bun 4 1/2 s.s	$0.17	$1.39		
	1 ea	Pickle Spears	$0.07	$29.40		
	1 sprig	Parsley\Fresh	$0.02	$0.65		
*	1 side	French Fries-Side Dish	$0.47	$0.47		
	5 oz	Roast Pork	$0.97	$3.11		
	2 foz	BBQ Sauce - Bull's Eye	$0.20	$12.49		
*	1 ea	Lettuce and Tomato Setup	$0.09	$0.09		

Method:

Courtesy of CostGuard (www.costguard.com).

- Portion quantities for inventory reporting.
- Sales totals.

A menu file may also store historical information on the actual number of menu items sold by meal period and date. Generally, after a meal period, the actual number of menu items served can be entered into the menu item file or automatically transferred from an integrated POS system. This data can be accessed by management or by sophisticated forecasting programs to project sales, determine the amount of ingredient quantities needed, and schedule needed production and service personnel. In addition, automated sales analysis applications can also access data in the menu item file to produce a variety of reports for management. When menu items, prices, or tax tables need to be changed, the menu item file is accessed and appropriate changes are entered according to procedures indicated by the system's vendor.

Sales Analysis

A POS system can store files that contain important data regarding daily food service operations. When a POS system is interfaced to an integrated food service management system, data maintained by POS system files can be accessed and applied in an automated process. A POS interface enables a sales analysis application to merge data from the POS files with data from files maintained within a recipe management application. The sales analysis software can then process this combined data into numerous reports to help management monitor and control operations in such specific areas as:

- Menu planning.
- Sales forecasting.
- Menu item pricing.
- Ingredient purchasing.
- Inventory control.
- Labor scheduling.
- Payroll accounting.

Exhibit 4 presents a sample sales mix of a dinner menu. Sales figures can be entered manually or imported from a POS system. The program calculates food cost and depletes inventory amounts accordingly. Food service management systems typically produce a variety of sales reports. A **daily sales report** summarizes all sales revenue activity for a day. Revenue is itemized by the following categories:

- Net sales
- Tax
- Number of guest checks
- Number of covers (customers served)
- Revenue per check
- Revenue per cover

Exhibit 4 Sample Sales Mix of a Dinner Menu

Sales Mix Info

Menu Name: Dinner Menu   Sales Date: 10/28/20XX

Comments:

Total Qty: 0   Total Cost: $0.00   Total Sales: $0.00   Total Food Cost: 0.00%

Sales Mix Details

Sort By: Menu Item   Search For:

PLU	Menu Item	Quantity Sold	Cost Unit	Cost Total	Sells For Unit	Sells For Total
7001	berries and cream		$1.49	$0.00	$5.95	$0.00
7002	brownie serving		$0.42	$0.00	$5.95	$0.00
2001	chicken alfredo		$3.13	$0.00	$10.95	$0.00
4002	Penne w/wine-pesto sauce w/veg		$2.04	$0.00	$9.95	$0.00
6002	rolls		$0.33	$0.00	$3.95	$0.00
4003	Rotini with vegetables		$3.47	$0.00	$11.95	$0.00
6001	salad, side		$1.61	$0.00	$4.25	$0.00
5001	Shrimp w/balsalmic vinegar and		$3.22	$0.00	$11.95	$0.00
1002	soup, minestrone serving		$3.78	$0.00	$5.95	$0.00
4005	spag w/meatballs		$42.44	$0.00	$10.95	$0.00

Courtesy of CostGuard (www.costguard.com).

- Sales category
- Day-part totals

In addition, affected general ledger accounts are listed and associated food costs and sales percentage statistics are noted. A **weekly sales spreadsheet** provides a weekly summary of information contained in daily sales reports.

A **sales category analysis report** shows relationships between amounts sold by sales category and time periods as defined by management. This report enables management to see at a glance menu item sales by time of day. Many POS systems also feature a **count down function** that provides a perpetual inventory (running count) of menu items. For example, if an operation has fourteen lobster tails at the start of dinner service and eight are sold, the POS system can report that six items remain available for sale. The count down mechanism also allows management to be aware of how close an item is to selling out as well as items that disappear or go to waste. A **marketing category report** compiles weekly totals summarizing revenue earned by food and beverage departments (or categories).

Menu Management

Most automated food service management applications sort and index data into timely, factual reports intended to help management answer such questions as:

- What is the most profitable price to assign to a menu item?
- At what price level and sales mix does a food service operation maximize its profits?
- Which current menu items require repricing, retention, replacement, or repositioning on the menu?
- How should daily specials and new menu items be priced?
- How can the success of a menu change be evaluated?

Menu engineering is a product management application used for evaluating decisions regarding current and future menu pricing, design, and contents. This application requires management to focus on the number of dollars a menu contributes to profit and not simply on monitoring cost percentages.

Menu engineering begins with an interactive analysis of menu mix (MM) and contribution margin (CM) data. Competing menu items are categorized as either high or low. A menu item is high when its MM is greater than or equal to 70 percent of its equal menu sales share and low when its MM is less than 70 percent of its equal menu sales share. The item's individual CM is similarly compared with the menu's average CM and categorized as either high or low. A menu item with a CM greater than or equal to the menu's average CM is considered high. It is low when its CM is less than the menu's average CM. A menu engineering analysis produces the following classifications:

- Menu items high in both MM and CM are stars (winners).
- Menu items high in MM but low in CM are plowhorses (marginal).

- Menu items low in MM but high in CM are puzzles (potential).
- Menu items low in MM and low in CM are dogs (losers).

The application goes a step further and identifies practical approaches by which to re-engineer the next menu to be more successful in terms of profitability and sales activity. For example, simple strategies include:

- Retain stars.
- Reprice plowhorses.
- Reposition puzzles.
- Remove dogs.

Following data input and selection of the analysis option, a menu engineering application begins its work. As the analysis progresses, a menu item's contribution margin and unit sales activity will be categorized as relatively high or low. The menu engineering output is composed of several reports that include:

- Menu item analysis.
- Menu mix analysis.
- Menu engineering summary.
- Four-box analysis.
- Menu engineering graph.

Menu Item Analysis

Exhibit 5 illustrates the initial report in a menu engineering analysis. This is an item-by-item listing accompanied by selling price, portion cost, contribution margin, and item count (number sold). The primary purpose of this report is to provide the user with a means by which to verify the data being analyzed. This can be helpful when data has been erroneously entered into the program either manually or automatically from a POS interface.

Menu Mix Analysis

Exhibit 6 illustrates a menu mix analysis report. This report evaluates each item's participation in the overall menu's performance. The percentage of menu mix (% *MM Share*) is based upon each item's count divided by the total number of menu items sold. Each percentage is then ranked as high or low depending upon its comparison with the menu engineering rule for menu mix sufficiency (the 70 percent rule). The percentage each item has contributed to the menu's total contribution margin is found in the column labeled % *CM Share*. Each item's contribution margin is then ranked according to how it compares with the menu's weighted average contribution margin (ACM). A menu classification for each item is determined by considering its MM group rank and CM group rank together.

Exhibit 5   Menu Item Analysis

Item Analysis

Item Name	Item Price	Portion Cost	Contr. Margin	Item Count
Fried Shrimp	7.95	4.85	3.10	210
Fried Chicken	4.95	2.21	2.74	420
Chopped Sirloin	4.50	1.95	2.55	90
Prime Rib	7.95	4.95	3.00	600
King Prime Rib	9.95	5.65	4.30	60
NY Strip Steak	8.50	4.50	4.00	360
Top Sirloin	7.95	4.30	3.65	510
Red Snapper	6.95	3.95	3.00	240
Lobster Tail	9.50	4.95	4.55	150
Tenderloin Tips	6.45	4.00	2.45	360

Exhibit 6   Menu Mix Analysis

Menu Mix Analysis

Item Name	MM Count	% MM Share	Group Rank	% CM Share	Contr. Margin	Group Rank	Menu Class
Fried Shrimp	210	7.00	HIGH	6.73	3.10	LOW	PLOWHORSE
Fried Chicken	420	14.00	HIGH	11.89	2.74	LOW	PLOWHORSE
Chopped Sirloin	90	3.00	LOW	2.37	2.55	LOW	<< DOG >>
Prime Rib	600	20.00	HIGH	18.60	3.00	LOW	PLOWHORSE
King Prime Rib	60	2.00	LOW	2.67	4.30	HIGH	?PUZZLE?
NY Strip Steak	360	12.00	HIGH	14.88	4.00	HIGH	**STAR**
Top Sirloin	510	17.00	HIGH	19.24	3.65	HIGH	**STAR**
Red Snapper	240	8.00	HIGH	7.44	3.00	LOW	PLOWHORSE
Lobster Tail	150	5.00	LOW	7.05	4.55	HIGH	?PUZZLE?
Tenderloin Tips	360	12.00	HIGH	9.12	2.45	LOW	PLOWHORSE

Menu Engineering Summary

Exhibit 7 illustrates a menu engineering summary report. Perhaps the most informative report produced by the menu engineering application, this analysis presents important information in capsule form to produce a concise statement of operations. The row labeled *Price* shows total menu revenue, average item selling price, lowest selling price, and highest selling price. The *Food Cost* row contains

Exhibit 7   Menu Engineering Summary

Menu Engineering Summary				
	Total	Average	Low	High
Price	22050.00	7.35	4.50	9.95
Food Cost	12374.70	4.12	1.95	5.65
Contribution Margin ...	9675.30	3.23	2.45	4.55
Demand Factor	3000	300	60	600
Food Cost Percentage	56.12%			
Number of Items	10			

total menu costs, average item food cost, lowest cost item, and highest cost item. The *Contribution Margin* row shows total menu CM, average item CM, lowest item CM, and highest item CM. The *Demand Factor* row lists total number of covers (guests), average number of covers, lowest item count, and highest item count. Much of the information in the body of this report is used elsewhere in the overall menu engineering system. For example, the lowest and highest selling prices on the menu are termed **price points** and can be used to help identify target market success. This report also contains the menu's food cost percentage and number of items sold.

Four-Box Analysis

Exhibit 8 illustrates a four-box analysis that indexes the menu classifications developed in the menu mix analysis report. Since menu engineering leads to a series

Exhibit 8   Four-Box Analysis

PLOWHORSE	STAR
Fried Shrimp Fried Chicken Prime Rib Red Snapper Tenderloin Tips	NY Strip Steak Top Sirloin
DOG	PUZZLE
Chopped Sirloin	King Prime Rib Lobster Tail

of decision strategies specific to each menu classification, this report provides the user with insight about the number of items found in each category. For example, Exhibit 8 displays a menu composed of five plowhorses, two stars, two puzzles, and one dog. Are five plowhorses too many? This type of evaluation process begins with the four-box matrix and continues as management strives to improve the menu.

Menu Engineering Graph

The menu engineering graph is usually considered the most powerful menu engineering report. The graph indicates the relative plotting of menu mix and item contribution margin. The vertical axis of the graph is scaled to the number of items sold, while the horizontal axis is calibrated in currency. Each menu item is then placed on a graph using its MM and CM coordinates. The graph is complete once all menu items are plotted and the 70 percent MM line and ACM line are added to the graph. It is important to note the creation of four quadrants, each depicting a separate menu engineering classification (dog, puzzle, plowhorse, and star). Exhibit 9 contains a menu engineering graph for the menu being analyzed.

Engineering the Menu

The benefits of menu engineering can accrue only if information gained from the menu engineering analysis is used to improve the menu. What should a food and beverage manager do with menu item classifications?

Managing Plowhorses. Plowhorses are items low in contribution margin, but high in sales. Guests like these items, but, unfortunately, plowhorses do not contribute a fair share to the operation's contribution margin. Possible strategies for managing a plowhorse menu item include the following:

- *Increase prices carefully.* Perhaps the item is popular because it represents a great value. If prices could be increased, the item may still represent a good value, may remain popular, and may generate a higher contribution margin. This alternative may be most effective when the item is unique to the property and cannot be obtained elsewhere (a signature item).

- *Test for demand.* If there is no strong resistance to price increases, it may be useful to complement an increased price with other strategies such as repackaging the item or repositioning it on the menu. These other strategies may be designed to maintain or increase the item's popularity while generating a higher contribution margin. If prices are to be significantly increased, it should probably be done in several stages rather than all at once.

- *Relocate the item to a lower profile on the menu.* Depending upon the menu layout, certain areas of a menu represent a better promotional location than others. A plowhorse may be able to be relocated to a less desirable area of the menu and continue to maintain its popularity. Since the item sells well, some guests will search the menu for the item. Others will be drawn to higher-profile areas of the menu that list more profitable items the operator desires to sell.

Exhibit 9   Sample Menu Engineering Graph

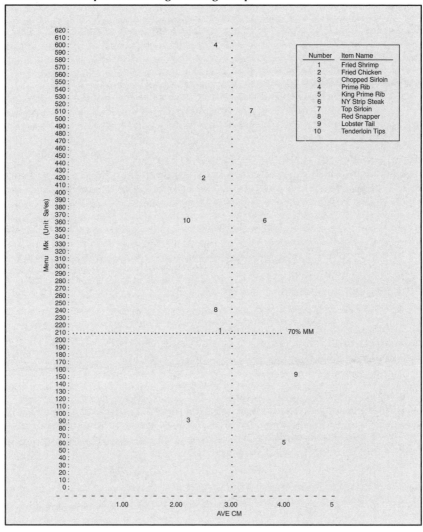

- *Shift demand to more desirable items.* Menu engineering allows management to determine which items to sell—those high in popularity and high in contribution margin. Servers using suggestive selling techniques, for example, should avoid recommending plowhorse items. Table tents and other point-of-sale tools should, likewise, promote stars and puzzles (with higher contribution margins); they should not suggest plowhorses.

- *Combine menu items with lower-cost products.* The contribution margin of a plowhorse can be increased if lower-cost meal accompaniments are offered to supplement the menu item. When higher-cost accompaniments may be replaced with less expensive items without reducing the item's popularity, the contribution margin will increase.

- *Assess the direct labor factor.* If there is a significant amount of direct labor required to produce a plowhorse menu item, then the item should be reconsidered.

- *Consider portion size reduction.* When a portion size is reduced, the product cost will be decreased and the contribution margin will correspondingly increase. This alternative must be viewed with caution, of course, since the guest's perception of value may decrease when the portion size is reduced.

Managing Puzzles. Puzzles are items that are high in contribution margin but low in sales—items management desires to sell due to a higher contribution margin. The challenge is to find ways to increase the number of items sold. Strategies include the following:

- *Shift demand to puzzle items.* Techniques include repositioning the item to a more visible area of the menu; renaming the item; using suggestive selling techniques; developing an advertising campaign; providing table tents, server badges, and menu boards highlighting the item; and other strategies to promote item awareness.

- *Consider a price decrease.* Perhaps the item is low in popularity because it does not appear to be a value to guests. If this is the case, the selling price might be decreased with the contribution margin still remaining higher than average. This could lead to increased sales, since a reduced selling price may represent an increased value to the guest.

- *Add value to the item.* Offering a larger portion size, adding higher-cost meal accompaniments or garnishes, and using higher-quality ingredients are among the ways that the item's value can be increased. These techniques may lead to increased popularity. The resulting lower contribution margin may still be higher than the menu's ACM.

Managing Stars. Star items are menu items that are classified as high in contribution margin and high in popularity. The best advice for managing stars includes:

- *Maintain rigid specifications.* Do not attempt to alter the quality of a star menu item.

- *If possible, move the menu item to a high-visibility location on the menu.* Stars are items that the operator wants to sell. Therefore, make sure guests are aware of their availability.

- *Test for selling price inelasticity.* Perhaps the star item is popular because it represents a significant value to the guest. Or perhaps the star is a signature item, not available elsewhere in the marketplace. These might be two instances in which the price could be increased without an offset in popularity.

- *Use suggestive selling techniques.* Some of the techniques aimed at shifting demand to puzzles might also be useful for stars.

Managing Dogs. Dog items are low in contribution margin and low in popularity. They are obvious candidates for removal from the menu. After all, dog items do not contribute a fair share of contribution margin and are not popular. Alternatively, the item's selling price could be increased, since this would at least generate a higher contribution margin whenever the item sold. When a dog requires a significant amount of direct labor, does not permit sufficient use of leftovers, and has a relatively short storage life, the reasons for removing the item from the menu become even more compelling.

Menu Item Pricing

Traditionally, food service operators have relied on cost-plus and cost-multiplier pricing strategies, which are based primarily on cost to the operation, i.e., food cost add-ons and food cost markups. While cost-plus and cost-multiplier methods are simple to apply, they often are misleading and inaccurate, and inadvertently limit revenue and profitability. The ACM pricing method is a more recent strategy, which some claim to be a result of the failure of the cost-plus and cost-multiplier pricing methods to reflect considerations for market pressure or activity, i.e., market demand. The following sections examine each of these three pricing strategies in detail.

Cost-Plus Pricing

In a cost-plus pricing scheme, management establishes a fixed financial component that is added to the food cost of each menu item. This add-on may be the result of transactional analysis, cost analysis, or arbitrary allocation. For example, a menu item costing $3.64 may be adjusted for menu pricing by adding a cost component that management has determined is required to cover costs beyond direct food costs. If in this instance the cost component added is $3.00, the item's total cost will equal $6.64 and will most likely appear on the menu with a rounded price of $6.99. While the cost-additive approach may help establish prices that appear to be successful, there is no consideration of market conditions, current menu mix, product demand, or menu contribution margin.

Cost-Multiplier Pricing

Historically the cost-multiplier pricing model has been a preferred and trusted industry formulation. Since a menu will project a potential food cost percentage, management can use that target in initially setting menu item prices. Given that actual food costs tend to vary on a regular basis, identifying accurate menu item costs may be more difficult to determine than anticipated. Once the item's cost is known, it is simply multiplied by the desired multiplier (100 percent divided by the desired food cost percentage) and adjusted for competition. For example, an operator who wants a menu item to have a 33⅓ percent food cost will use a cost multiplier of 3 (100 percent ÷ 33⅓ percent). Using the previous example, employing cost-multiplier costing for a menu item costing $3.64 when the cost multiplier is 3 will lead to a minimum menu price of $10.92, which, when adjusted for reasonable pricing, will most likely appear on the menu as $10.99. It is important to note that since cost-multiplier pricing focuses only on cost factors, it may artificially force menu items to a non-competitive price level. By inflating a menu item's price, demand may shift downward and result in lower profitability.

ACM Pricing

The average contribution margin (ACM) approach to menu item pricing is an offshoot of menu engineering aimed at new item pricing that improves current revenues and profitability. In terms of pricing, menu engineering uses percentages in a solely evaluative capacity; similarly, ACM pricing focuses on gaining a reasonable profit contribution from an actual menu mix rather than utilizing target markups or food cost percentages to determine pricing. Contribution margin (CM) is the most critical component to pricing because it deals specifically with each item's profitability; it is not, however, directly related to an item's food cost percentage.

Menu engineering uses the ACM to establish a benchmark for evaluating competing menu items. For example, if the entrées on a current menu produce an average contribution margin of $8.20, a quick means to approximate a new entrée's selling price is to add this ACM to the food cost of the candidate menu item. Hence, if a new seafood entrée costs the restaurant $3.64, then the minimum menu price for this item would be $11.84; more than likely, the published menu price for this item would be $11.99. By using ACM pricing, the food service operation is assured of at least earning its current ACM on new items without negatively impacting its bottom line.

Integrated Food Service Software

Perhaps the most common mistake in choosing a food service system is deciding on hardware before considering software. Hardware is typically purchased on the basis of brand, advertising, price, accessories, and the like. When hardware is purchased first, the difficult task of searching for software follows. Identifying effective software that is compatible with existing hardware can be time-consuming and frustrating. The best way to avoid this situation is to procure the software first and then get the hardware needed to operate it.

Generic Software

Standard word processing, electronic spreadsheet, and database management programs are powerful and versatile management tools, but can become a source of frustration if not properly applied. Consider the operator who selects a spreadsheet program to generate budgets, food costs, and daily reports. Each application requires that separate data be entered into specific cells located in distinct worksheet files. If the operator also decides to monitor inventory, the work it takes to support this set of automated applications may outweigh the savings in time and money. A food service operator who uses a word processing program for correspondence, an electronic spreadsheet program for financial analysis, and a database management program for inventory control may find that automation is more troublesome than anticipated.

The limitations of freestanding, nonintegrated, generic software become apparent when management attempts to exchange data between programs. Nonintegrated application software seldom achieves the primary objectives of electronic data processing (EDP). The objectives of EDP are:

- To minimize the time it takes to process input into output (throughput).

- To minimize the handling and rehandling of data (efficiency).

- To minimize the amount of unnecessary output (streamlining).

Integrated food service software applications enable the same data to pass directly from one application to another. Data is entered only once and is then applied where appropriate. The following section illustrates the differences between integrated and nonintegrated food service application software while describing precosting and postcosting applications.

Precosting/Postcosting Applications

Precosting is a special type of forecasting that compares forecasted guest counts with standard menu item recipe costs to yield an index of expense before an actual meal period. Precosting software applications can project costs on a portion, batch, or meal period basis. This projected cost of sales figure enables management to review and adjust operations before an actual service period begins. If precosting finds projected costs to be outside an acceptable range, management may consider raising prices, decreasing portion sizes, altering accompaniments, or substituting menu items.

Precosting predictions are based on three types of data: an accurate cost of every item contained in the ingredient file (FIDF); a set of standard recipes stored in the recipe file (RIDF) containing a precise list of ingredients, quantities, and production procedures; and a menu plan specifying each item on the menu from the menu file (MIDF) and the projected number of portions to be consumed during the meal period. A commercial restaurant with a fixed menu and standard recipes would need to focus most of its attention on maintaining current cost data and developing sound sales mix forecasts. An institutional food service operation would likely focus most of its attention on the meal plan and forecasted meal counts.

Although nearly all restaurants have access to the data needed for precosting calculations, few actually perform the analysis because it can be time-consuming and relies on assumptions. It can be even more time-consuming for restaurants with nonintegrated software packages. In a nonintegrated food service software design, the necessary data—ingredient costs, recipe formulations, and menu plans—most likely would reside in separate data files. Applying each ingredient data element against its recipe and menu plan would require intervention by the user, intermediate calculations, and re-entry of data, all of which is counter to the objectives of electronic data processing. To achieve accurate and timely precosting, the best approach is to use integrated software. Integrated file structures enable management to concentrate on designing menu plans without getting mired in repetitive clerical procedures. Exhibit 10 outlines the files accessed by a precosting management application.

   Postcosting multiplies the number of menu items sold by standard recipe costs to determine a potential food cost quotient. When actual recipe costs are known, these figures are multiplied by the number of menu items sold to produce an actual food cost figure. Exhibit 11 outlines the files accessed by a postcosting management application. Exhibit 12 summarizes popular food-costing algorithms.

Exhibit 10   Files Accessed by Precosting Applications

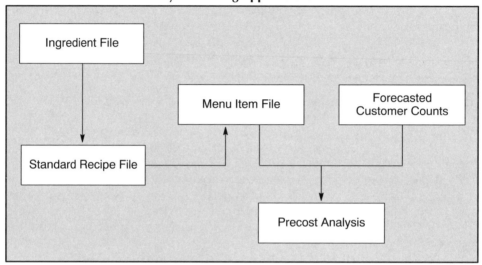

Exhibit 11   Files Accessed by Postcosting Applications

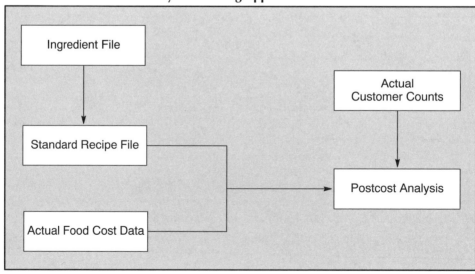

Exhibit 12 Popular Food-Costing Algorithms

Components	Costing Scheme
(Standard Cost) (Forecasted Counts)	STANDARD COSTING
(Standard Cost) (Actual Counts)	POTENTIAL COSTING
(Actual Cost) (Actual Counts)	ACTUAL COSTING

Automated Beverage System Reports

Automated beverage control systems record and store data that can be accessed to produce valuable reports for management. Data may include:

- Beverage items.
- Brand name items.
- Portion sizes.
- Selling prices.
- Total sales.
- Taxes.
- Tips/tip pooling.
- Bar check serial number (if appropriate).
- Server identification code.
- Service location(s).

Automated beverage control systems are programmed to access specific types of data and can generate a variety of reports. Reports produced by such a system are similar to those produced by a typical POS system. These reports may include sales mix analysis, inventory usage reports, check tracking reports, server productivity reports, and others. In addition, journal printers may be programmed to produce detailed accounting and financial reports.

For each shift and each service station during a shift, automated beverage control systems can produce separate reports indicating:

- Sales mix by beverage product.
- Sales mix by beverage category.
- Sales by time of day.
- Sales by server.
- Sales by settlement method.
- Open, closed, and missing guest checks.

Exhibits 13 through 19 show a series of reports generated by an automated beverage control system. The reports cover a single shift and integrate data from four separate service stations.

Exhibit 13 reports the expected beverage **sales by major beverage category** for the four separate service stations, as well as total sales figures combining the four stations. Exhibit 14 contains a **sales by beverage server report**. Note that the total sales figure at the bottom of this report ($5,524.05) is $30 less than the total standard beverage income listed in Exhibit 13 as $5,554.05 (total gross sales). An **outstanding guest checks report** (Exhibit 15) resolves this discrepancy. When a bartender closes a service station, the system generates a **settlement methods report** (Exhibit 16), which indicates the amount due in the form of electronic payment vouchers, house account charges, and cash. Note that the total of the settlement report (the amount of sales income that the bartenders will be held accountable for) does not include the $30 from the outstanding guest check.

Exhibit 17 shows a **net sales by time of day report**. This report is useful for forecasting sales and for scheduling servers and bartenders according to expected

Exhibit 13   Sales by Major Beverage Category Report

Ring Off #22	— 2:52 a.m.	1/06			
Accumulators Cleared	**— 8:00 a.m.**	**1/05**			
Sales by Major	Station 1	Station 2	Station 3	Station 4	Total
Category	Sales	Sales	Sales	Sales	Sales
Liquor	1,185.75	977.25	1,040.25	417.75	3,621.00
Beer	469.50	372.25	236.50	144.00	1,222.25
Wine	29.75	45.00	77.00	19.50	171.25
Soft Drinks	1.75	20.75	17.25	8.75	48.50
Misc A	34.50	61.15	88.70	117.90	302.25
Btl Wine	.00	.00	.00	.00	.00
Lookups	57.85	94.55	23.80	.00	176.20
Price Mode 1	3.00	77.00	110.25	.00	190.25
Mode 2	1,776.10	1,492.20	1,363.25	707.90	5,339.45
Mode 3	.00	1.75	10.00	.00	11.75
Tax—Mode 1	.00	.00	.00	.00	.00
Mode 2	.00	.00	.00	.00	.00
Mode 3	.00	.00	.00	.00	.00
Tips	1.50	.00	11.10	.00	12.60
Gross Sales	1,780.60	1,570.95	1,494.60	707.90	5,554.05
Net Sales	1,779.10	1,570.95	1,483.50	707.90	5,541.45
Accumulated Sales	919,058.24	43,281.83	50,696.30	30,780.18	
Transactions	16	190	24	93	323

Exhibit 14   Sales by Beverage Server Report

					(All Sales Include Tax and Tips)					
Server	Reported Tips	Total Sales	Cash	Visa	Dine	Amex	Prom	Comp	Disc	Dire
1	6.10	1252.05	1160.45	.00	.00	91.60	.00	.00	.00	.00
4	.00	197.45	197.45	.00	.00	.00	.00	.00	.00	.00
5	.00	223.40	223.40	.00	.00	.00	.00	.00	.00	.00
6	.00	493.50	493.50	.00	.00	.00	.00	.00	.00	.00
12	1.50	785.65	553.70	.00	179.70	52.25	.00	.00	.00	.00
15	.00	644.75	644.75	.00	.00	.00	.00	.00	.00	.00
16	.00	5.00	5.00	.00	.00	.00	.00	.00	.00	.00
17	.00	288.90	288.90	.00	.00	.00	.00	.00	.00	.00
27	.00	111.75	111.75	.00	.00	.00	.00	.00	.00	.00
35	.00	21.00	21.00	.00	.00	.00	.00	.00	.00	.00
37	.00	28.25	28.25	.00	.00	.00	.00	.00	.00	.00
39	.00	36.50	36.50	.00	.00	.00	.00	.00	.00	.00
40	.00	276.20	276.20	.00	.00	.00	.00	.00	.00	.00
41	.00	18.00	18.00	.00	.00	.00	.00	.00	.00	.00
43	.00	244.25	233.50	10.75	.00	.00	.00	.00	.00	.00
44	.00	5.95	5.95	.00	.00	.00	.00	.00	.00	.00
45	.00	85.95	85.95	.00	.00	.00	.00	.00	.00	.00
47	5.00	30.50	25.50	.00	.00	5.00	.00	.00	.00	.00
56	.00	166.25	166.25	.00	.00	.00	.00	.00	.00	.00
58	.00	84.25	84.25	.00	.00	.00	.00	.00	.00	.00
60	.00	7.75	7.75	.00	.00	.00	.00	.00	.00	.00
65	.00	13.00	13.00	.00	.00	.00	.00	.00	.00	.00
66	.00	235.50	235.50	.00	.00	.00	.00	.00	.00	.00
67	.00	2.50	2.50	.00	.00	.00	.00	.00	.00	.00
68	.00	21.00	21.00	.00	.00	.00	.00	.00	.00	.00
71	.00	24.25	.00	.00	.00	24.25	.00	.00	.00	.00
78	.00	208.25	208.25	.00	.00	.00	.00	.00	.00	.00
80	.00	10.50	10.50	.00	.00	.00	.00	.00	.00	.00
93	.00	1.75	1.75	.00	.00	.00	.00	.00	.00	.00
Totals	12.60	5524.05	5160.50	10.75	179.70	173.10	.00	.00	.00	.00

Ring Off #22 —2:52 a.m. 1/06
Accumulators Cleared —8:00 a.m. 1/05

demand. Exhibit 18 shows the **sales mix by major product report** for the shift. Managers use these reports to monitor product sales trends and to adjust par inventory levels when necessary. The **product usage report** shown in Exhibit 19 enables managers to minimize inventory control problems.

Automated beverage systems can greatly enhance managerial control of bar operations. At the least, the system provides accurate information about the number of drinks and/or ounces sold. At best, the system will not allow a drink to be served without it first being entered as a sale within the system.

An automated beverage control system may be limited by several factors, including:

- Some beverage products will not be listed within the system. For example, bottled beer is not listed, and a specialty mixed cocktail, such as a frozen daiquiri, will not generally be metered by automated beverage control equipment due to complexity in drink recipe monitoring.

Exhibit 15   Outstanding Guest Checks Report

| Ring Off #22 | — 2:52 a.m. | 1/06 |
| Accumulators Cleared | — 8:00 a.m. | 1/05 |

Outstanding Guest Checks	Server	Check Total
#4567	05	30.00
Total		30.00

Exhibit 16   Settlement Methods Report

Ring Off #22   —2:52 a.m.   1/06
Accumulators Cleared—8:00 a.m.   1/05

Settlement Methods	STATION 1 SALES	STATION 2 SALES	STATION 3 SALES	STATION 4 SALES	TOTAL SALES
Cash	1548.65	1560.20	1368.00	683.65	5160.50
Visa/MC	.00	10.75	.00	.00	10.75
Diners	179.70	.00	.00	.00	179.70
Amex	52.25	.00	96.60	24.25	173.10
Promo	.00	.00	.00	.00	.00
Company	.00	.00	.00	.00	.00
Discovery	.00	.00	.00	.00	.00
Direct Bill	.00	.00	.00	.00	.00
Total Settlements	1780.60	1570.95	1464.60	707.90	5524.05

- Dishonest bar personnel can almost always find a way to work outside or around the system.

- Should the equipment become inoperable, bar management likely will resume operations with an alternate system strategy.

Perhaps the best approach for controlling revenue with an automated beverage system is to ensure it complements the POS system used in the food and beverage operation.

🔑 Key Terms ───────────────────────────────

conversion tables—Automated programs that convert purchase units into issue and recipe units and track ingredients (by unit and by cost) as they pass through purchasing/receiving, storing/issuing, and production/service control points.

count down function—A POS feature that enables the tracking of individual item sales by perpetually monitoring inventory.

Exhibit 17   Net Sales by Time of Day Report

Ring Off #22	— 2:52 a.m.	1/06			
Accumulators Cleared	— 8:00 a.m.	1/05			
Net Sales by Time of Day	Station 1 Sales	Station 2 Sales	Station 3 Sales	Station 4 Sales	Total Sales
6 – 7 A.M.	.00	.00	.00	.00	.00
7 – 8	.00	.00	.00	.00	.00
8 – 9	.00	.00	.00	.00	.00
9 – 10	.00	.00	.00	.00	.00
10 – 11	.00	.00	.00	.00	.00
11 – 12	.00	.00	.00	.00	.00
12 – 1 P.M.	.00	.00	.00	.00	.00
1 – 2	.00	.00	.00	.00	.00
2 – 3	.00	.00	.00	.00	.00
3 – 4	.00	.00	.00	.00	.00
4 – 5	.00	3.25	16.50	.00	19.75
5 – 6	.00	14.00	32.25	.00	46.25
6 – 7	.00	43.00	68.25	.00	111.25
7 – 8	40.70	58.00	112.50	6.25	217.45
8 – 9	123.75	77.40	170.85	55.40	427.40
9 – 10	297.75	272.50	217.00	180.15	957.40
10 – 11	343.50	361.65	282.90	221.50	1,209.55
11 – 12	346.00	250.40	218.75	194.85	1,010.00
12 – 1 A.M.	276.90	276.05	208.50	49.75	811.20
1 – 2	233.00	183.45	126.00	.00	542.45
2 – 3	117.50	31.25	30.00	.00	178.75
3 – 4	.00	.00	.00	.00	.00
4 – 5	.00	.00	.00	.00	.00
5 – 6 A.M.	.00	.00	.00	.00	.00
Total Net Sales	1,779.10	1,570.95	1,483.50	707.90	5,541.45

daily sales report—Summarizes all sales revenue activity for a day. Revenue is itemized by the following categories: net sales, tax, number of guest checks, number of covers, dollars per check, dollars per cover, sales category, and day-part totals. Affected general ledger accounts are listed and associated food costs and sales percentage statistics are noted.

ingredient file—Contains important data on each purchased ingredient, such as ingredient code number, ingredient description, purchase unit, purchase unit cost, issue unit, issue unit cost, recipe unit, and recipe unit cost.

marketing category report—Compiles weekly totals summarizing the revenue earned by food and beverage departments (or categories).

menu engineering—A menu management application for evaluating decisions regarding current and future menu pricing, design, and contents. This application requires that management focus on the number of dollars a menu contributes to profit and not simply monitor cost percentages.

menu item file—Contains data for all meal periods and menu items sold.

Exhibit 18 Sales Mix by Major Product Report

Ring Off #22					
Accumulators Cleared	—2:52 a.m. 1/06				
	—8:00 a.m. 1/05				

Sales Mix by Major Product	STATION 1 SALES	STATION 2 SALES	STATION 3 SALES	STATION 4 SALES	TOTAL SALES
Scotch	30.00/ 12	46.00/ 22	45.00/ 18	15.00/ 6	136.00/ 58
Chivas	.00	.00	12.50/ 6	.00	12.50/ 6
Cutty	.00	.00	4.50/ 2	.00	4.50/ 2
Dewar's	46.75/ 17	30.00/ 12	36.50/ 14	46.75/ 17	160.00/ 60
J&B	11.00/ 4	8.25/ 3	32.00/ 12	.00	51.25/ 19
JW Black	8.25/ 3	13.75/ 5	2.75/ 1	2.75/ 1	27.50/ 10
Bourbon	47.50/ 19	15.50/ 7	21.50/ 9	5.00/ 2	89.50/ 37
Granddad	.00	5.25/ 3	.00	.00	5.25/ 3
WildTurk	5.50/ 2	8.25/ 3	.00	.00	13.75/ 5
JDaniels	74.25/ 27	90.75/ 33	65.25/ 27	35.75/ 13	266.00/ 100
Seag 7	52.50/ 21	13.00/ 6	13.00/ 6	30.00/ 12	110.50/ 45
MakrMark	5.50/ 2	18.25/ 7	2.75/ 1	11.00/ 4	37.50/ 14
Seag VO	22.00/ 8	40.00/ 16	45.75/ 17	27.50/ 10	135.25/ 51
Cr Royal	13.75/ 5	19.25/ 7	2.75/ 1	.00	35.75/ 13
C Club	8.25/ 3	82.00/ 32	35.75/ 13	8.25/ 3	134.25/ 51
Tanquray	60.50/ 22	46.75/ 17	51.00/ 20	22.00/ 8	180.25/ 67
Beefeatr	2.75/ 1	2.75/ 1	8.25/ 3	.00	13.75/ 5
Gin	25.00/ 10	10.00/ 4	7.50/ 3	2.50/ 1	45.00/ 18
Bombay	11.00/ 4	.00	.00	.00	11.00/ 4
Absolut	16.50/ 6	38.50/ 14	16.50/ 6	2.75/ 1	74.25/ 27
Vodka	145.00/ 58	130.00/ 52	205.50/ 85	45.00/ 18	525.50/ 213
Stoli	46.75/ 17	40.25/ 15	76.00/ 28	19.25/ 7	182.25/ 67
Smirnoff	24.75/ 9	13.75/ 5	.00	.00	38.50/ 14
Rum	30.00/ 12	5.00/ 2	28.00/ 12	5.00/ 2	68.00/ 28
Bacardi	.00	.00	.00	11.00/ 4	11.00/ 4
Trip Sec	.00	2.50/ 1	.00	.00	2.50/ 1
Peach	75.00/ 30	27.50/ 11	5.00/ 2	17.50/ 7	125.00/ 50
Sloe Gin	.00	2.50/ 1	.00	.00	2.50/ 1
Dom Beer	428.25/ 191	321.00/ 145	218.25/ 99	119.25/ 53	1086.75/ 488
Imp Beer	41.25/ 15	51.25/ 19	18.25/ 7	24.75/ 9	135.50/ 50
Tequila	5.00/ 2	.00	12.50/ 5	2.50/ 1	20.00/ 8
Cuervo G	2.75/ 1	24.75/ 9	5.50/ 2	.00	33.00/ 12
Gr Marn	.00	6.50/ 2	19.50/ 6	6.50/ 2	32.50/ 10
Brandy	12.50/ 5	.00	.00	.00	12.50/ 5
Menthe L	17.50/ 7	.00	7.50/ 3	.00	25.00/ 10
Menthe G	.00	.00	2.50/ 1	.00	2.50/ 1
Cacao Dk	2.50/ 1	.00	.00	.00	2.50/ 1
Drambuie	19.50/ 6	.00	6.50/ 2	.00	26.00/ 8
Di Saron	6.50/ 2	.00	3.25/ 1	.00	9.75/ 3
Amorita	19.50/ 6	.00	7.75/ 3	.00	27.25/ 9
Frngelco	.00	.00	3.25/ 1	.00	3.25/ 1
Chrdonay	.00	3.00/ 1	.00	3.00/ 1	6.00/ 2
Kamora	32.50/ 10	.00	4.50/ 2	.00	37.00/ 12
Midori	3.25/ 1	.00	.00	.00	3.25/ 1
Chablis	5.25/ 3	15.75/ 9	21.75/ 13	8.75/ 5	51.50/ 30
Sambuca	.00	26.00/ 8	45.50/ 14	.00	71.50/ 22
TiaMaria	.00	.00	7.75/ 3	.00	7.75/ 3
Zinfndel	21.00/ 7	21.00/ 7	36.00/ 12	6.00/ 2	84.00/ 28
Soda	.00	.00/ 1	1.75/ 5	.00/ 3	1.75/ 9
LemLime	1.75/ 2	.00	1.75/ 1	.00	3.50/ 4
SeagCool	.00	12.25/ 7	1.75/ 1	.00	14.00/ 8
Cola	.00	1.75/ 3	10.25/ 6	1.75/ 6	13.75/ 15
Tonic	.00	1.75/ 1	.00/ 1	.00	1.75/ 2
Diet	.00	5.00/ 3	1.75/ 1	7.00/ 6	13.75/ 10
Martini	10.25/ 3	13.75/ 4	21.25/ 7	78.75/ 23	124.00/ 37
Manhattn	3.25/ 1	3.25/ 1	40.25/ 13	.00	46.75/ 15
Mai-Tai	11.00/ 3	.00	.00	.00	11.00/ 10
Wh Sour	5.75/ 2	28.75/ 10	15.50/ 5	.00	50.00/ 17
TCollins	5.00/ 2	7.50/ 3	10.00/ 4	.00	22.50/ 9
Daiquiri	.00	.00	1.50/ 1	3.00/ 1	4.50/ 2
Bl Russn	13.00/ 4	2.25/ 1	2.25/ 1	.00	17.50/ 6
Rusty Nl	.00	.00	6.50/ 2	.00	6.50/ 2
Stinger	19.50/ 6	.00	.00	.00	19.50/ 6
Kamikaze	85.00/ 34	85.00/ 34	27.50/ 11	.00	197.50/ 79
Spritzer	1.75/ 1	3.50/ 2	17.50/ 10	1.75/ 1	24.50/ 14
Ice Tea	26.00/ 8	32.50/ 10	26.00/ 8	9.75/ 3	91.25/ 29
Lemonade	.00	6.50/ 2	.00	3.25/ 1	9.75/ 3
W Cooler	1.75/ 1	1.75/ 1	1.75/ 1	.00	5.25/ 3
Margrita	12.50/ 5	2.50/ 1	.00	.00	15.00/ 6
PeachDaq	.00	3.50/ 1	.00	.00	3.50/ 1
B-52	52.00/ 16	6.50/ 2	3.25/ 1	.00	61.75/ 19
V Hammer	.00	.00	.00	7.00/ 2	7.00/ 2
LaBoomer	.00	.00	3.50/ 1	.00	3.50/ 1
Spec Ctl	58.50/ 18	9.75/ 3	35.75/ 11	.00	104.00/ 32
Totals	1686.75	1415.25	1371.00	590.00	5063.00

Sales Mix by Product Lookup	STATION 1 SALES	STATION 2 SALES	STATION 3 SALES	STATION 4 SALES	TOTAL SALES
Moet Chandon	38.00/ 1	38.00/ 1	.00	.00	76.00/ 2
Cajun	.00	.00	6.95/ 1	.00	6.95/ 1
Barb Chick	6.95/ 1	13.90/ 2	.00	.00	20.85/ 3
Wild Mush	.00	6.95/ 1	.00	.00	6.95/ 1
Brie	.00	.00	4.95/ 1	.00	4.95/ 1
Thai Chick	6.95/ 1	.00	.00	.00	6.95/ 1
Reuben	.00	5.95/ 1	.00	.00	5.95/ 1
Mush Pep Sau	5.95/ 1	29.75/ 5	11.90/ 2	.00	47.60/ 8
Totals	57.85	94.55	23.80	.00	176.20

continued

Exhibit 19 Product Usage Report

Ring Off #22	—2:52 a.m.	1/06
Accumulators Cleared	—8:01 a.m.	1/05

Product Usage	Bottle Size	Ounces Poured	Bottles Emptied		Product	Size	Poured	Emptied
					Almond	Liter	4	
					Cacao Dark	Liter	3	
					Cacao Light	Liter	1	
Scotch	1.75 L	77	1		Menthe Green	Liter	1	
Chivas Regal	1.75 L	7			Menthe Light	Liter	15	
Cutty Sark	1.75 L	2						
Dewar's	1.75 L	82	1		Midori	Liter	2	
J&B	1.75 L	24			Peach Schnaps	1.75 L	68	1
JWalker Black	1.75 L	17			Sloe Gin	Liter	1	
					Triple Sec	1.75 L	42	1
Bourbon	1.75 L	54	1					
Jack Daniels	1.75 L	130	2		Di Saronna	1.75 L	3	
Jim Beam	1.75 L				Amorita	Liter	27	
Makers Mark	1.75 L	17			Drambuie	1.75 L	12	1
Old Granddad	1.75 L	3			Frangelico	750ml	1	
Wild Turkey	1.75 L	6			Grand Marnier	1.75 L	19	1
Canadian Club	1.75 L	64	1		Kahlua	1.75 L	4	
Crown Royal	1.75 L	17			Kamora	Liter	29	1
Irish Whiskey	1.75 L	1			Sambuca	750ml	28	1
Seagram's 7	1.75 L	60	1		Tia Maria	Liter	15	1
Seagram's VO	1.75 L	73	2					
					Chablis	1 Gal	234	1
Gin	1.75 L	43	1		Chardonnay	1 Gal	10	
Beefeater	1.75 L	6			Wht Zinfandel	1 Gal	159	1
Bombay	1.75 L	5						
Tanqueray	1.75 L	92	1		Margarita Mix	5 Gal	2	1
					Sour Mix	5 Gal	138	
Vodka	1.75 L	414	7					
Absolut	1.75 L	34	1		LemLime Syrup	1 Gal	32	
Smirnoff	1.75 L	18			Seagrams Coolr	1 Gal	7	
Stolichnaya	Liter	111	3		Cola Syrup	1 Gal	36	1
					Tonic Syrup	1 Gal	40	1
Rum	1.75 L	66	1		Diet Syrup	1 Gal	9	
Bacardi	1.75 L	5						
Myers's	1.75 L				Soda	1 Gal	799	6
					Water	1 Gal	42	
Tequilla	1.75 L	15						
Cuervo Gold	1.75 L	15						
Brandy	1.75 L	15	1					
Apricot	Liter							

continued

net sales by time of day report—A report produced by sophisticated automated beverage systems indicating hourly sales; the report is useful for forecasting sales and scheduling servers and bartenders according to expected demand.

outstanding guest checks report—A report produced by sophisticated automated beverage systems to resolve any discrepancy existing between the sales by major beverage category report and the sales by beverage server report.

postcosting—Multiplies the number of menu items sold by standard recipe costs to determine a potential food cost amount. When actual recipe costs are known, these figures are multiplied by the number of menu items sold to produce an actual cost figure.

precosting—A special type of forecasting that compares forecasted guest counts with standard menu item recipe costs to yield an index of expense before an actual meal period.

price point—The lowest or highest selling price on a menu.

product usage report—A report produced by sophisticated automated beverage systems indicating amounts of beverage products sold during a shift; the report enables managers to minimize inventory control problems.

recipe chaining—Including sub-recipes as ingredients for a particular standard recipe. This enables the computer-based restaurant management system to maintain a record for a particular menu item that requires an unusually large number of ingredients.

sales by beverage server report—A report produced by sophisticated automated beverage systems indicating the total sales of each beverage server during a shift.

sales by major beverage category report—A report produced by sophisticated automated beverage systems indicating the expected beverage income by major beverage category (liquor, beer, wine, etc.).

sales category analysis report—Shows relationships between amounts sold by sales category and day-parts defined by management; enables management to view at a glance which menu items sell and when they sell.

sales mix by major product report—A report produced by sophisticated automated beverage systems indicating how much of each beverage product was sold during a shift; the report is useful for monitoring product sales trends and adjusting par inventory levels when necessary.

settlement methods report—A report produced by sophisticated automated beverage systems indicating the amounts due in the form of cash, credit card vouchers, and house account charges for sales made during a shift.

sub-recipe—Recipes that are included as ingredients within a standard recipe record.

weekly sales spreadsheet—Provides a weekly summary of all information reported by relevant daily sales reports.

 Review Questions ————————————————————————

1. What three files does a recipe management application maintain?

2. How can other management applications use the data in recipe management files?

3. What does the term "sub-recipes" mean? How are sub-recipes used in an ingredient file of a recipe management application?

4. Why is it useful for a sales analysis application to be able to access POS system files?

5. How can managers use the results of menu engineering to improve the profitability of their operations?

6. Which pricing model has historically been preferred by the industry?

7. What problems could managers encounter when the restaurant operation uses generic software applications to manage information?

8. How can managers benefit from integrated software applications?

9. What do the terms "precosting" and "postcosting" mean?

10. How are menu management applications, such as menu engineering, different from most other management applications?

11. What are some of the reports produced by automated beverage systems that enhance management's control of operations?

Internet Sites ─────────────────────────

For more information, visit the following Internet sites. Remember that Internet addresses can change without notice. If the site is no longer there, you can use a search engine to look for additional sites.

Agilysys, Inc.
www.agilysys.com

Comtrex Systems Corporation
www.comtrex.com

Comus Restaurant Systems
www.comussoftware.com

CostGuard Foodservice Software
www.costguard.com

Infor
www.infor.com

iTradeNetwork, Inc.
www.itradenetwork.com

MICROS Systems, Inc.
www.micros.com

RMS-Touch
www.rmstouch.com

System Concepts, Inc.
www.foodtrak.com

Chapter 8 Outline

Sales Office Automation
    Group Guestroom Sales
    Function Room Sales
    Sales Filing Systems
    Sales Performance Reports
Revenue Management
    Elements of Revenue Management
    Using Revenue Management
    Revenue Management Software
Catering Software
    Off-Premises Catering
    Home Delivery Catering

Competencies

1. Identify characteristics of guestroom and function room sales that affect the design and operation of hotel sales software. (pp. 197–202)

2. Identify the types of files and reports used in the operation of a hotel sales office. (pp. 202–207)

3. Identify characteristics of revenue management in hotel operations that affect the design and operation of hotel sales software. (pp. 207–213)

4. Describe the features and functions of software designed for off-premises and home delivery catering operations. (pp. 213–217)

8

Sales and Catering Applications

Historically, sales offices and food service catering operations have relied on a large amount of paperwork, with a significant portion of each day spent managing the information collected through prospecting, selling, booking, servicing, and reporting. The development of specialty application software enables a platform for many of these time-consuming and expensive procedures to be handled through automation. Sales and catering application software can:

- Accomplish manually tedious tasks quickly and efficiently.

- Access sales information rapidly.

- Facilitate customized offerings through database marketing.

- Reduce data-handling errors.

- Decrease staff training costs by implementing standardized procedures.

- Access customer profile information for targeted promotions.

- Enhance communication linkages among affiliated properties.

The following sections explore hotel sales office automation, as well as banquet and catering software applications.

Sales Office Automation

Sales records are a vital part of sales office communications. Records can be helpful in establishing new accounts, servicing existing accounts, and generating repeat business. In a nonautomated sales office, it is necessary that salespeople familiarize themselves with sales form preparation and filing in accordance with office procedures. Many of the traditional mechanical and often detailed office procedures are streamlined or eliminated in automated sales office applications. Exhibit 1 highlights some of the differences between nonautomated and automated applications. The following sections compare nonautomated and automated sales office functions in relation to group guestroom sales, function and banquet room sales, and sales office filing systems. In addition, the sections describe sales forecasts and performance reports generated by automated sales systems.

197

Exhibit 1   Nonautomated vs. Automated Sales Systems

Nonautomated	Automated
1. Account and booking information is entered on a scratch sheet.	All information is entered directly into the computer. If the account is an established one, entering the first few letters brings the name, address, contact person, and all other relevant information onto the screen. If the new booking is similar to a previous booking, the old entry can be duplicated and modified if necessary.
2. The same account and booking information is entered into the group room control log—the log is summarized manually.	The log is updated automatically; summary and forecast are calculated automatically.
3. The secretary types up group room block and function information.	The recap is automatically printed and includes all details on the group room block and the function events.
4. The same account and booking information is retyped in a confirmation letter.	Confirmation is produced automatically.
5. The same information is retyped in a contract.	Contract is produced automatically.
6. The banquet event order is typed and retyped with corrections using the same information as well as detailed menus, resource items, and comments.	Banquet event order is automatically generated by selecting menus and resources from the screen. Costs, consumption, and use at the time of the event are displayed.
7. Related follow-up correspondence is typed, referring to the same account and booking information.	Follow-up correspondence is traced and generated automatically.
8. In order to execute market research and/or telemarketing activity, a database is built by re-entering the same booking and account information.	Integrated account booking information is available for database search for marketing, telemarketing, service history, and lost business tracking.
9. Reports are created by a review of the forecast books, diaries, and booking recaps. Summary of data is entered.	Diary is automatically updated each time a booking is entered; summary and forecast are automatically calculated.
10. Salesperson booking pace and productivity reports are created through manual tabulation.	Reports are generated automatically using data in the system.
11. Tracing is done by manual entry on 3- by 5-inch cards. Traced files are delivered by secretaries to sales manager where they pile up on desks.	All activities are traced to the salesperson in accordance with a pre-developed plan. Daily trace reports remind the sales staff of such critical account and booking details as contracts due, credit checks to be done, block pick-ups, menus, and follow-up sales calls. Tentative and definite bookings are displayed and traced for follow-up. Numerous user-defined account traces and booking traces are generated for action steps.

Source: Adapted from *HSMAI Marketing Review.*

Group Guestroom Sales

In most nonautomated sales offices, a **guestroom control book** is used to monitor the number of guestrooms committed to groups. Since front desk, reservations, and sales office employees are capable of booking guestroom business, it is important that all personnel be aware of timely and accurate group allotments to avoid overbooking.

Properties often implement revenue management strategies designed to maximize rooms revenue by establishing a desired mix of group, tour and travel, and individual guest business for specific time periods. Typically, a guestroom control book is used to guide guestroom booking activity by providing the sales office with the maximum number of guestrooms it can sell to groups on a given day. This quota is usually set by hotel management in consultation with the hotel's marketing and sales department. The remaining guestrooms (and any unsold guestrooms allotted to groups) become available for individual guests. In general, these guestrooms will be sold by front desk and reservations staff at higher rates than they would be sold to groups.

A major challenge of nonautomated sales offices is maintaining a current and accurate guestroom control book. Difficulties arise during busy periods when bookings or cancellations are not properly recorded as they occur. Therefore, before booking guestroom business, it is not unusual for a salesperson to double-check the reliability of guestroom control data by inquiring of other sales staff members.

Automated sales offices overcome many tedious operational problems simply because every salesperson with electronic access gains immediate access to guestroom control information. Bookings and cancellations can be quickly processed as they occur—even as the salesperson is in contact with the client. This helps ensure that every salesperson has access to exactly the same information, and that "definite" and "tentative" bookings are clearly identified to prevent errors.

Exhibit 2 shows the screen of a guestroom control log from a hotel sales program. For each day of the week, the screen shows the total number of rooms remaining available for sale, the number of rooms allocated to definite and tentative group bookings, and the number of rooms protected for front office sales to transient business. Room sales are coordinated in real time as salespeople and managers have instant access to the most current information. The booking evaluator, also shown in Exhibit 2, enables staff to assess the impact of individual group bookings on budgeted targets for room sales, average rate, and revenue per available room.

Function Room Sales

In nonautomated properties, the key to successful function and banquet space control is the **function book**. The function book indicates the occupancies and vacancies of specific function rooms (including banquet rooms) and is central to effective facility planning.

Function books normally are divided into pages for each day of the year, with sections set aside for each meeting or function room. Information recorded in the function book includes the organization or group scheduling the space; the name,

Exhibit 2   Guestroom Control Log

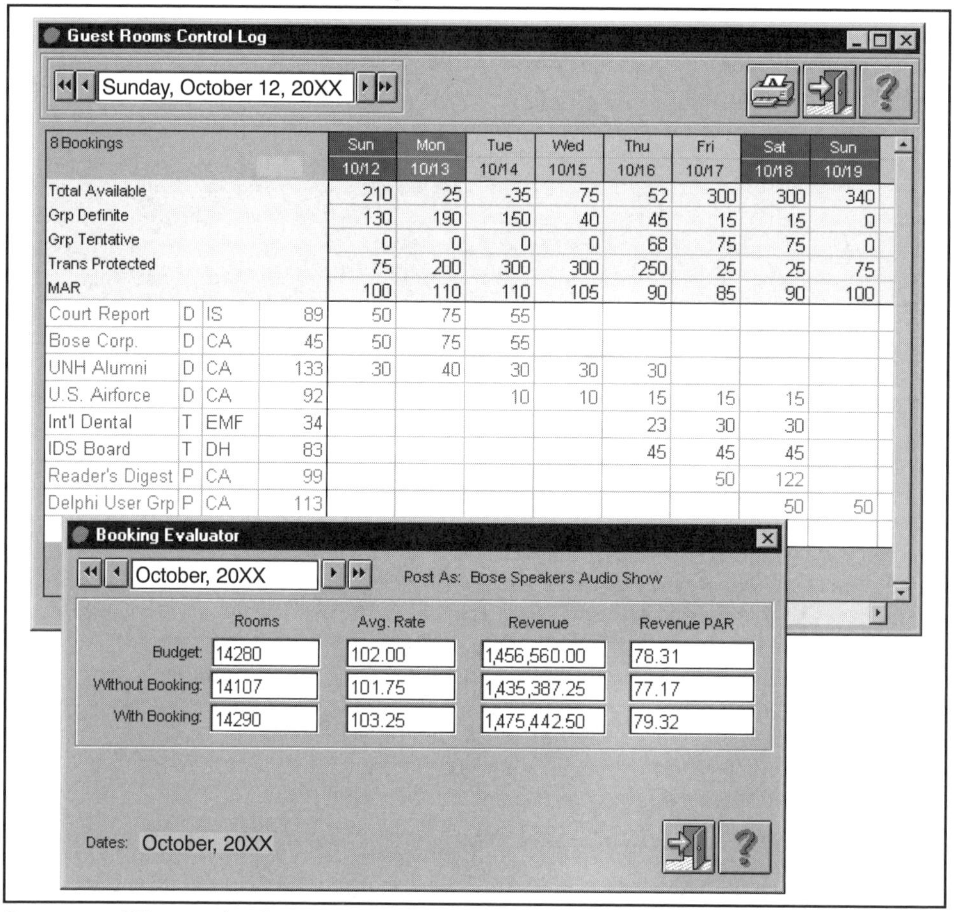

Courtesy of Newmarket International. For more information, browse the company's website at www.newmarketinc.com.

address, and telephone number of the group's contact person; the type of function; the duration of the function; the total time required for preparation, breakdown, and cleanup; the number of attendees expected; the type of setup(s) required; the rates quoted; the nature of the contract; and any pertinent remarks to help property personnel stage a successful function. Function book entries tend to be recorded in pencil because changes can occur even when a commitment seems firm. As with the guestroom control book, only one function book should be maintained to prevent mismatching of entries or double bookings.

Information from the function book and other files for events involving food or beverage service is eventually transcribed onto a **banquet event order (BEO)** form. Since a BEO generally serves as a final contract for the client and as a work order for the catering department, problems may arise should the function book contain inaccurate or incomplete information.

Automated sales office systems generate a BEO record as information is gathered and input into a client's account file. Exhibit 3 shows a system-generated BEO document. Advanced sales and catering software packages are generally able to supplement information contained in a BEO. For example, for a specific date or range of dates, an automated sales system can produce aggregated kitchen production reports (listing all menu items needed by preparation area), facility setup reports (listing all resource items requested for current events), and

Exhibit 3   Sample Banquet Event Order

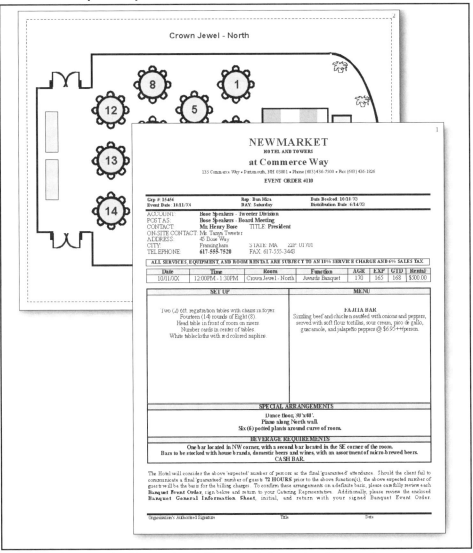

Courtesy of Newmarket International. For more information, browse the company's website at www.newmarketinc.com.

revenue forecast reports (based on anticipated revenue derived from business described on BEOs).

In a nonautomated application, coordination of the guestroom control book and the function book is critical. For example, consider the following scenario. A meeting planner phones the hotel and inquires about the best rate the hotel can offer for fifty overnight guestrooms for three nights in April with a general session meeting room (set up classroom style with a head table for five) and three break-out rooms (set up conference style) for the duration of the stay. To respond to this request, the salesperson must first match April guestroom availability dates in the guestroom control book with open dates for four meeting rooms in the function book. Next, the salesperson may feel the need to double-check the accuracy of each book's information with other members of the sales staff. Finally, the salesperson would likely have to check with the department managers before quoting a rate.

In an automated sales office application, a salesperson could respond much more quickly as rapid access processing is applied. Availability of both group guestrooms and function room space will be checked simultaneously. The salesperson will initiate a special search function to match the meeting planner's needs with the hotel's offerings. If there is not an equation of availability and inquiry, the system may generate a list of best available dates to accommodate the group (based on projected occupancy). This approach allows a hotel salesperson to quickly check the status of the meeting planner's preferred dates and to suggest alternative days if the requested days are booked. If the property's revenue management strategies are programmed into the system, the system would also provide a range of rates that the salesperson could negotiate without authorization from department management.

Exhibit 4 shows the screen of a function diary from a hotel sales program. Each function room is listed down the left side of the screen with each hour of a particular day listed across the top. Functions are blocked by room and time of day, with easy access to individual account information and room setup requirements. The program enables sales, banquets, and convention service managers to maximize function space and minimize room turns by attempting to schedule groups with similar or identical setup requirements in the same room at different times of the same day.

With sales office automation, a booking is entered into the system and is automatically integrated, tracked, and traced for management reports, contracts, proposals, and BEOs.

Sales Filing Systems

For maximum efficiency in the sales office, an effective filing system is required. Current information is essential for a successful sales effort, and information must be available quickly. Most nonautomated systems use three separate files for client information: the trace file, the account file, and the master card file. The exact contents of these files may vary from property to property.

Trace File. In nonautomated sales offices, a trace file (also known as a tickler file, bring-up file, or follow-up file) is used as a reminder to follow up on an account.

Exhibit 4   Sample Function Space Profile

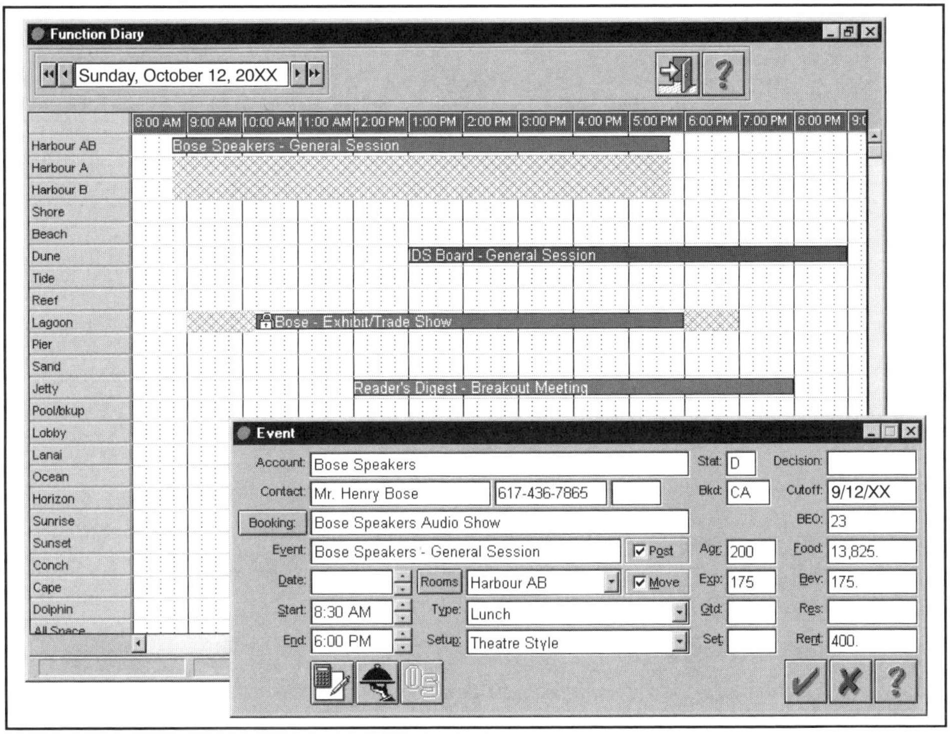

Courtesy of Newmarket International. For more information, browse the company's website at www.newmarketinc.com.

A reminder note or card may be filed in the trace file by month and date; as seen in Exhibit 5, daily dividers are arranged chronologically for the current month. The system is designed to remind the user of correspondence, telephone calls, or contacts to be handled on a particular date.

For example, suppose a client has reserved meeting room space for a training session at the property in April. The salesperson will need to contact the client no later than February 15 to finalize meeting plans, so the salesperson might place a note (often called a "trace card") dated February 15 into the February tickler divider. On February 1, the notes and trace cards for February would be reviewed and arranged according to date. The reminder note would be placed in the fifteenth slot.

A trace file system, as long as it is regularly updated and reviewed, tends to work well and takes little time to implement. However, the system also depends entirely on the accuracy and efficiency of the salesperson.

In an automated sales application, traces are activated on the appropriate dates and displayed/printed for each salesperson. The salesperson decides whether to act on the trace or to trace it to another date. Throughout the day, the salesperson uses a handheld device, notebook PC, or workstation PC to record

Exhibit 5 Sample Tickler File

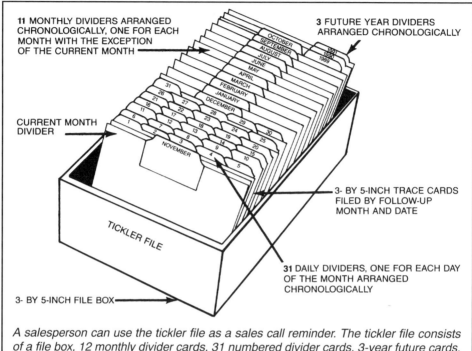

A salesperson can use the tickler file as a sales call reminder. The tickler file consists of a file box, 12 monthly divider cards, 31 numbered divider cards, 3-year future cards, and 3- by 5-inch index cards sometimes referred to as "trace cards."

notes regarding each trace. At the end of the day, the entries are processed. Traces that have been completed will no longer appear in the file, while those awaiting action will continue to appear until resolved.

Account File. In a nonautomated sales office, client accounts are maintained in standard-sized file folders. An account file is started at the time of initial contact with a prospective client and may include historical information related to previous conventions or meetings, convention bureau bulletins, or information relating to the organization that has appeared in the media. Sales reports and correspondence relating to previous sales efforts will also be placed in the file. All information in the account file should be in reverse chronological order, beginning with the newest paperwork first. Account files are usually filed alphabetically and color-coded by geographic location or market segment.

When an account file is removed, a guide card detailing the name of the account, file number, date of removal, and the initials of the person removing the file should be left in place of the file.

In an automated sales application, current account information is accessible by sales staff networked to account manager files. Typically, the salesperson accessing the files is able to determine the extent of the information displayed.

Exhibit 6 shows the screen of an account management system from a hotel sales program. From the main menu, an authorized salesperson can simply point and click to access current customer contact information (decision-makers, telephone numbers, etc.), account activity, past and future bookings, traces, and call reports.

Exhibit 6   Sample Account Manager Program

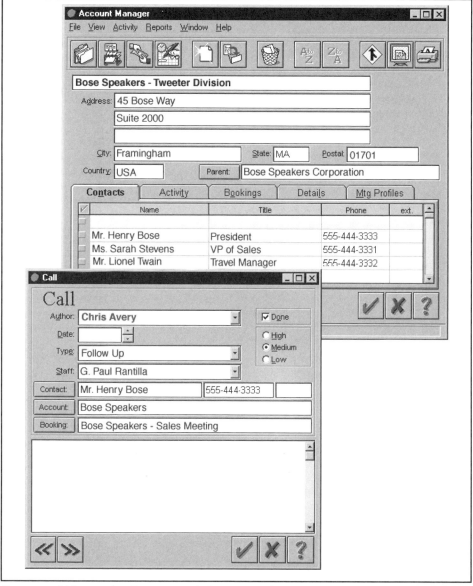

Courtesy of Newmarket International. For more information, browse the company's website at www.newmarketinc.com.

Master Card File. In nonautomated sales offices, a master card is created for each potential new account. The card contains a summary of information needed for an effective sales effort: the organization's name, names and titles of key executives, addresses, phone numbers, months of business meetings or other events, size of group, group meeting history, the group's decision-maker, and other pertinent data. Master card files can also be used to create mailing lists and to index addresses and phone numbers.

Master cards are often color-coded to specific areas of consideration: geographic location, months of meetings, follow-ups required, and size of group. Some properties also arrange master cards alphabetically by market segment. For example, IBM and Xerox would be sorted alphabetically under "Corporate Business." Other sales staff may not separate master cards by market segment, but may use a color-code system to easily identify specific market segments within the file. For example, an association account may be flagged in blue, a government account in yellow, and so on.

Some sales staff keep a geographic file of master cards. These cards are organized according to the geographic location of the decision-maker. This type of file enables sales personnel to quickly identify accounts in cities to which they are traveling. Salespeople can simply pull the names of the decision-makers located in the area and contact them during the sales trip.

Master card files can easily become overloaded with data as salespeople place more and more demands on the type of information they need to prospect, book, and service clients. In an automated sales application, the functions of a master card filing system are performed by search routines using select criteria. For example, a salesperson can access specific information needed for an account, whether it be the names of contacts, notes on follow-up calls, or remarks that can help other members of the sales team become knowledgeable about the account. In addition, a salesperson can use a search routine to search the database for accounts with specific characteristics or profiles. For example, a salesperson could search for only those accounts in northeast states that book in the month of July with a Sunday night arrival. If, on the first run, the generated list is too long, the salesperson could run a subsequent search with more narrow criteria, such as rate range or meeting space requirements.

Sales Performance Reports

An automated sales office application can produce reports that provide information on accounts, bookings, market segments, sales staff productivity, average room rates, occupancy, revenue, service history, lost business, and marketing data. The following sections describe representative system reports.

Cover Count and Revenue Summary Report. To produce a monthly catering sales forecast at a nonautomated sales office, someone must carefully review each page for a particular month in the function book and calculate (or estimate) each day's cover count and revenue forecast. This could take quite some time. Sales office software can generate an equivalent report in a matter of seconds. The daily revenue summary figures can be calculated on the basis of estimates (such as multiplying cover counts by check averages for meal periods), they can represent actual revenue figures drawn from completed banquet event orders, or they can be a combination of both estimated values and actual amounts.

Sales Performance by Market Segment Report. Sales office software packages can also produce reports related to sales performance by market segment. This report analyzes a salesperson's booking activity by market segment during a specified time period. This report is often helpful when evaluating the performance of salespersons.

Revenue Management

Revenue management, sometimes called yield management, is a set of demand-forecasting techniques used to determine whether room rates should be raised or lowered and whether a reservation request should be accepted or rejected in order to maximize revenue. The application of revenue management is based on factors related to supply and demand. Prices tend to rise when demand exceeds supply; prices tend to fall when supply exceeds demand. Pricing is a key to profitability. By increasing bookings on low-demand days and by selling rooms at higher prices on high-demand days, a hotel can significantly improve its profitability. In general, room rates should be higher when demand exceeds supply and lower (in order to increase occupancy) when supply exceeds demand.

One of the principal computations involved in revenue management is the **yield statistic**, which is the ratio of actual room revenue to potential room revenue. Actual revenue is the revenue generated by the number of rooms sold. Potential revenue is the amount of revenue the property would receive if all of its rooms were sold at full rack rates. There are many elements involved in implementing revenue management strategies.[1]

Elements of Revenue Management

Revenue management takes into account as many of the factors influencing business trends as possible. There are various approaches to revenue management, and each is modeled to meet the needs of the individual property or a group of affiliated properties.

Revenue management can be used to determine whether room rates should be raised or lowered—for example, when the hotel moves out of or into its traditional off-season—and whether selective room rate changes are appropriate. Revenue management becomes more complex when room rate changes are implemented on a selective rather than a general basis, and when a transaction involves selling rooms for which there may be competing buyers. Hotels frequently offer discounts to guests falling into certain categories (for example, senior citizens or government employees). Hotels must also decide whether to accept or refuse group business at a discounted rate.

The following elements are typically included in a successful revenue management strategy:

- Group room sales (room revenues)
- Transient room sales (room revenues)

- Food and beverage activity (non-room revenues)

- Local and area-wide conventions (other revenues)

- Special events (other revenues)

The following section focuses on group room sales.[2]

For many hotels, group business is the core business. It is common to have reservations for group sales months or even years in advance. Some international hotels and resorts, for example, report booking groups more than two years in advance. It is for this reason that understanding group booking requirements can be critical to the success of a revenue management strategy.

To clearly understand how group sales affect overall room revenue, the hotel should collect as much of the following data as possible:

- Business already on the books (reservations)

- Group booking pace (the rate at which group business is being booked)

- Business not yet on the books but likely to return (projected sales)

- Room booking lead time

- Displacement of transient business

Business Already on the Books. Management should determine whether the group blocks already in the reservation file should be reduced because of anticipated cancellations or overestimation of the group's size. If the group has a booking history at the hotel, management can often determine the likelihood of block reductions based on the group's booking history. Groups often block 5 to 10 percent more rooms than they need to ensure sufficient space for maximum potential attendees. Unnecessary group rooms can be deleted from the group block using what is called the **wash factor**.

Group Booking Pace. The rate at which group business is being booked is called the **group booking pace**. ("Booking" in this context refers to the initial agreement between the group and the hotel, not to the booking of individual rooms in the block by group members.) For example, suppose that in April of a given year, a hotel has 300 rooms in group blocks due to arrive in October of that year. If the hotel had only 250 group rooms booked for October at the same time the year before, the booking pace would be 20 percent ahead of the previous year's pace. Once a hotel has accumulated several years of operational data, it can often determine a historical trend that reveals the normal booking pace for each month of the year. While simple on the surface, this method of forecasting can become very complicated due to unanticipated fluctuations. Management should adopt a simple method for tracking the group booking pace.

Unbooked Business Likely to Return. Most national, regional, and state associations, as well as some corporations, have policies governing the locations of annual meetings. For example, a group may rotate among three cities, returning to each every three years. Although a contract may not yet be signed, management may be confident that a group will return according to its cycle. In addition, tentative bookings that await final contract negotiations are normally included in a revenue management analysis.

Booking Lead Time. Booking lead time measures how far in advance of arrival bookings are made. Some hotels have average lead times of two months. For many hotels, group bookings are usually made within one year of actual arrival. Management should determine its hotel's lead time for group bookings so that a booking trend can be charted. This trend can be combined with booking pace information on a graph to illustrate the rate at which the hotel is booking business compared with historical trends (see Exhibit 7). This information can be very important when determining whether to accept an additional group and at what room rate to book the group. If the current booking pace is lower than expected, or lags behind the historical trend, it may be necessary to offer a lower room rate

Exhibit 7   Lead Time/Booking Pace for Sample Hotel

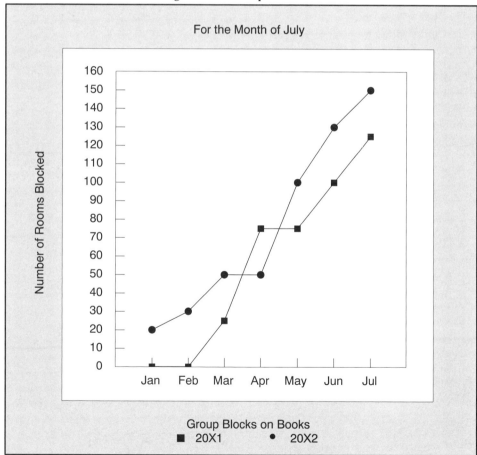

Source: Michael L. Kasavana, *Managing Front Office Operations,* 9th ed. (Lansing, Mich.: American Hotel & Lodging Educational Institute, 2013), p. 499.

to stimulate business through increased occupancy. On the other hand, if demand is strong and the group booking pace is ahead of anticipated or historical trends, it may not be appropriate to discount room rates.

Displacement of Transient Business. Management should consult its demand forecast when determining whether to accept group business. **Displacement** occurs when a hotel accepts group business at the expense of turning away higher-paying transient guests. Transient rooms are guestrooms sold to guests who are not affiliated with a group staying at the hotel. These guests, usually called transient guests or FITs (free independent travelers), are often businesspeople or vacationers. Since transient guests often pay higher room rates than group business, any situation involving displacement should be looked at very carefully.

Assume that a 400-room hotel has a **potential average rate** of $100, an actual transient rate of $80, an actual group rate of $60, and a marginal cost (i.e., the variable cost to service the room) of $15 per room. Consider the impact of a group requesting a block of sixty rooms during the following four days:

	Tuesday	Wednesday	Thursday	Friday
Room Nights Available	400	400	400	400
Definite Group Demand	140	140	150	150
Expected Transient Demand	200	180	220	210
Available Rooms	60	80	30	40
Suggested Group	60	60	60	60
Transient Displacement	0	0	30	20

If this group is accepted, no displacement occurs on Tuesday and Wednesday; the hotel clearly benefits on these days because it sells rooms it did not expect to sell (earning an additional $3,600 gross and $2,700 net room revenue each day). On Thursday and Friday, however, thirty and twenty transient guests, respectively, will be displaced. Still, as shown in Exhibit 8, Thursday's room revenue will rise by $1,200 gross and $750 net if the group is accepted. Friday's room revenue will rise by $2,000 gross and $1,400 net if the group is accepted. In other words, accepting the group business will increase the hotel's yield for all four days. Since it also

Exhibit 8   Revenue and Yield Calculations

	Tuesday		Wednesday		Thursday		Friday	
	Without Group	With Group	Without Group	With Group	Without Group	With Group	Without Group	With Group
Gross revenue	$24,400	$28,000	$22,800	$26,400	$26,600	$27,800	$25,800	$27,800
Contribution*	19,300	22,000	18,000	20,700	21,050	21,800	20,400	21,800
Yield**	61.0%	70.0%	57.0%	66.0%	66.5%	69.5%	64.5%	69.5%

*Based on a marginal cost of $15.
**Potential revenue = $100 potential average rate × 400 rooms = $40,000.

Source: Michael L. Kasavana, *Managing Front Office Operations,* 9th ed. (Lansing, Mich.: American Hotel & Lodging Educational Institute, 2013), p. 500.

raises the hotel's occupancy, the group business will probably increase non-room revenue as well.

Several factors help determine whether a group reservation should be accepted. As just illustrated, the hotel should first look at revenue factors. A group should probably be accepted if the expected revenue gain (including that from non-room revenue centers) offsets the transient guest revenue lost. In addition, management must consider what happens to the transient guests who cannot be accommodated. Whether they are frequent or first-time guests, they may decide not to return based on the treatment they receive. The point is that transient revenue lost may not be confined simply to the nights in question if frequent guests choose not to return. Of course, turning away group business may also reduce the chance that persons in that group will return. Deciding whether to accept a group that forces transient displacement is more than an issue of easily identifiable numbers. Management should also consider the long-term impact on future business.

Using Revenue Management

All elements of revenue management (group room sales, transient room sales, food and beverage activity, local and area-wide conventions, and special events) should be viewed together in order to make the appropriate decisions. While it is potentially complex, a failure to include relevant factors may make revenue management efforts less effective.

The hotel's yield statistic should be tracked daily. Tracking yield for past days can help reveal trends. However, to use revenue management properly, management must gauge yield outcomes for *future* days. Calculations must be done on a regular basis for a future period, depending on how far in advance the hotel books business. If management is currently projecting a 50 percent yield for a day three weeks away, there may be plenty of time to put strategies in place to enhance that number. Discounted rates may be opened to attract occupancy, or some discounts may be closed to raise average rate. It is the balance of occupancy and rate that achieves the highest yield. If achieving the potential room revenue is not possible (and it usually is not), management must decide on the best combination of rate and occupancy in order to get the highest yield.

Each segment of group business should be considered individually. Business should be compared to historical trends as well as to budget. A hotel usually establishes a group sales target or budgeted figure for each month. Each group should be examined to determine if it will help meet the budget. If demand is strong and the group will create low revenue, the hotel may decide not to book it. If demand is weak, the hotel may decide to accept the group simply to create revenue from rooms that would not otherwise be occupied. The group booking pace analysis will help management determine whether the hotel is on target to achieve its goals.

Another factor is the actual group booking pattern already on the books. For example, due to booked groups, a hotel may have two days between groups that are not busy. Management may take a lower-revenue-producing group just to fill the gap. The opposite may also occur. A group may want to come in over a period when the hotel is near attaining its goal of group room sales. The group may move the hotel past its business goal. While this appears to be good, it involves the displacement of higher-rated transient business. If management is committed to the group, it may quote a higher room rate that will help make up the lost revenue caused by the displacement of transient guests.

The same type of analysis is needed for transient business. For example, due to the discounts the hotel offers, corporate and government business may be assigned to standard rooms. As standard rooms fill, management may only have deluxe rooms left to sell. If demand is not strong, management may decide to sell the deluxe rooms at the standard rack rate to remain competitive. It is best to look at a combined picture (group and transient business) before making occupancy and rate decisions.

It is important to note that historical trends do not always apply. More recent trends must also be taken into consideration. For example, if historical trends have been strong, but recent business has been weak, it is better to plan for weak business and attempt to attract business through lower rates. Likewise, if recent occupancy is very strong, it is appropriate to follow that trend with higher rates.

Since the objective of revenue management is to maximize room revenue, tracking business by revenue source will also help management determine when to allow discounted business. Management may decide to allow specific types of discounted business, such as corporate business, since the corporation may be responsible for many additional room nights. As the various sources of business are determined, each should be analyzed to understand its impact on total revenue. Quite often, management will take discounted business if it generates frequent customers, since the long-term impact is very positive.

Revenue Management Software

Although the individual tasks of revenue management can be performed manually, doing so is very difficult and time-consuming. The most efficient means of handling data and generating yield statistics is through application software. Revenue management software can integrate room demand and room price statistics, and project an optimal revenue-generating room sales mix.

Revenue management software does not replace managerial decision-making. It merely provides information and support for sound decisions. The advantage of using revenue management software is that it can store, retrieve, and manipulate great amounts of data across a broad range of factors influencing room revenue. Over time, revenue management software helps create simulations showing the probable results of decisions; these models are based on historical, forecasted, and booked business.

Industries that have applied automated revenue management to business situations have achieved the following results:

- Continual monitoring: an automated revenue management system can track and analyze business conditions 24 hours a day, 7 days a week.

- Consistency: software can respond to changes in the marketplace, according to corporate or local management rules built into the software.

- Information availability: revenue management software can provide improved management information that, in turn, helps managers make more intelligent decisions more quickly.

- Performance tracking: an automated system is capable of analyzing sales and revenue transactions to determine how well revenue management goals were achieved.

Revenue management software is also able to generate a number of special reports. The following reports are representative of revenue management software output.

Market Segment Report. This report provides information regarding customer mix. This information is important to effective forecasting by market segment.

Calendar/Booking Graph. This graph presents room-night demands and volume of reservations on a daily basis.

Booking Overrides Report. A booking overrides report lists all bookings that fail to meet contribution margins or availability constraints as determined by management. The report provides management with information necessary to evaluate questionable bookings before contracts are sent to clients.

Future Arrival Dates Status Report. This report furnishes demand data for each day of the week. The report contains a variety of forecasting information that allows for the discovery of occupancy trends by comparative analysis of weekdays. It can be designed to cover several future periods.

Single Arrival Date History Report. This report indicates the hotel's booking patterns (trends in reservations). The report relates to the booking graph by documenting how a specific day was constructed on the graph.

Weekly Recap Report. This report contains the sell rates for rooms and the number of rooms authorized and sold in marketing programs with special or discounted rates.

Room Statistics Tracking Sheet. This report tracks no-shows, guaranteed no-shows, walk-ins, and turn-aways. This information can be instrumental in accurate forecasting.

Catering Software

While catering is similar in many ways to traditional restaurant operations, there are unique characteristics that are addressed by targeted software applications. There are two types of catering for which software applications have been developed: off-premises catering and **finished product** (or home delivery) **catering**.

Off-Premises Catering

There are many details involved in the proposal, planning, and execution stages of an off-premises catering activity. Initially, the caterer suggests a standard menu or set of menus to a client for consideration. The client either selects from available offerings or requests a special meal plan. In either case, the caterer develops a proposal for the function.

Caterers are responsible for food and beverage service and may also be contracted to provide furnishings, entertainment, decorations, and the like. Before an event, the caterer typically plans for necessary purchases, personnel, production, transportation, service, and rental equipment. Generally, the caterer arrives at a catered event with all these requirements, because supplemental equipment, product replenishment, and additional staff are usually not available at the catered site.

Catering software monitors and controls the activities associated with each stage of **off-premises catering service**. Many of the files created through the use of catering software packages perform functions similar to automated restaurant management applications. Typical files contained in a catering software package include:

- Ingredient file (FIDF).

- Recipe file (RIDF).

- Menu item file (MIDF).

- Proposal/contract file.

- Inventory file.

- General accounting files.

In addition to containing data on all purchased food and beverage products, the ingredient file includes data on such non-food items as labor, serving utensils, production equipment, rental equipment, disposable items, and entertainment options. The more complete this file, the easier it becomes for the caterer to assemble an entire catering service package.

While standard recipes for food service operations list ingredients and a set of assembly instructions, an off-premises catering recipe generally contains "ingredients" for non-food items as well. For example, a table and chairs recipe may be recorded in a recipe file to assist in determining the number of tables and chairs required for a particular catered event. A table that seats eight persons could be entered as a recipe into the catering (RIDF) file. The recipe for an eight-top table would have nine ingredients: a table and eight chairs. If the caterer were planning an off-premises catering activity for 240 persons, the table and chairs recipe would be automatically multiplied up to thirty tables and 240 chairs. In addition, the recipe file accesses cost data contained in the ingredient file to generate the cost of an event. The table and chairs recipe would serve as a sub-recipe within a larger recipe. Any number of sub-recipes can be chained to produce a single recipe that contains a large number and range of ingredients.

The menu item file contains meal plans for specific catered activities. Catering menu item files contain recipes for edible as well as non-food items. Some catering software packages allow users to create recipes for determining required gratuities, insurance, and taxes. All of these recipes are stored within a menu item file for the specific catered events.

A proposal/contract file accesses data contained in the menu item file, applies prices for menu items, and maintains a record of commitments. The inventory file and general accounting files perform functions similar to inventory and back office accounting applications.

Off-premises catering applications provide event calendars that list customer names, addresses, and notes that apply to specific events. A calendar may list events by a specific date, or it may cover a longer time period and list events assigned to a particular manager. Some applications convert information from the event calendars into production requirements for different preparation areas such as hot foods, cold foods, rentals, cutlery, and linen. This feature is particularly helpful because customers are likely to change the number of people expected to attend the event up to twenty-four hours before the event.

An event worksheet can be used to plan an event with a customer. Also, the manager of the event uses the worksheet as a checklist to ensure that all requested items are properly prepared and readied for the event. The worksheet lists the number of attendees, person in charge of the event, employees scheduled to work, customer's contact information, and the food, furniture, props, and other items required to fulfill the contract.

Once entered within the system, an event worksheet can be converted into a cost analysis report. A catering manager can use this information when pricing or evaluating a particular event. If a customer requests changes, an updated cost analysis can be prepared.

Home Delivery Catering

Some multi-unit food service operators have home delivery networks that function much like a hotel central reservation system. The focal point of the network is an order-taking center connected to remote production and delivery stations. As orders are transmitted to remote work stations, so too is the responsibility for fulfillment, delivery, and settlement.

In the case of single independent units, the order process originates with the order-taker entering the caller's telephone number and address into the home delivery system. The call-in system may be tied to a caller ID network to help confirm caller information. Entering caller data may trigger an internal database search through the system's customer master file, generating a customer history report.

If the customer has not placed an order before, a customer record will automatically be created as a consequence of the order-taking routine. With some systems, this routine begins with the order-taker using the system's street index to determine whether the customer is within the establishment's delivery area. If so, the order-taker enters a street code and the customer's address and telephone number. The system then generates a customer record and automatically completes mailing information (city, state, zip code, and e-mail) for future targeted promotions. Some systems also add map coordinates and route information to the customer record. This information automatically appears on the receipt for the customer's order, thus helping the delivery person deliver the order efficiently.

If the customer has placed an order at the establishment before, an electronic customer record is retrieved from the database. Exhibit 9 shows one type of order-entry screen format. Note that the screen displays the customer's total sales to date.

Exhibit 9   Sample Home Delivery Order Entry Screen

```
        F O O D M A N  -  Order-Taker  -  02/15          19:36

    1. Action:0  Telephone:447-5350      Order No:2023      Date:0125

    2. Name:  Paula Paterson            House#:345   Street:ZW
        Addr:  345 Shelton Avenue                    Del/PU:D
        Addr:  Apt 3b                                Del by: 9:00PM
        City:  Midland Park              State:NJ    Zip:07432    Sales
          SI:  Use rear of driveway                  Brthdy:0215   $263.12

   01 | 01 | LA  LL  LM  LR | Personal Pizza/Extra Cheese/Pepperoni/Mushrooms
   02 | 01 | EL             | Pepsi-Cola
   03 |    | (these are menu|
   04 |    | codes for the  | (Line items are displayed in this section
   05 |    | items ordered) |  for operator verification and read-back)

   Actions:  O = New Order  T = Take-out    C = Change Order | Price:   6.50
             S = Search     N = Next Order  I = Print Invoice | Tax:      .39
             D = Delete     P = Punch-in/out Q = Quit         | Total:   6.89
```

Source: Standard Commercial Systems, Englewood, New Jersey

Many automated home delivery systems also provide establishments with files for scheduling employees, recording time worked by employees, analyzing sales, and recording accounts payable data. Exhibit 10 shows a special check-out screen used by delivery drivers at the end of their shifts. The system prompts the

Exhibit 10   Sample Home Delivery Employee Check-Out Screen

```
        F O O D M A N  -  Operations Manager  -  02/15    12:00

    1.Action:0                    Employee:ARD

    Press F1 to start over if you make an error
    Enter ending mileage:004534    Total Mileage:  54
    Enter gasoline expense: 5.00      Deliveries:  12   Amount: 185.76
                                   Total Coupons:  17.00
                                   Car Allowance:
                                      Total Due:163.76

    Enter Coupons Below:

    Code:V1  Qty:6    Code:V2  Qty:11    Code:    Qty:
    Code:    Qty:     Code:    Qty:      Code:    Qty:

    Punch-In at:16:45              Occupation:D
    Punch-Out at:19:50 on 2/15     Total time was:03:05
```

Source: Standard Commercial Systems, Englewood, New Jersey

employee to enter ending mileage, coupons accepted (up to six different coupons), and any gasoline expense. The amount due from the driver is calculated. With this particular system, it is also possible to reimburse drivers who use personal cars. The compensation can be made on the basis of a percentage of the total deliveries.

Endnotes

1. For a complete discussion of these formulas, see Michael L. Kasavana, *Managing Front Office Operations,* 9th ed. (Lansing, Mich.: American Hotel & Lodging Educational Institute, 2013).

2. For a detailed discussion of the other major elements of revenue management, see Kasavana.

Key Terms

banquet event order (BEO)—Information from the function book and other files is eventually transcribed on a banquet event order (BEO). A BEO generally serves as a final contract for the client and as a work order for the catering department.

booking lead time—A measurement of how far in advance bookings are made.

displacement—The turning away of transient guests for lack of rooms due to the acceptance of group business.

finished product catering—Home delivery catering services.

function book—Book that indicates the occupancies and vacancies of specific function rooms (including banquet rooms).

group booking pace—The rate at which group business is being booked.

guestroom control book—Guides guestroom booking activity by providing the sales office with the maximum number of guestrooms it can sell to groups on a given day. The remaining guestrooms (and any unsold guestrooms allotted to groups) are available for individual guests.

off-premises catering service—A catering service that typically requires the caterer to be responsible for food and beverage production and service and possibly for providing furnishings, entertainment, decorations, and the like.

potential average rate—A collective statistic that effectively combines the potential average single and double rates, multiple occupancy percentage, and rate spread to produce the average rate that would apply if all rooms were sold at their full rack rates.

revenue management—A set of demand-forecasting techniques used to determine whether prices should be raised or lowered and whether a reservation request should be accepted or rejected in order to maximize revenue.

wash factor—The removal of unused and therefore unnecessary group rooms from a group block.

yield statistic—The ratio of actual room revenue to potential room revenue.

Review Questions ——————————————————————

1. What are the advantages an automated sales office has over a nonautomated sales office?

2. What are the advantages of using an automated sales system to create a function book and a banquet event order?

3. How does automation facilitate trace file, account file, and master card file systems?

4. What is the goal of revenue management?

5. What role does booking pace play in revenue management?

6. Why is transient displacement analysis so important in determining whether to accept a group reservation?

7. What does the term "off-premises catering" mean?

8. What does "finished product catering" mean?

9. What files are typically included in catering software packages?

10. What competitive advantages do automated home delivery systems offer?

 Internet Sites ————————————————————————

For more information, visit the following Internet sites. Remember that Internet addresses can change without notice. If the site is no longer there, you can use a search engine to look for additional sites.

CaterTrax
www.catertrax.com

CaterWare Inc.
www.caterware.com

Hospitality Sales and Marketing
  Association International (HSMAI)
www.hsmai.org

Newmarket International
www.newmarketinc.com

Waiter.com, Inc.
www.waiter.com

Chapter 9 Outline

Accounts Receivable Module
    Customer Master File
    Management Reports
Accounts Payable Module
    Vendor Master File
    Invoice Register File
    Check Register File
Payroll Module
    Employee Master File
    Payroll Register File
    Other Functions
Inventory Module
    Inventory Status
    Inventory Valuation
    Special Food and Beverage Concerns
Purchasing Module
    Purchase Order File
    E-Procurement
    Purchasing Reports
Financial Reporting Module
    Chart of Accounts
    Trial Balance File
    Financial Statements
    Ratio Analysis
    Enterprise Reporting
Labor Scheduling Applications

Competencies

1. Identify features and functions of an accounts receivable module for an automated accounting system and explain how managers use accounts receivable reports generated by the accounting system. (pp. 221–224)

2. Identify features and functions of an accounts payable module for an automated accounting system and explain how managers use accounts payable reports generated by the accounting system. (pp. 224–228)

3. Describe the functions typically performed by payroll modules in automated accounting systems. (pp. 228–232)

4. Explain how an inventory module addresses inventory status, inventory variance, and inventory valuation. (pp. 232–236)

5. Identify features and functions of a purchasing module for an automated accounting system. (pp. 236–241)

6. Identify features and functions of a financial reporting module for an automated accounting system. (pp. 241–247)

7. Identify features and functions of labor scheduling software applications. (pp. 247–251)

9

Accounting Applications

Hospitality industry back office software packages vary in the number of accounting applications they provide. This chapter focuses on software modules that are typically included in property management back office software packages:

- Accounts receivable
- Accounts payable
- Payroll accounting
- Inventory accounting
- Purchasing
- Financial reporting

The specific needs and requirements of individual properties help determine whether these modules are implemented and operated separately or are integrated with the front office modules of a complete property management system (PMS). Since much value (in terms of capitalizing on technology) is gained from a fully integrated system, this chapter treats each back office module as if it were part of a comprehensive PMS.

Accounts Receivable Module

The term **accounts receivable**, abbreviated A/R, refers to obligations owed to a lodging or food service operation from sales made to customers on credit. An accounts receivable software application typically performs the following functions:

- Maintains account balances
- Processes billings
- Monitors collection activities
- Monitors aging of accounts receivable
- Generates an audit report of accounts receivable transactions

Management can also set various credit limits to control accounts receivable and identify accounts with balances above an established credit limit. For each account, the module maintains a variety of credit history data. These data typically indicate the number of days elapsed between payments and the oldest invoice to which the last payment applied.

With an integrated system, A/R balances may be automatically transferred from a front office accounting module to a back office A/R module during the daily system update routine. The **city ledger** is a subsidiary ledger listing A/R balances for guests who have checked out, but had an outstanding balance on their folios. Data from the front office accounting module (such as balances from guest folios, non-guest accounts, bill-to accounts, credit/debit card charges, and others) form the **city ledger file** of the back office accounts receivable module.

Some front office systems simplify account billing procedures by creating semi-permanent and permanent folios. Semi-permanent folios are assigned to guest or non-guest accounts designated for direct billing (e.g., bill-to and third-party accounts). Permanent folios are assigned to credit/debit card companies and other long-term contracted financial relationships.

As payments are received or additional charges incurred, they are posted to the appropriate city ledger account. Payments or charges posted to the A/R module immediately update the city ledger file, thereby helping to ensure that all account balances remain current.

Customer Master File

A **customer master file** provides a basis for collecting and storing billing information for firms with which the hospitality business has a relationship, not guests. Customer data maintained in this file may include:

- Account number.
- Account name.
- Address.
- Telephone number.
- E-mail address.
- Website address.
- Contact person.
- Type of account.
- Credit limit.
- Last payment date.
- Last payment amount.
- Credit history.

Generally, management assigns an account name and number and designates the type of account. These accounts are not mutually exclusive and can be classified as transient, permanent, credit/debit card company, direct billing, and so on. Accounts receivable modules are capable of automatically generating individual account invoices.

Management Reports

An A/R module generally allows management to access data from any account stored in the A/R file. Part of this module functions as an **accounts aging file**, containing data that can be formatted into a variety of aging reports. An **aging of accounts receivable schedule** breaks down each account in the accounts aging file according to the date of the initial charge posting. Exhibit 1 illustrates a sample aging of accounts receivable report produced by a restaurant back office system.

Although aging schedules can be printed on demand, they are routinely generated during month-end file updates for tracking purposes. An A/R module can automatically produce standard dunning letters for all accounts in delinquent payment categories. A dunning letter is a generic term used to describe a demanding request for payment of an outstanding balance.

An A/R module can streamline and customize reports for various users. Much of the detailed information in an aging schedule may not be necessary for some accounting functions. In these cases, data maintained in the accounts aging file can be included or excluded according to the user's specific needs for customized aging reports. In addition, a summary aging of accounts receivable report is typically produced for management.

For audit purposes, some A/R modules issue an audit report listing all accounts receivable transactions. An audit report usually charts each account by

Exhibit 1   Sample Aging of Accounts Receivable Report

```
DATE:                        ACCOUNTS RECEIVABLE
                       AGED ACCOUNTS RECEIVABLE REPORT
                           01 - ABC RESTAURANT INC.                 PAGE: 1
                                 Aging Date:
```

--------CUSTOMER--------		--------INVOICE-----					
NUMBER	NAME	NUMBER	DATE DUE	CURRENT	OVER 30	OVER 60	OVER 90
1	AMERICAN EXPRESS	10577		0.00	2,442.53	0.00	0.00
1	AMERICAN EXPRESS	10776		567.71	0.00	0.00	0.00
				567.71	2,442.53	0.00	0.00
2	MASTERCARD	10578		0.00	1,676.77	0.00	0.00
2	MASTERCARD	10777		97.98	0.00	0.00	0.00
				97.98	1,676.7	0.00	0.00
10	JAMES JOHNSON	10774		122.56	0.00	0.00	0.00
10	JAMES JOHNSON	10775		165.36	0.00	0.00	0.00
				287.92	0.00	0.00	0.00

```
                        AGED ACCOUNTS RECEIVABLE TOTALS
                                 Aging Date:
```

---CURRENT---		---OVER 30---		---OVER 60---		---OVER 90---	
NO.	AMOUNT	NO.	AMOUNT	NO.	AMOUNT	NO.	AMOUNT
3	953.61	2	4119.30	0	0.00	1	0.00

account number, account name, invoice number(s), and dollar amount(s), for a specified time period.

Accounts Payable Module

The term **accounts payable**, abbreviated A/P, refers to liabilities incurred for merchandise, equipment, or other goods and services purchased by the hospitality operation with deferred payment. The accounts payable module can function as a stand-alone system or can be integrated with other modules of the PMS. This back office module is responsible for maintaining current payables records arising from the posting of transactions. Such processing helps prevent duplicate entries of invoices and provides management with up-to-date information on vendor invoices.

An A/P application maintains a vendor master file, an invoice register file, and a check register file, and typically performs the following functions:

- Posts vendor invoices

- Monitors vendor payment discount periods

- Determines amounts due

- Generates checks for payment

- Facilitates the reconciliation of used checks

- Generates management reports

With a fully integrated accounting system, an A/P module may be capable of accessing travel agent commission data from the front office reservations module to create travel agent commission checks. A/P modules without access to reservations data require staff to process commission checks by hand, treating them as individual accounts payable invoices.

Management reports that can be produced from data in A/P module files are payables aging reports, vendor status reports, vendor activity reports, and monthly check registers. A **check register** is a summary document containing a list of payment checks written during a specified time period. The checks can be sorted by vendor or by the invoice due date. An **accounts payable aging report** may contain several aging columns and list invoices by vendor number, vendor name, invoice number, and invoice date. Generally, this report can be generated on demand and streamlined to meet management needs. A **monthly check register** provides an audit trail of payments made by vendor. This report also identifies checks that have not been reconciled. Exhibit 2 contains a sample **vendor status report**.

Vendor Master File

The **vendor master file** maintains records of all current vendors. Data contained in this file may include:

- Vendor account number.

- Vendor name.

Exhibit 2   Sample Vendor Status Report

VENDOR STATUS REPORT BY VENDOR NUMBER

Vendor	Vendor Name	Balance Accruals	MTD Payments	MTD Accruals	YTD Payments	YTD
051462	Spunky's Produce	150.00	150.00	143.36	603.36	453.36
051562	Upton's Fish Market	0.00	-159.63	-159.63	0.00	0.00
051662	Cory Cow's Dairy Farm	0.00	0.00	101.92	101.92	101.92
051762	Capital Dry Goods	0.00	0.00	65.00	65.00	65.00
051862	Dolly Madison Bakery		0.00	0.00		
051962	Miltons Meat Market	0.00	0.00	269.00	269.00	269.00
052062	Amy's Amenities	0.00	0.00	500.00	500.00	500.00
052162	Denmark Data Forms	0.00	0.00	2500.00	2500.00	2500.00
052262	Suttons Pool Supplies		0.00	0.00		
121213	Carmen's Cleaning Service	92.00	92.00	0.00	92.00	
121214	S&S Quality Produce	1500.00	0.00	500.00	2000.00	500.00
121215	G&G Produce		0.00	0.00		
121217	Sounds of Music	0.00	0.00	890.00	890.00	890.00
121231	Coors Dist.	0.00	0.00	1300.30	1300.30	1300.30
121235	Nordic Princess Cheesecak		0.00	0.00		
121313	Southwest Laund	125.00	248.00	123.00	248.00	123.00
171717	Southern California		0.00	0.00		
1000000	ABC Lumber					
1212121	Pacific Bell	500.00	500.00	1000.00	1500.00	1000.00
1212129	Artistic Florist	0.00	0.00	175.00	175.00	175.00
1234698	Keenan's Uniform Supplies	0.00	0.00	15069.69	33659.02	33659.02
1256153	Martins Flower Shop	0.00	0.00	0.00	300.00	300.00
3249874	Eat Um Up Food Service	0.00	0.00	10002.38	10002.38	10002.38
4151265	Pacific Gas Company		0.00	0.00		
5261235	Bostonian Federal		0.00	0.00		
5468923	Halp Company		0.00	0.00		
6587463	Liquid Refreshment Inc.	0.00	0.00	2253.68	2253.68	2253.68
7878787	First Intermedian Bank	526.34	526.34	526.34	1052.68	526.34
8585858	Tony's Seafood		0.00	0.00		
9999999	Onetime Vendor	0.00	250.00	350.00	350.00	350.00
		2893.34	1606.71	35610.04	57862.34	54969.00

[405] 30 Items Listed.

- Contact name.
- Address.
- Telephone number.
- E-mail address.
- Website address.
- Vendor payment priority (if any).
- Discount terms.

- Discount account number (if different).

- Invoice reference number.

- Payment due date.

- Year-to-date summary.

A vendor status report, such as that shown in Exhibit 2, presents summary accounts payable information. A **vendor activity report** may contain gross amount invoiced, discounts taken, balance paid, invoice reference number, and other vendor data.

Invoice Register File

An **invoice register file** maintains a list of all invoices currently outstanding and payable. The A/P module can select invoices for payment by due date or by payment discount date. The **payment discount date** is the last day on which it is possible for the hospitality business to take advantage of a cash payment discount offered by the vendor. Many vendors offer a discount on the invoice amount if payment is made within a specified time frame. For example, the terms of an invoice could be stated as: 2/10 net 30 days, meaning that the buyer may apply a 2 percent discount to the invoice amount if payment is made within ten days of the date on which the invoice was issued; once the discount period has elapsed, full payment is expected within thirty days of the original invoice date. Tracking discount payment dates is often a tedious and time-consuming task in nonautomated back office accounting systems. The accounts payable module can be programmed to automatically identify those invoices with applicable discount payment terms. Early payments can represent significant savings.

Although A/P modules can automatically select invoices for payment, they also give management the ability to override selected invoices. **Override options** give management complete control over cash disbursements before the system is authorized to begin writing checks. Options that management may exercise include:

- Selecting invoices for payment that are not yet due.

- Making partial payments on certain invoices.

- Suspending payments on certain invoices.

- Adding reference data to invoices (to be printed on check stubs).

After management has exercised its options, a **cash requirements report** can be generated. This report lists all invoices selected for payment and the corresponding cash requirements to cover the payments. The report can be prepared by vendor number, vendor name, due date, transaction, or group code. A cash requirements report typically includes vendor number, vendor name, invoice number, due date, balance due, and amount being paid. Exhibit 3 contains a sample cash requirements report arranged by vendor number. A cash requirements report can be generated upon demand, based on the number of open invoices.

Exhibit 3   Sample Cash Requirements Report

Vendor	Vendor Name	Invoice	D/Due	Gross	07/15	07/22	07/29	08/05	08/12	08/19	Future
051462	Spunky's Produce	12312	06/15	150.00	150.00						
				150.00	150.00	0.00	0.00	0.00	0.00	0.00	0.00
121213	Carmen's Cleaning Serv	98798		25.00	25.00						
		1-6766	07/10	52.00	52.00						
		111	07/20	40.00	40.00						
				117.00	117.00	0.00	0.00	0.00	0.00	0.00	0.00
121214	S&S Quality Produce	121214	03/15	1500.00	1500.00						
				1500.00	1500.00	0.00	0.00	0.00	0.00	0.00	0.00
121313	Southwest Laundry	99998	08/10	125.00				125.00			
				125.00	0.00	0.00	0.00	125.00	0.00	0.00	0.00
1212121	Pacific Bell	12	07/20	500.00	500.00						
				500.00	500.00	0.00	0.00	0.00	0.00	0.00	0.00
7878787	First Intermedian Bank	1-6766	07/10	526.34	526.34						
				526.34	526.34	0.00	0.00	0.00	0.00	0.00	0.00
	Total for 6 Vendors			2918.34	2793.34	0.00	0.00	125.00	0.00	0.00	0.00

Check Register File

The **check register file** monitors the calculation and in-house printing of bank checks for payments of selected invoices. After printing checks, the A/P module deletes paid invoices from the invoice register file, preventing the possibility of double payments. With a fully integrated PMS, the check-writing routine updates account balances maintained by the general ledger module. After the checks have been written, the A/P module generates a check register by check number. The data in the check register can also be sorted by vendor number or invoice due date. The emergence of electronic or online banking is changing—even eliminating—the role of the check register file since there are no physical documents in circulation, only recordings of electronic fund transfers.

A/P modules can be modified to include electronic payments and voided checks. Generally, electronic payments and voided checks are highlighted on the check register report.

After all entries have been made, an **outstanding checks list** may be generated. This list details all payments that have been issued but remain outstanding.

The outstanding checks list can be used to reconcile checks issued against canceled checks and online payments appearing on bank statements. While actual procedures for **check reconciliation** vary, the procedure could prompt the user to enter check numbers and amounts from a bank statement. As each check is entered, the accounts payable module verifies the entry and removes (clears) the check from the outstanding checks list. When all checks and electronic payments have been reconciled, the system can produce a **reconciliation audit report**. This report balances the total of checks removed from the outstanding checks list with the total of cleared checks and electronic payments appearing on the bank statement.

Payroll Module

Calculating each employee's pay, developing the accounting records, and preparing the necessary reports required by federal, state, and local governments are recurrent tasks carried out by the back office accounting department. Payroll accounting can be time-consuming in nonautomated properties. Not only do pay rates vary with job classifications, but, in the hospitality industry, a single employee could also work at different tasks over a number of workshifts, each of which might have a different pay rate. Unlike many other accounting functions, payroll system requirements are defined by sources other than property management officials. Government agencies, unions, pension trust funds, credit unions, banks, and employees themselves often have input into how payroll information is stored and reported.

A payroll module must be flexible enough to allow a property to define its own pay period (daily, weekly, biweekly, or monthly). Payroll modules generally:

- Maintain employee master file.
- Calculate gross and net pay for salaried and hourly employees.
- Generate paychecks.
- Produce payroll tax register and related reports.
- Prepare labor cost reports for use by management.

Employee Master File

An employee master file maintains payroll and personnel data on each employee. Data contained in this file may include:

- Employee number.
- Employee name.
- Address.
- E-mail address.
- Social Security number.
- Job classification code(s).
- Wage rate code(s).

- Withholdings.
- Deductions.
- Other required information.

This file must be kept secure and confidential as it contains data that is proprietary to each employee. Appropriate deductions and withholding amounts are subtracted from each employee's gross pay to arrive at net pay. **Withholdings** are for income and Social Security taxes. Since federal tax regulations frequently change and since state withholdings vary across the country, many payroll modules are designed so that the user can make the necessary programming adjustments or receive regularly scheduled software updates. **Deductions** are usually voluntary and may be a function of the types of benefits available from the employer. Exhibit 4 lists some of the subtractions made from the gross pay of hospitality industry employees.

Payroll Register File

In order to calculate gross and net pay for hourly employees, the payroll module relies on a **payroll register file** to access the number of hours each employee worked during the pay period and other data that can require special tax calculations, such as sick leave and bonus pay, tips, and expense reimbursements.

In most properties, an **automated time-clock system** records time in and time out for employees. When a time-clock system is interfaced to a host system, data may be automatically transferred to the payroll module. Clocking in and out can

Exhibit 4   Sample Payroll Withholdings and Deductions

TAXES

- Federal, state, and city withholding amounts for income taxes
- Federal Insurance Contribution Act tax (Social Security tax)
- State unemployment compensation (selected states)

OTHER

- Savings bonds
- Medical insurance
- Life insurance
- Retirement contribution
- Charitable contribution
- Capital stock purchase plan
- Savings plan, credit union
- Charge for meals
- Payroll advance
- Garnishment of wages
- Union dues

be accomplished by a physical time card punch, employee number data entry, touchscreen selection, or biometric entry (finger, hand, or eye scan). Exhibit 5 depicts a scanner that requires biometric entry.

The payroll module must be flexible enough to handle several pay categories per employee and several non-tax deductions (which may be required on either a fixed or a variable basis). Payroll modules typically provide override options with which management can adjust pay. The two major concerns with payroll monitoring are overtime and lost time. Overtime is a concern as it requires a premium rate of pay once a basic threshold is achieved. Lost time refers to non-productive time for which an employee is being paid. Both can be controlled through payroll applications.

Other Functions

A payroll module can also be programmed to print paychecks, paycheck registers, payroll detail registers, and deduction registers. This module generally maintains a government reporting file for quarter-to-date and year-to-date federal and state tax histories. Deduction reports can be produced with year-to-date computations. Exhibit 6 contains a sample payroll check register produced by a food and beverage back office accounting system. The check register summarizes payroll information for each employee.

Exhibit 5   Sample Biometric Entry System

Courtesy of Kronos Incorporated (www.kronos.com).

Exhibit 6 Sample Payroll Check Register

```
DATE 09-08                  PAYROLL CHECK REGISTER                    PAGE 1
                            01 - ABC RESTAURANT INC
- - - - - - - - - - - - - - - - - - - - - - - - - - - - - - - - - - - - - - - - -
                         EARNINGS                        DEDUCTIONS
Employee              Category    Hours      Amount    Category    Amount
- - - - - - - - - - - - - - - - - - - - - - - - - - - - - - - - - - - - - - - - -
10                    Salary       50.00     500.00    Federal      59.99
Jones, Henry                                            FICA         35.75
                                                        State        13.12
                                                        Meals        17.50
                                                        Add'n Fed'l  12.00
                                                        Insurance     5.00
Check Number      125
Hours Worked       50.00
** Gross Pay      500.00
**** Net Pay      356.64
- - - - - - - - - - - - - - - - - - - - - - - - - - - - - - - - - - - - - - - - -
20                    Tipped Wages 40.00      80.40    Federal      36.61
Williamson, Johnny    Overtime     10.00      50.30    FICA         26.04
                      Rptd Tips               233.50   State         6.50
                      Gross Rcpts             2918.75  Uniforms      4.00
                      Tip Credit               53.60   Meals        17.50
                                                        Add'n Fed'l   7.32
Check Number      126
Hours Worked       50.00
** Gross Pay      130.70
**** Net Pay       32.73
- - - - - - - - - - - - - - - - - - - - - - - - - - - - - - - - - - - - - - - - -
***** END OF COMPANY SUMMARY *****
01                    Salary       50.00     500.00    Federal      96.60
ABC RESTAURANT INC    Tipped Wages 40.00      80.40    FICA         61.79
                      Overtime     10.00      50.30    State        19.62
                      Rptd Tips               233.50   Uniforms      4.00
                      Gross Repts             2918.75  Meals        35.00
                      Tip Credit               53.60   Add'n Fed'l  19.32
                                                        Insurance     5.00
No of Checks        2
Hours Worked      100.00
** Gross Pay      630.70
**** Net Pay      389.37                                             - - - -
- - - - - - - - - - - - - - - - - - - - - - - - - - - - - - - - - - - - - - - - -
***** EMPLOYER TAXES *****
Matching FICA     (630.7   +        53.60)    *     7.15% =    48.93
FUI Requirements                     0.00     *     2.00% =     0.00
SUI Requirements                   130.70     *     2.00% =     2.61
                                                               2.61
- - - - - - - - - - - - - - - - - - - - - - - - - - - - - - - - - - - - - - - - -
***** STATE TAX TABLE TOTALS *****
                 GA

                19.62
```

Similar to the accounts payable module, a payroll module can accommodate direct-deposit (electronic transfer) payroll checks and voided payroll checks. The module reconciles outstanding payments with paychecks and transfers appearing on a payroll summary report. Generally, at the end of a check reconciliation routine, the payroll module generates an updated list of outstanding checks.

In addition to printing paychecks, payroll modules can calculate sick leave and vacation hours accrued (earned) by employees in one of several ways: accrual each pay period, accrual periodically (for example, on the first pay period of the month), or accrual yearly on the basis of the employee's anniversary date.

Aggregating hourly and salaried employees' payroll expenses will produce a **labor cost report**. This report can be generated by operating department or job classification for management review.

Inventory Module

An accounting system may rely on an inventory module for tracking products, valuing products, and replenishing products. Internal control is essential to efficient inventory monitoring. Inventory data can be stored in an **inventory master file**, which typically contains the following information:

- Product name
- Product description (brief)
- Product code number
- Storeroom location code
- Product purchase unit
- Purchase unit price
- Product issue unit
- Product group code
- Vendor identification number
- Order lead time
- Minimum-maximum stock levels
- Date of last purchase

With this data, an inventory module can address three of the most common inventory concerns: inventory status, inventory variance, and inventory valuation.

Inventory Status

Inventory status is an account of how much of each item is in storage. Inventory status may be determined by a physical inventory or a perpetual inventory, or both. With a **physical inventory system**, staff periodically count items in storage. With a **perpetual inventory system**, a back office inventory module maintains an **inventory status file** that keeps a running balance of the quantity of issued/stored items. In general, this module carries over the ending inventory of the prior period as the beginning inventory of the current period, adds all newly purchased items as they enter storage areas, and subtracts all quantities issued from storage to other areas. Exhibit 7 contains a sample inventory directory report presenting a snapshot of stored items detailed in relation to purchase units, storage ("pack") units, and recipe units. Sorting options of the inventory module make it easy for managers to retrieve the precise information needed. When management uses a perpetual inventory system, a physical inventory is still taken at the end of each accounting period to verify the accuracy of inventory balances tracked by the perpetual inventory method.

Inventory modules may accommodate interfaces from handheld wireless mobile devices that can be used to significantly accelerate the process of taking physical inventory. These devices can also be used to monitor deliveries, create requisitions and transfers, and build purchase orders. In addition, some inventory modules can track product movement by separate inventory locations and print inventory count sheets that match the layout of each location. This feature will help speed up the process of taking a physical inventory.

The term **inventory variance** refers to differences between a physical count of an item and the balance maintained by the perpetual inventory system. Significant variances may indicate control problems requiring investigation and correction. Inventory modules may generate a variety of variance reports. The report shown in Exhibit 8 alerts managers to the difference between amounts of inventory

Exhibit 7   Sample Inventory Directory Report

Date: 8/19/200X
Time: 10:14 AM

Sorted by: Alpha

Inventory Directory
Wawa
Unit: SAMP

Item Name	PURCHASE Cost Desc	Last Priced	PACK Cost Desc	Size	Packs/ Purch.	RECIPE UNITS Cost Unit	# Per Pack	Shrink (%)
Almonds, Diced	$92.58 CASE	1/18/2002	$15.43 #10CAN	#10CAN	6.00	$0.24 OZ	64.00	0.00
Avocado	$68.00 CASE	1/18/2001	$2.43 EA	1 EA	28.00	$0.27 slice	9.00	25.00
Banana\Fresh	$0.61 LB	1/18/2002	$0.61 LB	LB	1.00	$0.24 EA	2.50	0.00
						$0.28 CUP	2.18	0.00
BBQ Sauce - Bull's Eye	$49.97 CASE		$12.49 GAL	GAL	4.00	$0.00	0.00	0.00
Bread-Burger Bun 4 1/2 s.s	$1.39 PACKAG	1/18/2001	$1.39 PACKAGE	PACKA	1.00	$0.17 PIECE	8.00	0.00
Bread-Rye Bread	$2.30 LOAF	1/18/2001	$2.30 LOAF	LOAF	1.00	$0.09 SLICE	27.00	0.00
Bread-White Bread 5x5	$1.91 LOAF	1/18/2002	$1.91 LOAF	LOAF	1.00	$0.09 SLICE	22.00	0.00
Breaded Chicken	$32.50 CASE	1/18/2002	$3.25 LB	LB	10.00	$0.81 PIECE	4.00	0.00
Cheese\Swiss	$2.96 LB		$2.96 LB	LB	1.00	$0.12 SLICE	25.00	0.00
Chocolate Syrup	$42.09 CASE		$7.02 CAN	CAN	6.00	$0.06 OZ	108.00	0.00
						$0.52 CUP	13.50	0.00
Coca-Cola	$7.04 CASE	1/18/2002	$0.29 BOTTLE	20 FLOZ	24.00	$0.00	0.00	0.00
Diet Coke	$6.84 CASE	1/18/2002	$0.28 BOTTLE	20 OZ	24.00	$0.00	0.00	0.00
French Fries	$18.67 CASE	1/18/2001	$3.11 BAG	4.5 LB	6.00	$0.00	0.00	0.00
Ham	$1.66 LB	1/18/2002	$1.66 LB	LB	1.00	$0.00	0.00	0.00

Courtesy of CostGuard (www.costguard.com).

Exhibit 8   Sample Inventory Variance Report

Date: 9/21/200X				Inventory Variance Alert Report								Page: 1
Time: 4:32 PM				Your Company Name Here								
From 1/1/200X to 12/31/200X (# of days: 365)				Unt: SAMP								
Details: Yes											Total Sales: $2651.85	
Range: Top 10 Items			Item		Actual Usage			Ideal Usage			Variance			Last	% of
Item Name		Unt	$	Unt	$	FC %	Units	$	FC %	Units	$	Counted	Sales
Whipped Topping	S GAL	38.95	6.0	233.70	8.8	0.3	9.99	0.4	5.7	223.72	01/21/02	8.4
Avocado	CASE	68.00	2.0	138.00	5.1	0.5	30.78	1.2	1.5	105.24	01/21/02	4.0
Oleo Blend Margarine	LB	1.08	70.0	75.80	2.9	2.4	2.57	0.1	67.6	73.03	01/21/02	2.8
Breaded Chicken	CASE	32.50	4.8	158.00	5.9	2.7	88.94	3.3	2.1	69.06	01/21/02	2.6
Lettuce Iceberg	CASE	24.00	2.0	54.00	2.0	0.2	5.20	0.2	2.0	48.77	01/21/02	1.8
Ice Cream Sherbet	TUB	12.78	5.0	67.41	2.5	1.7	21.36	0.8	3.3	46.05	01/21/02	1.7
French Fries	CASE	18.67	7.0	126.89	4.8	4.7	87.90	3.3	2.3	38.99	01/21/02	1.5
Strawberry Topping	CASE	42.95	1.0	40.89	1.5	0.2	6.87	0.3	0.8	34.20	01/21/02	1.3
Almonds, Diced	CASE	92.58	0.3	23.15	0.9	0.0	2.47	0.1	0.2	20.87	01/21/02	0.8
*** Grand Total			98.3	913.82	34.5	12.5	253.89	9.8	85.8	659.74		24.9

Courtesy of CostGuard (www.costguard.com).

that should have been used and what was actually used for a given time period. This enables managers to identify problem areas and take appropriate corrective actions.

Inventory Valuation

The term **inventory valuation** refers to the value of items in inventory. An **inventory valuation file** is used to determine the cost of goods sold and/or the replacement cost of items listed in the inventory master file. Exhibit 9 presents a sample screen from an inventory module that indicates the number of items in inventory expressed in purchase units and extends the inventory value of each item through a multiplication by purchase cost.

Since methods of inventory valuation differ, management must be careful to specify the format to be followed.

An inventory valuation file tracks the value of items in inventory by one of four generally accepted methods of inventory valuation:

- First in, first out (FIFO)
- Last in, first out (LIFO)
- Actual cost
- Weighted average cost

When a **first in, first out (FIFO)** method of inventory valuation is used, the products in storage areas are valued at the level of the most recently purchased items in storage. (In other words, the costs "used" first—those assigned to issues and used as cost of goods sold—are those that have been in inventory the longest, leaving the more recent costs still in inventory.) With a **last in, first out (LIFO)** method, the inventory value is assumed to be represented by the cost of items that were placed in storage the earliest. Under the **actual cost** approach, each unit is marked with its actual cost when it enters inventory; the sum of these unit costs is the inventory value. The **weighted average** method values inventory by considering the quantity of products purchased at different unit costs. This method "weights" the costs to be averaged based on the quantity of products in storage at

Exhibit 9   Sample Inventory Module Screen

Sub	Item Name	Count Purch\Pack	Purch\Pack Units	Purch\Pack Cost	Extension $
	chocolate, unsweetened bak ba	2	CASE\brick	$90.12\$7.51	$180.24
	croutons	1	CASE\case	$9.00\$9.00	$9.00
	flour	1	BAG\lb	$4.10\$0.41	$4.10
	garlic, chopped in water	2	JAR\jar	$12.34\$12.34	$24.68
	macaroni, elbow	2	CASE\lb	$5.30\$0.53	$10.60
	noodle, fett	2	CASE\lb	$20.13\$2.01	$40.26
	noodle, spaghetti	2	CASE\lb	$22.56\$2.26	$45.12
	noodles, penne	2	CASE\lb	$20.76\$2.08	$41.52
	noodles, rotini	2	CASE\lb	$19.65\$1.97	$39.30
	oil, olive	3\2	CASE\gal	$42.57\$10.64	$149.00
	oil, vegetable	2	CASE\gal	$21.45\$5.36	$42.90
	olives, black, Canned	1	CASE\#10can	$16.23\$2.71	$16.23
	onion, yellow large	1	BAG\lb	$11.32\$0.23	$11.32
	oregano, dried	2	CONTAINER\co	$12.56\$12.56	$25.12
	pepper, ground	2	CONTAINER\co	$19.57\$19.57	$39.14
	pesto, jar	2	CASE\jar	$36.57\$3.05	$73.14
	salt, canister	2	case\CONTAINE	$9.35\$0.78	$1.56
	stock, chicken prepared	2	CASE\qt	$32.54\$2.71	$65.08
	sugar	2	BAG\lb	$6.34\$0.63	$12.68
	tomato paste	4	CASE\can	$28.76\$4.79	$115.04
	tomato, diced canned	4	CASE\can	$31.45\$5.24	$125.80
	vinegar, balsamic	2	CASE\gal	$34.29\$8.57	$68.58
	wine, white	3	CASE\l	$36.79\$3.07	$110.37

Count Information

Count Date 7/21/20XX   Counted By

Location storeroom   Verified By

Courtesy of CostGuard (www.costguard.com).

each cost. Note that, except for actual cost valuation, the method of valuation does not relate to the actual flow of items through storerooms. Instead, it refers to the financial value of inventory.

Special Food and Beverage Concerns

From the point of view of food and beverage managers, an inventory application is perhaps the most important part of a back office package. But inventory applications tend to be the least uniform of all food service software. Modules vary widely with respect to file capacity and design. The usefulness of inventory reports produced by the system depends on the details within file records and the aptness of the formulas used.

The creation of a food and beverage ingredient file and subsequent file updates (daily, weekly, monthly, etc.) can be overwhelming tasks for some food service operations. Also, if errors are made when initially entering data, all subsequent processing will be unreliable and system reports will be relatively worthless. In addition, applications that do not support integrated files can be cumbersome because users must re-input data from several files in order to execute an application.

Some inventory applications provide file space for more than one ingredient designation, such as item file code number, inventory sequence number, internal customer code, and so on. The ability to work with additional designations can increase the efficiency of the inventory control system, enabling a user to print ingredients on a physical inventory worksheet according to the order in which they appear on a storeroom shelf, for example.

Inventory is critical to a food service operation, because many POS systems cannot track an item as it passes through the control points of receiving, storing/ issuing, and production. The data maintained by the inventory files of a back office package must be specific to each of these control points, because most ingredients are purchased, stored, and used in different quantities. Food and beverage inventory applications should enable users to specify tables for converting and relating purchase units, issue units, and recipe units for individual inventory items. When conversion tables are not part of the application's design, data processing may have to be supplemented by cumbersome and time-consuming manual procedures.

Another concern is how usage is charted by the inventory application—by unit, by cost, or by both unit and cost. A system that charts items by unit might be able to report changes in stock levels, but might not provide financial data necessary for food costing. On the other hand, a system that charts items primarily by product cost may not facilitate spot-checks of items in storage. The most effective inventory applications are those that track both product unit and cost.

Management needs to understand how basic food service concepts are defined within an inventory application design. For example, is an inventory item considered "used" (for costing purposes) at the time it is received, when it is issued to the kitchen, or at the time it is sold? The time frame that suits management's needs should be the time frame built into the application's design.

Purchasing Module

Effective purchasing methods are extremely important because cost savings can directly affect bottom-line profitability. Since a significant percentage of sales income is spent on purchasing, it is critical that all procedures include effective controls. A back office purchasing module greatly enhances management's control over purchase ordering and receiving practices. The steady growth of electronic procurement (e-procurement) and online buying procedures reinforces the importance of purchase order processing.

Purchase Order File

Back office purchasing modules maintain a purchase order file that is typically organized by vendor account and purchase order number. The value of a purchasing module lies in its ability to generate purchase orders and internally update subsequent tracking files.

A purchasing module can generate purchase orders by accessing and analyzing minimum/maximum (sometimes referred to as *mini-max*) inventory data or par stock data. **Minimum/maximum inventory levels** help managers determine when products need to be purchased and how much of each product to order. For each purchase item, management sets a minimum quantity below which inventory levels should not fall and a maximum quantity above which inventory levels should not rise. The minimum level is the safety level—the number of purchase units that must always remain on hand. The maximum level is the largest number of purchase units permitted in storage. Using minimum/maximum inventory levels, data transferred from the inventory module to the purchasing module can be applied to generate purchase orders based on an order point established through usage rate and lead-time factors.

The usage rate is the number of purchase units used per order period. This is an important factor for determining when more purchase units need to be ordered. In addition to usage rates, managers must also determine a lead-time quantity for each purchase item. **Lead-time quantity** refers to the anticipated number of purchase units taken from inventory between the time an order is placed and the time it is delivered. Purchase units are counted in terms of normally sized shipping containers.

The order point is the number of purchase units in stock when an order is placed. The order point is reached when the number of purchase units in inventory equals the lead-time quantity plus the safety (minimum) level. If products are ordered at the order point, the quantity in inventory will be reduced to the safety (minimum) level by the time the ordered products are received. When the order arrives, the inventory levels for the product will be brought back to the maximum level.

An alternative to the mini-max approach is the par stock inventory method. In the par stock system, a maximum value (similar to the mini-max maximum) is established. This level is termed the par value. To determine a purchase quantity to replenish inventory, a physical inventory is conducted. For each item, the difference between what is on-hand (physical inventory) and the par level for the item is the order quantity. In other words, the quantity ordered brings the item to par level. The information contained in Exhibit 10 indicates the variables that managers can use when generating purchase orders.

Purchase orders can also be generated by a purchasing module that analyzes sales forecast data. This method assumes a zero-based inventory system (i.e., nothing in storage) for developing purchase orders. Rather than reference existing inventory levels, the purchasing module forecasts anticipated sales, projects needed inventory items, and automatically generates the necessary purchase orders.

Regardless of the method by which purchase orders are produced, purchasing modules typically provide override options allowing management to alter items

Exhibit 10   Generating Purchase Orders

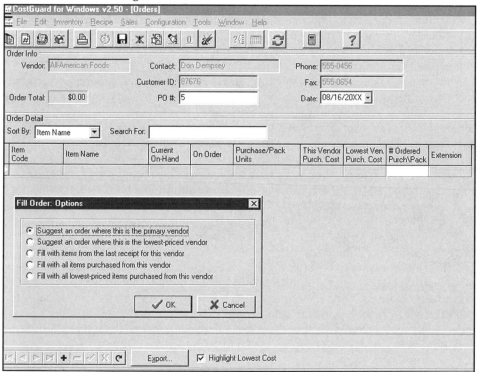

Courtesy of CostGuard (www.costguard.com).

and quantities before the final preparation and distribution of purchase orders. In addition to override capabilities, systems can add routine purchases (furnishings, amenities, supplies, food, and the like) to vendor orders by predetermined date. For example, the ordering of one case of bathroom cleaner each month can be automatically added to a purchase order, thereby eliminating the possibility of omission in ordering.

A growing trend among system vendors and food service purveyors is to install automated networking capabilities to enable rapid purchase order transfer to suppliers. The property must first develop its own purchase order file and then use communications software to transmit purchase orders to the vendor's system. The screen shot shown in Exhibit 11 presents a sample vendor's order guide that managers use to import bids and export orders.

E-Procurement

The biggest challenge facing purchasing managers is how to make the procurement process more efficient and cost effective. In the hospitality industry, minimal savings in procurement costs may result in a disproportionate increase in profitability.

Exhibit 11   Sample Vendor Order Guide

Item Name	Item Code	Case Cost	Pu De
ICE CREAM VAN CLASSIC	1921089	$15.53	CS
ICE CREAM CHOC	6412852	$13.63	CS
ICE CREAM STRAWBERRY	1921105	$16.46	CS
CHEESE MOZZARELLA LOAF PRT	2170215	$16.24	CS
OMELET EGG CHEESE	2232965	$30.54	CS
CREAM SOUR CUP NO FAT	2343333	$8.98	CS
ICE CREAM CUP VAN NFAT/NSA	2403582	$13.68	CS
ICE CREAM CUP CHOC NFAT/NSA	2403590	$13.68	CS
ICE CREAM CUP STRAW	2403608	$13.68	CS
CREAMER HALF & HALF CUP UHT	2444669	$8.19	CS

Courtesy of CostGuard (www.costguard.com).

E-procurement refers to the online purchasing of goods and services. Using a web browser, buyers are able to review product catalogs, identify vendor services, conduct product comparisons, place orders, and settle transactions. There are three approaches to online purchasing:

- Sell-side model
- Buy-side model
- E-marketplace model

The **sell-side model** involves placing an order directly with a supplier over the Internet. In this many-to-one environment (many buyers, one seller), the buyer generally accesses the supplier's website to research products and services and make purchases. The sell-side model applies to companies using web technologies to sell goods and services to other companies (a business-to-business relationship).

The opposite of the sell-side model is the buy-side model. In the **buy-side model**, there is one buyer and many sellers. Buyers purchase web-based services or buy products from approved vendors electronically. When using a buying service, buyers may have access to customized catalogs of goods and services offered by multiple suppliers. Once an order is placed, the buying service transmits the order to the supplier. The buyer and supplier then complete the financial transaction while the buying service provides fulfillment tracking support. Several major hotel chains and related purchasing groups use this model.

Companies can choose to operate their own electronic purchasing environment, but would need to assume the responsibility of managing content and technology. The buy-side model offers key opportunities to reduce procurement, production, and operating costs by streamlining the purchasing process. It focuses on quick and thorough searches to compare desired product offerings, minimize paperwork, and generate consistent product and vendor information, thereby reducing ordering errors.

The **e-marketplace model** represents a virtual shopping mall where many buyers and many sellers transact business. Such communities connect customers directly with suppliers to serve a targeted business segment. An e-marketplace typically appeals to a larger universe of buyers, often formed into purchasing groups that consolidate the volume from otherwise unrelated businesses interested in purchasing similar products and services. By bundling orders of like goods, costs are reduced.

The key benefit to buyers under each of the three approaches is the ability to view online catalogs containing detailed product descriptions, receive timely pricing information, complete order placement online 24/7, and reduce costs by eliminating ordering errors and unnecessary paperwork. The buy-side model and the e-marketplace model offer the added advantage of pooling many customers' orders to create buying economies and achieve volume discounts. An additional benefit of these two models is the added cost savings of fully automating the purchasing process from order placement through payment, as well as the ability to track and analyze purchases through all stages of the purchasing cycle.

E-procurement solutions have broad appeal because they span all hospitality industry sectors. E-procurement can deliver significant cost reductions through a variety of techniques, including automation of manual processes, improved contract compliance, and empowerment of purchasing staff.

Purchasing Reports

Properties dealing with multiple vendors may collect competitive bids and store them in a **bid specification file** containing the specific characteristics of purchased items. Vendors can then submit price quotations for products that meet or exceed stated specifications. Once bids are obtained, they can be automatically entered into the system, and the purchasing module can sort items to be purchased by vendor and bid price.

Back office purchasing modules may also simplify product delivery and receiving practices. Receiving practices in nonautomated properties can be tedious and time-consuming, as each item needs to be recorded and counted. Typically, a receiving clerk manually verifies shipments received by cross-checking each item against the original purchase order. The list of items received is used by the accounting office for price extensions. That is, the quoted price of each purchased item is multiplied by the quantities received to yield an approximate cost of goods purchased. Price extensions can later be used to scrutinize billings from vendors. Following price extension, the quantities received are entered on an inventory worksheet alongside the name of the inventory item.

Automated purchasing modules can streamline receiving practices and simplify inventory updating. A receiving clerk may verify shipments by cross-checking items received against a list of product names and ordered quantities. Or a property may institute a blind receiving practice by supplying the receiving clerk with a list of product names only and requiring the clerk to record quantities received.

Once receiving is completed, amounts can be entered into the purchasing module by accessing and updating the stored purchase order. When the purchase order quantities reflect received quantities, inventory files can be instantly updated with a release to inventory function. All items and quantities on the receiving list (the updated purchase order) are added to the former perpetual inventory quantities to reflect updated quantities on hand.

The purchase price variance report, designed to notify purchasers, accounting personnel, and others when the recent price of an item exceeds the level of variance previously established by management, is another popular purchasing report. This report enables management to react to price changes on a timely basis. With an integrated system, data from the purchasing module can be transferred to the accounts payable module so that a projected cash requirements report can be generated.

Financial Reporting Module

The financial reporting module, also called a general ledger module, maintains account balances and is used to prepare trial balances, financial statements, and a variety of reports for management. In order to assist accounting personnel in the preparation of statements and reports, the financial reporting module must have access to account balances maintained by other system modules. When the financial reporting module has limited access to data maintained by external modules or when the module serves as a stand-alone general ledger system, data may be entered directly into the module's files. Most modules can generate reports relating to individual operating departments, support centers, divisions, or entire properties (for multi-unit corporations).

Many financial reporting modules can be adapted to the needs and requirements of individual hospitality properties. Flexible codes, screen designs, and report formats allow properties to customize applications. Management may design the format of the property's financial statements by controlling headings, spacing, indentation, subtitles, underlining, and other formatting features.

Chart of Accounts

An industry-accepted uniform system of accounts provides a logical approach to back office design because it guides accounting personnel in the preparation and presentation of financial statements by standardizing formats and account classifications. This standardization permits users of financial statements to compare the financial position and operational performance of a particular hospitality property to similar types of properties in the industry. For new businesses entering the hospitality industry, a uniform system of accounts serves as a turnkey accounting system that can be quickly adapted to meet the needs of the business.

A **chart of accounts** lists general ledger accounts by type of account, including account number and account title. The account names found in the **chart of accounts file** are listed in a sequence that parallels the order of their appearance on the financial statements and general ledger. The **general ledger** is the principal accounting ledger containing all of the balance sheet and income statement accounts.

A chart of accounts shows no account balances. The main purpose of a chart of accounts is to serve as a "table of contents" to guide bookkeepers as they enter the results of business transactions in accounting records. Bookkeepers are generally not allowed to use an account unless it specifically appears on the company's chart of accounts.

For hospitality businesses, the chart of accounts arranges accounts according to their major classification. Accounts are classified as either asset, liability, equity, revenue, or expense accounts. Asset, liability, and equity accounts form the basis for preparation of a balance sheet. Revenue and expense accounts form the basis for preparation of the income statement. The typical sequence of major account classifications appearing on a chart of accounts is:

1. Asset accounts

2. Liability accounts

3. Equity accounts

4. Revenue accounts

5. Expense accounts

Automation in the input (recording) phase requires that each account be assigned an account number. The account number is usually designed so that the first digit(s) represents one of the major account classifications (asset, liability, equity, revenue, or expense accounts). The digits that follow normally define the individual account's sequential relationship within that classification.

For example, assume that management has designed a three-digit account numbering system. Since the first major account classification is assets, the number 1 might be assigned as the first digit for all asset account numbers. The number series of 1xx will therefore include all asset accounts. Since cash is typically the first account to appear within the sequence of accounts classified as asset accounts, the three-digit account number assigned to the cash account will be 101. Since liabilities are the second major account classification, the number 2 can be assigned as the first digit for all liability accounts. Thus, the number series 2xx includes all liability accounts.

A hospitality business can use any account numbering system that meets its particular requirements. Some general ledger systems accommodate up to twelve-character account numbers and maintain an array of accounts for multiple corporate properties. The type of accounts and the design of numbering systems can vary from business to business, depending on the company's size and the detail of management information desired.

Trial Balance File

A **trial balance file** maintains a list of accounts with debit and credit balances. For a hotel property management system, the daily system update is responsible for transferring data from front office and back office modules to the general ledger, ensuring that the balances held in the financial reporting module are current. A **trial balance** is prepared to test the equality of these balances (debits and credits). In a nonautomated back office system, the trial balance is prepared as follows:

1. Determine the balance of each account in the ledger.
2. List the accounts and show debit balances in one column and credit balances in a separate column.
3. Add the debit balances.
4. Add the credit balances.
5. Compare the totals of the debit and credit balances.

When the total of debit balance accounts equals the total of credit balance accounts, the trial balance is in balance. If debits and credits do not balance, the bookkeeper has made errors in recording the transactions, in determining the balances of each account, or in preparing the trial balance. It is important to note that a balanced trial balance is not proof that all transactions have been properly recorded. It merely indicates that debits equal credits.

Preparing a trial balance in a nonautomated system can be an error-prone and time-consuming task. In an automated system, the general ledger function of the financial reporting module can generate an accurate trial balance upon demand.

The general ledger function of the financial reporting module also simplifies the closing process at the end of an accounting period. The module audits accounting files for any out-of-balance conditions. It also searches for invoices or journals that are not fully posted to the general ledger and produces a report disclosing all errors.

Some modules allow the current period to remain open while postings are made to future periods. When the current period closes, the module computes opening balances for the next accounting period. Once a period is closed, errors are generally corrected with journal entries made to the current period. Some modules, however, are able to reopen previously closed periods for correcting entries.

Financial Statements

A back office financial reporting module can access relevant data from front office and back office modules and generate balance sheets and income statements. Most modules can also produce statements of cash flows.

The **balance sheet** provides important information on the financial position of a hospitality business by showing its assets, liabilities, and equity on a particular date. Simply stated, assets represent anything a business owns that has commercial or exchange value, liabilities represent the claims of outsiders (such as creditors) to assets, and owners' equity represents the claims of owners to assets. On a balance sheet, the total assets must balance with the combined totals of liabilities and equities. In essence, the format of the balance sheet reflects the fundamental accounting equation:

$$\text{Assets} = \text{Liabilities} + \text{Equity}$$

Financial reporting modules should be able to produce balance sheets (and other financial statements) that compare current figures with those of prior periods. In addition, modules should be able to generate comparative and common-size balance sheets for managerial review.

Comparative balance sheets present two sets of figures for each balance sheet line item. One set of figures is from the current balance sheet and the other set is from the balance sheet of a prior period. Changes in amounts of line items from one period to the next are reported in both absolute and relative terms. Absolute changes show the change in dollars between two periods, while relative changes (also referred to as percentage changes) are calculated by dividing the absolute change by the amount shown for the previous period. Significant changes are brought to management's attention.

Common-size balance sheets also present two sets of figures for each balance sheet line item, one set from the current balance sheet and the other set from a prior balance sheet. All amounts are reduced to percentages of an account classification. That is, the total assets on each balance sheet are set at 100 percent, and each asset category is reported as a percentage of total assets. This same procedure is followed for the total liabilities and owners' equity sections. The percentages found on the two balance sheets are then compared and significant changes are brought to management's attention.

The **income statement** (also called the profit and loss statement) provides important financial information about the results of operations for a given period of time. The time period may be as short as one month and does not usually exceed one business year. The business year is called the **fiscal year**. Since this statement reveals the bottom line (net income for a given period of time), it should be one of the most important financial statements managers use to evaluate the success of operations. It may also be an important measure of managerial effectiveness and efficiency. Most financial reporting modules are able to generate both comparative and common-size income statements. Exhibit 12 shows a comparative income statement produced by a restaurant back office accounting system.

Financial reporting modules also produce condensed income statements comparing results of the current month with previous months, the same month of previous years, and budgeted amounts. These reports may also compare year-to-date results with results of previous years.

Some financial reporting modules have extensive graphics capabilities. Although graphs do not usually provide detail, managers can track recent performance trends more easily by reviewing results through line drawings.

Exhibit 12 Sample Comparative Income Statement

Comparative Income and Expense

Description	Curr Month This Year	% Of Total	Curr Month Last Year	% Of Total	Y-T-D This Year	% Of Total	Y-T-D Last Year	% Of Total
REVENUE								
Food	186,682.00	68.0	174,645.00	68.9	2,683,148.19	69.9	2,267,895.00	70.1
Beverage	86,500.00	31.5	77,880.00	30.7	1,145,800.00	29.8	959,245.00	29.7
Miscellaneous Income	1,200.00	.4	800.00	.3	7,500.00	.2	7,500.00	.2
TOTAL REVENUE	274,382.00	100.0	253,325.00	100.0	3,839,348.19	100.00	3,234,640.00	100.0
COST OF SALES								
Food	76,410.00	27.9	74,100.00	29.3	1,087,651.63	28.3	947,650.00	29.3
Beverage	750.00	.3	1,156.00	.5	11,486.00	.3	9,432.00	.3
Cost of Well Brands	7,273.00	2.7	7,191.00	2.8	95,549.00	2.5	87,750.00	2.7
Cost of Call Level 1	5,326.00	1.9	4,980.00	2.0	69,238.00	1.8	58,145.00	1.8
Cost of Call Level 2	4,547.00	1.7	4,750.00	1.9	64,111.00	1.7	58,250.00	1.8
Cost of House Wines	1,234.00	.5	679.00	.3	12,510.00	.3	10,555.00	.3
Cost of Fine Wines	554.00	.2	1,915.00	.8	12,756.00	.3	10,775.00	.3
Cost of Brandy & Liqueurs	925.00	.3	1,470.00	.6	17,523.00	.5	14,225.00	.4
Cost of Bar Garnishes	231.00	.1	182.00	.1	2,772.00	.1	2,327.00	.1
Cost of Bar Mixes	205.00	.1	224.00	.1	2,460.00	.1	2,239.00	.1
TOTAL COST OF SALES	97,455.00	35.5	96,647.00	38.2	1,376,056.63	35.8	1,201,348.00	37.1
GROSS PROFIT	176,927.00	64.5	156,678.00	61.9	2,463,291.56	64.2	2,033,292.00	62.9
OTHER INCOME								
Vending Machines	2,406.00	.9	2,145.00	.9	24,812.00	.7	22,600.00	.7
TOTAL OTHER INCOME	2,406.00	.9	2,145.00	.9	24,812.00	.7	22,600.00	.7
TOTAL INCOME	179,333.00	65.4	158,823.00	62.7	2,488,103.00	64.8	2,055,892.00	63.6
CONTROLLABLE EXPENSES								
Salaries and Wages	75,320.00	27.5	65,900.00	26.0	960,640.00	25.0	810,650.00	25.1
Employee Benefits	14,125.00	5.2	12,800.00	5.1	197,050.00	5.1	166,550.00	5.2
Direct Operating ExpeNses	17,560.00	6.4	16,995.00	6.7	258,720.00	6.7	237,220.00	7.3
Music and Entertainment	2,410.00	.9	2,240.00	.9	34,020.00	.9	28,400.00	.9
Marketing	5,130.00	1.9	4,750.00	1.9	73,960.00	1.9	62,000.00	1.9
Energy and Utility Serv's	5,600.00	2.0	5,050.00	2.0	80,200.00	2.1	67,800.00	2.1
Administrative/General	18,000.00	6.6	18,400.00	7.3	222,800.00	5.8	188,900.00	5.8
Repairs and Maintenance	4,200.00	1.5	4,710.00	1.9	58,800.00	1.5	50,100.00	1.6
TOTAL CONTROLLABLE EXPENSES	142,345.00	51.9	130,845.00	51.7	1,886,190.00	49.1	1,611,620.00	49.8
INCOME BEFORE RENT & OTHER OCCUP. COSTS	36,988.00	13.5	27,978.00	11.0	601,913.56	15.7	444,272.00	13.7
RENT & OTHER OCCUP. COSTS								
Rent And Other Occ. Costs	11,330.00	4.1	10,000.00	4.0	132,260.00	3.4	115,900.00	3.6
INCOME BEFORE Interest	25,658.00	9.4	17,978.00	7.1	469,653.56	12.2	328,372.00	10.2
INTEREST	1,850.00	.7	2,000.00	.8	25,900.00	.7	22,000.00	.7
Depreciation	4,733.00	1.7	5,000.00	2.0	66,266.00	1.7	56,950.00	1.8
TOTAL RENT & OTHER OCCUP. COSTS	17,913.00	6.5	17,000.00	6.7	224,426.00	5.9	194,850.00	6.0
INCOME BEFORE PROVISION FOR INC. TAXES	19,075.00	7.0	10,978.00	4.3	377,487.56	9.8	249,422.00	7.7
PROVISION FOR INC. TAXES								
Income Taxes	6,625.00	2.4	5,625.00	2.2	92,750.00	2.4	78,575.00	2.4
TOTAL PROVISION FOR INC. TAXES	6,625.00	2.4	5,625.00	2.2	92,750.00	2.4	78,575.00	2.4
NET INCOME	12,450.00	4.5	5,353.00	2.1	284,737.56	7.4	170,847.00	5.3

Departmental expenses can be shown using pie charts, departmental revenue using bar charts, and so on. Charts tend to be easy to understand, and they can be used to demonstrate operational results more successfully than the traditional financial statements, which may at times appear as a confusing list of numbers.

Ratio Analysis

Hospitality industry financial statements contain a lot of information. A thorough analysis of this information may require more than simply reading the reported facts and figures. Users of financial statements need to be able to interpret the contents of these documents so that critical aspects of the property's financial situation do not go unnoticed. Interpretation is often accomplished through **ratio analysis**. A **ratio** gives mathematical expression to a relationship between two figures. It is calculated by dividing one figure by the other.

Ratio results are meaningful only when compared against useful criteria. Useful criteria against which to compare the results of ratio analysis normally include:

- Corresponding ratios calculated for a prior period.

- Corresponding ratios of other properties.

- Industry averages.

- Planned ratio goals.

Ratio analysis can be extremely useful to owners, creditors, and managers in evaluating the financial condition and operation of a hotel. Users of ratio analysis must be careful when comparing two different properties because the accounting procedures of one may differ from those of another. Moreover, ratios are only indicators; they do not resolve problems or reveal what problems may exist. At best, ratios that vary significantly from past periods, budgeted standards, or industry averages indicate a reason for investigation. When problems appear to exist, considerably more analysis and investigation are necessary to determine appropriate corrective action.

Assuming that necessary financial data are stored, ratio statistics can be generated almost at will. Many ratios need not be calculated on a daily basis. In fact, if their analysis is based on too short a period of time, they may fail to provide meaningful information. It is important that management officials determine which ratios are to be calculated and how often. If all ratios were calculated daily, there could be a risk of information overload. In other words, so many statistics would be generated that the manager would not have the time—or the inclination—to search for critical information.

Operating ratios may be an exception to this rule. They can be very useful when prepared on a frequent basis. For example, when a hotel's night audit is automated, many operating ratio computations (such as average daily rate, occupancy percentage, double occupancy percentage, and others) are a by-product of the system update routine. These statistics can then be compared against budgeted goals to present management with a timely (and convenient) measure of operational success.

Enterprise Reporting

Enterprise information systems are designed for hospitality corporations and management companies that need to consolidate multi-unit data into useful reports for corporate staff as well as for managers at the unit level. Some of these systems resemble data warehouses since they have extremely large databases and are designed to support decision-making within organizations. The database is structured to conduct a variety of analyses, including elaborate queries on large amounts of data that can require extensive searching.

Enterprise information systems enable corporate managers to monitor transactions and affect unit-level operations such as:

- Sorting data from units grouped by regions, price points, or other variables.

- Implementing pricing changes for a single unit, the entire company, or for a select group of business units.

- Implementing accounting changes (such as a new tax table) for a single unit, the entire company, or for a select group of business units.

With data warehouses, data are typically historical and static and may also contain numerous summaries. Some application software features a quick index summary referred to as a dashboard. The dashboard is designed to present management with sufficient detail to formulate an opinion on the effectiveness of business operations. With enterprise reporting via an Internet connection, real-time reporting enables management to monitor sales, promotions, labor costs, etc., from a web browser anytime, anywhere. User names and passwords control the degree of online access granted to various management levels.

Labor Scheduling Applications

The old adage "time is money" is proven daily in the hospitality business. For an industry facing a shrinking, more expensive labor force, labor scheduling software applications have become popular. Traditionally a tedious and error-riddled manual process, the construction of shift schedules can be automated. Basically, labor management software deals with containing payroll costs, reducing nonproductive time, restricting overtime, and ensuring shift coverage.

Automated labor management systems provide assistance in forecasting, scheduling, reporting, analyzing, and controlling time worked and use of time worked. Effective labor scheduling can be accomplished through PC-based applications, web-based applications, and POS-integrated applications. Each of these approaches can streamline labor-related processes while enhancing workforce controls. Managers are often surprised to discover the bottom-line impact of cost containment through improved labor scheduling.

Cost Containment. While labor cost containment can be accomplished in a variety of ways, most software applications focus attention on lost time and overtime as major strategies for labor savings. Reducing or eliminating lost time, which results from unauthorized early time-in and/or late time-out entries, can represent meaningful savings. Consider the scenario in which a server scheduled to begin work at

9 A.M. clocks in at 8:45 A.M. but doesn't report to the dining room to work until 9 A.M. The dining room supervisor will consider the worker reliable and on time, unaware he clocked in fifteen minutes early. The payroll office, unaware that the worker was not scheduled to report until 9 A.M., will inadvertently pay for an extra fifteen minutes of nonproductive time. This additional time wasn't forecasted by management and therefore results in overspending within the labor budget. Similarly, late clock-outs can represent unexpected additional labor costs and lead to unscheduled higher-priced overtime. Note that a fifteen-minute savings for ten employees per day, for a 360-day year, at an hourly rate of $8.00, equals $7,200 annually.

Controlling Lost Time. In a labor management system, early sign-ins and late sign-outs are tightly controlled. Even though some labor scheduling systems allow employees to clock in before their scheduled start time, the system will not authorize wages until individually assigned scheduled times occur. In the previous scenario, for example, the server may have clocked in fifteen minutes early, but the system will not authorize a payroll transaction to begin until the scheduled time of 9 A.M. arrives. Similarly, staff can clock out late but will not be paid beyond the limit of the scheduled shift termination time. For an employee to be paid outside the parameters of a stored labor schedule, there must be managerial/supervisory authorization. Hence, exceptions to predetermined scheduled times, arising from unforeseen circumstances, can be adjusted through the system's override procedure.

Overtime Monitoring. As many practitioners can attest, controlling overtime can be especially critical to labor cost containment. While management often finds the unpredictability of business does not always allow for the elimination of overtime, labor management software does provide a means to restrict overtime to pre-approved overtime. In other words, with an automated process, there are few, if any, unanticipated overtime expenditures. Most operators cite the monitoring of overtime as a key factor in the successful implementation of a labor scheduling system. The system allows staff to earn overtime only if it occurs in a controlled environment. In essence, management is notified as an employee's hours worked approach the overtime threshold. The system then only permits overtime to occur with managerial approval.

Shift Coverage. In a labor scheduling software application, shift coverage is accomplished through a series of forecasting, scheduling, and analysis functions. Labor forecasts are typically constructed based on historical data and intuitive guesswork. Some labor management systems offer operators the option of system-developed schedules or provide an accessible file for user determination. An analysis of forecast information and previous schedules can help reveal weak or limited coverage periods requiring reconsideration. It is for this reason that software packages give users the ability to fine-tune or modify preliminary system-generated schedules. In larger firms, departmental managers may generate and refine departmental schedules and then submit them to the payroll office for official entry into the system. From there, schedule data can be downloaded to the system time clocks for monitoring and control. Finalized schedules are used to establish authorized payroll expenditures through sign-ins and sign-outs.

Payroll Processing. Since payroll practices vary widely, a labor management system may need to be interfaced to a payroll accounting module to produce a finalized payroll ledger and/or payroll checks. Labor scheduling software is primarily limited to time and attendance accounting and the computation of gross pay. Payroll processing and paycheck generation can be accomplished via an add-on program or through exporting to a specialty application package. The two primary objectives of automated labor management systems are cost containment and improved shift coverage.

Authentication Media. Newer time clocking systems allow operators to select among several time recording media: traditional paper time cards, magnetic stripe plastic cards, electronic keypad, and biometric recordation. Traditional time card systems rely upon punches to record time in/out data. Heavy paper time cards require a storage rack, effective printing capability, and an accurate time stamp. Clocks featuring automatic card alignment minimize over-punching and incorrect recordation. Improved paper card clocks contain data-handling techniques that can recognize magnetic stripe and bar code information that may be placed on the card.

Plastic magnetic (mag) cards, which can also serve as employee identification badges, provide enhanced sign-in and sign-out functions but may not provide employees with a printed copy of time in attendance. Badge-based data collection requires the insertion of a recognizable input format (magnetic stripe or bar code) for processing. Magnetic stripe cards are capable of storing an employee's identification number and scheduled shift number.

One concern with magnetic stripe cards is that, unlike a time card format, there may be no provision for providing verifiable documentation for employees. Such a device places the burden of proof on the employee to prove which work shifts he or she worked.

Card-less and badge-less systems require employees to enter their employee number through a keypad, similar to an ATM. These systems rely upon keypad entry to initiate system functions. Since employees may desire a printed copy of time and attendance data to ensure proper payroll processing, some keypad-based systems provide output through an attached printer. A main advantage of keypad entry systems is eliminating card storage racks and not needing to create and maintain magnetic stripe cards.

A file server or desktop computer can be connected to the time clock to poll data collected by the clock. Data polling enables exportation of captured data to other application software and other systems. For example, detailed labor analysis software packages are available from numerous payroll system vendors. Operators that rely on off-premises payroll service bureaus may use communication equipment capable of directly relaying stored data to remote computing sites.

While not all labor management systems operate identically, the following six functions are representative of system capabilities:

1. Labor requirement forecasting

2. Employee scheduling

3. Time and attendance recordation

4. Overtime/lost time monitoring

5. Labor cost analysis

6. Payroll processing

Labor requirement forecasts are developed from performance parameters such as sales or budgetary information. Employee scheduling is designed to ensure shift coverage based on employee availability, skill inventory, and labor requirement forecasts. It is for this reason that a majority of labor management systems are considered schedule-driven systems.

Time and attendance data can be recorded by time card, plastic badge, or keypad entry. Systems aim to classify captured time as regular time, overtime, or special time (with each of these categories being associated with different pay rates and scheduling considerations). This enables the system to separate individual events for labor costing by job. For example, a property catering a private party would be able to identify each employee assigned to the function and apply the cost of time worked to the specific event. This allows labor cost reporting by event, department, and employee. This is an inherent strength of a labor management system.

Daily labor reports, labor distribution reports, budget to actual reports, projected overtime reports, and the like combine to provide a base of financial information for managerial consideration. Although labor management systems typically do not generate payroll registers and paychecks, they do perform important calculations that simplify eventual completion of the payroll cycle. Labor management systems that interface with external systems can save additional time while providing a mechanism for enhanced labor analysis.

A labor management package may also possess a sales and tip data collection function, often essential to effective human resources management. Employees who are required to track sales and/or tips can enter this data at clock-out and the data will be tracked for them. Similarly, management can aggregate revenue data for determination of tip pooling shares and government reporting. Such systems can generate sales performance reports, tip allocation reports, detailed distribution reports, and related reports.

System Reports. There are a variety of reports available through a labor management system. Representative reports include:

- *Work Schedules*—by department, employee, date, shift, hour, function, and other criteria. Schedules are built upon worker profile, shift coverage needs, and worker availability data.

- *Overtime Reports*—containing the names of employees approaching or incurring overtime pay.

- *Tardy/Absent Report*—tracking attendance abuse and lateness.

- *Projected Hours Report*—a projection of scheduled hours and expenditures that is comparable to actual data after the fact.

- *Availability Report*—a summary of work shift availability and skill index data for construction of shift coverage plans.

- *Labor Distribution Report*—a breakdown of labor hours by employee, unit, department, function, or other criteria. Reports typically summarize regular, overtime, and special time totals and assist in labor allocation decisions.

PC-Based Applications. PC-based labor management applications may require two hardware components: a time-capture device (i.e., time clock) and a desktop computer. An automated time-capture device may be intelligent and/or programmable. Most clock devices store critical data internally and operate independently (off-line) of the file server. The main purpose of a time clock is to capture punch (sign-in and sign-out) data for eventual transmission to a remote payroll accounting program. Time clocks typically contain microprocessors with plug compatibility for connecting monitors, keyboards, printers, and communication equipment. In essence, some time clock devices have evolved into stand-alone computing units.

Web-Based Applications. There are an increasing number of software products being marketed as web-based (or web-hosted) workforce management solutions. Most application packages offer enhanced forecasting capabilities, scheduling functionality, and more flexible interfaces for extensive report generation. A web-based application tends to be structured as a closed-loop system for managing a single site labor force (including forecasting, scheduling, time and attendance, and real-time reporting). In addition, a graphical snapshot capability with actionable alerts and consolidated reports can be configured as an essential system component.

POS-Integrated Applications. Automated work schedules often require modification as sales volumes and availability of workers change. In a seasonal business, for example, perhaps only one-third of the peak workforce may be retained. Developing a labor scheduling process designed for a small workforce becomes problematic when expansion to peak time staffing is needed. The dynamic nature of seasonal business fluctuations can lead to less than ideal system utilization, as the data required during peak business volumes can bring the system to a halt. As workers' schedules change and business needs vary, a labor management system may struggle to keep pace. It is for these reasons that some integrated applications have begun to appear in the marketplace.

Consider sophisticated labor scheduling software packages that rely upon POS data to populate workforce forecasting and scheduling modules. The POS data is used to determine the jobs, tasks, and workload necessary to optimally operate the hospitality enterprise. By dynamically matching worker profiles, skill sets, and availability data to an internally generated labor forecast, the system is able to construct shift coverage (by worker and department) within budgetary constraints.

 **Key Terms** ———————————————————————————————————

Accounts Receivable Module

accounts aging file—Contains accounts receivable data that can be formatted into a variety of aging reports that segment accounts in the file according to the date the charge originated.

accounts receivable—Obligations owed an organization from sales made on credit.

aging of accounts receivable schedule—Segments each account in the accounts aging file according to the date the charge originated.

city ledger—A subsidiary ledger listing accounts receivable balances of guests who have checked out, and other receivables as well.

city ledger file—Contains data from the front office guest accounting module, such as balances from guest folios, non-guest accounts, bill-to accounts, credit card billings, and others.

customer master file—Sets up billing information. Customer data maintained in this file includes: account code, name of guest or account, address, telephone number, contact person, type of account, credit limit, last payment date, last payment amount, and credit history.

Accounts Payable Module

accounts payable—Liabilities incurred for merchandise, equipment, or other goods and services that have been purchased on account.

accounts payable aging report—Contains several columns listing invoices by vendor number, vendor name, invoice number, and invoice date.

cash requirements report—Lists all invoices selected for payment and the corresponding cash requirement totals; prepared by vendor number, vendor name, due date, item, or group code and typically including vendor number, vendor name, invoice number, due date, balance due, and amount to be paid.

check reconciliation—Balancing the total of checks removed from the outstanding checks list with the total of cleared checks appearing on the bank statement.

check register—After the check writing routine, the accounts payable module prints a check register by check number. The check register also may be sorted by vendor or by invoice due date.

check register file—Monitors the calculation and printing of bank checks for payments of selected invoices.

invoice register file—Maintains a complete list of all invoices currently outstanding and payable.

monthly check register—Provides a hard copy audit trail of payments made to vendors. This report also identifies checks that have not yet been accounted for.

outstanding checks list—Details all checks that have been issued but remain outstanding; can be used to reconcile checks issued against canceled checks appearing on bank statements.

override options—Provide management with complete control over cash disbursements before engaging the automatic check writing feature of the accounts payable module.

payment discount date—The last day on which it is possible for a lodging operation to take advantage of a cash payment discount that may be offered by a specific vendor.

reconciliation audit report—Balances the total of checks removed from the outstanding checks list with the total of cleared checks appearing on the bank statement.

vendor activity report—Lists gross amount invoiced, discounts taken, number of invoices, and other vendor data.

vendor master file—Maintains records of all current vendors. Data contained in this file includes: vendor number, vendor name, contact name, address, telephone number, vendor payment priority, discount terms, discount account number, invoice description, payment date, and year-to-date purchases.

vendor status report—Presents summary accounts payable information.

Payroll Module

automated time-clock system—Records time in and time out for employees.

deductions—Subtractions from gross pay that are usually voluntary and depend on the types of benefits available from the employer.

labor cost report—Shows labor costs by department or job classifications.

payroll register file—Maintains the number of hours each employee works during a pay period and other data that may require special tax calculations, such as sick leave pay, bonus pay, tips, and expense reimbursements.

withholdings—Subtractions from gross pay for income and Social Security taxes.

Inventory Module

actual cost—A method of inventory valuation. Values inventory only in relation to actual costs of items stored. The value of stored products is, then, the value represented by the sum of individual unit costs.

first in, first out (FIFO)—A method of valuing inventory; the products in storage areas are valued at the level of the most recently purchased items to be placed in inventory.

inventory master file—Maintains basic inventory data, such as item name, item description (brief), inventory code number, storeroom location code, item purchase unit, purchase unit price, item issue unit, product group code, vendor identification number, order lead time, minimum-maximum stock levels, and date of last purchase.

inventory status—An account of how much of each item is in storage. Inventory status may be determined by a physical inventory or a perpetual inventory.

inventory status file—In a perpetual inventory system, keeps a running balance of the quantity of issued/stored items.

inventory valuation—The value of items in inventory.

inventory valuation file—Contains data for determining the cost of goods sold and the replacement cost of items listed in the inventory master file.

inventory variance—Differences between a physical count of an item and the balance maintained by the perpetual inventory system.

last in, first out (LIFO)—An inventory valuation method that assumes that the products that are most recently purchased are used first. The inventory value is assumed to be represented by the cost of items placed in storage the earliest.

perpetual inventory system—An inventory system that keeps records up-to-date by tracking all additions to and subtractions from stock.

physical inventory system—An inventory system in which property employees periodically observe and count items in storage.

weighted average—An inventory valuation method that considers the quantity of products purchased at different unit costs. This method "weights" the prices to be averaged based on the quantity of products in storage at each price.

Purchasing Module

bid specification file—Contains the specific characteristics of purchased items. Purveyors are asked to quote prices for products that meet or exceed stated specifications.

buy-side e-procurement model—A "one buyer, many sellers" approach. Buyers purchase web-based services or use self-supported systems to buy from approved vendors electronically.

e-marketplace e-procurement model—Represents a virtual shopping mall where many buyers and many sellers transact business. Such communities connect customers directly with suppliers to serve a broad array of business segments.

e-procurement—Purchasing goods and services over the Internet.

lead-time quantity—The anticipated number of purchase units withdrawn from inventory between the time an order is placed and the time it is delivered.

minimum/maximum inventory levels—Help managers determine when products need to be purchased and how much of each product to order. For each purchase item, management sets a minimum quantity below which inventory levels should not fall and a maximum quantity above which inventory levels should not rise.

sell-side e-procurement model—Involves placing an order directly with a supplier over the Internet. In this many-to-one environment (many buyers, one seller), the buyer generally accesses the supplier's own website to do research and make purchases.

Financial Reporting Module

balance sheet—Provides important information on the financial position of a hospitality business by showing its assets, liabilities, and equity on a particular date.

chart of accounts—Lists general ledger accounts by type of account including account number and account title.

chart of accounts file—Lists the names of accounts in a sequence that parallels the order of their appearance on the financial statements and general ledger.

common-size balance sheet—A special type of balance sheet that presents two sets of figures for each balance sheet line item, one from the current balance sheet and the other from the balance sheet of a previous period. All amounts are reduced to percentages of their account classification.

fiscal year—Twelve consecutive months that define a business year.

general ledger—The principal accounting ledger containing all of the balance sheet and statement of income accounts.

income statement—Also called the profit and loss statement, provides important financial information about the results of operations for a given period of time.

ratio—Gives mathematical expression to a significant relationship between two figures. It is calculated by dividing one figure by the other.

ratio analysis—Analysis of financial statements and operating results through the use of ratios.

trial balance—Tests the equality of debit and credit account balances.

trial balance file—Maintains a list of accounts with debit and credit balances.

Review Questions

1. What functions are performed by an accounts receivable module?

2. How can management use an aging of accounts receivable schedule?

3. What functions does an accounts payable module perform?

4. What override options provided by accounts payable modules may be useful to management?

5. What are some uses of the cash requirements report produced by an accounts payable module?

6. What functions are performed by a payroll module?

7. What are some of the characteristics of hospitality operations that complicate the design of a back office payroll module?

8. How can differences among purchase units, issue units, and standard recipe units complicate the design of a back office inventory module?

9. What are two basic ways by which a purchasing module may automatically generate purchase orders?

10. What functions does a financial reporting module perform?

Internet Sites

For more information, visit the following Internet sites. Remember that Internet addresses can change without notice. If the site is no longer there, you can use a search engine to look for additional sites.

Hospitality Accounting Organizations

Hospitality Financial and Technology
  Professionals (HFTP)
www.hftp.org

Hotel Property Management Systems with Accounting Applications

CMS Hospitality
www.cmshospitality.com

MICROS Systems, Inc.
www.micros.com

Food and Beverage Systems with Accounting Applications

Agilysys, Inc.
www.agilysys.com

iTradeNetwork.com
www.itradenetwork.com

Comtrex
www.comtrex.com

RMS-Touch, LLC
www.rmstouch.com

CostGuard
www.costguard.com

System Concepts, Inc.
www.foodtrak.com

Labor Scheduling Software

Advanced Tracker Technologies Inc.
www.advancedtracker.com

Loki Systems Inc.
www.lokisys.com

Amano USA Holdings, Inc.
www.amano.com

Radiant Systems, Inc.
www.radiantsystems.com

Automatic Data Processing, Inc.
www.adp.com

ScheduleSource, Inc.
www.schedulesource.com

Data Management, Inc.
www.timeclockplus.com

Timeco
www.timeco.com

Knowledge Touch Pte Ltd.
www.knowledgetouch.com

Chapter 10 Outline

Management Information System
    MIS Personnel
Electronic Data Processing
    Advantages of Electronic Data
        Processing
    Types of Data
    Binary Coding
Database Management
    Files, Records, and Fields
    Database Structures
    Input/Output Specifications
    Database Management Commands
Multidimensional Databases
    Customer Relationship Management

Competencies

1. Define the purpose of management information systems, and describe the typical responsibilities of managers and staff working in the information systems area of a hospitality operation. (pp. 259–262)

2. Describe the data processing cycle and cite the advantages of electronic data processing. (pp. 262–264)

3. Identify the types of data and discuss binary coding. (pp. 264–265)

4. Identify major features of database management software and describe how they can be used by hospitality operations. (pp. 265–272)

5. Distinguish multidimensional database structures from traditional database structures and explain their use in customer relationship management. (pp. 272–274)

10

Information Management

THE INFORMATION SYSTEMS of automated hotels and restaurants can produce a nearly unlimited amount of reports for managers. However, simply distributing reports does not in itself ensure an effective information system. To achieve the full potential of an automated information system, system functions must align with management's information needs.

Information systems also streamline the process of collecting and recording data and expand the ways in which information is organized and reported. These systems enable management to accelerate the process by which useful information is made available to decision-makers.

This chapter examines the design and functions of a management information system and describes the major responsibilities of information system managers. The fundamentals of data processing and database management are also addressed. The chapter closes with an overview of how databases are used to provide management with information to better manage relationships with guests.

Management Information System

A **management information system (MIS)** is designed to provide managers with the information necessary to plan, organize, staff, direct, and control operations. An effective MIS is built around the information needs of managers. It can be designed so that system applications support decision-making activities at all levels within the organization. An effective MIS extends its power beyond routine report generation and provides managers with the information they need to:

- Monitor progress toward achieving organizational goals.
- Measure performance.
- Identify trends and patterns.
- Evaluate alternatives.
- Support decision-making.
- Assist in the identification of corrective action.

An MIS supports strategic planning, tactical decision-making, and operational decision-making. Strategic planning refers to decision-making activities through which future-oriented goals and objectives of an organization are established. Tactical decisions relate to activities required to implement strategic planning decisions. Operational decisions address specific tasks that normally follow previously established rules and patterns.

Once the information needs of managers have been identified, an MIS is designed to perform the following functions:

- Enable managers to better monitor and administer business transactions and activities.

- Provide a high level of operational and internal control over business resources.

- Produce timely and comprehensive reports formatted to the specific needs of management.

- Reduce managerial paperwork and operational expenses by eliminating unnecessary source documents and streamlining data transfer and recording procedures.

To perform these functions effectively, an MIS uses a variety of information technology and decision support systems. **Information technology (IT)** establishes a communication process in which data are transferred from related systems, such as a hotel's reservations system, front office modules, point-of-sale system, accounting applications, or sales applications. The transferred data are processed according to pre-established decision-making rules, financial models, or other analytical methods. The processed data are then stored in information formats tailored to the needs of individual managers and become available on demand or at set intervals.

Information technology also includes simulation capability and the incorporation of expert systems. Decision support systems with simulation capability enable managers to explore "what if" possibilities. These systems are interactive information systems that use decision models and a comprehensive database to provide information customized to support specific business decisions. Expert systems differ from decision support systems in that they apply specialized problem-solving expertise and are used to indicate the most probable solution. Therefore, an expert system may complement or replace an expert to solve problems.

MIS Personnel

In large, fully automated hospitality properties, the MIS management staff may consist of a property systems manager and department systems supervisors. Generally, the **property systems manager** participates in the evaluation, selection, and installation of system hardware and is trained in network operations for specific software applications used throughout the property. The property systems manager, also known simply as the systems manager, provides on-premises systems support and, when necessary, functions as a network administrator and/or an applications software analyst. **Department systems supervisors** are typically individuals already employed within a specific department who receive extensive training in the operation of specialty hardware, software, and network components used in the operating departments. Department systems supervisors train others within their operating departments and provide technical support services as appropriate. Professional certification in the area of hospitality technology is offered by Hospitality Financial and Technology Professionals (HFTP). For more information about HFTP and professional certification, visit HFTP's website at www.hftp.org.

The property systems manager has a wide range of responsibilities. More often a generalist than a technician, the systems manager must understand advanced technology (including hardware, software, network, and security components), information-processing techniques, and interrelations of functional areas within the property. Without this understanding, it would be difficult to direct the MIS to meet the specific information needs of managers throughout the property. The systems manager must also be skilled in system vendor relations and provide a reliable and efficient information distribution system for management and staff. Other duties of a property systems manager include:

- Planning and controlling MIS activities, which includes identifying the processing priorities within the system.

- Selecting department systems managers and establishing training programs.

- Managing multiprocessor environments, which includes developing system configuration and design alternatives in relation to the placement and processing capabilities of system components.

- Designing and implementing information back-up and security controls.

- Oversight of local and wide area networks, including elements of access and security.

In addition to the above responsibilities, the systems manager also periodically reviews the MIS and presents requests for system modification, including upgrades, to management. If the modifications are approved, the systems manager discusses desired changes with appropriate system vendors. Subsequent system changes are documented by the systems manager.

The systems manager is also responsible for planning, maintaining, and securing the hardware configuration. The most common hardware configuration for property-based systems is the client-server model. This model uses a powerful file server computer to store application software, including database management technology, and to communicate with distributed workstations within a local area network (LAN).

There is justification for keeping software applications separate and distinct, as it reduces the chance of one application interfering with another and simplifies troubleshooting. Placing too many applications on a single server may save hardware costs, but it increases the property's vulnerability to server failure.

An alternative property management system configuration is the application service provider (ASP) model, more properly called a remote-server model. In this system structure, the application software may be physically located somewhere other than at the property, such as at the chain's headquarters, a system supplier site, or a remote website. The users' workstations at the property are connected to the server over a wide area network (WAN), virtual private network (VPN), or via the Internet (cloud computing) and supported on a fixed monthly fee or per-transaction fee basis.

A majority of remote functions rely on the Internet, which may provide greater guarantees of security and performance than a comparable dedicated private network. The benefit to the property is greater confidence in server reliability, data security, and software upgrades, since the website provider takes responsibility for ensuring accessibility. The tradeoffs are the long-term cost of using external system components, which influence access and control over data, and vulnerability to the loss of network connectivity. It's an analysis potential WAN users must consider.

Electronic Data Processing

Data are facts and/or figures to be processed into useful information. **Data processing** involves transforming raw facts and isolated figures into timely, accurate, and useful information. Every day, hospitality managers are bombarded with facts and figures about the results of operations. These individual pieces of data are relatively meaningless until they are organized or manipulated into useful information.

Information, the result of data processing, is clearly one of the most valuable resources of a hospitality business. Information can increase a manager's knowledge regarding guests, service, labor, finance, and other areas of concern. Information may reduce the uncertainty that managers may experience when making decisions. And, after decisions have been made, information can provide managers with important feedback on the effectiveness of their decisions and may indicate new areas of concern that call for corrective action.

Data processing is not unique to the world of business; it is an important function that occurs in everyday life as well. Everyone processes data. For example, consider what may happen on a typical payday. After receiving a paycheck, a person may consider all of the items he or she would like to purchase, the cost of those items, and the difference between the amount of the paycheck and the total amount of the desired purchases. If the amount of the paycheck is greater than the amount of planned purchases, the person may decide to place the surplus amount in a savings account. If, on the other hand, the total amount of desired purchases is greater than the amount of the paycheck, the person may reconsider the purchase options or perhaps consider applying for a bank loan.

In this example of data processing, a collection of data (the amount of the paycheck and the purchase options) is processed (totaled and compared) and transformed into information (surplus or deficit) useful in making decisions (what to buy, how much to save, or how much to borrow).

The conversion of data into information is accomplished through a cycle of events identified as input, process, and output. In this example, the paycheck and the purchase options are inputs; totaling the planned purchases and comparing that total with the amount of the paycheck is the processing; and the resulting surplus or deficit is the output. The sequence of input, process, and output forms the basic data processing cycle as illustrated in Exhibit 1.

During input, data are collected and organized to simplify subsequent processing. During processing, input data are mathematically manipulated or logically

Exhibit 1 Data Processing Cycle

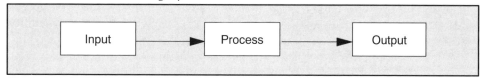

arranged to generate meaningful output. The output can be reported for immediate use or saved for future reference.

The speed, accuracy, and efficiency required for an effective information system are often best achieved through electronic data processing. The difference between data processing and electronic data processing lies in the automation of the process and the addition of a memory unit. Exhibit 2 illustrates the electronic data processing cycle.

Electronic data processing is an automated system that results in faster and more efficient operation. The addition of a memory unit allows for the storage and retrieval of data or instructions for more accurate and reliable processing.

Advantages of Electronic Data Processing

Electronic data processing transforms data into information by reducing throughput, streamlining output, and minimizing the handling of data.

Throughput (formerly termed "turnaround time") refers to the time that elapses between data input and information output. Simply stated, throughput is a measure of data processing efficiency. Automated systems are able to minimize throughput for almost all data processing tasks. Inquiry and search procedures are usually performed within an acceptable response time. For example, if a hotel front desk employee needs to find in which room a guest is registered, the information should be generated quickly. Also, a busy food and beverage manager would appreciate the speed and accuracy of an effective automated system when spot-checking the inventory levels of expensive ingredients immediately following a meal period.

Streamlining the output of an automated system means generating only those reports requested by those who will use the information. A frequent criticism of

Exhibit 2 Electronic Data Processing Cycle

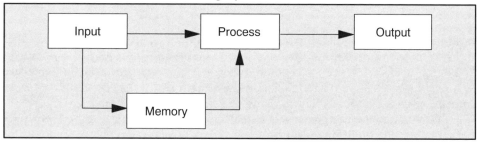

electronic data processing is that automated systems produce large volumes of irrelevant information. This criticism is misdirected. If an automated system over-whelms management with useless information, it is not the fault of the system—it is the fault of the information system design. Instead of generating a generic daily report of operations, for example, management may develop a summary report of critical metrics (often called a "dashboard" report).

Reducing the number of times that data must be handled enhances both the speed and accuracy of data processing tasks. Consider the difference between a manual accounting system and an automated accounting system.

In a manual accounting system, the amounts of invoices that are received must first be recorded in a journal. The amounts are carried over to a ledger. Amounts recorded in the ledger are then used to prepare financial statements. During each of these steps, it is possible for a bookkeeper to make any number of mistakes, such as recording the wrong number, failing to include a number, reversing a number's digits, calculating a total incorrectly, and so on. The more times the same data must be handled, the greater the possibility for error.

In an automated accounting system, an invoice amount is entered only once. The amount can then be accessed by the programs that prepare the journal, ledger, and financial statements. Therefore, when the amount of the invoice is entered correctly, all of the subsequent financial statements will be mathematically correct. If the amount is entered incorrectly, but the mistake is identified and corrected, the correction automatically flows from the journal through to the financial state-ments. With electronic data processing, there are fewer opportunities for error, because it is not necessary to rehandle the same data.

Types of Data

There are three distinct types of data. One type is called "alpha data" because it consists only of letters of the alphabet. For example, the names of menu items, employees, and hotel guests are examples of alpha data. A second kind of data is called "numeric data" because it consists only of numbers. Menu prices, room numbers, transaction amounts, and occupancy percentages are numeric data. The third type of data is termed "alphanumeric data" and is composed of both letters and numbers. A hotel's street address, a menu item's description, and personnel records are examples of alphanumeric data.

Classifying data by type can be very helpful when users are operating in an automated environment. When a data processing system is programmed, each data element must be "introduced" to the system so that the type of data and the maximum number of characters it may contain can be specified. Once the system is programmed with this information, it will not allow users to input data that does not meet specifications. For example, if a reservation system expects the tele-phone number of a guest to have ten numeric characters, and a user mistakenly enters nine numbers and a single letter, the system will refuse the data entry and inform the user that he or she has made a mistake. This feature reduces the poten-tial number of data entry errors and enhances the reliability of the data processing cycle by initially qualifying input elements.

Binary Coding

Regardless of whether alpha, numeric, or alphanumeric data are to be entered into an electronic data processing system, in order for the system to process it, the data must be translated into a binary code. The **binary code** is a counting system based on two digits, zero and one. This is the easiest way for an automated system to handle data because electronic circuits have two natural states: "on," usually represented by binary digit one; and "off," represented by binary digit zero.

A **bit** is the smallest unit of electronic data. The term bit is short for a *BI*nary digi*T* (which is either zero or one). All characters are represented by a special sequence of binary digits. For example, the character "A" can be converted into binary code as 01000001.

A special sequence of bits representing a single character is called a **byte**. A byte is a group of adjacent bits that work, or are operated on, as a unit. Theoretically, a byte may be any length, but the most common length for a byte is eight bits.

Bytes take up memory space. A **kilobyte** represents approximately one thousand bytes (1,024 bytes). Kilobyte is often abbreviated as "K" or "Kb" and is used to describe memory capacity. A **megabyte**, abbreviated as "Mb," represents approximately one million bytes (1,048,576 bytes). A **gigabyte**, abbreviated as "Gb," represents approximately one billion bytes (1,073,741,834 bytes). A **terabyte**, abbreviated as "Tb," represents approximately one trillion bytes.

Database Management

Database management is a term for applications that allow users to catalog and store information about their businesses for future use. A **database**, also referred to as a data warehouse, is a collection of related facts and figures designed to serve a specific purpose. For example, a personal checkbook is a database; it collects facts and figures that are designed to monitor personal finances. Other common databases include address books, telephone books, dictionaries, online search engines, and information warehouses.

The design and organization of such databases are essential to users. The data within an address book, telephone book, and dictionary are sorted alphabetically so that users can quickly access the particular data they need. The checks in a personal checkbook are numbered sequentially. If an individual keeps to this numbered sequence when issuing checks, the returned canceled checks can be stored in the same numbered sequence, enabling the person to easily retrieve any particular check. An online search engine or information warehouse may use various techniques to index and identify content based on relevance or recency.

A database management system can be compared to a filing cabinet. The way information is organized within a filing cabinet will depend on the kind of information that is stored and the particular needs of the user. File cabinets have separate file drawers. Each file drawer contains separate file folders. The folders within each drawer typically contain similar records of related information. Each record within a folder contains specific facts and/or figures.

Exhibit 3 diagrams the similarity between a typical office file cabinet and a database management system. In the language of database management, the file

Exhibit 3   Database Files, Records, and Fields

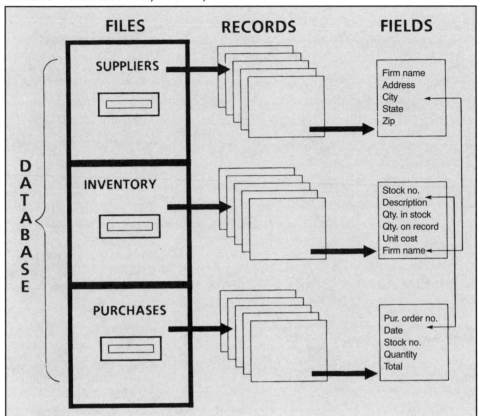

cabinet is called the database, the drawers of the cabinet are called **database files**, the folders within the drawers are called **database records**, and the detailed facts and/or figures in the records are called **database fields**.

For example, a database might be set up for inventory control. Assume that this database is made up of a single file. The file would contain one record for each inventory item, and each record would contain a number of fields, such as the item's name, number, cost, quantity on hand, reorder point, and so on. Users of the system could access this database to perform any number of desired functions, such as:

- Generate inventory checklists to assist managers and supervisors in conducting a physical inventory.

- Perform variance analyses on the differences between actual quantities of items on hand (physical inventory) versus the quantities projected (perpetual inventory).

- Calculate the total financial value of items in inventory.

There are hundreds of uses for database management applications in the hospitality industry. These applications are used in relation to personnel file management, payroll processing, marketing research, general ledger accounting, tax reporting, direct mail advertising, sales reporting, and countless other areas.

Database management applications control the structure and organization of databases as well as the means by which data are handled within a system. Database technologies are designed to limit the number of times that data must be handled and ensure that users accessing the database are working with identical information. In addition, database management software can enable users to create, access, and merge data files; to add, select, and delete data; and to index, sort, and search data files for information that is generated for use by management.

Files, Records, and Fields

In a database management system, fields are labeled by categories that identify the kind of information they contain. Records are identified in terms of a primary key field, which contains unique information. The name of the primary key field becomes the basis for searches through a data file for a particular record.

Consider the organization of a master payroll file. The file would contain a record for each employee. Each record would be made up of fields identified by labels such as employee number, employee name, address, pay rate, withholdings, deductions, and so on. One of these fields would be designated as the primary key field, which could be used to search the data file for a particular record. Since the primary key field must contain unique information, the employee number field would function best as the key field of the master payroll file. Two employees may, by chance, have the same name, but when a company assigns employee numbers on a sequential basis, it guarantees that a particular number in the sequence identifies one employee named John Smith, who lives at a specific address, and so on.

The database of a hospitality business may be organized into many data files (such as personnel files, financial data files, guest history files, etc.). These files may contain dozens of records and scores of fields containing thousands of pieces of data. Database management applications structure the relationships among files, records, and fields in a way that ensures rapid access to information. However, not all database management software applications structure a database in the same manner.

Database Structures

Database management applications structure a database by organizing data files, records, and fields in ways that facilitate searching for data, updating data, and generating reports for management. Database applications manage databases through either hierarchical structures or relational structures.

A **hierarchical database structure** arranges data files, records, and fields into formations that resemble the structure of the roots of a tree. As the trunk of a tree leads into major roots, which in turn branch off into entire networks of roots, so a hierarchically structured database begins with a data file (the trunk), which opens onto a number of master records (the major roots), which in turn lead to intricate networks of other subordinate records. Exhibit 4 illustrates the structure of a hierarchical database. In order to access data contained in subordinate records, the database management system must first access the data file, then the parent root, then a key field of the subordinate record network.

Database management applications that arrange data in hierarchical structures are able to carry out precise data searches and generate comprehensive statistical analyses. However, they are dependent upon rigid parameters that define the nature of fields and records. It may be difficult and time-consuming to incorporate new data definitions into a hierarchically structured database.

Relational database structures have become popular because of the simplicity of data arrangement, the ease of data manipulation, and the flexibility of data handling. The data files of a relational database management program are formatted as rectangular tables of rows and columns and are similar in design to electronic spreadsheets. Column headings identify fields (some relational database management packages refer to fields as attributes) such as an employee's number, name, address, work history, pay rate, skill code, and so on. When a column is read down through the rows, it reveals the same type of attribute data about many employees. Each row is a record. When a row is read completely across the columns, it reveals all the different types of data that have been input regarding a single employee. A key field (such as employee number) is used to identify the record. Exhibit 5 illustrates how the same data presented in Exhibit 4 would appear in a relational database structure. Exhibit 6 uses personnel data to illustrate the difference between hierarchical and relational database structures.

Input/Output Specifications

Database applications require users to define an input area for data entry, a criteria area for directing queries, and an output area for directing results. Although database applications usually provide predetermined specifications (also referred

Exhibit 4   Hierarchical Database Structure

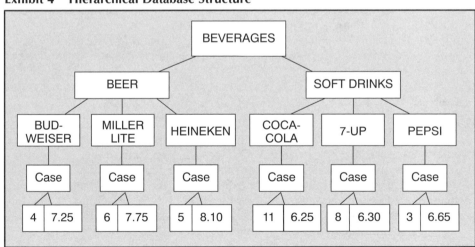

Exhibit 5   Relational Database Structure

Beverages	Brand	Unit	Qty.	Cost
BEER	BUDWEISER	Case	4	7.25
BEER	MILLER LITE	Case	6	7.75
BEER	HEINEKEN	Case	5	8.10
SOFT DRINK	COCA-COLA	Case	11	6.25
SOFT DRINK	7-UP	Case	8	6.30
SOFT DRINK	PEPSI	Case	3	6.65

Exhibit 6   Personnel Data

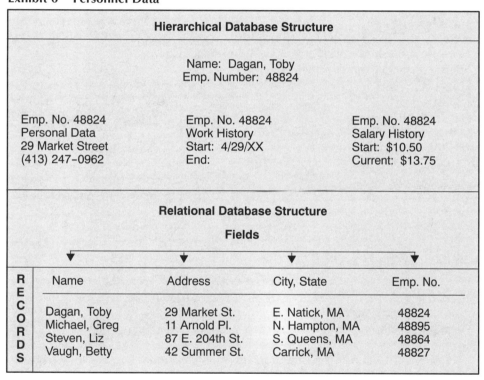

to as default settings), users are encouraged to define specifications for these areas that best meet their needs.

Input area specifications define data entry procedures. Screen templates can be designed to guide users with data input responsibilities. For example, the display monitor at the front desk of a hotel may guide front desk employees in entering specific data regarding guests during check-in. The use of a screen or window template would ensure that important data are collected and properly entered into the system.

Criteria area specifications define query procedures. A query is usually a request for data that does not necessitate the completion of a lengthy report, such as information regarding a guest's credit limit. Most database management programs support a query language that enables users to formulate requests. Criteria area specifications define the necessary sequence of data entry. For example, inputting a query may necessitate the following selections:

- Entering a command or selecting a predetermined option

- Defining the scope of the command

- Specifying command conditions

Database management commands are usually entered by identifying a simple word (such as DISPLAY, SUM, COUNT, LOCATE, LIST, and so on). Defining the scope of the command identifies which areas of the database will be affected by the command. Specifying command conditions stipulates the circumstances under which the command will operate. For example, given a particular database management program, entering the following sequence: DISPLAY NAME, ADDRESS, CITY, STATE FOR SOCSEC + '384-42-1999' will lead the system to carry out the command (DISPLAY) for the field names listed (NAME, ADDRESS, CITY, STATE) when a specified condition is met (the existence of a Social Security number of 384-42-1999). The system will respond by displaying the person's name, address, city, and state only if there actually is an employee in the database with the specified Social Security number.

Output area specifications control the generation and formatting of reports and additional database files. Since data stored in a database are independent of its application, database applications are able to separate related information and generate a variety of reports.

Database Management Commands

Once a database has been designed and the data input, records within database files can be accessed by a number of users, and various types of information can be obtained through database management commands or system options. Database management applications provide a number of commands that enable users to organize records within database files and to search for information that may be contained in several files. A few of the more common commands are briefly described in the following sections.

Organizing Records in Database Files. Two of the most frequently used commands that organize records in database files are the "index" and "sort" commands. The index command does not rearrange the records of a database file. Instead, it provides a limited working file that identifies records containing certain data, somewhat as the index of a textbook identifies page numbers containing information on a certain subject. When a database file is retrieved and the sort command issued, a new database file is created that is equal in size and content to the original (source) file. However, the sort command changes the order of the records in the source file according to a field category designated by the user.

Assume that a large hospitality company is considering increasing the life insurance benefits of employees who have been continuously employed by the firm for more than ten years. A user retrieves the personnel database file and the records containing employee numbers, names, addresses, length of employment, and so on, and discovers that the records are arranged by employee number. Through the database management application, the user issues a command to sort the file and reorder the records by length of employment. The sorted file can then be generated as a report revealing the employees affected by the new insurance benefit, or the sorted file can become the basis for further processing.

It is important to note that an indexed file generally maintains a direct connection with the source file from which it was created. Therefore, the indexed file will immediately reflect any changes that are made to the source file, and vice versa. This is not the case with sorted files. A sorted file is generally independent of the source file from which it was created. Therefore, any changes made to the source file, such as updating the records, will have to be transferred to the previously sorted file. If extensive updating of database records occurs regularly, new sorted files must be created.

Searching Records. The "find" or "locate" command is used to search for specific records in database files. The find command normally functions more quickly than the locate command. However, it generally works only with files that have been indexed in terms of the specific field category for which the user is searching. The locate command functions by matching file entries with the character string for which the user is searching. Searches issued by the locate command tend to be less efficient and more time-consuming than searches issued by the find command, especially when large database files are involved.

Multiple Searches. An important feature of a database management application is its ability to perform multiple searches across a broad spectrum of field categories. For example, consider the advantages of a multiple-search routine for processing an overnight room request from a walk-in guest. Assume that a guest arrives at the front desk of a large hotel and requests an upper-floor suite with two double beds. The front desk employee conducts a multiple search through the rooms availability database file. The first search indexes the database file in terms of a primary key field, which is the broadest field category involved in the search. In this example, the primary key would be the type of room—a suite. Subsequent searches focus on secondary keys, which order and limit the primary key field. In this example, the number of beds in a room and floor location would be the secondary keys that order the primary key field of suites. Using the multiple-search feature of a database management application, the front desk employee would have the necessary information to room the guest within seconds.

Multiple-search routines can be extremely useful when working with large or complex databases. Consider how a restaurant manager could use a multiple-search routine to find a substitute server who is available on Tuesday evenings between 4 and 7 P.M. Initially, a personnel database file would be searched for all persons qualified as food servers. Subsequent automatic search passes through the file would result in a selective deletion of names whose work availability schedules fail to coincide with the day and time criteria. Remaining records are those that satisfy the multiple-search criteria.

Calculations. Most database management applications have built-in calculators that are capable of carrying out basic arithmetical and statistical operations. Standard mathematical conventions are adhered to, with multiplication and division taking precedence over addition and subtraction. The calculator feature can be accessed at any point.

Since the results of calculations can be automatically stored and later referenced, the calculator dimension extends the usefulness of the application. For example, a specific command files the results of calculations under a named memory variable. A hotel's average room rate, which is calculated by dividing rooms revenue by the number of rooms sold, can be computed and filed under a unique name, such as "ADR." Later, when the data are needed, they can be referenced and retrieved.

Database management applications allow the user to store both numeric and alpha data as memory variables. This feature enhances the recall capabilities of the application without necessitating the creation of separate database files that would have to be indexed, sorted, or searched.

Multidimensional Databases

For decades, hospitality businesses have electronically captured and stored transactional data. However, the manner in which they did so made it difficult to access and analyze data for decision-making purposes. Information technology enables individual properties as well as chain organizations to more easily identify relationships, patterns, and trends within large, centralized databases also known as data warehouses. A **data warehouse** is a database designed to support decision-making in an organization. The data in a data warehouse are structured to support a variety of analyses, including elaborate queries on large amounts of data that may require extensive searching. When the data warehouse is organized or segmented by department or function, it is referred to as a **data mart**, i.e., a small unit within the overall data warehouse. Dividing a data mart into its component parts results in a set of **data cubes**. For example, all hotel data form the warehouse, rooms division data is a mart, and suites within the rooms department are a cube.

Online analytical processing (OLAP) is decision support software that allows the user to quickly access data and analyze information that has been summarized into multidimensional views and hierarchies. OLAP works with databases that are structured as multidimensional cubes rather than as the two-dimensional rows and columns typical of relational databases. Data are stored as dimensions or subject domains, and the cube structure allows different views of the data to be displayed quickly. The ability to quickly switch between one slice of data and another allows users to analyze information in small palatable chunks instead of through a comprehensive report. The data cube presented in Exhibit 7 contains three dimensions. If data were filled in the cube, "Months" could be listed across the top, "Actual," "Budget," and "Forecast" could be listed down the top, and "Payroll Departments" could be listed down the side.

Exhibit 7   Multidimensional Data Cube

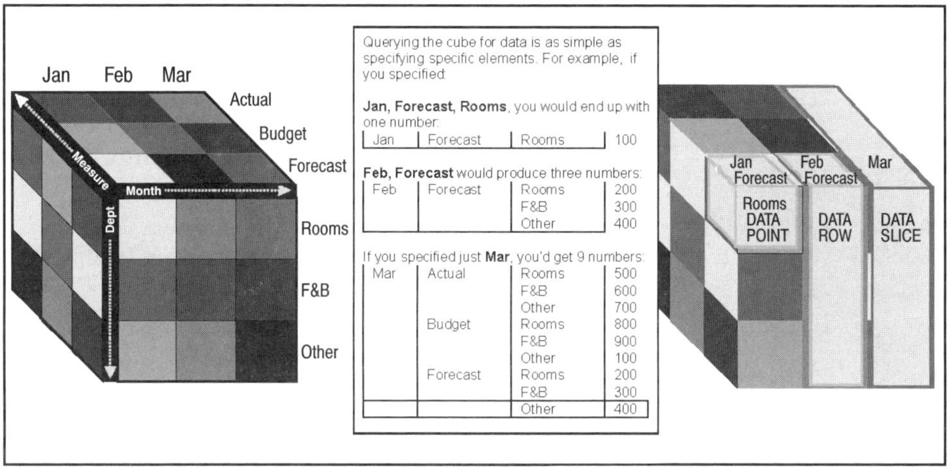

Source: Datavision Technologies, Inc. (www.datavisiontech.com).

The dimensions, or subject domains, are defined in terms of decision support requirements. Traditional hospitality database systems are organized around operational transactions such as reservations, registration, rooms management, guest accounting, etc. Multidimensional databases, on the other hand, can be organized around subject areas such as guests, spending patterns, bundled purchases, length of stay, etc. These dimensions are created to support managerial decision-making, not simply to reflect business processes. OLAP tools enable managers to drill down into masses of data to isolate only that data needed for specific decision-making purposes. For example, when managers are seeking data about guests from New York State, with only three clicks of the mouse, they can "drill down" from "World" to "North America" to "U.S.A." to "New York." **Data mining** is the process of exploring (digging through data) to uncover patterns and relationships relevant to the decision or issue at hand. Data mining can be done manually by slicing and dicing the data until a pattern becomes obvious, or it can be done with programs that analyze the data automatically.

Customer Relationship Management

The hospitality industry deals with large market segments (such as business travelers, leisure travelers, corporate business, etc.) and targets specific groupings, or segments, of guests and potential guests within these markets (such as working women between the ages of twenty-five and forty). Advances in information technology and database management tools have made it possible to create a market of one. Given the appropriate technology and transaction history, marketing and sales staff can access the significant information (room types, spending pattern, preferred entrées, etc.) needed to understand an individual guest, contact that guest, and sell additional hospitality products and services that directly meet the guest's needs. This process is termed **customer relationship management (CRM)**.

A popular form of one-to-one marketing is the use of personalized communications, including personalized website content and e-mails. These are generally permission-based programs in which guests opt-in, or agree, to receive messages from the hospitality company. Examples include frequent-traveler loyalty programs and frequent-diner affinity programs.

Key Terms

customer relationship management (CRM)—The process of using significant guest information to understand an individual guest, contact that guest, and sell additional hospitality products and services that directly meet the guest's needs.

department systems supervisor—An individual already employed within a specific department who receives extensive training in the operation of hardware, software applications, and network components, and afterward conducts training sessions for others and provides some technical support services.

information technology (IT)—Technology that establishes a communication process in which data are transferred from related systems; processed according to pre-established decision-making rules, financial models, or other analytical methods; and stored in information formats tailored to the needs of individual managers.

management information system (MIS)—A system designed to provide managers with the necessary information needed to plan, organize, staff, direct, and control operations.

property systems manager—Participates in the evaluation, selection, and installation of system hardware and is trained in the operation of software applications used throughout the property; provides on-premises systems support and, when necessary, functions as a network administrator and/or an applications software troubleshooter.

Data Processing

binary code—A code based on only two digits, zero and one. This is the form of data a computer can handle with the greatest ease because electronic circuits have two natural states: "on," usually represented by the binary digit one; and "off," represented by the binary digit zero.

bit—The smallest unit of electronic data. The term is short for *BInary digiT* (which is either zero or one). All characters (letters, numbers, and symbols) are represented by a special sequence of binary digits.

byte—A special sequence of bits (electronic data) representing a single character. A byte is a group of adjacent bits that work, or are operated on, as a unit. Theoretically, a byte may be any length, but the most common length for a byte is eight bits.

data—Facts or figures to be processed into useful information. Three types of data are alpha data, numeric data, and alphanumeric data.

data processing—A cycle of events identified as input, process, and output that transforms raw facts and isolated figures into useful information.

gigabyte—Often abbreviated as "Gb," equal to 1,073,741,834 bytes, and commonly used to describe computer memory capacity.

kilobyte—Often abbreviated as "K" or "Kb," equal to 1,024 bytes, and commonly used to describe computer memory capacity.

megabyte—Often abbreviated as "Mb," equal to 1,048,576 bytes, and commonly used to describe computer memory capacity.

streamlining—An electronic data processing practice of generating only those reports that are requested by staff members who will actually use the information.

terabyte—Often abbreviated as "Tb," equal to one trillion bytes, and commonly used to describe computer memory capacity.

throughput—An electronic data processing term referring to the time that elapses between data input and information output.

Database Management

data cube—Individual component parts of a data mart.

data mart—A multidimensional database organized for one department or function.

data mining—The process of exploring a database to uncover patterns and relationships relevant to the decision or issue at hand.

data warehouse—A database designed to support decision-making in an organization; structured to support a variety of analyses, including elaborate queries on large amounts of data that can require extensive searching.

database—A collection of related facts and figures designed to serve a specific purpose.

database fields—The detailed facts or figures contained in database records.

database files—A collection of database records and fields.

database records—A collection of database fields.

hierarchical database structure—In database management software, arranges data files, records, and fields into formations that resemble the structure of the roots of a tree.

online analytical processing (OLAP)—Decision support software that allows the user to quickly analyze information that has been summarized into multidimensional views and hierarchies.

relational database structure—A database structure in which the data files are formatted as rectangular tables of rows and columns and are similar in appearance to electronic spreadsheets.

 # Review Questions

1. What is the purpose of a management information system?

2. What are the typical duties and responsibilities of a property systems manager? Of a department systems supervisor?

3. What are the three phases of the data processing cycle? Describe the functions performed in each phase.

4. What does the term "binary code" mean?

5. What is the difference between a bit and a byte? A kilobyte and a megabyte? A megabyte and a gigabyte? A gigabyte and a terabyte?

6. What does the term "database" mean? How can database management programs be useful to managers of hospitality operations?

7. What are "files," "records," and "fields"? How are they organized within hierarchical and relational database structures?

8. How do primary and secondary keys function in relation to multiple searches across a broad spectrum of field categories within a large database?

9. What is the difference between data warehouses and data marts?

10. How can personalized communications work as a marketing tool?

 Internet Sites ——————————————————————

For more information, visit the following Internet sites. Remember that Internet addresses can change without notice. If the site is no longer there, you can use a search engine to look for additional sites.

Agilysys, Inc.
www.agilysys.com

MICROS Systems, Inc.
www.micros.com

CMS Hospitality
www.cmshospitality.com

NCR Corporation
www.ncr.com

Comtrex
www.comtrex.com

System Concepts, Inc.
www.foodtrak.com

Datavision Technologies, Inc.
www.datavisiontech.com

Chapter 11 Outline

Information Needs
Sales Literature
System Requirements
Request for Proposal
    Site Survey
    Evaluating Proposals
    Vendor Product Demonstration
Contract Negotiations
    Contract Provisions
    Contractual Arrangements
Installation Factors
    Training
    Site Preparation
    Design of Materials
    Data Entry
    Acceptance Testing
    System Conversion
    Documentation
    Contingency Planning

Competencies

1. Describe ways in which hospitality managers can analyze current information needs. (pp. 279–280)

2. Identify ways in which managers can collect sales literature to get information about technology systems. (pp. 280–285)

3. Explain how managers can establish basic technology system requirements. (pp. 285–286)

4. Explain the purpose of a request for proposal (RFP). (pp. 286–289)

5. Describe how managers can evaluate proposals submitted by technology system vendors. (pp. 289–291)

6. Describe how managers can get the most value out of technology product demonstrations. (pp. 291–292)

7. Identify provisions and arrangements that hospitality managers generally negotiate with vendors of hospitality technology systems. (pp. 292–295)

8. Identify factors involved in the installation of technology systems in hospitality operations. (pp. 295–300)

11

System Selection

THE IDENTIFICATION, EVALUATION, AND SELECTION of hospitality technology systems can be complex and time-consuming. Many properties appoint a project team. The project leader generally has overall responsibility for purchasing the technology system. This person determines a schedule for the purchasing process and monitors the team's progress. The process begins as the team analyzes the current information needs of the business, collects relevant technology sales literature, and establishes system requirements. The results of this preliminary research are used to formulate a request for proposal (RFP) from vendors. The process continues with the evaluation of proposals and product demonstrations, contract negotiations, and the implementation of the new system. Throughout the process, it is helpful to keep the "nevers" of technology purchasing in mind:

- Never purchase hardware before software. After selecting software first, identify the hardware it requires.

- Never make a purchase decision based solely on cost. Too often, economic factors are given a disproportionate weight in the decision process.

- Never lose control of the purchasing process. Develop request for proposal documents, script on-site vendor demonstrations, and apply uniform criteria when evaluating vendor proposals.

- Never rely on enhancement promises. A system feature that is advertised, but not yet available for sale, may not actually become available for some time.

- Never be the first system user. New systems have no operational history and, therefore, are difficult to evaluate.

- Never allow technology to dictate operations. Changing operations to fit the demands of the technology is reverse logic (i.e., the tail wagging the dog).

- Never be the largest system user. Pushing the capabilities of a system's processing speed, file parameters, memory capabilities, and other functions may lead to a series of problems, many of which may not be resolved in a timely manner.

- Never be the last system user. System maintenance, ongoing technical support, enhancements, and the like may be difficult or impossible to obtain once the vendor has abandoned the product.

- Never allow a vendor to rewrite the business's technology requirements. The focus must be on business needs, and a system that meets vendor specifications may not meet business needs.

Information Needs

The first step in analyzing the information needs of a business is to identify the types of information that various levels of management use in the course of operations. This can be done by compiling samples of reports currently prepared for management—for example, the daily operations report, basic financial statements, and reports similar to those identified in Exhibit 1. Once collected, the reports can be analyzed in relation to such variables as purpose, content, distribution, and frequency.

Report analysis identifies the types of information management uses, but does not necessarily reveal the information needs of the business. A separate survey needs to be conducted to evaluate the effectiveness of the format and content of current reports. Survey findings can provide the basis for immediate improvements in the information system and enable a more in-depth analysis to include flowcharts and a property profile.

Flowcharts use specially designed symbols for diagramming the flow of data and documents through an information system. Flowchart symbols have been standardized by the American National Standards Institute. Some of the more commonly used symbols are illustrated in Exhibit 2. Standardization is achieved by using common symbols and also by drawing flowcharts according to established procedures.

Since flowcharting reveals the origin, processing, and final disposition of a document, it can be a valuable technique for evaluating the business's current information system. Weaknesses, overlapping functions, and other redundancies can be identified.

An alternative to detailed flowchart depictions is a series of written narrative descriptions. Written narratives are less efficient than flowcharts and are time-consuming to develop and review. A written narrative of six to eight pages may be needed to communicate the same information a detailed flowchart presents in a single page.

A **property profile** compiles statistics about the installed information system. Exhibits 3 and 4 illustrate sample property profile formats for lodging operations and food service operations, respectively. The types of categories and number of individual entries will vary from property to property. A property profile can be invaluable when communicating information needs of the business to system vendors. A well-designed property profile allows vendors to compare the property's information needs to those of similar properties. In addition, a property profile enables management to conduct a more informed and efficient review of technology sales literature.

Sales Literature

After creating a property profile, management should collect sales literature on a variety of technology systems that meet the general information needs of the business. Literature collection can result from:

- Sending inquiries to state and national hospitality trade associations.
- Attending hospitality industry trade shows.

Exhibit 1   Typical Management Reports

Report	Frequency	Content	Comparisons	Who Gets It	Purpose
Daily Report of Operations	Daily, on a cumulative basis for the month, the year to date.	Occupancy, average rate, revenue by outlet, and pertinent statistics.	To operating plan for current period and to prior year results.	Top management and supervisors responsible for day to day operation.	Basis for evaluating the current health of the enterprise.
Weekly Forecasts	Weekly.	Volume in covers, occupancy.	Previous periods.	Top management and supervisory personnel.	Staffing and scheduling; promotion.
Summary Report— Flash	Monthly at end of month (prior to monthly financial statement).	Known elements of revenue and direct costs; estimated departmental indirect costs.	To operating plan; to prior year results.	Top management and supervisory personnel responsible for function reported.	Provides immediate information on financial results for rooms, food and beverages, and other.
Cash Flow Analysis	Monthly (and on a revolving 12-month basis).	Receipts and disbursements by time periods.	With cash flow plan for month and for year to date.	Top management.	Predicts availability of cash for operating needs. Provides information on interim financing requirements.
Labor Productivity Analysis	Daily. Weekly. Monthly.	Dollar cost; manpower hours expended; hours as related to sales and services (covers, rooms occupied, etc.).	To committed hours in the operating plan (standards for amount of work to prior year statistics).	Top management and supervisory personnel.	Labor cost control through informed staffing and scheduling. Helps refine forecasting.
Departmental Analysis	Monthly (early in following month).	Details on main categories of income; same on expense.	To operating plan (month and year to date) and to prior year.	Top management and supervisors by function (e.g., rooms, each food and beverage outlet, laundry, telephone, other profit centers).	Knowing where business stands, and immediate corrective actions.
Room Rate Analysis	Daily, monthly, year to date.	Actual rates compared to rack rates by rate category or type of room.	To operating plan and to prior year results.	Top management and supervisors of sales and front office operations.	If goal is not being achieved, analysis of strengths and weaknesses is prompted.
Return on Investment	Actual computation, at least twice a year. Computation based on forecast, immediately prior to plan for year ahead.	Earnings as a percentage rate of return on average investment or equity committed.	To plan for operation and to prior periods.	Top management.	If goal is not being achieved, prompt assessment of strengths and weaknesses.
Long-Range Planning	Annually.	5-year projections of revenue and expenses. Operating plan expressed in financial terms.	Prior years.	Top management.	Involves staff in success or failure of enterprise. Injects more realism into plans for property and service modifications.
Exception Reporting	Concurrent with monthly reports and financial statements.	Summary listing of line item variances from predetermined norm.	With operating budgets.	Top management and supervisors responsible for function reported.	Immediate focusing on problem before more detailed statement analysis can be made.
Guest History Analysis	At least semi-annually; quarterly or monthly is recommended.	Historical records of corporate business, travel agencies, group bookings.	With previous reports.	Top management and sales.	Give direction to marketing efforts.
Future Bookings Report	Monthly.	Analysis of reservations and bookings.	With several prior years.	Top management, sales and marketing, department management.	Provides information on changing guest profile. Exposes strong and weak points of facility. Guides (1) sales planning and (2) expansion plans.

Exhibit 2   Common Flowchart Symbols

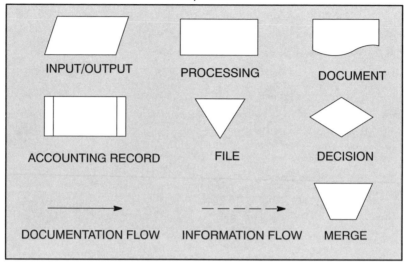

- Visiting local technology system suppliers.
- Distributing broadcast mailings to hospitality technology vendors.
- Conducting online searches for hospitality technology vendors.

State, national, and international hospitality trade associations, such as the American Hotel & Lodging Association (AH&LA), Hospitality Financial and Technology Professionals (HFTP), National Restaurant Association (NRA), Club Managers Association of America (CMAA), International Hospitality Information Technology Association (*i*HITA), and the International Association of Conference Centers (IACC), provide information services for their members. While these organizations are not likely to recommend specific products or suppliers, they will refer members seeking information about technology applications to specialty providers. The Internet sites of these associations provide links to hospitality technology vendors.

In addition, trade associations and other organizations regularly sponsor state, regional, and national trade shows. Attendance at trade shows typically places management in direct contact with hospitality technology vendors.

Management can also secure product information by visiting local system suppliers. This approach, however, can be time-consuming and may not provide a representative view of the range of products on the market.

Perhaps the most effective approach to fact-finding is using the information obtained from trade associations, attendance at trade shows, and visits to local vendors to formulate a general interest inquiry to be mailed or e-mailed to vendors of hospitality technology systems. This can be an efficient means of securing necessary information on various system solutions. Management may also choose to use broadcast mailings to secure more specific information, such as:

Exhibit 3   Sample Lodging Property Profile

General

___ Type of property (resort, hotel, motel, convention, condo, roadside, etc.)
___ Total number of rooms
___ Annual occupancy
___ Average room rate
___ Number of types of rooms
___ Number of suites
___ Percentage of annual occupancy from groups (tours, airlines, travel agencies, etc.)
___ Seasonal period(s); seasonal rates
___ Average length of stay
___ Number of permanent guests
___ Number of meeting rooms
___ Arrival/departure patterns
___ Number of revenue centers and locations

Reservations

___ Volume of reservation transactions (phone, telex, letter, etc.)
___ Volume of each type of reservation transaction
___ Percentage of reservations that require special handling (deposits, confirmations, etc.)
___ Hours of coverage
___ Average wage per employee
___ Annual overtime costs
___ If unionized department—will employees get raises because of automation?
___ Outside reservation services
___ Travel agent handling
___ Forecasting
___ Number of employees

Switchboard

___ Number of positions at switchboard
___ Type of equipment
___ Number of employees per shift (average/maximum)

Housekeeping

___ Number of floors
___ Number of rooms per floor (average)
___ Number of rooms or units cleaned per room attendant
___ Number of room attendants
___ Number of inspectors
___ Number of room attendants per inspector

Food and Beverage

___ Number of outlets
___ Location of outlets
___ Volume of sales
___ Number of sales
___ Number of menu items
___ Type of service

___ Number of covers
___ Average check
___ Present food and beverage registers
___ Present form of check used
___ Prechecking techniques (if applicable)
___ Inventory control methods
___ Inventory volumes
___ Percentage of sales charged to guestrooms
___ Number of employees
___ Number of function rooms

Accounting

___ Number of A/R accounts
___ Number of A/P accounts
___ Total A/R revenue handled per month (average/maximum)
___ Total A/P revenue handled per month (average/maximum)
___ Number of employees for A/R
___ Number of employees for A/P
___ Number of employees for general ledger
___ Number of employees for payroll
___ Number of employees for other accounting functions
___ Total number of employees on payroll (average/maximum)
___ Number of service bureaus presently employed
___ Cost of service bureaus
___ Number of travel agent accounts
___ Number of corporate accounts
___ Number of airline accounts
___ Number of special accounts
___ Present back office equipment
___ Cost/value/maintenance of present equipment
___ Supply cost of present equipment

Front Desk

___ Number of registration windows
___ Number of cashiering windows
___ Can registration and cashiering be done by same clerk?
___ Present equipment in use
___ Cost/value of present equipment
___ Maintenance of present equipment
___ Cost of supplies for present equipment (tapes, forms, etc.)
___ Number of employees per shift (average/maximum)
___ Average wage and benefit cost per employee
___ Number of registrants per day (average/maximum)
___ Number of check-outs per day (average/maximum)
___ Number of postings per day (average/maximum)

Exhibit 4   Sample Food Service Property Profile

FILE AND TRANSACTION VOLUMES

Sales and Cash Receipts

___ Number of seats
___ Number of covers per day
___ Number of daily menu items
___ Total number of menu items

Food Inventory

___ Number of inventory items (ingredients)
___ Daily inventory receipts (vendors)
___ Number of inventory items
        (classifications) per receipt
___ Daily inventory requisitions (from
        storeroom)
___ Number of recipes
___ Number of ingredients per recipe

Liquor Inventory

___ Number of inventory items
___ Daily storeroom requisitions (item
        classifications)
___ Number of recipes

Accounts Payable

___ Number of vendors
___ Invoices per day
___ Expense distributions per invoice
___ Checks (disbursements) per day

Accounts Receivable

___ Number of house accounts
___ Number of daily charges on account
___ Number of external charge media
        (American Express, etc.)
___ Number of daily receipts on account

Payroll and Labor Analysis

___ Number of employees
___ New hires per year
___ Number of W-2s prepared

General Ledger

___ Number of accounting periods
___ Number of accounts
___ Standard (recurring) monthly (journal
        entries)
___ Monthly general ledger postings (journal
        entries)

- Hardware documentation.

- Software documentation.

- Netware documentation.

- Lists of installed users.

- Sample report formats.

- Sample training materials.

- Suggested training and implementation scheduling.

- Annual financial statements of the vendor's business.

- Purchase/lease options.

- User support and maintenance programs.

- Sample system contract.

Gathering this information early in the process may prove valuable later when standardizing the response form that selected vendors will be required to complete when submitting system proposals to management. Before formulating the issues and categories of responses that will appear on the request for proposal document, management must analyze the needs of the business in light of the sales information collected.

System Requirements

Having analyzed the business's information needs and collected relevant sales literature, management's next step is to establish system requirements. This does not mean that hospitality managers must become experts in technology system design. Instead, management must be able to:

• Determine what data needs to be processed.

• Establish how that data will be processed.

• Identify how processed data will be stored and reported.

Determining what data to process involves identifying the information tasks that can best be performed by the automated system. Management must carefully weigh what is to be gained through technology. Will automation improve guest services? Will it increase operational efficiency? Will it enhance management's decision-making effectiveness? Other factors to consider when determining which data to process include the ease of identifying, collecting, entering, and coding data. These factors are essential to the timely processing and output of information.

Determining how data is to be processed is a matter of ensuring that the algorithmic design of the software programs corresponds to the formulas management prefers. The term "algorithm" refers to a prescribed set of well-defined, unambiguous rules or procedures leading to the solution of a problem. Too often, management assumes that hospitality industry jargon, such as "occupancy percentage" and "food cost percentage," means the same thing to all system designers. The truth is that hospitality properties differ in terms of the variables incorporated into these calculations.

Throughout the lodging industry, occupancy percentage is calculated by dividing the number of rooms sold by the number of rooms available for sale. Unfortunately, properties may vary in definition of the terms "rooms sold" and "rooms available for sale." Actual occupancy percentage calculations produced using this formula necessitate an understanding of how complimentary rooms, out-of-order rooms, no-show rooms, and other room status situations will be interpreted. Similarly, in relation to food service operations, the formulas used to calculate food cost may vary widely. Some properties may cost food when received, others when it is issued to the kitchen, others when the food is sold, and so on.

In order to ensure that the selected system will process data according to the property's standards, management should survey individual operating departments seeking detailed explanation of how formula variables are to be handled. This master list of formulas and the accompanying explanations identify major system requirements that vendors need to address when submitting a proposal to management.

Determining the formats in which processed data will be output as information involves decisions that may change the structure and style of current business forms, guest folios, guest checks, management reports, and other materials. The information needs of the business and the format preferences of managers should dictate the choice of the system's output capabilities. The sample report formats collected from various vendors during the early fact-finding stage should serve as a starting point for management's determination of preferred formats for reporting. If the vendors solicited have installed systems in other hospitality operations, management should request sample designs for review, including:

- Reservation confirmation notices (electronic and printed).
- Registration processing (system-based and self-service).
- Guest folio files (electronic formatting).
- Third-party billings (electronic and printed).
- Payroll accounting (e-checks, direct deposit, and printed).

Request for Proposal

After translating information needs into system requirements, management is ready to request a property-specific proposal from industry suppliers. A **request for proposal (RFP)** is typically made up of three major sections. One section informs the vendor about hospitality business operations; a second section establishes bidding requirements for vendor proposals; and a third section deals specifically with user application requirements.

The first section of the RFP should contain an overview of the hospitality business, list objectives and broad operational requirements for the system, and briefly outline the scope of vendor relations and support services. The overview of the hospitality business should include a detailed property profile based on its information needs. Listing objectives and operational requirements for the system offers management the opportunity to identify and designate particular system features as mandatory or optional, thus assisting vendors in the preparation of responsive proposals. An outline of the vendor's responsibilities should include the proposal submission deadline and should encourage vendors to submit as much information as possible relative to such areas as:

- Network configurations.
- Application descriptions.
- Maintenance and support services.
- Installation and training programs.
- Guarantees and warranties.
- Payment plan options.
- Future expandability of the proposed system.

The second section of the RFP establishes bidding requirements for vendor proposals. Allowing vendors to formulate bids using a proprietary or arbitrary format will force management into using an unstructured evaluation process. All proposals should be submitted in a standardized response form supplied by management to facilitate price and performance comparisons. Exhibit 5 shows a sample cost summary table. Note that structured formatting enables management to conduct comparisons between proposals using a common set of dimensions. Vendors should also be required to include a statement of financial history and stability.

The final section of the RFP needs to address specific system application requirements. Exhibit 6 shows a sample RFP form that structures vendors' responses to application requirements. Since all vendors are required to use the identical response format, management will be more efficient in evaluating competing proposals.

Once created, the RFP (printed, electronic, or online) is distributed to the vendor community for response. After receiving an RFP, most vendors will contact management and conduct a site survey.

Site Survey

After receiving an RFP, vendors typically contact the property to perform a **site survey**. The purpose of a site survey is to allow the vendor to better understand the specific business operations of the property that may affect system design. The physical parameters of a property help determine appropriate types of hardware and network configurations.

Exhibit 5   Sample Cost Summary Table

REQUIREMENTS	PRICE	MAINTENANCE	COMMENTS
Hardware Software Other (specify) Discount Subtotal			
NON-RECURRING COSTS	**PRICE**	**MAINTENANCE**	**COMMENTS**
Site Prep Delivery Installation Training Other (specify) Discount Subtotal			
Total			

Exhibit 6   Sample Format for Listing Application Requirements

Instructions: Vendors are to indicate the applications they offer that are identical to those desired by the user (YES—Same), similar in function to those desired by the user (YES—Similar), function not now available but will develop (NO—Soon), or function not available (NO).

*   check appropriate column   *

FUNCTION:	YES Same	YES Similar	NO Soon	NO
Ingredient file of food items				
Recipe file of ingredients				
Menu file of recipe and subrecipes				
Inventory file of food items				
Payroll master file of employees				
Purchase order file by purveyor				
Check register of issued checks				
Daily transaction register				
Payroll register				
Accounts receivable ledger module				
Accounts payable ledger module				
General ledger module				
Income statement				
Balance sheet				

During a site survey, a vendor may analyze many other characteristics specific to business operations that are important to overall system planning. Details regarding management and workforce organization, business policies and procedures, and daily operations will directly affect the vendor's system proposal in relation to such areas as:

*   Training and retraining programs.

*   Hidden cost considerations.

- Electronic community (wired vs. wireless).

- Installation schedules.

- Number of workstations.

- Backup system requirements.

- Communication links.

- Security requirements.

- System support services.

In order to secure all the information necessary to complete a proposal, vendors may require information from several operating departments that will involve the cooperation of personnel within the property. Management may assign a staff person as a representative to facilitate the vendor's access to such information and minimize disruptions to operations. When several vendors are scheduled to conduct site surveys, it is wise to appoint the same representative to serve as coordinator. The coordinator should note the efficiency with which vendors conduct a survey, as this information may become a contributing factor when comparing vendors.

Evaluating Proposals

After conducting a site survey, the vendor completes a system proposal and submits it for consideration. While there are many ways to evaluate a proposal, a multiple rating system can be an efficient and effective method.

A multiple rating system applies the same criteria to judge the worth of each vendor's proposal. Generally, the criteria consist of several issues that management considers critical to the business. Management then rates the vendor's response to each issue on a scale from 1 to 100. The higher the rating, the better the proposal is deemed to address the issue. Since some issues will always be considered more important than others, simply totaling the ratings on key issues may not necessarily identify the best system proposal. In order to identify the best proposal, management must rank the issues in the order of their importance. This can be accomplished by assigning a percentage value (or weight) to each criterion, denoting its relative importance within the overall evaluation scheme. The ratings for each issue are multiplied by their appropriate percentage values and *then* totaled to yield an overall score for each vendor proposal. The proposals receiving the highest overall score identify the vendors with whom management should seriously consider scheduling product demonstrations. The following example illustrates how a multiple rating system can be used to evaluate proposals from three different vendors.

Assume that a business receives three proposals, one each from vendor A, vendor B, and vendor C. Assume further that management has decided to evaluate each proposal on three key issues—product performance, vendor's business reputation, and system cost.

The issue of product performance focuses on how well the proposed system fits the information needs of the business. Each vendor's proposal is studied and given a rating from 1 to 100. For the sake of this example, assume that vendor

A receives a rating of 80, vendor B a rating of 70, and vendor C a rating of 50. Further assume that management decides that product performance is the most important of the three issues and assigns this issue a relative value of 45 percent. Each vendor's rating on the first issue is then multiplied by 45 percent to arrive at a score that is relative to the entire evaluation scheme. Vendor A would therefore be awarded 36 points (80 × 0.45); vendor B given 32 points (70 × 0.45); and vendor C assigned 23 points (50 × 0.45).

The second issue focuses on the vendor's business reputation and includes such factors as success in the marketplace, the degree of system support that the vendor can provide, and the financial stability of the vendor's business. In relation to this issue, management will be interested in answers to such questions as:

- How long has the vendor been in the hospitality technology business?

- Are hospitality systems the vendor's principal business?

- How many installations does the vendor currently support?

- How satisfied are current users?

- Is the vendor's business financially stable?

- Is the vendor expected to remain in the hospitality technology business?

Each vendor's proposal is studied and given a rating from 1 to 100. Vendor A receives a rating of 60, vendor B a rating of 95, and vendor C a rating of 80. Management assigns the issue of business reputation a value of 30 percent. Each vendor's rating on the second issue is then multiplied by 30 percent to arrive at a score. Vendor A scores 18 points (60 × 0.30); vendor B earns 29 points (95 × 0.30); and vendor C totals 24 points (80 × 0.30).

The third issue centers on economic factors such as direct, indirect, and hidden costs of purchasing the technology. Assume that management designed a portion of the RFP requiring respondents to estimate the **direct costs** of individual system components. The identification of system components enables management to:

- Evaluate the benefits of installing the system in phases or modules.

- Eliminate unnecessary hardware devices or software programs.

- Conduct comparative price shopping for system components.

The RFP should have directed vendors to estimate **indirect costs**, such as taxes, insurance, shipping, and other costs that may result from:

- Modifying air conditioning, electrical, and communication networking.

- Establishing contingency backup and security procedures.

- Installing uninterruptible power sources, system access points, and related products.

- Maintaining an inventory of spare parts.

Vendors should also be required to estimate additional expenses, sometimes referred to as **hidden costs**, which include such items as supplies, training, overtime pay, and data conversion costs.

Each vendor's proposal is evaluated in relation to these factors and given a rating from 1 to 100. Vendor A receives a rating of 90, vendor B a rating of 70, and vendor C a rating of 80. Cost issues are assigned a relative value of 25 percent. Each vendor's rating on the third issue then is multiplied by 25 percent to arrive at a score that is relative to the entire evaluation scheme. Vendor A scores 23 points (90×0.25); vendor B receives 18 points (70×0.25); and vendor C earns 20 points (80×0.25).

Exhibit 7 shows the results of the multiple rating system used in this example. Vendor C's proposal will probably not receive further consideration as it did not score well on any of the three key issues. Also, note that although vendor A was judged best in terms of product performance, vendor B received the highest overall score. However, since the overall scores of vendors A and B are close, both vendors would likely be invited to schedule a product demonstration.

The previous example is meant only to illustrate a multiple rating system. A hospitality business should take care to identify and rank key issues that relate specifically to the needs and requirements of individual operations. Similar to how issues and relative order of importance will vary, so will the relative percentage values assigned to each key issue.

Vendor Product Demonstration

A product presentation is intended to allow management to view, firsthand, how the proposed system components operate to achieve the promised results. In order to control this process, management should consider using a scripted demonstration format.

Scripted product demonstrations (scripted demos) prevent vendor presentations from becoming a confusing show of "neat system tricks." With scripted demos, management provides each vendor with a script indicating which applications to demonstrate, ensuring that the session addresses features relevant to the business. This approach also provides a standard to ensure that every demonstration covers the same functionality.

When preparing scripts for vendor presentations, management must determine the most important system capabilities to be demonstrated. To develop this

Exhibit 7   Multiple Rating Results

CRITERIA	VENDORS		
	A	B	C
Product Performace	$80 \times 0.45 = 36$	$70 \times 0.45 = 32$	$50 \times 0.45 = 23$
Vendor Reputation	$60 \times 0.30 = 18$	$95 \times 0.30 = 29$	$80 \times 0.30 = 24$
System Cost	$90 \times 0.25 = 23$	$70 \times 0.25 = 18$	$80 \times 0.25 = 20$
Overall Score	77	79	67

list, management may need to meet with staff to determine potentially problematic areas.

In addition to adhering to the provided script, the vendor should be required to use the actual hardware components and application software included in the proposal. It is essential that all components needed to execute the scripted scenarios be included in the demonstration. For example, if a review of the output from a remote workstation printer is part of one of the scripted scenarios, the vendor should include a remote printer in the demonstration. If contactless payment readers, handheld terminals, or other units are included in the vendor's proposal, the vendor should be required to demonstrate these capabilities during the scripted demonstration session.

If applicable, develop guest scenarios to be scripted. Have members of the staff propose typical guest behaviors and transactions and describe unusual patterns of business to be monitored by the system. For example, have invited vendors program a POS system with the menu items offered in the restaurant to closely simulate actual orders, modifications, and settlement procedures.

Arrange scenarios in a logical sequence, but stagger the processing of transactions to simulate actual business conditions. Scripted demos are intended to test the system's ability to perform a variety of functions in random fashion. During the presentation, vendors should demonstrate the scripted guest scenarios one at a time and in the sequence established by management. Scenarios should not be modified or rearranged or reorganized. This will ensure that all demonstrations adhere to the identical script and form a basis for benchmarking and comparative evaluation.

Identify future events that may be relevant to the system, such as physical plant expansion, changes in staff size, online reservations management, satellite system interfacing, e-procurement, and so on.

Management must limit each vendor's demonstration time. Time constraints direct the vendor to address features and functions that management and staff are most interested in reviewing rather than features the vendor is most interested in showing. A ninety-minute presentation period should be sufficient for a twelve-to-fifteen transaction scenario script.

Vendors should be informed that those who successfully pass the scripted demo stage will be invited back for a second visit. At that time, vendors may demonstrate any additional system features that the scenarios failed to illustrate. A second visit provides an opportunity to establish product differentiation among competitors. After that stage of review, management should be able to select the most appropriate product and begin contract negotiations with the vendor.

Contract Negotiations

Before entering into contract negotiations with a vendor, management should secure copies of several standard contracts used by vendors of hospitality technology applications. These standard contracts are typically written in favor of the vendors and may not provide the kind of protection that the hospitality business may require. Management should examine these contracts carefully and obtain legal advice from a qualified attorney. If the attorney has no working knowledge of technology applications, management may also need assistance from an experienced technology applications consultant. In any case, the standard contract offered by a vendor serves as the starting point for contract negotiations. Since the actual sale has not yet been completed, management (the buyer) maintains a great deal of leverage in negotiating changes to the vendor's standard contract.

Contract Provisions

The general contents of a technology contract tend to be divided into several areas. While some areas may be executed as separate contracts or subcontracts, management may find that one master contract best meets the needs of the business. Three basic areas of a system contract are:

- General provisions (including saleability).

- Hardware provisions (including maintenance).

- Software provisions (including enhancements).

  General contract provisions specify standard contractual terms, including:

- Terms of delivery.

- Terms of payment.

- Survival past delivery.

- Saleable product warranty.

- Catastrophic remedies.

- Product warranty conditions.

- Provisions for breach of contract.

Survival past delivery refers to the responsibilities of both parties once the product arrives on the buyer's premises. Saleable product warranty provides the buyer assurance that the seller has a legal, marketable right to warrant the purchased product. Catastrophic remedies refer to penalties and relief in the event of a major product failure.

Hardware contract provisions relate to the purchase and operation of the technology equipment, including the operating system software, network configuration, and system security. Key areas addressed in the hardware section of a contract include:

- Specifications and performance criteria.

- Delivery, installation, and testing requirements.

- Costs and terms of payment.

- Reliability tolerances.

- Maintenance program options.

- Security requirements.

Software contract provisions tend to be more difficult to negotiate because of the complex nature of software ownership. Since application software is a compilation of ideas and processes proprietary to the seller, title is not automatically transferred to the buyer. Instead, the software often remains the property of the seller and the buyer is granted a nonexclusive license to use the software. Key areas of a software contract are similar to those listed for hardware; however, the contract should demand that a copy of the source code in which the software was originally written be placed in escrow (in care of an independent third party) and released to the buyer should the vendor fail to carry out provisions stated within the contract or leave the hospitality technology business.

Contractual Arrangements

In relation to hospitality technology, there are several types of contractual arrangements. Three common agreements are:

- Single-vendor contracts.
- Multi-vendor contracts.
- Other equipment manufacturer (OEM) contracts.

A **single-vendor contract** refers to an agreement to purchase hardware, software, and netware from the same vendor. In most cases, the vendor makes the necessary hardware, software, and netware modifications before system implementation. A single-vendor contract clearly identifies the vendor's responsibilities in relation to system performance and security and avoids the kind of confusion that may arise in other contractual arrangements when the lines of responsibility are not so clearly defined.

A **multi-vendor contract** refers to an agreement to purchase system components from more than one vendor. The hardware components may be purchased directly from the manufacturer or purchased through a software vendor, who serves as a value-added reseller. In either case, the hardware components or the accompanying operating system may require modifications by the software provider in order to perform effectively. Similarly, network features may require modification based on hardware and software specifications.

When a business purchases hardware components from one source that must be modified to perform according to specifications set by another source, confusion can arise with respect to guarantees and warranties. For example, when a software vendor modifies hardware components in order for the system to support special application programs, the hardware manufacturer's guarantees and warranties could become invalid. Hardware manufacturers generally assume responsibility for product performance only in relation to designated performance specifications. Whenever hardware components must be modified, management should insist that whoever modifies hardware, software, or netware provide guarantees and warranties similar to those originally provided by the manufacturer or developer.

Another area of concern in multi-vendor contracts relates to troubleshooting and maintenance. For example, when a problem arises in a hotel's reservation system, the reservations staff may scramble to implement a backup operation while management contacts the hardware vendor. The hardware vendor may consider management's description of the problem and conclude the reservation system problem is a software problem. Management then contacts the software vendor who, after listening to management's description of the problem, may conclude that the hotel's problem is a hardware problem. Meanwhile, managers waste time, tempers shorten, and reservation traffic may be lost.

An **other equipment manufacturer (OEM) contract** refers to a situation in which a business agrees to purchase hardware, software, and netware from a single source, and the single source takes responsibility for the performance of the technology application. OEM contracts generally involve purchasing a complete system that arrives at the property ready for installation. This kind of contractual arrangement provides a business with the equivalent of a single-vendor contract, as all hardware, software, and netware customization is performed by the OEM.

Installation Factors

After completing contract negotiations, management must make final decisions on such installation factors as:

- Training.
- Site preparation.
- Design of materials.
- Initial entry of database elements.
- Acceptance testing.
- System conversion.
- Documentation.
- Contingency planning.

The following sections discuss each of these installation factors.

Training

Training should begin before installation and continue throughout the implementation process. The primary users of the system will be those individuals responsible for data entry, report generation, and system maintenance. These persons should begin active (hands-on) training with hardware components and software applications before installation. Training sessions are normally conducted by vendor staff members or vendor representatives using manuals, books, CDs, DVDs, video, web, and other media.

Training is most effective when conducted at the user's site. Management should insist that training sessions involve hardware and software identical to that being installed at the property. Although the costs of training are negotiable, the hospitality business generally assumes responsibility for the cost of training as well as any out-of-pocket expenses incurred by the vendor at the user's site. In addition, the hospitality business might have to bear the costs of securing additional training equipment needed to accommodate larger employee groups at the property.

Vendor representatives usually provide instruction on specific topics, ranging from technology application overruns to the details of particular software programs. There has been an expansion of training sessions offered by system vendors.

Technology training through text materials (books or manuals) can be laborious and confusing for first-time technology users. Written materials, however, have a permanence other media may not possess. Text materials can also be helpful for introducing sequential software applications.

Video, web-based, and related media have proven to be highly effective training methods. Videotapes, CDs, and DVDs designed to teach specific applications generally allow a learner to progress through the materials at his or her own speed. Web-based training materials permit a learner to progress in a non-linear fashion, jumping over previously mastered areas to concentrate on applications considered more difficult.

The amount of training managers need will vary based on prior exposure. Generally, managers are not directly involved in the input and processing functions of the technology application. However, since management depends on system output, it is vital that managers understand system capabilities. Successful implementation often is a function of management involvement and commitment. Management must provide support and encouragement for personnel training.

Site Preparation

Site preparation refers to architectural or engineering changes that must occur before an automated system can be installed. The extent of these changes depends on the size of the property and the kind of technology being installed. Site preparation may include:

- Modifications to the property's air handling system, electrical system, and communication system.

- Construction of individual workstation furniture to accommodate system components, cabling, and access points.

- Installation of an uninterruptible power supply.

- Construction of a technology room.

- Development of a security system.

These facets of site preparation must be carefully planned and executed in order to prevent disruptions to operations during and after installation.

Design of Materials

Details regarding any printed materials output or used by various applications must be resolved before implementation. This is also true of guest-related touch point applications (a touch point being any area of the business with which the guest interacts).

Lodging properties may choose to design both printed and electronic formats for reservation confirmation, website interfacing, broadcast mailings, guest folios, billing statements, payroll checks, and many management reports. Materials that may be redesigned for food service businesses include guest checks, broadcast mailings, menus, promotional materials, and management reports.

Other questions related to such materials include:

- Which forms will be printed or distributed in multiple copies?

- Will different qualities of paper stock be used for different printed materials?

- Which printed or electronic forms, documents, and reports will require the business's logo or other artwork?

Answering these questions during system development will ensure smoother installation of the technology and enable management to refine materials during acceptance testing of an application. In addition, appropriate personnel will receive specific training in order to prepare and distribute forms, documents, and reports.

Data Entry

Before system installation, management and vendor representatives must develop a plan for data entry that will populate the application database. This is a critical area of technology planning that often is overlooked. Once the system is installed and implemented, the content of the database is necessary to define the scope of potential applications.

While database design specifications are usually the mutual responsibility of the vendor and management, the actual entering of data elements according to design specifications is the responsibility of trained property employees. Initial data entry can be a time-consuming and costly process that can be a significant hidden cost of implementation. For most lodging properties, initial data entry involves inputting room types, room numbers, room rates, revenue management codes, employee identification numbers, transaction posting codes, settlement options, sales history data, guest history files, and so on. For most food service operations, initial data entry entails inputting ingredient lists, recipe and sub-recipe files, meal plans, menu prices, settlement options, historical menu mix (sales) data, and more. It is extremely important that initial data entry be completed within a time frame that permits extensive acceptance testing before the business considers the system fully implemented.

Acceptance Testing

Before adopting or upgrading an application, management should conduct extensive acceptance testing of the candidate technology. Acceptance testing involves more than simply checking whether the application works. Tests should be developed to determine whether automated operations function according to standards defined by management. Fundamental areas of acceptance testing include:

- Hardware efficiency.

- Software reliability.

- Data integrity.

- Network security.

Hardware efficiency refers to the ease of use of system equipment and the suspense time involved in searching for necessary data. These areas must be tested using industry metrics and found acceptable. Users must be able to retrieve necessary data in a timely manner without unnecessary procedures or user intervention.

Software reliability refers to the accuracy with which the programs process data. The reliability of application software programs as well as embedded algorithms (formulas) should be challenged with a set of test data. This can be done by processing a known set of data through the application and comparing the system's output with calculated results generated by previous computation. Lodging operations can input data from a previous month and process a series of statistical reports and financial statements. These reports and statements can then be compared with the actual reports and statements prepared by the previous technology. Similarly, food service operations can input data from a prior period and test the accuracy of the application software in calculating food cost percentage, menu counts, and payroll expenses. In any case, the use of previously processed data can be extremely helpful in verifying the algorithmic design of the new system.

Data, or system, integrity refers to the degree of software integration. Sharing files to produce comprehensive reports is typically a major issue in system selection. Acceptance testing should prove that such integration exists and meets management's standards. Network security involves testing firewalls and other techniques that ensure the safety of proprietary data and information.

System Conversion

System conversion is the process of transitioning from an installed (legacy) system to a new system. System conversion within a hospitality operation can be difficult and trying. Two commonly used conversion strategies are parallel conversion and direct cutover conversion.

With **parallel conversion**, the property continues to operate the legacy system while incrementally installing application modules of the new system. The two information systems operate simultaneously. Usually, both systems are maintained for one accounting period with incremental transitioning between the old and new systems. When comfortable with the new system's operation, management will direct a complete conversion to the new system. While there is relatively little risk involved with parallel conversion, it incurs the high costs of operating two information systems simultaneously. It also assumes a lack of urgency in adopting the new system.

With **direct cutover conversion**, management chooses a date on which the property is to switch from the current system to the new system. Direct cutover is also called "cold turkey" because it involves a complete withdrawal from the previous information system on a targeted date. This approach may be especially effective when the previous system is perceived as cumbersome and inadequate, or when the new technology is perceived as a major enhancement over the former system. The main advantage of a direct cutover conversion is that the hospitality business is not required to operate two information systems simultaneously. A disadvantage is the potential risk of adopting a new system without the ability to revert to old processes and procedures should operational confusion or system failure ensue.

There are a number of conversion strategies that combine aspects of both parallel conversion and direct cutover strategies. For example, lodging properties may choose to immediately convert areas such as reservations, rooms management, and guest accounting, but maintain parallel conversion procedures for payroll and general ledger accounting applications. Whatever the selected strategy, balance operational costs against risks. Risks can often be minimized by careful attention to acceptance testing, training, and contingency planning.

Documentation

Adequate system documentation for each component is critical to the success of system operations beyond the initial training period. Documentation is essential for ongoing training of staff and for identifying underused system capabilities and possible weaknesses within the system design. The three most important forms of documentation, whether they be available in printed, electronic, or online format, are the operator's guide, technical manuals, and system flowcharts.

Operator's guides, also called user's guides, are training materials for specific application procedures. Some vendors provide a single, all-encompassing guidebook or online resource, with a table of contents or search engine. However, the documentation for a system with extensive application options might be most effective when segmented by job function, with a separate user's guide for a specific staff position (for example, cashiers, front desk agent, sales staff, and so on).

Technical manuals, also called systems manuals, focus on the engineering features of the technology. Technical manuals typically include schematic diagrams of electronic circuitry and may include troubleshooting hints for service and repair workers. Managers of some businesses fail to request this kind of technical documentation because they do not foresee using it themselves. However, technical manuals can be valuable resources in emergencies or during system upgrades.

While system flowcharts may not be part of the standard documentation package, management should request this documentation, as it offers insight into the operation and interconnectedness of applications. System flowcharts illustrate the input-process-output logic, file structures, program subroutines, interprogram relationships, and the level of program integration within the system. These flowcharts provide a way to analyze the effectiveness of the information system and may prove invaluable when software or hardware modifications are considered.

Contingency Planning

The purpose of contingency planning is to define procedures that are to be followed when an automated application does not function properly. Contingency planning is an important aspect of technology implementation. There are four basic parts to an effective contingency plan.

The first part designates an emergency team. The systems manager (or supervisor) typically leads the emergency team, which is made up of representatives from various operating departments. Each team member is assigned specific responsibilities that may range from installing spare parts to troubleshooting or performing sophisticated diagnostic routines.

The second part of a contingency plan identifies detailed information about hardware components, network configurations, software design, supplier contacts, environmental requirements, and site considerations. This information is typically stored in a secure location and is made available only to members of the contingency team.

The third part of the plan identifies secure operational and backup sites (such as local service bureaus, web-hosted service providers, etc.) and sources of substitute equipment.

The final section of a contingency plan details procedures for data recovery and file capture and for implementing temporary nonautomated operations while the system remains inoperable.

Key Terms

direct costs—In relation to the purchase of a technology system, the costs of individual system components.

direct cutover conversion—In relation to the implementation of a technology system, management chooses a date on which there is to be a complete switch from the current system to a new system. Also called going cold turkey.

flowchart—Specifically designed symbols to diagram the flow of data and documents through an information system.

hidden costs—In relation to the purchase of a technology system, costs associated with supplies, customized forms, training, overtime pay, and data conversion normally not included in the system purchase price.

indirect costs—In relation to the purchase of a technology system, these costs include taxes, insurance, shipping, and other costs that may result from modifying the property's air conditioning, electrical, and telephone wiring systems; establishing contingency programs; installing uninterruptible power sources; and maintaining an inventory of spare parts.

multi-vendor contract—In relation to the purchase of a technology system, an agreement to purchase hardware and software from separate sources.

other equipment manufacturer (OEM) contract—In relation to the purchase of a technology system, a contract in which a business agrees to purchase hardware components and software packages from a single source, and this single source takes full responsibility for the performance of the system. An OEM contract generally involves purchasing turnkey packages.

parallel conversion—In relation to the implementation of a technology system, a property operates a legacy system and a new system simultaneously until confident enough to move entirely to the new system.

property profile—Compiled statistics about aspects of the current information system; useful when communicating information needs of the business to vendors of technology systems.

request for proposal (RFP)—In relation to the purchase of a technology system, a three-part document prepared by management. The first section orients the vendor to management's business operations; the second section establishes bidding requirements for vendor proposals; and the third section deals specifically with user application requirements.

single-vendor contract—In relation to the purchase of a technology system, an agreement to purchase hardware and software from the same vendor. In most of these cases, the vendor makes the necessary hardware and software modifications before system implementation.

site survey—In relation to the purchase of a technology system, visits by vendors to identify important factors regarding specific business operations within a property that may affect system design.

system conversion—The process of switching from the current information system to the capabilities of a new system.

Review Questions

1. How can management go about analyzing the current information needs of a hospitality operation? How can flowcharts be used as a method of analysis?

2. What are some of the ways management can collect product literature regarding technology systems?

3. What factors must management take into account when determining system requirements?

4. What does the term "algorithm" mean? How does this term relate to management's task of determining system requirements?

5. What are the three major sections of a "request for proposal"? Why is it important for management to ask vendors to follow the same format when submitting proposals for review?

6. In relation to purchasing a technology system, what do the terms "direct costs," "indirect costs," and "hidden costs" mean? What are some examples of each?

7. What are the three areas typically addressed in a contract for the purchase of a technology system?

8. What are the major differences between single-vendor, multi-vendor, and other equipment manufacturer contracts? What are the advantages and disadvantages of each?

9. Upon completing contract negotiations, what factors must management officials address regarding the installation of a technology system?

10. Why is securing adequate documentation of each system component critical to the success of system operations beyond the installation period? What are the three critical forms of documentation?

Internet Sites

For more information, visit the following Internet sites. Remember that Internet addresses can change without notice. If the site is no longer there, you can use a search engine to look for additional sites.

Hospitality Organizations

American Hotel & Lodging Association
www.ahla.com

American Hotel & Lodging Educational Institute
www.ahlei.org

Club Managers Association of America
www.cmaa.org

Hospitality Financial and Technology Professionals
www.hftp.org

National Restaurant Association
www.restaurant.org

Restaurant Technology Systems

Agilysys, Inc.
www.agilysys.com

CMS Hospitality
www.cmshospitality.com

Comtrex
www.comtrex.com

System Concepts, Inc.
www.foodtrak.com

Point-of-Sale Systems

AccuPOS
www.accupos.com

Action Systems Inc.
www.rmpos.com

ALOHA POS
www.ncr.com

Dinerware POS
www.dinerware.com

MICROS Systems, Inc.
www.micros.com

PAR POS
www.partech.com

Pixel Point POS
www.pixelpointpos.com

Squirrel Systems
www.squirrelsystems.com

Chapter 12 Outline

Competencies

1. Identify three general threats to information systems and the private data they hold and describe security precautions to take against these threats. (pp. 305–306)

2. Describe basic operational precautions that help protect system integrity. (pp. 306–308)

3. Identify and describe three fundamental security measures. (pp. 308–312)

4. Outline the procedures that should be covered in contingency plans dealing with planned or unplanned system downtime. (pp. 312–322)

12

System and Security Maintenance

THERE IS A SAYING that the only completely secure system has no inputs or outputs, is encased in concrete, and lies at the bottom of the sea. Hospitality information systems accept data, process it, store it, and report it as output through both on- and off-premises applications. Maintaining systems security is an essential, never-ending task that strives to achieve perfect results. Even the best technical security will never be absolute. Therefore, users must have a sense of potential threats or problems and how to best resolve issues.

There's a balance to be struck between operating an open system and implementing too many security precautions. The adoption of reasonable precautions to protect information is essential.

The weakest security link in any system is human fallibility. The application software programs used to perform business functions are written by people for people. People sometimes make mistakes and aren't always honest. In fact, some may believe they have reason to corrupt or destroy information.

This chapter reviews the main threats to information and offers practical guidelines to making systems as secure as is reasonable without interfering with daily routines.

System Security and Data Privacy

Proprietary guest information and operational statistics are among the most valuable assets that a hospitality property can possess. Paper and electronic records are subject to physical damage from fire, flood, and so forth. Electronic records may also be vulnerable to threats that aren't as visible, but can be just as devastating as physical threats. The flexibility and interconnectedness that make networked systems so valuable also make them subject to internal and external threats, both deliberate and random. There are three broad categories of system security threats:

- *Environmental.* Environmental threats include situations or events that threaten the infrastructure of the system. Major concerns include fire, flood, earthquake, power failure, and loss of external network connectivity. Hospitality properties need to protect all locations housing essential system components, as well as design and implement a disaster recovery plan (DRP). A DRP provides a detailed explanation of system maintenance in the event of a major catastrophe. An effective DRP must be frequently reviewed, rehearsed, and updated.

- *Electrical.* Data can be corrupted accidentally or on purpose through viruses, hacker attacks, and other malicious acts distributed across network resources. System administrators must be mindful of "phishing" and "pharming" attacks. Phishing is the term used to describe a situation in which a hacker attempts to get a user to enter a legitimate password and/or other proprietary data into a website that resembles a trusted company, but is actually a front for the hacker. Pharming relies on domain spoofing (providing a web address that redirects the user elsewhere) for the purpose of obtaining personal or financial data. While phishing targets one user at a time, pharming targets groups of users simultaneously. The installation of an **uninterruptible power supply**, **firewall** protection, and **anti-virus software** is critical to system security.

- *Operational.* Accidental or intentional data entry errors, programming bugs, system circumvention, accidental deletions or modifications, and deliberate data corruption by current or former staff form a significant set of security threats. Restricting data access through biometric identification, password authorization, or other means is important to data integrity and security. Also important are access coding and encryption, as well as policies governing the use of software, personal media devices (including USB drives and recordable disks), and e-mail.

Hospitality managers become the guardians of a great deal of sensitive guest and employee information. An expectation of privacy is a basic component of guest-hotel and employee-employer relationships. For some time now, data privacy has been codified in both statutory and case law. Guests' and employees' expectations concerning data privacy are paramount. If a hotel company is not vigilant about proper data collection and protection processes, potential security threats are likely to arise. The threat of undesirable publicity, litigation, or fraud serves as a driver for industry adoption of sound privacy practices. Articulating and executing strong privacy policies typically strengthens and reinforces guest and employee relations.

Operational Precautions

The human element will always be a factor, through accidents such as data entry errors, bumping hardware, opening suspicious e-mail attachments, or physical damage caused by disgruntled current or former employees. All staff members using the systems must understand that they are responsible for maintaining the integrity of the system and its data. There's no way to prevent all forms of data entry errors, but taking the time (for example) to check whether a caller already has a guest history record instead of simply creating a new one may well pay off in terms of improved guest service and more repeat business. It's worth emphasizing that the more consistent and accurate the data input, the more valuable the informational output.

Education and reinforcement help staff members understand the nature of potential risks and realize that there are sound reasons for operating procedures and policies.

Restricted Access

In the same way that bank safe-deposit boxes are locked—inside a locked vault, inside a locked building—access to data must be partitioned. Users must be required to sign in with unique passwords that change regularly, and must be restricted to data and functions required for their specific job functions.

Systems must be designed to restrict individual users' access to various combinations of menu functions, further divided into "read-only" or "modify" capabilities for each, combined with detailed audit trails to identify who made data entries or alterations. If summary information from a restricted area would be useful to a staff member, then the information could be provided to the user without the detail behind the analysis being disclosed. It is a powerful inducement to use a system properly and professionally when staff know that all data processing functions can be traced.

The access privileges and passwords of any terminated staff member must be revoked immediately, and system passwords changed.

Written Policies

Having written policies and procedures in place and requiring all users to read and sign them before being provided system access enhances security awareness. Typical information system policies address:

- Application software.
- Portable storage media.
- E-mail and Internet use.
- Passwords and user names.
- System security.

Application Software. Limit applications to a clearly defined standard set, with no other software permitted on the system workstations. Some operating systems automatically enforce this policy through a **lock down** of the terminal's desktop configuration. This approach is highly recommended. All users should understand that supporting a standard application set will maximize its performance and maintainability. Additional applications can be added to the standard set as required, but only after approval by management based upon compatibility and usefulness.

Portable Storage Media. Personal software should not be allowed on portable storage media. The danger of contamination is too great; users may not take the time to scan media for viruses before running programs or copying data.

E-mail and Internet Use. Clear e-mail and Internet access policies are needed. Policies need to address whether personal Internet or e-mail access is permitted and under what circumstances. Whatever policy management sets, it should be in writing and signed by each employee.

Passwords and User Names. Passwords and user names must be used responsibly. Passwords should be changed regularly (at no less than three-month intervals) and monitored by system management. When personnel leave the organization, passwords and user names should be deleted immediately.

System Security. Computer room security must be maintained at all times. The room should be located away from heavy traffic areas (most definitely not in a through area), with access permitted only to those authorized to work on or manage the system. The room should have a self-closing, self-locking door and be properly air conditioned.

General Principles

At the core of all security measures are three fundamentals, without which any other precautions will be far more difficult to manage. These are:

- System backup—duplicate copies of important data must be properly indexed and stored off-site.
- System documentation for all component (inventory, support services, etc.) hardware, software, and netware.
- Security audit—reviewed no less often than annually, to ensure that system precautions are current.

The sample documents and schedules that appear in this chapter are only guidelines. Some items will not apply to all operations. Other system configurations will have additional items to append to the guidelines. Property system configurations are unique and must be documented to suit the circumstances.

System Backup

Backups are very important, both in terms of having manual procedures to fall back on and in having duplicate copies of data and system software. Operationally, even without a functioning system, both guest and transactional data can be current and accurate as long as there are predefined contingency procedures for control and coordination. It also helps if standby kits of the appropriate forms, materials, and supplies are kept handy and fully stocked. An example of manual operations guidelines is provided in the appendix at the end of this chapter.

The best insurance against system failure or data loss is a comprehensive backup copy of data and system files. Restoring a system from a backup file is usually the only way of recovering lost data, apart from reentering it from printed records. Even if you have to manually reenter all changes since the last backup was run, that is still far preferable to losing it all.

Backups should be created on a regular basis, using large-capacity, reliable storage media. A complete system backup of the network should be performed on a weekly basis. This procedure will take more time than the daily data backup, and therefore should be scheduled for the least busy time of the week. Operational data should be backed up every day, with the event recorded in the backup log (see Exhibit 1).

Backup media should be stored in a secure fire- and heat-proof location somewhere away from the system it is backing up, so the backup is not subject to the same conditions as the system if a catastrophe occurs.

Exhibit 1   Sample Media Backup Log

Day/Date	Time Started	Time Finished	Medium Used	Comments (errors/problems)
1.				
2.				
3.				
4.				
5.				
6.				
7.				
8.				
9.				
10.				
11.				
12.				
13.				
14.				
-------	-------	-------	-------	-------
-------	-------	-------	-------	-------
29.				
30.				
31.				

Media Backup Log

Month:_____ Year:_____

A set of backup media should be secured off-site at all times. A designated person should take the most current set of backup materials to an off-site storage location and bring the oldest set back to the property for recycling. Backup media may also be picked up and traded with a specialty service firm or a banking delivery company, such as Wells Fargo or Brinks.

However essential backups are, they do take time to reload onto the system, and all transactions that have occurred since the backup was created will have to be reentered to make the system data current again. To keep the system operating while this procedure is being completed, many properties print reports on key information at intervals throughout the day. To save paper, some properties copy important data to files on portable storage media. A laptop PC, which relies on batteries, will not be subject to a power outage that takes down the system. This can be a viable alternative for nearly all properties.

Downtime reports or files should provide all essential hotel status and guest billing information. These should be produced every two hours. If more than one department will need the same information, be sure that sufficient copies are generated. Suggested reports or backup files include:

- In-house guest list.
- Room availability list.
- Expected arrivals list (next five days).

- Current folio balances.

- Expected departure list.

- Guest messages.

- Room availability forecast (thirty days).

If it is known in advance that the system will be down, printing guest folios for all occupied rooms and house accounts is sensible. If time permits, housekeeping should generate the following reports:

- Late check-out list

- Room change report

- Early departure list

- Room status list (dirty and/or vacant rooms)

System Documentation

Documentation can be tedious to create and maintain (although automated tools can help with both functions), but it can also prove invaluable. Even in day-to-day operations, efficiency and confidence can be gained from having detailed and complete system documentation. Documentation needs to cover hardware, software, and netware components, listing:

- Component identification.

- Model and version/release number.

- Name and contact information of support service.

- Update log (changes since installation).

- Service call log.

A system description summary sheet should be completed for each system component. Exhibit 2 presents a sample form used to summarize a POS system. Interfacing the POS system to the property management system enables a food and beverage outlet to transmit postings to the appropriate guest folio. Exhibits 3 and 4 present additional generic forms.

In addition, there are two network diagrams that are especially useful. One is a physical schematic of hardware (PCs, printers, etc.) connectivity to various network topologies. This diagram includes all hardware on each network segment, with each item labeled with its make/model, IP address, and other relevant data. The second diagram is a software schematic that illustrates how the different applications are integrated and interact with each other. A software schematic can be useful when determining the impact of an application failure. The diagram should reflect interactions, flows, and data transfer methods.

Security Audit

A **security audit** is intended to verify that backup procedures and documentation are accurate and comprehensive. It serves as a check on every aspect of the system

Exhibit 2   Sample System Description Summary Sheet

POINT OF SALE (POS) SYSTEM AND PMS INTERFACE

System Description

Vendor/Model:_____   Software Level:_____

Purchased from:_____   Contact Name: _____

Phone:_____   Fax: _____

Comments: _____
_____
_____
_____
_____
_____
_____
_____

Service Information

Support Department Contact Name:_____   Phone:_____

Support Hours of Service:_____

Systems Engineer:_____   Phone: _____

Marketing Rep.: _____   Phone: _____

Comments: _____
_____
_____
_____
_____
_____
_____
_____

backup procedures, documentation, physical safeguards, password management, and so on. The audit process is normally guided by a checklist of requirements. Exhibit 5 presents a sample checklist for an information system audit. Industry practitioners suggest that an outside agency review the contents of the audit to ensure it is sufficient.

If a hospitality property is part of a management group, each property can audit another. For independent properties, outside consultants may be retained to perform the same service. It is important to note that the specifics of an installed configuration will determine the extent of auditing appropriate at a specific property.

Exhibit 3   Summary of Software Licenses

Software Type, Vendor, Application Name/Version	Number of Licenses Purchased	Installed on Server (S) or PC (PC)?	If on Server, Number of Users with Access	If on PCs, Number Installed

Detailed lists to be kept separately.

Manual Operations Plans

The following plans and procedures are suggested as an outline for use whenever a property management system is down for a significant time. Exhibit 6 outlines immediate actions to take to establish clear control and coordination responsibilities. Each property should prepare its own version based on its operational needs and should prepare similar documents for all other critical systems (POS, sales and catering, etc.). Plans should be reviewed periodically to ensure they remain current.

The key to effective manual operations is well-organized communication between management and all departments, especially the front office, reservations, and housekeeping departments. Most employees will never have worked in a manual environment and will be used to relying on electronic data processing. Consequently, instructions to employees should be clear and precise, and the plans should be practiced regularly. Ensuring quality guest service is of utmost importance during this period.

Management/Staff Roles

The following roles are suggested for key management and operations staff. The task assignments should be customized to the nature of each operation. For example, while many properties may not have a systems manager, they should have one person who has responsibility for coordinating support activities on automated systems. It is most important that the responsibility for performing each task is clearly understood by all.

Exhibit 4 Sample Service and Support Call Log

Before calling for hardware service, get approval from one of the following managers:
Name/Position:_____ Phone Extension:_____
Name/Position:_____ Phone Extension:_____
Name/Position:_____ Phone Extension:_____
Name/Position:_____ Phone Extension:_____
Name/Position:_____ Phone Extension:_____

Hardware Maintenance Vendor:_____
Contact Name: _____
Business Hours Phone:_____
Fax:_____
After Hours Phone:_____
Comments: _____
             _____
             _____
             _____

Critical Equipment
The following key items are covered by a 24x7 maintenance contract:

Equipment:	Location:

Important Equipment
The following hardware is on "normal hours" maintenance contract with service provided five days a week during business hours:

Equipment:	Location:

Low-Priority Equipment
The following equipment is not on a maintenance contract. All service will be billed as incurred at a per call rate of _____:

Equipment:	Location:

General Manager/Hotel Manager

- Authorizes notification of all management personnel.
- Receives status reports from the system personnel.
- Makes/approves operational decisions regarding system downtime.

Exhibit 5   Sample Information System Audit

Information System Audit
(Please comment on or explain any "No" responses.)

A.   Computer Room/Physical Systems

1.   Is the computer room in a quiet area, not on an outside wall, and not where it might be subject to flooding?
2.   Does it have a self-closing, self-locking door? What kind of lock is fitted?
3.   Who has access?
4.   Is there a separate air-conditioning unit for the computer room?
5.   Are temperature and humidity measured on a periodic basis to confirm that they are within specified ranges?
    a.   Who performs the measurements?
    b.   Attach copy of most recent page of log.
6.   Is there a fire alarm/smoke detector in the computer room?
7.   Is it a local alarm system? If not, where else does the alarm get indicated?
8.   When was it last tested?
9.   Is there a local fire extinguishing system in the computer room?
    a.   What type?
    b.   When was it last inspected? (Attach copy of log.)
10. Is the power for all critical systems on a separate electrical circuit with clearly marked outlets?
11. Are all critical systems on UPSs with sufficient battery backup for at least 20 minutes?
    a.   When was the last check of the backup's reliability under full load performed?
    b.   Do the battery backup systems provide automatic shutdown of the computer after a specified length of time?
    c.   When was this last tested?
12. Are all peripherals (PCs, printers, scanners, etc.) connected to surge-suppressing power strips?
13. Are preventive maintenance inspections being performed regularly? (This includes physical hardware—filter changes, etc.—and any software preventive maintenance such as NT server re-boots, re-booting the PMS to reclaim memory, etc.)
14. Is the computer room kept clean?
15. Is all cabling tidy and clearly labeled?
16. Is there a network diagram? (Attach copy.) Are procedures in place to keep it current?
17. Is there an inventory of all computer hardware?
    a.   How often is it checked, and by whom?
    b.   What is done if something is missing?

Exhibit 5　*(continued)*

18. Is there an inventory of all software applications and operating systems?
    a. How often is it checked, and by whom?
    b. Do proper licenses exist for all software?
    c. What is done if the number of copies in use exceeds the number of legal licenses?
19. Are there full, written descriptions of all computer systems and interfaces, including configuration, support information, current version level and modification history?
20. Are procedures with regard to fire, flood, or other emergencies posted in the computer room and understood by all who have access to the room and equipment?
21. Is there a disaster recovery plan? (Attach copy.)
    a. When was the last time it was tested?
    b. Where is the plan posted?

B.　Information Security

1. When are full/partial backups done? (Attach copy of plan.)
    a. Who performs the backups?
    b. Attach copy of log.
2. Where are the backups stored?
    a. In what type of container?
    b. Who has access to the media?
    c. Where is the off-site storage location?
3. How are verifications done to ensure the backup is working properly?
4. When was the last verification done?
5. Are downtime reports run to a specific schedule? (Attach copy.)
6. Are obsolete reports destroyed?
7. What redundancy is there for the critical computer systems?
    a. Are there complete backup computers/hardware?
    b. When were the computer/software maintenance contracts last reviewed for all critical systems?
    c. Is there an action plan for failure of the backup?
    d. When was it last tested?
8. Are all support contact numbers posted by the equipment?
9. Are the trouble logs kept with the systems or in an accessible location? (Attach copy.)
10. Are written procedures for manual operations posted at all appropriate locations?
    a. When were they last practiced?
    b. Are "crash kits" of office supplies, pre-filled forms, etc., kept available and fully stocked?

(continued)

Exhibit 5 *(continued)*

C. Network Security

1. How often are system and user passwords changed?
   a. Who determines the passwords?
   b. Are they secure? (At least six characters, mixed case and alpha/numeric, not easily connected with any specific user.)
2. Is a procedure in place to ensure that employees leaving the company have no access to the systems?
3. Does the current password list match the personnel list?
4. Are all operating system patches/fixes up to date?
5. Is a network-wide anti-virus program installed?
   a. Are all the virus signatures/software updates current?
   b. How often are the servers scanned for viruses?
   c. Is there a written policy regarding the use of diskettes?
6. Are there any outside connections to the local area network?
   a. If the connections are made using a modem on an individual computer, who has control over the connection(s) and the account(s)?
   b. If it is a direct connection into the LAN by a router or other similar device, who maintains the connection, hardware configuration, and passwords for the device?
   c. Is there a firewall?
   d. Who maintains it?
7. Have password-cracking programs or external security consultants been employed to help determine the level of security?

D. Employee Security

1. Are new employees required to sign a written policy regarding computer usage and abuse?
2. Are there written procedures and policies for access to the Internet, including e-mail and browsing?
3. Are there written procedures for securing the computer systems when an employee is terminated? (Attach copies of all such policies and procedures.)

Systems Manager

- Determines magnitude of problem, estimates system downtime, and determines status of all correction activities in progress.

- Notifies response team on the severity of problem and recommends the degree of contingency to implement.

- Ensures that all necessary functions and personnel are prepared to begin manual operations, if needed, and notifies appropriate service/vendor personnel.

Exhibit 6   Downtime Quick Response Checklist

Quick Response Checklist

1. Alert managers.

2. If the system is down because of a power failure, *turn off all equipment immediately.* Failure to do so could result in further hardware damage. If the critical items are on uninterruptible power supplies (UPSs) with automated shutdown routines, monitor these to ensure that they are in fact closing down correctly.

3. Distribute the most recent downtime reports and destroy prior lists.

4. Designate a rack clerk, responsible for maintaining the room inventory and status, to begin to record all check-ins, check-outs, etc.

5. Designate a posting clerk, responsible for writing all charges on the guest folios.

6. Alert the outlets that the system is inoperable and that they must close checks to the manual key. All room charges must be taken to the front desk for manual posting.

7. Alert the audit staff members no later than four hours before their shift that the system is down and that they should report early to begin a manual audit.

8. Alert the central reservation help desk of the situation and estimated downtime, and arrange an alternative for continued delivery of reservations and feedback of hotel availability status.

9. The rooms division manager should write a letter to all in-house guests and arrivals notifying them of the situation.

10. Issue battery-operated radios to all key personnel, including PBX.

- Keeps management updated regarding contingency status.
- Supervises repair, restoration, and replacement of data, components, systems, or entire computer room as needed.
- Prepares reports for hotel management detailing the problems, causes and solutions, plan performance, and suggestions for modifications as needed.

Front Office Manager

- Coordinates front office activity with the systems manager and reservations manager.
- Supervises the front office activity during downtime.
- Monitors controls and audit trails during downtime.
- Supplies food and beverage outlets with current guest list, no-post list, and cash guest list.
- Documents observed or perceived problems in plan operation for review and/or revision.
- Coordinates reconstruction of data once the system is restored.

Front Desk Supervisor

- Monitors and controls registration functions.
- Maintains room status control sheet.
- Maintains walk-in list.
- Communicates status changes to housekeeping.
- Maintains status change log.
- Supervises the bucket clerk.
- Supervises reentry of check-ins, check-outs, and moves once the system is restored.

Reception Agents

- Control filing of guest charges and maintenance of current balances. Supervise generation of source documents, vouchers/receipts, etc.
- Assist cashiers in balancing shift.
- Assist with posting of charges and payments once the system is restored.

Reservations Manager

- Distributes thirty-day and one-year room availability reports to all reservation agents.
- Supervises manual booking of reservations.
- Maintains manual reservations file.
- Maintains a manual room availability control chart.
- Supervises reentry of reservations once the system is restored.

PBX Operator

- Notifies technology staff when the system is down.
- Maintains and updates the telephone reference list with assistance of front office.

All Outlet Managers

- Coordinate the food and beverage contingency plan with the systems manager.
- Supervise the execution of the contingency plan in all food and beverage outlets.
- Supervise manual operation of outlets, including ordering, service, payment, and posting of all checks.
- Supervise entering of all information once system is restored.
- Assist in the balancing process during downtime.

Cashiers

- Distribute three-part check and check control sheet to outlet cashiers.
- Monitor the manual tip control sheet and disbursement of charge tips.

Assistant Controller

- Coordinates accounting department activity with the systems manager.
- Supervises execution of the contingency plan in the accounting office.
- Supervises data reconstruction after the system is restored.

Accounts Receivable Manager

- Works with the front desk supervisor and bucket clerk on maintaining the manual guest ledger.
- Maintains manual banquet billings.
- Coordinates advance deposit refunds with accounts payable during extended downtime.
- Maintains manual credit card account balances.
- Monitors advance deposit activity.
- Supervises the restoration of data.

Housekeeping

- Supervises manual room status controls.
- Establishes initial room status sheet (P.M.) housekeeping report.
- Supervises vacant room inspection.
- Supervises distribution of updated room status lists to front desk.
- Supervises manual assignment of room attendants.
- Maintains room status change log.

Night Reception Manager

- Performs regular audit functions when and where necessary.
- Helps generate manual reports during extended downtime.
- Supervises the night clerks during downtime.
- Assists in the restoration of data.
- Updates and distributes reports.
- Balances hotel accounts at the end of the day.

Manual Front Desk Overview

Exhibit 7 lists items and staff needed to manually operate the front desk. It is wise to be sure that a room rack report (see Exhibit 8) or its equivalent and any standard forms are prepared in advance (with the room numbers and other data that do not change). In addition, "crash kits" stocked with necessary office supplies (pens, cards, pads, tape, etc.) should be placed in an area that is convenient to the front desk. The appendix at the end of the chapter contains steps outlining the basic manual operation of the front desk, followed by more detailed procedures for manual check-in, check-out, and other typical functions.

Exhibit 7   Items and Staff Needed for Manual Front Desk Operations

Forms:	Manual Room Rack	
	Cash Guest Report	
	House Count Sheet	
	Registration Cards (handwritten or preprinted)	
	Guest Folios (handwritten or preprinted)	
	Reservations Forms (handwritten or preprinted)	
	Most recent downtime reports from system	
Miscellaneous:	Index cards and alphabetical file	
	Calculator with tape (battery-operated)	
	Pencil with eraser	
	Credit card imprinters	
Personnel:	Posting Clerk:	Responsible for posting all charges to guest folios
	Rack Clerk:	Responsible for maintaining room inventory and current status
	Runners:	Responsible for communications between departments, ensuring that departments are passing information correctly and that everyone is following the manual operating procedures

Returning to Automated Operations

Once the system becomes fully operational again, it must be brought up-to-date by manually entering transactions that occurred in the interim. This requires an organized effort on the part of management to keep all postings on the correct day. If night audit work is organized into batches, staff is able to concentrate on one day's activity at a time. A night audit routine must be executed for each day that the system was down in order to bring the system up to the current date. Manual downtime procedures must be maintained until the system is functioning properly and data has been verified as up-to-date. General steps involved in bringing the system up-to-date include:

1. Process the first day's work. Process all activity that was not posted on the day the system crashed, including check-ins, check-outs, all transactions, and room status changes.

2. Some systems (POS, call accounting, minibars, pay movies, etc.) that use an interface to post charges to guest folios may hold charges in a buffer memory storage area. If these systems continued to function during the time the PMS did not, charges may post automatically when the interface is restored. This could result in charges being posted to the wrong accounts, double posting of charges, phones or minibars being turned off or on inappropriately, and so on. Each of these systems should have a backup printer to report charges (including date, time, and room number) that were unable to be transferred to the PMS. This is the information needed to post charges manually to the correct guests' folios, but the reports do not imply that charges are not still being held in a buffer. Management needs to inquire with each vendor of an interfaced system to learn how the system works when the interface host is nonfunctional.

Exhibit 8   Sample Manual Room Rack Report

Manual Room Rack

Floor Number _____   Section Number _____

Room #: _____	Room Type: _____
Status: _____	Guest Name: _____
Room Features: _____	Check-Out: _____

Room #: _____	Room Type: _____
Status: _____	Guest Name: _____
Room Features: _____	Check-Out: _____

Room #: _____	Room Type: _____
Status: _____	Guest Name: _____
Room Features: _____	Check-Out: _____

Room #: _____	Room Type: _____
Status: _____	Guest Name: _____
Room Features: _____	Check-Out: _____

Room #: _____	Room Type: _____
Status: _____	Guest Name: _____
Room Features: _____	Check-Out: _____

Room #: _____	Room Type: _____
Status: _____	Guest Name: _____
Room Features: _____	Check-Out: _____

Room #: _____	Room Type: _____
Status: _____	Guest Name: _____
Room Features: _____	Check-Out: _____

Room #: _____	Room Type: _____
Status: _____	Guest Name: _____
Room Features: _____	Check-Out: _____

Room #: _____	Room Type: _____
Status: _____	Guest Name: _____
Room Features: _____	Check-Out: _____

Room #: _____	Room Type: _____
Status: _____	Guest Name: _____
Room Features: _____	Check-Out: _____

Room #: _____	Room Type: _____
Status: _____	Guest Name: _____
Room Features: _____	Check-Out: _____

3. Perform a rooms and financial audit for the day.

4. Conduct a night audit routine within the system.

5. Once the above procedures are complete and the system moves on to the next day, process the remaining days' transactions in a similar manner. Perform an end-of-day procedure for each failed day until the current day and time are reached.

Key Terms

anti-virus software—Programs that search for binary signatures (patterns) of known viruses that have attached themselves to executable programs. As new viruses are discovered, the signature database has to be updated in order for the anti-virus program to be effective. Vendors generally offer downloads via the web in order to keep clients current.

downtime—The time during which a computer is not functioning due to hardware or system software failure.

firewall—A method for keeping a network secure from intruders. It can be a single router or a combination of routers and servers, each performing some type of firewall processing.

lock down—An action designed to restrict the functionality of a system. For example, network administrators can lock down client desktops so that users can perform only certain operations.

security audit—An examination of networks and computer systems to determine an organization's vulnerability to criminal invasion (hackers, viruses, arson, etc.), natural disasters (fire, tornadoes, earthquakes, etc.), and other threats.

uninterruptible power supply (UPS)—Backup power used when the electrical power fails or drops to an unacceptable voltage level. Small UPS systems provide enough battery power to power down the computer in an orderly manner. Sophisticated systems tied to electrical generators can provide power for days.

Review Questions

1. What installations are critical to electrical system security?

2. What is provided in a disaster recovery plan (DRP)?

3. In what ways can user access to data be restricted?

4. What applications policy can be enforced through a lock down?

5. What is a major precaution that can be taken to guard against system failure or data loss?

6. Which two network programs are useful in system documentation?

7. What is the purpose of a security audit?

8. What are suggested tasks for hotel managers when a property management system is down?

9. Which staff member should be responsible for maintaining the room status change log when a property management system is down?

10. What steps are necessary to bring up to date a property management system that was previously down?

 Internet Sites

For more information, visit the following Internet sites. Remember that Internet addresses can change without notice. If the site is no longer there, you can use a search engine to look for additional sites.

Captain Information Technology Inc.
www.captainresq.com

Returnstar Technology Co., Ltd.
www.iqboard.net

Data Security Management Systems Inc.
www.dsmsystems.com

Symantec Corporation
www.symantec.com

Home PC Firewall Guide
www.firewallguide.com

Zone Alarm
www.zonealarm.com

Chapter Appendix

Manual Front Desk Operations

Manual Room Rack

1. Establish a manual room rack on the rack sheets with an accurate and complete status of all rooms. Obtain as much information as possible about the status of each room from the downtime reports, the bucket, and the housekeeping reports. Use your staff (including security, bellpersons, and others if needed) to resolve any discrepancies.

2. Record the status of each room on the room rack sheets. Use the status codes most familiar to your hotel.

3. For each occupied room, complete the data on the room rack sheet.

Posting Clerk

The posting clerk should create a folio for each registered guest and carry forward the last balance from the last occupancy report. A sample downtime guest folio is presented in Figure 1. Attach the folio to each registration card in the bucket. If manual posting becomes necessary, the posting clerk will post charges to this folio and will carry the balance forward as they post. If departure folios are relatively current, they may be filed in the bucket in lieu of manually preparing folios. Include the rate and tax on the folio. This process may take some time, and you may need to assign employees from other departments to assist with it.

Housekeeping

1. The housekeeping floor supervisors update the executive housekeeper on room status.

2. Hourly, the executive housekeeper updates the front office manager and the reservation manager with the current status of the hotel rooms. The front office manager is responsible for updating the rack clerk. These four people are responsible for maintaining an accurate house count.

Rack Clerk

The rack clerk generates an updated rack report that will be distributed to each department.

1. Gather the registration cards for all arrivals and all departures since the time of the last backup list. Enter them on manual arrival and departure logs, and write "SYSTEM DOWN" after the last entries so that arrivals and departures before and after the downtime can be determined.

Figure 1   Sample Downtime Guest Folio

Date: _____

We're sorry, but we are unable to print a copy of your folio at this time. Please review the amounts listed below and note any corrections. A final folio will be mailed to you as soon as possible. Thank you!

Guest Name: _____   Room Number:_____

Mailing Address: _____

_____

_____

Balance as of: _____ at _____ $_____
                         Date   Time

Room Charge for the Night of: _____ $_____
                                        Date
Room Tax: $_____

Other Charges:

_____ $_____

_____ $_____

_____ $_____

_____ $_____

_____ $_____

_____ $_____

Total: $_____

Amount Paid: $_____

Balance: $_____

Form of Settlement (circle):   Cash   Direct Bill   Amex   Visa/MC   Diners   Discover
                                         (attach voucher for credit card settlement)

Time of Departure: _____   Charges Posted: ___   Clerk: _____

Clerk Number: _____   Check-Out: ___   Clerk: _____

Folio Mailed: ___   Clerk: _____

2. The rack clerk keeps track of the house count, including in-house guests, expected departures, 6 P.M. arrivals, etc.

Check-In

1. At 5 P.M. the rack clerk, front desk manager, and executive housekeeper should compare their reports for discrepancies. These discrepant rooms should be rechecked manually; notify housekeeping once there is an accurate accounting of the house status.

2. For new check-ins, the front desk clerk handwrites a folio, attaches it immediately to the registration card, and passes it to the posting clerk for placement in the bucket.

3. Record cash-paying guests on the cash guest report and distribute this to the outlets on a regular basis.

PBX

Fill out index cards for each occupied room for placement in an "in-house guest" accordion file for PBX operators. Include each guest's last name, first name, room number, check-out date, and credit status. The credit status is needed to determine if long-distance phone service should be allowed for this guest. Make note of any guest requiring accessible accommodations. Because this process may take some time, employees from other departments may be assigned to assist.

Posting Clerk

At a time designated by management, the posting clerk should be stationed in the cashier/count-out room and begin posting all charges from the outlets. Information on the folio includes date, charge/outlet, reference number, and the amount.

Shift Closing

At the end of the shift, the posting clerk totals all outlet charges by outlet, runs a tape, balances each stack of charges, and places all charges in the night audit basket.

Check-Out

1. Pull the registration card and folio from the bucket. Make certain room and tax has been posted each night; if not, manually post the appropriate amount with date.

2. Post any adjustments or paid-outs manually using the appropriate form. Ensure that the type of adjustment, account code, date, and amount are recorded accurately on the folio.

3. Re-add all charges on the folio to ensure that the balance is correct and collect the payment. Attach a copy of the folio, credit card voucher, and any miscellaneous vouchers to the registration card, and file it with the appropriate method of payment in the shift work.

4. Advise guests at check-out that all charges may not appear on the bill they've just been given and that a revised statement will be sent to them.

5. Tell the rack clerk that this guest has checked out. The rack clerk will then change the status of the room on the rack sheet.

6. The rack clerk notifies housekeeping and PBX of the status change.

7. PBX removes the index card for that guest from the folder.

Miscellaneous Posting

Items needed: Preprinted posting slips for miscellaneous charges, adjustments, and paid-outs. The posting clerk will post all guest charges manually.

1. When charges are brought to the front desk from the outlets, the posting clerk will write the amount, time, date, and source of charge on the guest's folio.

2. The posting clerk should initial the charge voucher.

3. A copy of the charge voucher should be placed in the bucket along with the guest folio. If the copy machine is not functioning, make a manual copy and mark it as a copy.

4. The posting clerk should set a copy of the charge voucher aside for end-of-shift balance.

Paid-Out

In hotels that routinely post charges from outlets that are not a part of the hotel (gift shop, etc.) as paid-outs, the following procedures should be followed:

1. Fill out a paid-out voucher and attach it to the receipt that the outlet presented to you for posting.

2. Present the receipt with the paid-out voucher to the posting clerk for posting to the guest folio.

3. The posting clerk will include the copy of the receipt in the bucket with the folio.

4. A copy of the receipt and the paid-out voucher will be included with the posting clerk's shift work.

Shift Closing

Shift closing will be conducted in the usual manner with the exception of balancing to the computer. Accounting personnel should be available to assist during shift closings.

1. Complete the cash drop form and run a calculator tape to determine the total cash taken in.

2. Drop the correct amount of cash in the deposit envelope, leaving your bank at the correct starting amount.

3. Add each type of posting voucher you posted. This includes adjustments, miscellaneous vouchers, phone, restaurant, bar, etc.

4. Add each credit card payment by type (AX, VA, etc.).

5. Complete a shift-closing report.

6. Place the shift-closing packet in the night audit basket, including the shift closing report and the totaled posting vouchers by account and any miscellaneous notes.

Night Audit

Each night, the night auditor and any additional personnel designated by the controller will perform an audit to ensure that revenue was posted properly. Special attention should be paid to each individual folio to ensure that they are all totaled correctly. Each morning the controller and designated representatives from the front office and accounting will record and audit all transactions that have been manually posted from the previous day, producing a manual revenue report. NOTE: The accounting department should create and attach additional documentation for this section describing specific functions to be performed by the audit staff and the posting clerks.

Housekeeping

The housekeeping department will keep a manual record of the status of all rooms on a daily basis. It should generate manual section assignments, which could be implemented at any time. The following procedures should be followed once the rack and current house status have been completed:

1. In the morning, generate room assignments using the rack report prepared by the rack clerk.

2. Housekeeping floor supervisors will update the executive housekeeper on room status as rooms are cleaned.

3. Hourly, the executive housekeeper will update the front office manager and the reservation manager; the front office manager is responsible for updating the rack clerk. These four people are responsible for maintaining an accurate house count.

4. Report discrepancies immediately to the front office manager as they occur throughout the day.

5. The rack clerk will periodically generate an updated rack report for distribution to each department. At 1 P.M., housekeeping, the front office manager, and the rack clerk should verify the status of the expected departures. Conduct a physical check of the rooms expected to depart.

6. At 5 P.M., the rack clerk, front desk manager, and housekeeper should compare their reports for discrepancies. Discrepant rooms should be rechecked manually. Notify housekeeping once there is an accurate accounting of the house.

7. Begin filling out the manual assignment sheets for the next day's housekeeping assignments. Any minor changes due to late check-in should be passed by the rack clerk to housekeeping the next morning. Setting up the reports the evening before ensures prompt guest service and maintains housekeeping productivity.

PBX and Call Accounting

The systems that make up your phone system (PBX, call accounting, voice mail, and property management system interface) could fail individually or simultaneously.

If the PBX system fails, your phones will not function. To be prepared, the hotel should have several direct lines that do not go through the PBX that can be used if the PBX fails. Your PBX may also have specific power-failure phones that are designed to work when the PBX system loses power.

If the PBX interface to your property management system fails, phones and message lights must be turned on and off manually.

If the call accounting system fails, most PBX systems will buffer the phone call information until the call accounting system is restored. Back charges will then be processed automatically.

If the call accounting interface to your property management system fails, most call accounting systems will buffer the phone charge information until the call accounting interface is restored. Back charges will then be processed automatically. Most call accounting systems also have a backup printer that prints all charge information, which can be used should manual posting of guest folios be required. However, be wary of duplicating charges when the interface connection is restored.

Check to see if the voice mail system has also failed, by attempting to leave and retrieve a test message. If the system is not accepting messages, notify the PBX operators, and have them take manual messages. Check with your PBX, call accounting, and voice mail vendors to find out how your systems work and what backup and downtime procedures should be practiced by your hotel.

Locating Guests

Operators will create an index card for each in-house guest using the latest occupancy report, indicating the guest's name and room number. These cards will be filed alphabetically in the accordion file or file box for use in locating a guest.

Manual Posting Calls

If manual postings of call charges are necessary, the following steps should be taken:

1. The operator will fill out a telephone charge voucher for each call placed, indicating the room number, time, charge, and type of call (local or long distance), and will send it to the posting clerk for action.

2. The posting clerk will keep a manual ledger of postings so that the night audit can balance the phone charges that were posted during the day.

Reservation Center

Notify the central reservations help desk of the situation and estimated downtime. Arrange an alternative procedure for receiving reservations and passing back changes to availability.

Manual Reservations

All reservations should be taken on manual reservation forms, passed to the supervisor to modify future days' inventory, and placed in an accordion date file for later use. Reservations taken during this time should be filed by the date the reservation was made for proper entry into the system when it is back up and running. All requests for specialty rooms should be forwarded to a supervisor. If your hotel has the ability to transfer phone calls automatically to the reservation center, consider implementing this.

Index